Reluctant Power

Information Policy Series

Edited by Sandra Braman

The Information Policy Series publishes research on and analysis of significant problems in the field of information policy, including decisions and practices that enable or constrain information, communication, and culture irrespective of the legal siloes in which they have traditionally been located as well as state-law-society interactions. Defining information policy as all laws, regulations, and decision-making principles that affect any form of information creation, processing, flows, and use, the series includes attention to the formal decisions, decision-making processes, and entities of government; the formal and informal decisions, decision-making processes, and entities of private and public sector agents capable of constitutive effects on the nature of society; and the cultural habits and predispositions of governmentality that support and sustain government and governance. The parametric functions of information policy at the boundaries of social, informational, and technological systems are of global importance because they provide the context for all communications, interactions, and social processes.

Reluctant Power

Networks, Corporations, and the Struggle for Global Governance in the Early 20th Century

Rita Zajácz

The MIT Press
Cambridge, Massachusetts
London, England

This book was set in Stone Serif by Westchester Publishing Services. Printed and bound in the United States of America.

Library of Congress Cataloging-in-Publication Data

Names: Zajácz, Rita, author.
Title: Reluctant power : networks, corporations, and the struggle for global governance in the early 20th century / Rita Zajácz.
Description: Cambridge, MA : MIT Press, [2019] | Series: Information policy | Includes bibliographical references and index.
Identifiers: LCCN 2018049350 | ISBN 9780262042611 (hardcover : alk. paper)
Subjects: LCSH: Communication policy--History--20th century. | Geopolitics--History--20th century. | Ionospheric radio wave propagation--Government policy--History--20th century. | Radio broadcasting--Political aspects--History--20th century.
Classification: LCC P95.8 .Z267 2019 | DDC 384.09--dc23
LC record available at https://lccn.loc.gov/2018049350

10 9 8 7 6 5 4 3 2 1

To Tim, Robi, and Reni

Contents

Series Editor's Introduction

At one end of the spectrum are the "research industries," the production lines that repetitively investigate the same research questions over and over again, perhaps with slightly different exemplars as the target subjects—the spectrum, that is, of whether or not research in the social sciences and humanities is getting us anywhere at all. Work produced in this industrial manner does get published, does earn tenure and promotion for academics, and is read at least by others who are working in the same industry and those they teach. The answers, though, can be given as soon as the questions are asked, not needing the detail provided for the purpose of demonstrating the ability of the author(s) to produce and reproduce the commodity. What industrial research of this type does *not* do is move our understanding meaningfully and effectively forward, a matter that may contribute to the relative disregard for the social sciences and humanities among policymakers, the general public, and indeed often among university administrators. No one in physics, after all, is publishing or holding a job in the twenty-first century by asking what will happen to a ball held in one's hand if the hand is opened and the ball let go.

At the other end of the spectrum, with many variants in between, are those works that look at what we may think of as known phenomena, processes, or events and find in them worlds of unasked research questions, driving our knowledge to ever more fundamental levels as they are addressed. The analogue in physics would be the research that has moved us from attending to molecules, to atoms, to subatomic particles, and to quarks, leptons, quantum mechanics, and on. Rita Zajácz's *Reluctant Power: Networks, Corporations, and the Struggle for Global Governance in the Early 20th Century* falls at this far, and far too rare, end of the spectrum. Her analysis of how the United States came to dominate global communication networks during the period from 1899 to 1934 not only overturns received histories but also provides theoretical foundations and a research agenda for those struggling to understand what is going on with the Internet and other communication networks today.

Zajácz's conceptual and theoretical innovations developed out of her immersion in a massive amount of archival material as well as a seemingly exhaustive review of literatures across multiple disciplines. With the invaluable and also rare gift of being able to move with ease up and down levels of abstraction, she makes visible the issues as they were understood and negotiated during that era. We tend to forget that one of the first issues that needed to be decided upon by those who were involved in the early stages of the design of what we now call the Internet was how many bits should be included in a byte for network purposes. The history told in this book begins in a time when, as the author describes it, "radio was a type of telegraphy, when communication policy was primarily naval policy, and when the nature of the multinational corporations (MNCs) that managed communications networks was a mystery to all" (p. 1). The questions over which Britain, the United States, and others struggled between 1899 and 1934 were fundamental not only to networks but to the nature of the economy and law-state-society relations: What is a corporation? What comprises a network connection? How should the nationality of a connection or of a corporate entity be determined? What does it mean to serve the public interest in an international context? Which features of a technological system require differential regulatory treatment, and which can be treated analogically?

There are surprises along the way, such as the importance of an insurance company (the British insurer Lloyd's) as the first entity to have licensed the radiotelegraph, which allowed ships to communicate with each other and with the shore, and to control an international network of this type. Some matters that have been grasped intuitively or only in the most broad terms by others, such as the fact that all "domestic" network policy issues are actually also matters of foreign relations, are fully developed empirically and theoretically. Notions that have commonly been conflated are, importantly, unbundled; early twentieth-century battles over what has previously been referred to as access to immaterial *airwaves* were, more accurately and with significant consequences for which factors were influential and how contention took place, conflicts over control of very material *stations*, and both must be analytically distinguished from efforts to control *information*. Some features believed to be unique to the Internet environment are, to put it simply, not, such as the importance of amateurs to network governance.

The "general idea" of network control has been around for decades, but in the hands of others, except as regards very specific issues such as governance of the Internet's domain name system (DNS), has been so vague as to be impossible to operationalize and thus, frankly, of limited analytical value irrespective of how often cited. One of the most important theoretical contributions of this work is Zajácz's theory of network control as involving decision-making ability over three things—territory, capital, and technology—that allows one party "an uninterrupted flow of information, while denying the same to its opponent." (Note the unusual and invaluable inclusion of the negative as well as the positive dimension, on beyond Max Weber.) This theory is much more fully articulated in chapter 1 and proves useful in analysis of and is supported by the evidence discussed in the rest of the book. Here it is worth highlighting her insight that it is the difficulty of controlling all three at once that makes the histories of electronic communication networks so complex; studying intersections between any two of these is particularly fruitful analytically.

The author is an excellent guide to her own work, not just identifying broad areas in which her analyses differ from those scholars who have come before but also pointing readers to the specific claims in particular works to which she is providing the contra (pay attention to the "cf." citations). There are historians of networks who claim archival foundations for their work but leave the reader wondering, often nervous about how much to trust the work, because those authors do not provide the references to specific documents that such research should yield; Zajácz does. She is assiduous about marking the boundaries of what is known and what is not known—which archival materials have been mined and which have not, which questions have been addressed and which are yet to be pursued. Single paragraphs in which she situates her perspective relative to that of existing literatures provide outlines deserving of full semester-length treatment by students and their equivalent by scholars working in these areas.

Reluctant Power should now be the book with which study of the development of global communication networks at the turn of the twentieth century and during its first decades begins, but this is not where the value of this book ends. Zajácz's challenges and contributions to how we think about network governance, political economy, and globalization in the present as well as in the past are profound. Thank you, Rita.

Acknowledgments

This book has been a long time in the making. Among the institutions that made their resources available, I would like to express my thanks especially to the National Archives, the Manuscript Division of the Library of Congress, the Public Record Office, and the archives of British Telecommunications. When my book expanded in scope, I received help on several other visits from the same collections and added the Herbert Hoover Presidential Library, the papers of Franklin Delano Roosevelt, and the Special Collections section at St. Lawrence University to the list. I wish I knew the names of all the staff who helped me locate and tirelessly pulled all the materials I requested at these locations. I appreciate all your work.

At Indiana University, Herbert A. Terry and Michael McGregor offered advice (along with rides to Goodwill to get what seemed like a bookshelf but was called a "headboard") while providing support collecting and organizing what seemed like a monumental pile of facts. The research programs of Harmeet Sawhney and William R. Thompson influenced the two main strands of the book: common carrier regulation as the application of enduring ideas to new technologies, and geopolitical competition to set policy for the world system.

The flexibility and generous assistance of the University of Iowa were instrumental in helping me turn my research and ideas into a book. Most important of all, I am grateful for the patience of the university to allow me to write the book I wanted to write. I was able to take leave without pay to recover from childbirth and to finish my book, received a tenure extension after the births of my children and family emergencies, and found financial support for archival research in the form of the Old Gold Fellowship. I am pleased to thank my colleagues at the Department of Communication Studies and in the professional communities that cluster around the Communication Law and Policy and the Communication History divisions of the International Communication Association. Two of my colleagues, Joy Hayes and John Durham Peters, read multiple chapters of this manuscript, providing insight and crucial encouragement.

At MIT Press, I would like to thank Sandra Braman, the editor of the Information Policy series, for her unwavering enthusiasm as I figured out the final shape of the book, starting with a grant submission. She was there at conference presentations, workshops, and deadlines, listening to multiple iterations of the project as it took shape and offering additional sources and perspectives along the way. If she ever doubted whether it would be completed, she never showed it. I am grateful to acquisitions editor Gita Manaktala, who took on this project, and to the anonymous reviewers who provided professional expertise, thoughtful criticism, and encouragement in equal measure. Their attention to both the big picture and the details of the work was invaluable. Finally, I appreciate Hal Henglein's keen eye for both the intricacies of the language and the historical context as well as the timely assistance of production editor John Donohue at Westchester Printing Services.

Alongside the privilege of a flexible and stable academic position that allows one to even attempt a book like this one, inevitably there are sacrifices. In the case of an immigrant to the United States, many of those are borne by others. I would like to thank my friends and family members as well as the tireless employees of Debrecen Megyei Jogú Város Szociális Szolgálat and the Hajdúbagosi Idősek Otthona for their efforts in caring for my mother. Without the timely interventions of Dobó Istvánné Zajácz Irén, Dobó Katalin, Dobó István, Dakosné Nováki Zita, and Nováki Patrícia, she would not have had the chance to recover from an accident as well as she did. Balogh László Zoltánné provided both timely information and invaluable assistance with the recovery process. I would also like to thank Sue Campney and David Kearns for support with family issues during these past few years, as well as my friends Maria Tsitsekli and Urbánné Dicső Ágnes for always listening and never judging.

The greatest debt I have incurred along the way goes to my husband, Timothy Havens, who put up with a project that had expanded by two-thirds by the time it was finished. There were trips to archives, more trips to archives, ideas that may have been simple but somehow not for me, drafts to read, babies and sitting for them, little kids and playing with them while I was working during weekends and nights, and several apartments to empty on his own—all of this requiring a seemingly endless amount of patience. I dedicate this book to him and to Robi and Reni, the two other highlights of my day.

1 Network Control

Control over global communications networks is central to world leadership, but much remains unclear about the relationship between the two. During the late nineteenth century, when Britain's dominance in the international system seemed to be at its apex, both the high seas and the global submarine cable network were widely perceived to be under British control. This perception was strengthened by the reported cooperative relationship between the British government and the Eastern and Associated Telegraph Companies, the cable monopolist headquartered in Britain. Communications superiority and naval superiority reinforced each other: cable communications allowed the Royal Navy to direct its forces, and naval power protected the cable links.

As concerns about British control over global communications mounted in the 1899–1934 period, the country's geopolitical rivals looked to circumventing technologies such as radiotelegraphy, a point-to-point application of radio technology. One of the most important rivals that could achieve autonomy from Britain in communications and even exert control over the global network was the United States. This book takes us back to a time when radio was a type of telegraphy, when communications policy was primarily naval policy, and when the nature of the multinational corporations (MNCs) that managed communications networks was a mystery to all. In the chapters that follow, I will trace the way American policymakers sought to gain control over the global radio network in an effort to advance the position of the United States in the world system. At the end of a complex set of maneuvers, American policymakers achieved autonomy and settled on policies furthering expansion. The way this eventually happened, however, went against the best judgment of the government department most fervently pursuing this objective, the U.S. Navy.

A step-by-step analysis of U.S. policy efforts over three decades would not be possible without a preliminary understanding of what it takes to control a global network. How does a state, which can credibly claim control over territory alone, assert control over a global communications network? At the heart of my story is the concept of *network control*, a concept often unstated or casually applied in previous scholarship but sharpened here to mean decision-making ability regarding *territory*, *capital*, and *technology* through which one party secures an uninterrupted flow of information while denying the same to its opponent. This definition combines the *purpose* of control with three *sites* of control—technology, territory, and capital—that serve as sources of leverage and countervailing influence. Two *levels* of control round out the framework. On the tactical level, parties turn to existing sources of leverage, which includes control over territory for the state, while the structural level refers to the ability to influence the rules of the game via such tools as general policy principles and discursive framing.

The network control concept captures both policymakers' aspirations and their wish list: *why* they aspire for control, *what* is necessary to obtain it, and *how* it can be acquired. The historical analysis here reveals the extent to which American policymakers were able to realize their objectives during the time period under study. In order to explain the purpose of network control, I draw on naval theory. Sea power doctrine, as I will show, has long provided a template for state control beyond national territory, which was already a tall order. If the sea is nature's infrastructure, however, the global communications infrastructure is man-made. The fact that networks require both technological expertise and capital investment introduces different challenges. To take charge of a global network, dominance over all three sites of control is necessary, but the difficulty of achieving a monopoly over all of them simultaneously makes network control unstable and the illusion of control difficult to sustain. The most promising venues for analyzing efforts to establish control over a global network therefore seem to be at the intersections between any two, or all three, forms of leverage.

Here I will specifically focus on the territory-capital nexus, the intersection most relevant for global networks. States that vie for control over global communications must expand abroad and are likely to meet resistance from other countries ill disposed toward foreign governments operating strategic technologies in their territories. As a result, my analysis highlights the critical role that intermediaries play in network control. The multinational corporation, the intermediary most relevant for control over the physical infrastructure during the early twentieth century, mediated between national control and global reach. It served as a buffer zone between the clashing interests of sovereign states and raised unexpected problems of its own. Rather than being pliant targets of regulation, early MNCs were independent players in their own right that sought to exploit fissures within and among states and demanded a central role in shaping both domestic and global communications policy. As a result, American policymakers faced the challenge of controlling the intermediaries who managed the network.

The two *levels* of network control answer the "how" question, directing our attention to policy, rather than superior technology, as a significant reason for American ascendancy in radiotelegraphy. The tactical level involves the struggle over relational power, where one party gets the other one to do what it wants via existing forms of leverage. For the state, for example, the primary form of leverage is control over territory. On the structural level, the focus centers on game-changing developments, which include general policy principles and discursive framings that attempt to shift the advantage to the state. Although developments on the two levels are related, my main focus will be on the structural level, where decisions are aimed at changing the structure of global communications. By analyzing the development of communications policy with this framework, I hope to further our understanding of the role of the global communications infrastructure in geopolitical rivalry.

Radiotelegraphy is worth our attention not simply because it anticipates so much of the early twenty-first-century digital norm of people sending written messages to distant receivers but also because it lays bare the fascinating power struggles over global communications and the discursive struggles over the identities and loyalties of the early multinational corporations managing the network. Radio technology was initially developed for ship-to-shore communications and provided navies and shipping lines with connectivity at sea that was not available with the submarine cable. The pioneering British Marconi company quickly established subsidiaries, among them the Marconi Wireless Telegraph Company of America (hereafter American Marconi), to offer service in the largest markets. Long-distance communication, in competition with the cable network, was the objective from the very beginning. For Britain's geopolitical rivals, two questions quickly emerged: Would radiotelegraphy simply reinforce British control over global communications? And, if so, what could be done to prevent that outcome?

Here I want to underscore that policies aimed at network control are foreign policies, whether incorporated in domestic legislation, enacted in an international convention, or pursued abroad. Thus, the customary separation of the domestic and international realms is not tenable. All three major pieces of radio legislation in the early twentieth century—the Radio Act of 1912, the Radio Act of 1927, and the Communications Act of 1934—were shaped by American policymakers' desire to harness radiotelegraphy for geopolitical purposes. The goal of policies such as interconnection and licensing was to ensure autonomy of communications and thwart British Marconi's attempts to determine the configuration of the global network. The policies facilitating American expansion, in turn, sought to match the expansion of homegrown MNCs, including the Radio Corporation of America (RCA) and International Telephone and Telegraph (ITT), with the gradual expansion of the American sphere of influence. When this goal proved to be a great deal more challenging than originally imagined, naval policymakers started to theorize the impact of international expansion, via cartels and foreign direct investment (FDI), on the identities and loyalties of corporations. Eventually they would offer national ownership, limited foreign direct investment, and intermodal (or "type") competition (i.e., the competition between cable and radio networks) as appropriate solutions. Significantly, some policy measures that embodied the general principle of national ownership (e.g., the various types of foreign ownership regulations) brought the problem of American corporate nationality to the fore, which became a central concern for policymakers throughout the early twentieth century.

American policymakers ventured into uncharted territory as they attempted to exert control beyond stations on U.S. soil. Because there was no master plan that guided policymakers through the three decades analyzed here, policy analysis reveals as much about the transformation of policymakers' mind-sets as it does about the policy measures furthering American ascendancy. Radio policy was largely devised in the Navy Department and was profoundly shaped by the defensive mind-set of a challenger whose central concern with autonomy influenced even the policies aimed at expansion. Under the Navy Department's influence, the United States was a "reluctant power" in global communications, desirous of a larger role but wary of expanding too far beyond the American sphere of influence. By the 1930s, U.S.-headquartered multinationals and the State Department would chafe at these constraints.

I hope to show that American ascendancy in radiotelegraphy was the result of three reinforcing and interconnected factors: concrete policies, the perception that some of these policies worked, and a conceptual shift to the confident vision of an aspiring world leader. Significantly, the "therapeutic" functions of policy were as important as the specific measures aimed at American ascendancy. That is, each successful measure reassured policymakers that control over a global communications infrastructure, and even over global capital, was both possible and within reach. Perhaps the most important development in American radio policy at this time was conceptual: while working tirelessly to acquire more control, policymakers got used to more uncertain forms of control, chiefly those exercised by private corporations, as the country's overall position in the world system improved.

The 1899–1934 period encompasses the decisive decades when the conceptual and policy foundations of American ascendancy were laid. This time frame begins with the appearance of radiotelegraphy in the United States and ends with the Communications Act of 1934. The main focus on one industry, one country, and the territory-capital nexus, in turn, makes it possible to grasp some key connections between policy and political economy, domestic legislation and international expansion, imperialism and geopolitics, and material and discursive struggles. It might seem apparent that placing early radio policy into its geopolitical context should take us right to the intersection of two bodies of literature, those of communications policy and international political economy. Instead, radio history is currently bifurcated between domestically oriented critical and cultural histories and internationally oriented diplomatic and military histories, which pay little heed to the systemic context. The following section briefly reviews the main questions and blind spots of these studies, laying the groundwork for the contribution that a synthesis of communications policy and international political economy could provide.

Radio History

Infrastructure industries are vitally important to state power, but most American radio history has hitherto focused on broadcasting as a form of domestic political persuasion. *Critical and cultural radio histories*, in particular, understand radiotelegraphy as the "prehistory" of broadcasting (Douglas, 1989, p. xvi). In the best-regarded histories of the period, attention to the international dimension of radio policy decreases in direct proportion to researchers' focus on broadcasting as opposed to wireless (Aitken, 1985; Douglas, 1989; Streeter, 1996). Since they are most interested in the gradual elimination of the democratic potential of radio technology, these researchers foreground the airwaves, rather than the network, as well as the conflict between the amateurs and "large institutions." Two related consequences follow. First, the fact that radiotelegraphy was a strategically important, emerging *global* industry does not figure into the analysis. As a result, recurrent, visible conflicts between the state and large corporations are dismissed as family quarrels between parties with largely similar interests.

For policy analysis, these blind spots are debilitating. In the early 1900s, policymakers understood radio as a kind of telegraphy and sought to regulate it as a common carrier. Once this is taken into account, the very emergence of the spectrum in policy discussions becomes an open question. When and why did the spectrum become important for radio policy? Moreover, the company whose expansion policymakers sought to block was widely identified as a British corporation. The amateurs were indeed marginalized, but the effort to lump together American Marconi and RCA under the umbrella of "large corporations," and the interests of both of these entities along with those of the U.S. government, misses an important part of the story. From a transnational, network-oriented perspective, large institutions fought for control among themselves, and the United States was faced with integration into a network developed in the interests of a geopolitical rival.

Second, *diplomatic and military historians* position communications networks as subject to, rather than tools of, control, and they typically examine the timing and the reasons for the transition from British to American leadership in global communications. This literature treats radiotelegraphy alongside the submarine cable as a strategic technology used for point-to-point communications, seeking to place developments in these industries into the context of contemporary military affairs and foreign relations. Communications networks are highly useful for geopolitical purposes and are inevitably fought over. This vein of scholarship has been dubbed "the struggle for control" school, drawing on the title of a rare book on policy analysis (Winseck, 2013). Analyses of struggle for control, including this volume, help us better understand the role of the global communications infrastructure in geopolitical rivalry rather than the role of geopolitical rivalry in the development of the global media system (cf. Winseck, 2013; cf. Winseck & Pike, 2007). The transition to American world leadership depended not only on control over global communications but also included other strategic industries, such as petroleum or international finance (see Hugill, 2014, for a recent contribution). Strategic communication, on the other hand, is only one strand in a complex web of interactions that shaped the development of the global media system.

Diplomatic and military historians take their cues from Hugh Aitken's *The Continuous Wave* (1985) in foregrounding the role of technological leadership—specifically, the invention of continuous-wave radio—in America's ascendancy in radiotelegraphy. Based on Aitken's study, there is general agreement that the United States had achieved technological leadership by 1914 (Aitken, 1985, p. 253; Headrick, 1991, p. 180). Policy, on the other hand, played "almost no role in the rise of American power in telecommunications," historian Daniel Headrick offers, attributing it instead to the country's wealth, aided by technology (Headrick 1991, p. 276; Winkler, 2008, p. 202). When American policy is present, it is judged to have failed (Winkler, 2008, p. 271). Indeed, ascendancy in radiotelegraphy or in global communications took place in the context of shifts in many different industries, but even favorable combinations of those factors couldn't, by themselves, guarantee U.S. predominance. Exactly how is technological leadership in radiotelegraphy related to leadership in the industry, let alone to leadership in the broader field of global communications? Policy analysis does provide answers, but only if the exclusive focus on technology is abandoned.

When technology is stressed as the key to ascendancy, researchers investigate how policymakers control access to strategic technologies such as the Alexanderson alternator, which was central to the operations of RCA in the early years, rather than how a state obtains control over both ends of a *circuit* connecting two countries and the collection of circuits that make up a global network. Corporations are understood as equipment manufacturers, rather than as telecommunications service providers, and recede into the background. The lack of emphasis on *networks*, in turn, prevents researchers from identifying specific starting and ending points of ascendancy while foreclosing connections between domestic legislation and policies designed for international expansion. By investigating how the United States sought to exert control over the global radio network, whether imaginary, under development, or fully built out, this book invites attention to the companies acting as network managers, identifies key steps of American ascendancy to 1934, and focuses on policy in order to explain how policymakers sought to align the identities and decisions of companies with their geopolitical objectives.

The Radio Network in the Context of International Political Economy

During the early twentieth century, the global communications infrastruc-ture was an "essential facility" of strategic advancement. Domestically, tele-communications networks were critical infrastructures, one of four types of industries so vital to U.S. economic and public life as to be regulated in the public interest, alongside banking, energy, and transportation (Wu, 2010, p. 58). Perhaps not coincidentally, the same four industries were identified as "strategic goods" central for world leadership (Winkler, 2008, p. 278). From a commercial standpoint, companies like British Marconi were in the busi-ness of message handling for the *New York Herald* and the *New York Times* as well as for passengers on ships. From a military and geopolitical perspective, however, the radio network was an auxiliary of sea power and mapped onto established trade routes. In order to examine how American policymakers sought to wrest control over the global communications infrastructure from Britain, we need (1) some key terms as well as specific starting and ending points of U.S. ascendancy, (2) a political economic framework that brings developments in the American market and those abroad into analytical focus in the same case, and (3) a combination of policy analysis and a polit-ical economic perspective that can accommodate change over time. This section takes up the first two tasks, and the following section addresses the third, laying out the intellectual background that underlies the network control framework proposed in the second half of the chapter.

Companies that control income-generating assets in more than one country have, since the 1960s, been analyzed under various terms: the multinational corporation, the multinational enterprise, the transnational corporation, and the global corporation (Fieldhouse, 1986, p. 9; Schiller, 1992; Sinclair, 2007; Strange, 1996; Vernon, 1971). Researchers use different terms in part to avoid implications that a firm is equally identified with the several different countries in which it operates or that it is mindful of the interests of any particular state (Evans, 1981, p. 203). Although I will use the term "the multinational corporation" because of its widespread presence in the litera-ture, I am not signaling any particular theoretical position about the identities and loyalties of these entities. In the early twentieth century, the MNC was an emerging institution whose very nature policymakers sought to understand. A central strand of this book follows how they attempted to pin down the identities and loyalties of these firms.

The key to the global expansion of multinational corporations is foreign direct investment. Researchers distinguish between "inward" and regular FDI, where the former refers to flows of investment into a country and the latter to an outflow of capital. FDI, manifested in equity ownership in subsidiaries doing business abroad, allows the parent company to direct its global assets according to a common management strategy (Vernon, 1974, p. 1). Companies involved in radiotelegraphy were public utility MNCs and one of four types of multinational corporations that had existed since the late nineteenth century. For such MNCs, their engagement in foreign direct investment was the direct result of providing the service (Fieldhouse, 1986, pp. 24–25).

Thinking about companies as MNCs divides states into two categories: "home states," where the parent company has its headquarters, and "host states," the recipients of FDI, where the subsidiaries conduct business. Significantly, FDI confers direct managerial control over assets. Because the MNC controls elements of a foreign economy, much has been written about the threat it poses to the sovereignty of host states (Lipson, 1985, p. xv). What may be a prudent business decision on the level of the individual firm quickly becomes a thorny problem of political economy in a strategic infrastructure industry.

The three companies discussed in this book—British Marconi, RCA, and ITT—qualify under all but the narrowest definition of the MNC. Public utility MNCs followed the strategy of horizontal integration characteristic of the service industries by setting up foreign subsidiaries similar to those in the headquarters country (Lipson, 1985, p. 6). The number of subsidiaries and the extent of control over them are central to classifying companies as MNCs. British Marconi and ITT met a six-subsidiary "standard" set out in the business management literature by the end of the first decade of their existence (Fouraker & Stopford, 1968, p. 57; Vernon, 1971, p. 4). Both companies owned a percentage of stock in their subsidiaries that far exceeded the minimum 10–15 percent that could prove sufficient to exercise "a controlling interest" in legal terms (Vagts, 1961, p. 1535). RCA, on the other hand, did not have subsidiaries abroad but was still a multinational. Its lack of FDI, as chapter 6 shows, was the direct result of geopolitical pressures, which channeled company expansion into contracts with foreign telegraph administrations for traffic handling, as well as into cartels and joint ventures with companies headquartered outside the United States. RCA would therefore qualify as an MNC under recent studies in business administration, which downplay the importance of equity ownership and look to other forms of capitalist control over companies, such as licensing arrangements, joint ventures, and contracts (Winder, 2006, p. 790).

The terms reviewed here help describe the United States in the first decade of the twentieth century. The country had a powerful economy and was developing a large navy, but it lagged behind in control over global communications links. The United States was a host state subject to media imperialism, or the process whereby the ownership and structure of the media in any given country are subject to "substantial external pressures" from the media interests of other countries "without proportionate reciprocation of influence by the country so affected" (Boyd-Barrett, 1977, p. 117). Because British government control over radio stations was not a possibility, the external pressure in radiotelegraphy came from British Marconi, a private service provider, which offered connections to the outside world. How, then, did the United States transform itself from being subject to media imperialism into an imperialist power in its own right?

Jill Hills's (2007) typologies of network control, developed with the submarine cable industry in mind, have hitherto contributed the most to our understanding of control over the global communications infrastructure. I will rely on three of her models—end-to-end control, the Western Union model, and the European state-to-state model—in order to establish the specific starting and ending points for American ascendancy (Hills, 2007, pp. 5, 11). End-to-end control involves foreign investment and conceptualizes the network as one without regard for national borders. Its defining feature is control in the hands of one organization, without any requirement for interconnection. The absence of borders, physical or legislative, means that states play no role. Under this model, British Marconi could erect stations anywhere in the world, including the United States, and companies like RCA might establish stations even in the British Empire. This level of control by a single firm or government administration was particularly uncommon, especially in radiotelegraphy, among geopolitical rivals.

Far more prevalent were manifestations of Hills's two other models, in which states play a more assertive role. The Western Union model, for example, is a form of asymmetric end-to-end control whose key feature is protectionism of domestic markets. Under this arrangement, the cables of one country, say Britain, can freely enter the territory of another, such as Brazil, but the borders come down on the other end, and cables established by Brazilian firms are denied entry into Britain (Hills, 2007, pp. 11–12). This is the territory of media imperialism, and was the dream of British Marconi, though it was the exception in the submarine cable industry, where the British government pursued a policy of free trade in landing rights (Kennedy, 1971, p. 742). Under the Western Union model, British Marconi would be free to roam the earth without even interconnecting with any other firm, while no company established outside Britain could enter the territory of the British Empire. Finally, under Hills's state-to-state model, state-owned telecommunications administrations exchange traffic at the border under "traffic agreements" (Hills, 2007, pp. 10–12). Formally, this was an arm's-length relationship; any inequality in power relations must be analyzed via the terms of specific agreements.

If the United States hoped to get ahead, it would need to thwart the possibility of a Western Union model exercised by British Marconi and install its own version in its place. Therefore, the effectiveness of policies in general and of the policies aimed at American ascendancy in particular cannot be understood without a time frame of several decades. The starting point of American ascendancy in radiotelegraphy was the very possibility of asymmetric end-to-end control by a British corporation. Its ending point was "direct communication" with Britain (i.e., American companies' access to the territory of the British Empire), which policymakers did not accomplish until 1945. This book follows the major turning points of American ascendancy to 1934, when the conceptual and policy foundations of the transition were laid.

The current political economic frameworks underlying the established radio histories cannot handle domestic and international developments together because they ignore the network managers. Critical and cultural histories focus on ownership (table 1.1),[1] drawing the key analytical distinctions between public and private ownership as well as between for-profit and nonprofit ventures within the latter. The domestic orientation of the

Table 1.1

Domestic political economy of communications in the United States, 1899–1934.

		Content	
		Point-to-point	Mass
Ownership	Public	Post	N/A
	Private	Telephony Telegraphy	Broadcasting

Table 1.2
International political economy of electric communications in the United States, 1899–1934.

		Content	
		Point-to-point	Mass
Private ownership (for profit)	Domestic	Telephony Telegraphy	Broadcasting
	Foreign	Submarine cables Radiotelegraphy	N/A

industries is assumed both in institutional and in cultural analyses. The concept of "corporate liberalism," outlining how liberal thought adjusted to the rise of the large corporation, has no room for the large *multinational* corporation or the resulting distinction between home states and host states (Streeter, 1996).

Researchers studying global communications networks narrow their focus to private ownership (table 1.2). They assume the for-profit orientation of companies, and give analytical priority to the distinction between domestic and foreign ownership, but do not foreground the intermediaries managing the network. This leads to difficulties in linking the domestic and the international realms (see Winkler, 2008, for progress in this direction).

"Networks breach borders," as Hills asserts, and the interdependence of international operations and domestic distribution was well understood in the telegraph industries of the time (Hills, 2007, p. 11). For example, the U.S.-headquartered network provider Western Union was a monopolist in the American market and linked the country to the world via submarine cables after 1911. It was also one of the two companies providing distribution outlets for radio traffic arriving in the United States from abroad. Yet, diplomatic and military histories do not typically explore the links between the domestic and the international realms. A key aspect of the transition to U.S. leadership in radiotelegraphy was the transformation of the country from a host state into a home state of MNCs expanding abroad. For a brief period in the 1910s, the United States played both roles. Even the U.S. government itself sought to establish stations abroad, as the example of the 1914 Panamanian government decree reveals. By further narrowing the focus from "private ownership" to "foreign ownership," table 1.3 shows how the

Table 1.3
Political economy of point-to-point radio communications involving the United States, 1899–1934.

			Point-to-point radio
Foreign ownership	Public	Home	Panama, 1914 decree (chapter 5)
		Host	N/A
	Private	Home	Federal Telegraph (chapters 5 and 6); United Fruit (chapters 5 and 7); RCA after 1919 (chapter 6); ITT (chapter 7)
		Host	American Marconi (chapters 2, 3, 4, and 5)

United States sought to gain control over radiotelegraphy both inside and outside its own territory.

In the chapters that follow, I will specify how American policymakers at the beginning of the twentieth century established national borders via legislation and sought to extend the country's territorial control indirectly, via U.S.-headquartered MNCs. To this end, however, we need to be familiar with how policymakers thought about corporations with international operations, which is not possible without interpretive work. The concept of "foreign ownership," in particular, presupposes a clear separation of "us" and "them," but it was precisely this categorization that policymakers struggled with in the early twentieth century. In the course of considering the wisdom of unrestricted—inward or regular—FDI, American policymakers were asking and answering the kinds of questions that policymakers and policy analysts still debate today. Were American Marconi, Western Union, or ITT "American" corporations? Even RCA did not escape this line of questioning. I will revisit this problem as it relates to several different bodies of literature. In the following section, I will make a case for the necessity of interpretive analysis to address the questions raised earlier and for the integration of policy analysis with realist world systems analysis, the political economic framework most attuned to geopolitical rivalry over time.

World Systems Theory and Communication Policy

While the mainstream international political economy framework helps to integrate analysis across the domestic-international boundary, it is better suited to snapshots in time than to examining change over time. World systems theory, a system-level political economic perspective, provides an approach that allows analysis over a longer duration. Control over global communications networks is currently not central to the realist long-cycles research program, which has led communications scholars and researchers in other fields to stretch it to accommodate this research problem (Hall & Preston, 1988, p. 32; Hugill, 1999, p. 19). My aim is to stretch the long-cycles framework even further by inviting attention to the crucial role of intermediaries in global communications for understanding the transition from one leader to the next and to the necessity of linking political economic and policy analyses. This discussion rounds out the conceptual background that informs the network control framework.

World systems theory suggests that the international system is hierarchical rather than anarchic. If researchers are interested in states at all, they are typically concerned with the roles that home and host states play in the system. This is not the place to sketch the contending approaches to the world system, but I will note the key concepts of the long-cycles school. In this research program, states compete to set policy for the system as a whole. The "world leader" exerts disproportionate influence, and "challengers" seek to displace it. Though all varieties of world systems analysis are interested in the relationship between long-term political and economic processes, they disagree about who the leaders are, how they emerge, the characteristics of economic or political cycles, and what drives these cycles (Arrighi, 2010; Thompson, 2000; Wallerstein, 2004). Even the use of a hyphen between "world" and "system" is contested. According to the long-cycles framework, for example, innovation drives economic change, which results in leading economic sectors. Leading sectors cluster in particular countries and transform them into the lead economies of the world. This is a "historical-structural" research program, so named because history serves as material for theory building, which in turn seeks to explain the transformation of system structure over time. Thus, the early twentieth-century transition to American leadership is an example of a hegemonic transition, which is a recurring feature of the world system (Hall & Preston, 1988; Hugill, 1999). Four lead economies—Portugal, the Netherlands, Britain, and the United States—assumed leadership positions in the past five hundred years, succeeding each other in five one-hundred-year leadership cycles, with Britain taking two turns (Modelski & Thompson, 1996, pp. 25–26). These countries were the centers of commerce, finance, and military power, and their decline initiated a period of "transition crisis" (p. 222).

Under the long-cycles framework, shifts in core state position change the structure of the system (cf. Wallerstein, 2004, p. 29). Because of researchers' interest in tracing systemic change as a whole and in the emergence of leading economic sectors as catalysts, however, this framework does not capture how important global communications networks seemed to policymakers in the early twentieth century, nor does it foreground the relationship between states and multinational corporations. Perhaps these blind spots are worth a second look. Critical infrastructures undergird both industrial development and strategic advancement, and policymakers in the early twentieth century were particularly preoccupied with their potential as auxiliaries of sea power. While geopolitical rivalry influenced developments in these industries, governments rarely dealt with one another. Instead, state-to-state relationships were mediated by multinational network managers, a necessity that introduced unique challenges. While the long-term trajectories of world leaders and multinational corporations are typically seen as intertwined, central to this book is the conceptualization of capitalism and territorialism as "opposite logics of power" (Arrighi, 2010, p. 34; Modelski & Thompson, 1996, p. 66). States' political and military strategies are aimed at territorial expansion, whereas those of capitalists are focused on individual advantage and capital accumulation (Harvey, 2003, pp. 26–27).

Treating developments at home and abroad together depends as much on the selection of the political economic framework as it does on the connection between political economy and policy. In structural theories, whether material or symbolic, the political economic or discursive structure sets the boundaries of what is possible, and it is just a matter of time before policymakers take advantage of them. Realist political economy offers the notion of "the perceptual transitional lag" to explain why the policies adopted do not always match a country's objective interests, as identified by the researcher (see also Krasner, 1995, p. 34; Thompson, 2000, p. 180). Policymakers afflicted with a perceptual transitional lag may continue to reason from the mind-set of an inferior power, for example, even as the world around them is changing to their advantage (Friedberg, 1988, p. 18). This concept is important because it highlights the disconnect between a country's changing economic position and its policymakers' decisions. I accept the premise of world systems analyses—that economic factors underlie a country's rise—without necessarily engaging in the debate about what these factors are. My interest here lies less in comparing policies to states'

objective interests than in establishing how underlying economic and technological changes filtered into policymakers' consciousness and influenced
the policies they deemed acceptable.

Policies aimed at network control are shaped by where policymakers see
their country in the international pecking order. Policy matters, despite what
historians and world systems researchers have said about its irrelevance.
Whatever the underlying strengths of a country, world leadership does not
happen by accident. *Whether, when,* and *why* those underlying strengths
filtered to the surface and *how* they influenced decisions are the bread and
butter of the scholarship. Answering such questions, in turn, requires
a national-level analysis, which takes into account the basic insight of
humanities scholarship that what happens in the world has meaning for its
inhabitants (Hollis & Smith, 1990, p. 68). What follows is, in part, an insider
account of the rise of a hegemon that seeks to understand how policymakers came to terms with America's rise at the same time that they sought to
improve its position in global communications.

Understanding radio policy in the context of hegemonic transition
requires a definition of the state that shifts the focus away from the regulatory commission, an institution that has dominated communications and
media history. That regulators at the Federal Radio Commission (FRC) or the
Federal Communications Commission (FCC) are subservient to industry
demands seems to be common sense in the literature today. The debate, if
there is one, centers on the level of, and reasons for, their subservience (see
Horwitz, 1989, for theories of regulation, and see McChesney, 1993, for an
example). Much of the analysis of U.S. radio policy relies on the structural
Marxist capitalist state theory, which locates the autonomy of the state in
its role as the protector of the long-term interests of capital (Horwitz, 1989,
pp. 41–42; Streeter, 1996, pp. 35, 109, 178). It is because of the influence of
this theory, which easily accommodates the state's efforts to overrule the
interests of any one company, that visible and recurrent conflicts between
the state and large corporations are dismissed out of hand (Rossi, 1985, p. 40;
Trumpbour, 2002, pp. 101–105). The theory has been evaluated as being
impervious to empirical examination (Horwitz, 1989, p. 43).

Therefore, much is at stake in defining the state as "the foreign policy
executive"—that is, the White House, the State Department, or, more generally, "high-ranking bureaucrats charged with the overall conduct of defense
and foreign affairs" (Krasner, 1978; Lake, 1988, p. 70). The state in general

and the military departments in particular are among the primary users of communications networks. Because of its interest in ship-to-shore and ship-to-ship communication, the government department responsible for radio policy was the Navy, which in 1904 successfully argued that it had the predominant stake in the technology. Naval policymakers maintained their influence in radiotelegraphy during the time period examined in this book, since the regulatory agencies that acquired authority over the technology were preoccupied with other industries (Aitken, 1985; Douglas, 1989, p. 125; Horwitz, 1989, p. 100). I will periodically combine the analysis of naval policymakers' views with those of others in the foreign policy executive in order to outline the debate whereby American radio policy was brought in line with the country's improving economic position. In contrast to the regulatory agency, the autonomy of the foreign policy executive stems from its position at the intersection of the international system and domestic society, as well as its broad mandate to further the nation's general interests (Krasner, 1978, p. 11; Lake, 1988, p. 67). Regardless of their political positions, researchers agree that when national security, geopolitical advancement, or broad ideological conceptions of U.S. world hegemony are involved, the state enjoys a level of autonomy unheard of in other issue areas (Rosenberg, 1982; Skocpol, 1985, p. 13; Strange, 1996, p. 53).

Radiotelegraphy does not fit easily within the corporate liberal framework or capitalist state theory. In the domestic realm, corporate liberalism is ill suited to public service industries where "public service liberalism," which imagined a much larger role for the state, prevailed (Stone, 1991). Arguably, the extension of the public service classification to more and more industries signaled the expansion of state power in the American economy (Novak, 2010).[2] Policymakers' attempt at classifying radiotelegraphy as a public service industry in the first decade of the twentieth century and the Navy's push for government ownership in the following decade were not minor skirmishes between parties of largely similar interests. At the very least, capitalist state theory must account for the precise interests of capital that are best served by the potential elimination of an entire industry that the government ownership proposal represented.

Moreover, all theories positing a common interest between the state and capital assume that companies and policymakers share the same allegiances. Policymakers in the early twentieth century were not quite sure. In international industries, in particular, where the public interest is understood as the national interest, state autonomy is often intertwined with nationalism. Because the incentives of global expansion for capital and for nations often collide, even homegrown MNCs posed a problem for nationalism. To which country MNCs belonged was never obvious, and the possibility of control over them was always tenuous. If policymakers could not count on the loyalty of companies with international operations, such as ITT, why would they support their expansion? The line of academic thinking that presumes that policymakers seek to preserve the long-term viability of "capital" does not ask whether and why they would also seek to preserve the viability of global capital in general. By contrast, I will show that the national interest was far from "a corporate liberal trope" (cf. Streeter, 1996, p. 224).

Since my purpose is to explain radio policy in a systemic context, I will treat the international system and the foreign policy executive as integrally related (Amoore et al., 2000, p. 61; Friedberg, 1988, p. 6). For the purposes of the national-level analysis that will take up much of this book, the international system will be understood as policymakers' knowledge about the system. Policymakers form part of an interpretive community, which is the source of shared meanings (Streeter, 1996, pp. 114–115). Law, as Thomas Streeter points out, is "a way of turning forms of knowledge into action" (Streeter, 1996, p. 8). The knowledge that informed early radio policy, however, was not entirely domestic. In the early twentieth century, American naval elites participated in a "transatlantic discursive community" that circulated knowledge about the system and informed their outlook on international matters (Bönker, 2012, p. 5). The boundaries of the interpretive community were likely even larger. Daqing Yang's (2009) research has revealed that Japanese policymakers' objectives with regard to communications networks mirrored those of their European counterparts. Thus, naval policy provides the link between system structure, technological leadership, and hegemonic leadership in the field of radio communications. Policymakers at the turn of the twentieth century were theorists of the world system and of the multinational corporation at the same time that they had the ability to make decisions to effect change.

If policy matters, then system structure is transformed through actions on the national and international levels, and American geopolitical objectives could be served through domestic legislation (licensing, foreign ownership rules), international law (the 1906 convention), and bilateral negotiations (e.g., the 1914 decree issued by the Republic of Panama).

Insofar as legislation was required to achieve American geopolitical objectives, policymakers had to maneuver between the ideas emerging from the geopolitical interpretive community and a domestic legal tradition that sought to incorporate radio as a public service industry while also straining to adjust to the new institutional development that was the multinational corporation. As a result, three types of knowledge were developing during the early twentieth century: knowledge about the world system, about radiotelegraphy, and about the multinational corporation.

American policymakers' conception of system structure at the turn of the twentieth century was similar to that of world systems theory: it was hierarchical and attentive to historical succession, placing the United States in a long line of challengers to British power (Bönker, 2012, p. 70; cf. Headrick, 1991, p. 102). In general, policymakers' knowledge about the system, their "geopolitical code," includes a definition of a state's interests, the identification of its enemies, and planned responses to external threats (Gaddis as cited in Taylor, 1993, pp. 91, 64). While the general framework they used for world affairs was shared among members of the geopolitical discursive community, the specifics were confidential. During the course of three decades, policymakers both in Britain and in the United States reevaluated where their country stood in the world system and revised their views about the other country as well. Neither security nor power were self-defining, and plans for using new technologies or the new corporate form for geopolitical advantage were closely held. Before American policymakers could unite behind general policy principles for radiotelegraphy, they had to agree that the country was no longer a challenger in need of defensive policies but was rather an aspiring world leader. The policies they developed, perhaps not surprisingly, did not emerge in response to domestic political pressures but instead are best understood as the response of self-seeking nation-states to perceived international structures.

Before leadership in radiotelegraphy could aid American ascendancy, policymakers needed to give up their view of radiotelegraphy as an inferior substitute for the submarine cable and see the technology as an opportunity for structural change in global communications. It would take the systemic perspective of naval policymakers to give weight to radiotelegraphy's independence from the cable network while at the same time downplaying its technological shortcomings, such as susceptibility to interference and interception. In the balance of the book, I develop the third aspect

of knowledge, policymakers' understanding of the multinational corporation, in the most detail. In order to facilitate the analysis of policymakers'
perspectives under the structural level of network control, the following
section also lays out researchers' views on corporate nationality.

Network Control

The chapters that follow trace the steps of American ascendancy toward a
Western Union model of control while analyzing policymakers' attempts
at defining what constituted American control. Thus, I will be looking at
"control" in two different ways. On the one hand, researchers studying documents years later may have insights that policymakers at the time did not.
On the other hand, policymakers acted only on the information available to
them. My definition of network control therefore is largely independent of
policymakers' understanding of the concept and general enough to facilitate
comparisons between developments in different contexts (for the difficulty
of combining historical "understanding" with social scientific "explanation," see Hollis & Smith, 1990, p. 91). Since the strategically significant
radio network used the airwaves for connection, the airwaves eventually
also became subject to geopolitical rivalry, as did the information that went
through the network. During much of this period, however, control over
the network was seen as an indirect approach to controlling information.
Control over the network, the airwaves, and information were all on the
table in early twentieth-century radio policy, but this work only follows the
first problem at length.

　　One of the best-known attempts to examine power and networks in relation to each other is Manuel Castells's sociological approach to the network
society. The similarities between the network control framework offered for
consideration here and Castells's theory, however, are superficial. Whereas
Castells understands networks broadly, as "the fundamental pattern of life"
(Castells 2013, p. 21), I understand them narrowly, as the telecommunications infrastructure. Castells invites his readers to identify and understand
power relationships as a process specific to each network (Castells, 2013,
p. 46). Understanding power on the level of each network, however, requires
a different framework for each one. Unlike gossip or financial networks,
physical networks follow "the economic laws of rival resources and the
political laws of sovereign jurisdiction and control" (Nye, 2011, p. 19). Once

the network-specific development of sovereign control is addressed, we would still have a long way to go to understand how a country uses the unique features of the network to exert influence over individuals in specific instances, either within its own territory or worldwide.

Since the physical infrastructure is shaped by geopolitical and economic desires, states loom large in the management of telecommunications networks. They seek control over what they see as a weapon of war and do so to achieve geopolitical advantage. Castells defines the state broadly as all kinds of institutions of governance on various levels: national, regional, and international (Castells, 2013, p. 39). Using this definition, he draws connections between the local realm of human experience and the global social structure, effectively bypassing world powers. By contrast, the distinction between world powers and less powerful states is analytically salient in this volume, which foregrounds the actions of the former states on the global stage. The similarities between the types of power states exercise and the types Castells has identified are for future research to discover. It is sufficient to note here that asserting control over the physical infrastructure may well require some distinct strategies that are not applicable to using these networks to influence the global public.

Network control involves decision-making ability over territory, capital, and technology through which one party secures an uninterrupted flow of information while denying the same to its opponent. This formulation broadens the analysis from "what" states seek to control, which is currently the most developed aspect of the concept, to "why" and "how" questions (Aitken, 1985, p. 252; Bar & Sandvig, 2008, p. 546; Goldsmith & Wu, 2008, p. 68; Hugill, 1999, p. 95). The network control framework ties together the structural level, which presents an insider's understanding of control, and the tactical level, which enables us to trace the geographical expansion of American interests in radiotelegraphy. Though I will periodically comment on the tactical level, the full analysis of American expansion is left for another time. For now, combining the network control framework with historical analysis helps us understand core states' objectives and the challenges they face when attempting to control global communications networks. In this section, I will address the three sites of network control to narrow the inquiry to the territory-capital nexus, which is the most relevant for control over global networks. Next, I will explain how the security establishment understands the purpose of network control. Finally, I will sketch how states seek to control global communications networks defining the tactical and structural levels of control.

The Territory-Capital Nexus

States seeking control over global communications networks have an immediate advantage in control over territory. What makes the intersections among the three forms of leverage—technology, territory, and capital—analytically promising, however, is that they have the potential to provide countervailing influences to each other. Each of the three intersections relevant for network control—territory-capital, territory-technology, and capital-technology— deserves a study in its own right. My focus in the chapters that follow will be on the territory-capital nexus, analyzing policymakers' responses to the challenge that the global expansion of early telecommunications companies posed for the state. The *technology-territory* nexus includes, for example, a country's attempt to keep new technologies on its territory, such as the Admiralty's attempt recounted in chapter 2, or a struggle over the values embedded in the network. Tech-savvy experimenters such as the amateurs in the past and hacktivists today may threaten the state's ability to secure and maintain control of the network (Douglas, 1989; Streeter, 1996; see Zajácz, 2013, for a contemporary example). The *capital-technology* nexus— most apparent during this period in the switch from the era of the individual inventor to corporations handling patent libraries—is beyond the scope of this book. I will treat patents as already attached to companies and discuss their use on the tactical level as one of the ways for MNCs to piece together control over a global network on a country-by-country basis, but I will not address intercorporate competition for patent rights in detail either.

The network control framework is useful for analyzing the territory-capital nexus because Giovanni Arrighi's insight that capitalism and territorialism act as opposite logics of power manifests itself in a unique manner when applied to global infrastructure industries. In general terms, the source of the multinational corporation's authority is its "command over the nature, location and manner of production and distribution of goods and services" (Strange, 1996, p. 45). This assumption leads to the idea of the "footloose" corporation, which can shift its activities from country to country in pursuit of global profits (Strange, 1996, p. 45; Vernon, 1971, p. 10). States, in turn, appear helpless in the face of mobile capital. The idea of the footloose MNC puts conflicts between territory-bound states and global capital front and center but overemphasizes the leverage that control over capital provides MNCs.

In global communications, the underlying sources of leverage are distributed far less clearly. Because infrastructure development is costly, companies have not relied solely on capital markets for financing but also have often received public subsidies. Thus, states can also control the capital that companies need. The flip side is also true: unlike MNCs involved in, say, detergent manufacturing, public utility MNCs must control territory. Rather than weighing multiple countries for investment, an infrastructure MNC must piece together a global network by establishing stations on the territories of "desirable" countries. Once public utility MNCs establish facilities, capital is fixed in investments of long duration and companies lose most of the bargaining power they may have had at the outset (Harvey, 2003, pp. 109–110). Economic powerhouses enjoy the most leverage in their dealings with public utility MNCs. Because companies cannot bypass their territories, they must deal with their foreign policy executive. The key issue of the territory-capital nexus in global infrastructure industries is that states and MNCs, whether homegrown or headquartered elsewhere, compete to control territory around the world.

If MNCs involved in infrastructure industries are far more "fixed" than their counterparts in other areas of the economy, world powers are far more "mobile," precisely because they can exercise influence indirectly. World systems researcher Immanuel Wallerstein argues that, on the international level, control exercised by states does not necessarily accompany ownership of territory and, conversely, it can be asserted in the absence of ownership (Wallerstein, 2004, pp. 52–55). Unable to erect stations in the territories of other sovereign states, global powers expand via intermediaries. The British government, for example, could not place Admiralty cable or radio stations anywhere it wished. However, regional and world powers using public utility MNCs can extend their influence further than a conception of control centered on territorial acquisition alone would allow, if only they could trust these companies. It is therefore not surprising that a key question occupying policymakers ever since communications multinationals appeared was whose interests they served.

The United States, as a host state, faced the classic challenge of FDI: because the physical placement of radio stations on U.S. soil was vital for the Marconi Company, American policymakers were forced to compete for control over the choicest locations for stations on American territory. As soon as American Marconi erected its stations and British Marconi made its bid to run the marine communications of the world, questions emerged regarding the relationship between the two companies. Was American Marconi, in fact, "American"? If its policies were made in Britain, should British Marconi decide the policies governing the radio network and determine its scope? How should the United States act toward companies operating on American soil that presumably acted in the interest of other states?

Our current understanding of radio policy assumes that policymakers sought to control access to the airwaves, but what if they started out by seeking to control the stations and considered both the airwaves and information in the context of this objective? During the early twentieth century, commercial stations on American territory were integrated into a global network established in Britain, and a foreign MNC decided whether even the U.S. Navy could access a station on American territory. From the perspective of the United States as a host state, unrestricted FDI meant a lack of borders and a loss of sovereignty that was untenable from a national security standpoint. This was the problem, and incorporating the airwaves into policy discussions became a key part of the solution.

For the United States acting as a home state, on the other hand, the central problem was how to control the identity and loyalty of the MNC as well as its plans for territorial expansion. American policymakers faced the challenge of matching the expansion of U.S.-headquartered MNCs with the gradual expansion of the American sphere of influence. The emergence of homegrown MNCs was accompanied by the now familiar fixation on corporate nationality, which led to questions about the impact of international expansion on the identities and loyalties of network managers. How should the United States approach the expansion of its own MNCs into other countries? Could corporations with international operations retain their loyalty to the United States?

Investigating the territory-capital aspect of network control has much to offer if we hope to understand control over the global communications networks in general and American ascendancy in radiotelegraphy in particular. Global capital and world powers may well use each other's power to strengthen themselves, as Arrighi contends, but capital's side of the story will be left for another day (Arrighi, 2010, p. 172). How early radio companies imagined global economic and strategic relations, how they secured technology or interfaced with the financial system to raise money for expansion, and the way they maneuvered with and around states is for future research to explore. If, however, researchers abandon the state entirely in favor of analyzing hegemony as the product of a transnational capitalist class, as some have suggested, they are likely to miss an important part of governing global communications networks (Robinson, 2005). In the following section, I will take a closer look at the motivations of the state and trace the origins of policymakers' approaches to controlling global communications networks to sea power doctrine.

The Purpose of Network Control

At the turn of the twentieth century, sea power doctrine, a line of thinking with a centuries-long pedigree, was adapted to the task of controlling the communications infrastructure and yielded the concept of "autonomy of communications" as the central policy objective. Admiral Alfred Thayer Mahan, the architect of American naval strategy, asserted that the key to winning a decisive conflict with a strong rival was command of the sea: the ability to use the sea and deny the same to one's opponents (Hannigan, 2002, p. 19). Over time, naval theorists have scaled back the scope of the doctrine to use or deny only some seas, but the dual emphasis on the ability to use and deny remains (see Till, 2013, chap. 6; Turner, 1974, p. 8). The following discussion represents a preliminary entry into a broader problem of exactly how the geopolitical imagination and the legal framework interact to shape our understanding of communications networks. When and why were messages flowing through networks modeled after troops crossing a bridge or after goods carried via the railroad in interstate commerce? And what was the consequence of invoking one framework or the other?

Command of the sea implies control over "a medium of communications," where the word "communications" refers to transportation and the word "medium" draws on an older use of the term as a channel facilitating action at a distance (Till, 2013, p. 65). When a fleet has the ability to use the sea, it can send large forces across great distances (Posen, 2003, p. 13). As the concept of sea control morphed into autonomy of communications, messages sent across the distance replaced troops, but the focus on the unobstructed transmission and reception of information remained. In the most immediate military context, autonomy of communications meant the ability to transmit and receive confidential information between the

Navy Department in Washington and units of the fleet. In a geopolitical context, control over a network was thought to facilitate its availability for both confidential and public use.

Radiotelegraphy, though largely neglected in media history, illustrates the ongoing and deep connections between transportation and communication. As naval policymakers sought to fit the logic of controlling a transportation network onto a communications infrastructure, they emphasized control over the network to secure the passage of information. They operated on the assumption that the best way to protect maritime communications was to patrol the trade routes that ships had to pass through. Protecting trade routes, in turn, required control over the geographic bottlenecks through which the enemy had to pass. The concept of "chokepoint control" indicated the importance of controlling key territories that could give one's forces an advantage (Turner, 1974, p. 8). The roots of this approach lay in the "sea-lane" metaphor: the Navy would protect the sea-lanes as the Army protected roads (Till, 2013, p. 216). Although the Navy would soon abandon this strategy as unworkable, it would still influence policymakers' thinking about communication networks.

Autonomy of communications emerged from the transatlantic discursive community to become a shared objective among naval elites worldwide. "All countries of the world consider autonomy of communication a basic tenet in national defense," a Japanese government official commented in connection with Japan's annexation of Korea in 1910, adding, "All aspire to possess their own communications systems" (cited in Yang, 2009, p. 235). What policymakers in each country would come to recognize as "their own" independent network system and how autonomy could be squared with expansion would be worked out in the next several decades.

Over the past century, the desire for autonomy of communications has come to inform the military's approach to each subsequent communications network. As a British admiral noted in another context, "instruments alter, principles remain" (Till, 2013, p. 218). Securing the ability to communicate and denying the same to the enemy have been central to discussions about network-centric warfare, cyberwar, and the use of the global commons (Clarke & Knake, 2010, p. 44; Der Derian, 2009, p. 241; Posen, 2003, p. 8; Winseck, 2008, p. 424). Even the specific idea of chokepoint control carried over into proposals to secure the internet (Clarke & Knake, 2010, p. 161). Since these ideas form an enduring element of the way the national security establishment approaches communications networks, analyses of state control over global communications networks would be deficient without them.

Levels

I have adapted political scientist Susan Strange's distinction between tactical and structural power to help define the levels of network control (Strange, 1996, p. 136). The *tactical* level involves the struggle over relational power, where one party gets the other one to do what it wants via existing tools available in a given conflict. The *structural* level refers to the ability to influence the rules of the game, including general policy principles, discursive framing, or the values embedded in technologies. Attention to the two reinforcing levels allows us to follow the emergence of policies aimed at changing system structure. Because the United States was a challenger in the early twentieth century, policymakers focused more on securing for the country the ability to communicate via general policy principles and discursive framing rather than on denying that ability to others. Delineating the problem in this fashion naturally omits denying the use of the network in the military context of World War I, including the examples used here to illustrate the tactical level (see Winkler, 2008, for the use of radio in military maneuvers).

The boundaries between the tactical and the structural levels are at times less than clear-cut. Tactical-level actions facilitate change on the structural level, which in turn prepares the ground for the geographical expansion of American interests in radio communications. What was once part of the structural level can become part of the tactical level, though the process does not typically work in reverse. By introducing licensing in the 1910s, policymakers changed the radio environment to the advantage of the state, but the policy is now a fixture in the state's arsenal. Analyzing change on these two levels is the dynamic aspect of the network control framework and can usefully be combined with historical analysis.

The tactical level highlights the use of immediately available forms of leverage. The ultimate form of leverage for the state is control over territory, which is fully realized when the legal claim to sovereignty is accompanied by economic and military might (on different forms of sovereignty, see Krasner, 1999). Control over British territory, for example, made it possible for Britain to deny Germany the ability to communicate by severing most of the Atlantic cables at the beginning of World War I or for American policymakers in peacetime to prevent Western Union from landing a cable in

Miami (Winkler, 2008). Using territory to such advantage, however, may be difficult for many small and weak countries, even on their own territories. Cable landing rights, railroad rights of way, and, by extension, radio licenses, on the other hand, are the codification of the state's control over territory captured in the legal concept of jurisdiction. These policy measures operate on the structural level of network control, freeing the state from continually relying on control over its territory in order to achieve its objectives. The metaphorical transformation of intangible things into "territory," in turn, is an important element of exercising control over them.

American ascendancy is the story of territorial gains, actual and metaphorical. Direct reliance on U.S. territory as a form of leverage, however, will be relevant mostly in part I, which focuses on achieving autonomy of communications. American ascendancy began in the first decade of the twentieth century against the backdrop of asymmetric end-to-end control by a British corporation, and both levels of network control were intertwined during these early years. Because the United States was a host state subject to media imperialism, American policymakers sought to reclaim the country's own communications space. Policymakers pursuing interconnection and licensing on the structural level of network control relied on tactical control over U.S. territory while also seeking U.S. government control over radio stations abroad. This book, however, is primarily a study of the structural level. The following section outlines the concepts necessary to follow how American policymakers sought to bring the multinational corporation under territorial control and how they sought to influence the strategies of U.S.-headquartered MNCs as they expanded their networks to territories outside the United States.

Discursive Framing and Policy Decisions   One of the central problems of communications policy analysis is that policy is not only a site of knowledge but also a site of action. The specific policies that American policymakers developed to improve the country's position in global communications were shaped by participants' perceptions about the world system, about radio technology, and about corporations expanding internationally. The enactment of legislation, in turn, transformed both policymakers' perceptions and the structure of global communications networks. The difficult part of the analysis is in describing how this process takes place. Given the importance accorded to knowledge about the world system, radio technology, or the corporation, how are we to understand the relationship between discursive framing and policy decisions? How is knowledge turned into action? I will address this question in the conclusion.

In the discussion that follows, I will use "discursive framing" and "knowledge" to refer to the currents of thought surrounding specific topics but will leave the fine-grained distinctions among metaphors, ideology, framing, and discourse to the specialists. The following chapters will focus less on how policymakers' views of system structure, the spectrum as a natural resource, or the corporation as a migrant subject emerged and more on the way these ideas figured into policies aimed at American ascendancy.

Corporate Nationality The multinational corporation was a new force in the global economy during the early twentieth century and posed serious questions to policymakers. It is worth noting that the definitive study examining the relationship between early MNCs in the communications industry, their subsidiaries, and the states they came into contact with is yet to be written. As a result, we don't know how executives at British Marconi and other companies in this book understood the nature of their firms. The relationships these companies had with their subsidiaries and how the British government influenced the actions of the parent company or its subsidiaries also remain unclear. In the chapters that follow, I will investigate how American policymakers sought to grapple with the MNC and discuss the influence of their emerging knowledge on communications policy. The analysis will sever the easy relationship between corporate interests and the national interest that is the staple of much policy analysis in the field today.

The problem of corporate nationality, which had plagued policymakers from the outset, is central to the analysis. In 1969, business professor Howard Perlmutter distinguished between ethnocentric (home country–oriented), polycentric (host country–oriented), and geocentric (world-oriented) corporations. Much has happened since then, but I will use Perlmutter's typology to sketch the general contours of assumptions about the relationship between multinational corporations and their home states in several fields of inquiry, in addition to reviewing scholarship related to communications networks.

The ethnocentric corporation is the policymaker's dream. The underlying assumption is that U.S.-based MNCs, no matter the extent of their international operations, are "American" and will act as extensions of their home states (Gilpin, 1975, p. 15; Schiller, 1992, p. 60). This is because, for world powers at least, the relationship is understood to be mutually beneficial.

The accumulation of capital depends on a stable international legal order, which the hegemon provides. Thus, the success of MNCs depends on the power of their home state abroad (Modelski & Thompson, 1996, p. 66; Taylor, 1993, p. 189). The hegemon's status as the lead economy in the world, in turn, depends on the innovation and the accumulation of capital that its companies provide. Analysts of communications networks have implicitly agreed that when ITT expands, the United States does as well (Hills, 2007, p. 11). Only recently have historians started looking at archival documents to establish relationships between companies and states, such as the interactions between British Marconi and the British government (Winkler, 2008, p. 96).

Historically, policymakers have drawn connections between corporate nationality and loyalty. Loyalty is identity in action. One by-product of the expectation of corporate loyalty is the assumption that companies will favor their home countries in wartime (Gilpin, 1977, p. 28; Vernon, 1971, p. 145). However, when companies are transformed as a result of international expansion, two types of disloyalty may occur. First, companies may be hijacked by their host states and act as agents of foreign governments—a development most likely for the "polycentric corporation" (Moran, 1990, p. 61; Vernon, 1974, p. 12). From a realist perspective, which prefers autarkic self-reliance in key economic sectors to protect national security, this is the greatest concern. Purely domestic corporations are the least likely to compromise the state's security objectives, but working with MNCs introduces uncertainty (Moran, 1990, pp. 63, 67).

Another form of disloyalty may occur when a multinational's global strategy subordinates each affiliate to the needs and strategies of the multinational network as a whole. Such "geocentric" MNCs strive for independence from every state they operate in and become, in fact, stateless (Barber, 1995, p. 56; Gilpin, 1975, pp. 9–10). Contemporary researchers in communications and media studies who see corporations as "deterritorialized" from their home states presuppose an uncomplicated past where states had more control (Sinclair, 2007, p. 139). Historical studies operating from this perspective, however, have no such illusions and have provided evidence that early MNCs presented "whatever national identity suited [their] purpose" to the various governments they came into contact with (Winseck & Pike, 2007, p. 59). But if corporate executives represented themselves in patriotic garb for an audience of policymakers, did policymakers buy these representations? Moreover, can academic theories that investigate the relationship between MNCs and their home states but ignore the position of the home state in the world system be descriptively accurate?

Table 1.3 left off with the United States emerging as the home state to its indigenous MNCs. The integration of political economic analysis with policy analysis will produce another set of figures that will map the possibilities of foreign control over the American communications space, starting from an extreme hypothetical—British government dominance over all aspects of radio communication under institutional control—and ending with naval policymakers' last-ditch efforts to tie both the holders of radio licenses and their parent companies to the United States.

Precisely at the time when the large corporation created a problem for liberal thought, its multinational variant presented a problem for nationalism. Autonomy of communications as a policy objective immediately posed an epistemological dilemma: how would a country tell when it possessed "its own" communications system? Both "American" and "control" required interpretation as policymakers and corporate executives negotiated the national identity of communications companies. The process by which policymakers sought to yoke the corporation to the national interest was therefore characterized by recurrent struggles over the discursive framing of corporate nationality. Policymakers' views about corporate nationality and loyalty influenced the development of general policy principles and were informed by a theory, however rudimentary, of the globalization of business. I will show that policymakers developed a nationalist critique of the MNC well before there were any words to describe the phenomenon. By theorizing what could be termed "the hegemon-centric corporation," or an MNC loyal to the most powerful state in the world system, naval policymakers' systemic perspective offers an intriguing corrective to contemporary academic theories of the relationship between multinational corporations and their home states.

Natural Monopoly Theory and Imperialism The network control framework extends beyond autonomy of communications and helps us understand expansion as well. Because the acquisition of territory abroad would prove to be impossible in all but the most dependent countries, most U.S. expansion in radiotelegraphy proceeded via U.S.-headquartered MNCs. I will show that relying on these companies was a structural-level decision, which policymakers only reluctantly accepted.

Policymakers' and corporate executives' attention to control over territory flowed from natural monopoly theory, a staple of economic theory in the early twentieth century. This theory and its legal counterpart—the essential facilities doctrine—identify industries where a single firm provides a service or product most efficiently (Lipsky & Sidak, 1999, p. 1187). Because of network effects, whereby each participant increases the value of a network, the network with the largest user base becomes the most viable (Katz & Shapiro, 1994, p. 94). Because there was only enough traffic to support one company, the reasoning went, duplication of facilities was undesirable. The ideal under natural monopoly theory was one service provider to a circuit, which in turn entailed exclusive control over territory. Even though both telephony and telegraphy fit uneasily with the assumptions of natural monopoly theory (John, 2008, p. 512; Mueller, 1997, pp. 15–16), the theory informed the calculations of industry players, the General Board, and those in the Navy Department who were in charge of radio policy (for critiques of natural monopoly as an ideology, see Cowhey, 1990, p. 183; Streeter, 1996).

Despite limits on the number of providers, the theory was compatible with a variety of policy options regarding the service provider itself, which could be a government, a single company, a joint venture, or a cartel. From a domestic perspective, natural monopolies were regulated in the public interest based on a number of criteria, which included decisions about whether the well-being of competitors or subscribers should be paramount (John, 2010, p. 407). After regulators classified an industry as a public utility, a common carrier, or both, monopoly was possible in the domestic context. This was the reward for accepting regulation. But how would this regulatory framework play out in the case of radiotelegraphy, an emerging global industry in which the public interest was replaced by the national interest? Would American policymakers grant monopoly status to the American subsidiary of a British firm? Since the industries clothed with the public interest were also essential to world leadership, how did natural monopoly theory dovetail with American ascendancy?

The fact that natural monopoly presupposed one service provider to a *circuit* calls attention to the problem of imperialism. In its broadest form, imperialism describes formal or informal foreign control over the assets and decisions of a weaker country. The most widely recognized form of imperialism is territorial acquisition and direct rule, where a political authority sets itself up as sovereign over a foreign territory and its people (Smith, 1981, p. 6). Here I understand imperialism in relation to the communications infrastructure from the vantage point of the state as an expansionist foreign policy that seeks to improve the country's position in the world system. When I comment on particular cases, I will examine the parts of the world that corporate executives and policymakers considered central (for critiques of the Euro-Atlantic emphasis of this line of analysis, see Hampf & Müller-Pohl, 2013; Hugill, 2009). Though I periodically address the perspectives of corporate executives, tracing the territorial gains of expansionist American firms would require a much larger study.

Exercising control over a circuit has the potential to signal expansion, since circuits have two ends and one of the stations is on the territory of another state. Who would run the foreign station, and under what conditions could it establish connections with the American station? If control over circuits with one end in the United States was potentially expansionist, control over circuits where both ends were outside the United States was definitely so. But what happened when more than one core state competed for control over a circuit? We can capture this dynamics better if we think of imperialism as intertwined with geopolitical rivalry rather than as an alternative to it (cf. Winseck & Pike, 2007, p. 104). Of course, *which* core state controls the communications space of peripheral countries may make little difference from the perspective of the periphery, particularly if core states treat peripheral countries the same way. Methodologically, however, an analysis of governments' views about particular industrial agreements, as seen in chapter 6, for example, can usefully complement the current reliance on quantitative indicators of dominance in media imperialism research.

Chapter Outline

Like the hero in an action movie clinging by his fingertips atop a tall building, Britain's grip over global communications slipped off one metaphorical finger at a time during the first three decades of the twentieth century. What follows, then, is by no means a comprehensive history of radio policy but is instead an analysis of the development of policy measures that facilitated American ascendancy. Part I of this book, "Autonomy," chronicles how American policymakers sought to prevent the country from being integrated into an emerging global radio network controlled by Britain. The book begins with the possibility of centralized control over the global radio network implemented by British Marconi, a multinational corporation widely perceived to be under British control. *Interconnection, licensing,* and *national ownership* fragmented the network under development while reasserting a kind of American border around radio. The following three chapters address these policies in order. Chapter 2 analyzes the rejection of the Marconi Company's claim to international public utility status at the 1903 and 1906 international conferences and the acceptance of interconnection as a general policy principle governing the operation of marine radio. Chapter 3 traces the way licensing, which ended unrestricted foreign direct investment in radiotelegraphy, was codified in the Radio Act of 1912 along with an interconnection requirement. Chapter 4 addresses how a corporation became "American" by linking foreign ownership regulations, the key alternative to government ownership, to tighter legal definitions of corporate nationality. Many of these measures pushed back against contemporary legal protections that facilitated the expansion of multinationals, including unrestricted foreign direct investment and the extension of full legal personality to corporations. By putting these measures in place, the United States achieved autonomy of communications over the transatlantic circuit that connected the United States to Europe. Communications policy came into its own as a tool of territorial control.

Part II, "Expansion," tells the story of how American policymakers came to settle on the forms of expansion for U.S.-headquartered MNCs. If the first part of the book reveals the emergence of a nationalist framework for radio policy, this part examines the unexpected challenges that U.S.-headquartered MNCs posed to the emerging framework. I will recount the prolonged process by which companies with a global orientation and a challenger country whose expansionist vision only gradually encompassed the entire world came to accommodate one another. Chapter 5 investigates American policymakers' efforts in the 1910s to obtain control over the U.S.–Latin America circuit. I analyze how policymakers realized the limits of territorial control and settled on an independently financed, brand new, "100 percent American" corporation—the future RCA—as the only possible avenue for American expansion. Chapter 6 details the experiences of American policymakers as they were challenged by expansionist corporate strategies, such as cartels and FDI, which drove toward the integration of the global radio and cable industries. Eventually, policymakers would settle on type competition, or the separation of these two industries, in combination with limited FDI, as the approach that best preserved the independence of American radio. Chapter 7 focuses on the enactment of direct and indirect foreign ownership regulations and traces the incorporation of the latter provision in the Communications Act of 1934 to naval policymakers' theory of the internationalization of business. As the interactions between industry and naval policymakers widened to include the State Department, which operated from the mind-set of an aspiring world leader, the Navy's perspective was being marginalized. Taken together, the last three research chapters trace how American nationalist thinking transitioned from being fixated on corporate purity to accepting, and even valuing, an institution as murky as the multinational corporation. By focusing on general policy principles, the book addresses the conceptual transformation of the United States into the leader in global communications and contributes to a better understanding of the role of global communications networks in geopolitical rivalry.

I Autonomy

2 Interconnection: Common Carrier Regulation, Spectrum Allocation, and Geopolitics at the 1903 and 1906 International Radio Conferences

Radio, after all, is a child of the telegraph.
—Russell Conklin, 1926

In March 1902, the German embassy called the attention of the U.S. State Department to an agreement between the Marconi Wireless Telegraph and Signal Company, registered in Britain, and the marine insurance organization Lloyd's of London, also established in Britain, inquiring whether the United States was interested in joining an international agreement to regulate ship-to-shore communication via radio.[1] The German draft proposal was aimed directly at the Marconi Company's "non-intercommunication" policy, which contractually bound ships and shore stations using a Marconi apparatus to communicate only with ships and shore stations that also carried a Marconi apparatus.

The linchpin of the German draft proposal, forwarded along with the invitation, was "free intercommunication": organizations should transmit and receive ship-to-shore messages regardless of the system being used. At stake, however, was not access to the airwaves, which the Marconi Company did not control, but access to the company's network of shore stations. Access to these stations, in turn, meant nothing less than access to the territory of Britain, which commanded the principal trade routes of the world. Policymakers at this time sought connectivity at sea for their countries' ships—a global economic and strategic matter of primary importance. Since radio was understood as a type of telegraphy, policymakers gathered to regulate an incipient public service and sought to transfer the principle of interconnection, well established in telegraph regulation, to radio. Regulation of the spectrum would eventually form an important part of an international agreement, but the German draft proposal did not so much as mention the airwaves or interference.

When the governments participating in the 1903 and 1906 conferences arrived at free intercommunication as the policy principle governing the operations of global marine radio, they put an end to the Marconi Company's attempt to shape network structure via private contracts. Not only did policymakers solve the geopolitical problem of marine communications, but they also left open the possibility for an alternative long-distance network to emerge. Wireless telegraphy, they would find, was no ordinary public service, since its potential to provide an alternative to submarine cables was well understood. Control over the technology—and any future network developed based on it—would also confer military advantage. The principle of free intercommunication thus worked on the structural level of network control: by undergirding fragmentation as a viable alternative to centralization, it laid the groundwork for American ascendancy in radio communications.

In order to follow this line of argument, several aspects of received wisdom need a closer look: that interference led states to gather in conference, which in turn focused on the management of a global resource; and that these conferences were ineffective (Codding, 1995, p. 503; Hills, 2002, p. 103; Hugill, 1999, p. 92). Importantly, the principle of free intercommunication would not have been adopted without Britain's adherence to the 1906 convention. Understanding why Britain adhered, in turn, is inseparable from grasping how the earliest form of spectrum management emerged in the context of a telegraph convention. Since radio communications relied on the airwaves for connection, the extension of the interconnection principle to the radio network pointed up a recurring problem of telegraph regulation: what exactly counted as a "connection?"

The Lloyd's Contract and the Development of Radiotelegraphy as a Systems Market in a Geopolitical Context

The German inquiry to the United States and other maritime powers came in the wake of a widely publicized affront to Kaiser Wilhelm's brother, Prince Henry, who was unable to send a message via the Nantucket lightship. Prince Henry's ship carried the Slaby-Arco apparatus, manufactured by the Allgemeine Elektrizitäts Gesellschaft (AEG), registered in Germany, while the lightship was equipped with a Marconi apparatus (Douglas, 1989, pp. 120, 138). At the heart of the German invitation, however, lay a complaint about the impact of the Lloyd's contract. Behind the scenes, the September 1901 agreement embodied a compromise between the respective commercial interests of the Marconi Company and Lloyd's, as well as the military objectives of the British Admiralty.

The newcomer in the group was the Marconi Wireless Telegraph and Signal Company, incorporated in 1897 to capitalize on Guglielmo Marconi's patents. Several aspects of the company's business strategy were formed early on as a way to work around the monopoly of the British Post Office over telegraph traffic, which extended to the United Kingdom and its territorial waters (Pocock, 1988, pp. 146, 150). Since the Marconi Company sought a foothold in the telegraph business but could not charge for individual messages, executives decided to offer ship wireless service to customers under contract. Steamship lines would lease Marconi equipment and pay a monthly fee for access to the network, a certain number of words, and the company's services (Pocock, 1988, p. 150).[2] In contemporary terms, steamship lines were on a *plan*. A central element of the Marconi Company's strategy was to present radiotelegraphy as "a system" and to encourage the simultaneous adoption of ship wireless service and the equipment necessary to receive that service (Douglas, 1989, p. 131). This was a closed system: since sending messages in Morse code required technical assistance, the company furnished the apparatus and provided trained operators (Aitken, 1976, pp. 231–233).[3] All operators, Managing Director Cuthbert Hall would later declare to American policymakers, were controlled by the Marconi Company.[4] The business plan was legal because the service was limited to intracompany traffic, but the presence of British subjects at Marconi stations worldwide would soon raise eyebrows.[5]

During the early years, the Marconi organization was developing two kinds of service, "maritime signaling" and "sea telegraphy." Maritime signaling covered a relatively narrow class of information, specifically related to ship movements. Navies and shipping lines welcomed the improvement over optical telegraphs and fast torpedo boats, which had made confidential communications difficult. In fair weather, everybody could see the semaphore signals; in fog or during a storm, nobody could see anything, which led ships to run into each other or ram lighthouses (Pocock, 1988, pp. 29, 32). Sea telegraphy, on the other hand, included "the receipt and transmission of messages to and from passengers in vessels" as well as "public news transmitted to or from vessels."[6] Inventor Guglielmo Marconi would soon conjure a future in which newspapers were printed aboard ship every day.[7]

The Lloyd's contract connected Marconi's pioneering technology to a global organization specializing in maritime signaling. Leading an industry with an immense need for accurate information meant that Lloyd's had set up "a global information network" consisting of numerous stations for semaphore signaling and 1,300 agents and subagents involved in collecting and forwarding the latest news of ship movements (Aitken, 1976, p. 235; Hodgson, 1984, p. 68).[8] The Lloyd's network relied on modern lighthouses, which had been developed in the British Empire, to provide warning to ships approaching the shore, and the organization continuously upgraded its technology. Wireless was a great advantage to companies dealing with risk: when prompt assistance was sent to vessels in distress or when ships were diverted to different ports, both people and perishable cargo could be saved, obviating the need for insurance claims (Hancock, 1974, pp. 15–16).

The Lloyd's network was also a strategic asset, which became an extension of the Royal Navy in wartime. The company employed naval reservists as signalmen, and the Admiralty had the right to occupy any of the Lloyd's stations in an emergency.[9] These stations would save the Admiralty the expense and inconvenience of establishing its own "War Signal Stations."[10] Anticipating wartime use, Lloyd's permitted the Admiralty to exercise effective veto power over the placement of the organization's stations.[11] Instead of control over the air, which the flags and the colored lights used for signaling disturbed, these arrangements provided the Admiralty with control over the Lloyd's stations and facilitated the Royal Navy's command of the seas. Command of the seas, in turn, was central to world power, and radiotelegraphy would soon come into its own as an auxiliary of sea power.

The suggestion for a contract between the Marconi Company and Lloyd's came from the Admiralty,[12] which had become dependent on Marconi technology[13] but was convinced that "one controlling power" was necessary to work a global network.[14] Before the success of Marconi's longdistance experiments, two features commended wireless to the Admiralty: safety at sea and instantaneous communication. Wireless was invaluable for coordinating fleet movements and raised hopes for better protection of the Empire's trade routes (Pocock, 1988, pp. 151–153, 157). With the introduction of the new technology, admirals could broadcast an order to all of their ships in a given region at once (Headrick, 1991, p. 121). The

Admiralty was in fact the quintessential large, multilocation organization that economists have placed at the forefront of adopting communications networks. Such organizations internalized network effects; in effect, they "communicated with themselves" (Katz & Shapiro, 1994, p. 97).

The Lloyd's contract was a patent licensing agreement—with a geopolitical edge. The Marconi International Marine Communications Company (MIMCC), which focused on the commercial work of reporting ships,[15] licensed Lloyd's to use the company's system for maritime signaling, or such information about shipping and insurance as Lloyd's had already collected and disseminated via semaphore telegraphy.[16] Lloyd's would act as an operating company, and the Marconi Company would furnish and maintain all apparatuses for Lloyd's free of charge while reserving sea telegraphy for itself.[17] In practice, this meant that most shore stations were controlled by Lloyd's, but there existed freestanding Marconi stations as well. The revenue from sea telegraphy went to the Marconi companies, and the revenue from maritime signaling went to Lloyd's.[18]

A few months after signing the commercial contract, policymakers and company executives were putting the finishing touches on a tripartite agreement, which included the Admiralty as well.[19] Lloyd's agreed to comply with any "conditions and regulations the Admiralty thought necessary in the public interest,"[20] and the long-standing agreement for the use of the company's stations in time of war was extended to cover the new technology.[21] The Marconi Company agreed not to erect any installations either in the United Kingdom or abroad without first giving Lloyd's the option to do so and promised to supply installations only to Lloyd's and the British government.[22] In the end, the Admiralty would deal with a single, "semipublic" network manager and keep the technology in British hands, while Lloyd's would remain the clearinghouse for maritime information.[23] By tying the Marconi Company to Lloyd's and Lloyd's to the Admiralty, naval officers ensured control in the operating side of the business by a hierarchy of command. The agreement would soon fall apart, but not before it alerted policymakers in maritime countries to the dangers of yet another British monopoly over global communications.

The non-intercommunication policy, missing from both the Marconi Company's 1901 contract with the Admiralty and from its early propositions to the U.S. Navy, was a central component of the Lloyd's contract.[24] Lloyd's agreed not only to equip all of its stations with a Marconi apparatus but also to exchange messages only with ships equipped with Marconi's apparatus. Rather than "a master stroke of corporate strategy," the non-intercommunication policy was incorporated in the contract as a consolation prize for relinquishing traffic handling for maritime signaling (cf. Aitken, 1976, p. 237).[25] From the perspective of an equipment manufacturer, the policy was advantageous because it ensured that shipping lines contracting with Lloyd's for service ordered equipment from the Marconi Company. For a company planning to carve out a niche in the telegraph business, the agreement was less than satisfactory.

Most importantly, the contract put Lloyd's in charge of the global network now equipped with wireless. This was a setback to British Marconi, which had already begun its global expansion. Putting ships in any part of the world in touch with each other and with the shore had meant global expansion because ship wireless was both a short-haul and a global technology. The development of the commercial radio infrastructure followed the established and lucrative trade routes: ocean liners traveling the transatlantic route were the first to subscribe to radio service in order to prevent loss of life and property (Aitken, 1976; Hancock, 1974). Before the contract, the Marconi Company had been developing its business to serve shipping lines around the world by licensing its patents to subsidiaries established on several continents (Hancock, 1974, p. 24).

By early 1903, the parent company had supplemented MIMCC with four subsidiaries: one in the United States, one in Canada, one in Belgium, and one in France.[26] Executives at MIMCC referred to the company as an "international corporation," while British Marconi executives described the parent company as "an association of affiliated national companies."[27] At the time, however, only entities created by a treaty were recognized as "international corporations," so British Marconi was working to cobble together subsidiaries created under the laws of different countries (Vagts, 1970, p. 740). In a few decades, such companies would be termed "multinational" corporations.

The single most important consequence of conceiving of the Marconi Company as an operating company for ship wireless service had been the erection of the company's own shore stations. Before 1904, the British government placed no conditions on the establishment of private stations, and the Marconi Company had put up forty-five stations of ordinary power and three "stations of great power."[28] Now that the Marconi organization had joined forces with Lloyd's, the two companies controlled access to a global network and could also deny access to it. Lloyd's would soon require steamships to be equipped with the Marconi system in order to get the best insurance rates.[29] Though the rates were advantageous, shipping lines were nudged toward a preferred manufacturer. Everyone who wanted access to the Lloyd's network of information and insurance agents had to have a Marconi set (Aitken, 1976, p. 236). This was because shore stations were disproportionately valuable for the functioning of the network as a whole. All ships eventually needed to get in touch with the shore.

The importance of shore stations for a public network poses a challenge to economic theory, which ties the value of a network to the number of participants. As the concept of "network effects" makes clear, users pay for the ability to get in touch with other users: demand for a service depends on who else has subscribed (Aitken, 1976, p. 239; Mueller, 1997, p. 27). The perceived importance of user-to-user connection influenced what was considered the most valuable part of the network. In telephony, this was the switchboard, which negotiated the connection between users. Ship wireless, however, was a global service, whose users bought safety at sea and coordination, which placed a premium on shore stations. The head of the British delegation to the 1906 conference would compare shore stations to "a common center" from which telegraph wires radiated.[30] Interacting with this "switchboard" was as valuable as interacting with other users via the switchboard.

Describing the first decade of the twentieth century as the period of "unlicensed devices" or unowned public space therefore misses how much of radiotelegraphy was embedded in contemporary business and geopolitical relations (cf. Benkler, 1998, p. 295). Researchers have long associated the non-intercommunication policy with contractual "fences" around the spectrum in order to make the enforcement of property rights easier (Aitken, 1985; Douglas, 1989; Hills, 2002, p. 97). But the non-intercommunication policy did not restrict the use of the airwaves. Amateurs could exchange sports scores and entrepreneurs could broadcast opera without ever connecting to a Marconi station. Marconi instruments, on the other hand, were subject to patent, contract, and, soon, common carrier law. Ship and shore "devices" differed wildly in importance, and the value of shore stations, as we will shortly see, was determined by the economic position of the country where they were located.

Though the agreement between Lloyd's, British Marconi, and the Admiralty was a workable alternative to both wartime takeover and government monopoly,[31] it did not survive the introduction of long-distance radiotelegraphy. While ship-to-shore traffic covered short distances, the endgame for the Marconi Company was competition with the submarine cable network. The company kept its focus on the lucrative transatlantic trade route and, in December 1901, turned transatlantic wireless transmission into reality by sending the letter S across the Atlantic. Shortly after a ship in the mid-Atlantic received intelligible messages from a Marconi station over 1,500 miles away, Cuthbert Hall made it clear to both the British and the American navies that "unless [we] could do transatlantic and transocean business generally there was no money in wireless telegraphy."[32] The success of Marconi's long-distance experiments quickly led to speculation that wireless would replace the submarine cables, and the price of cable shares began to fall (Jacobsen, 2010, p. 235; Kurylo & Susskind, 1981, p. 147; Masini, 1995, p. 161).

Now, the Marconi organization sought to take the place of Lloyd's at the center of a global network. Rather than a monopoly over the invisible and communal ether, company executives pursued a monopoly over traffic handling and recognition as an international public utility (cf. Douglas, 1989, p. 101). Aiming at control over the choicest locations, the company began freezing Lloyd's out of the operating business by refusing to equip the latter's shore stations if they were in the same place as Marconi installations (Maclaurin, 1949, p. 37). Marconi executives claimed that the Lloyd's contract gave Lloyd's no rights to transoceanic telegraphy, and they would soon sue Lloyd's for the privilege of working several shore stations that Lloyd's was operating at the time (Raboy, 2016, p. 205n).

Naval policymakers were quick to notice the cracks in the agreement.[33] "Marconi erects stations when & where he pleases," the First Lord of the Admiralty, Lord Selborne, found out.[34] That control over technology favored the Marconi organization was apparent when the Admiralty, though anxious not to be perceived as "throwing over" Lloyd's,[35] switched to an arrangement with the Marconi Company. After all, Lloyd's did not develop radio technology and would not, on its own, improve it.

Fresh off its technological achievement, the Marconi organization faced the problem of monetizing access to its network and opening it to public correspondence. Would the non-intercommunication policy be as advantageous for a telecommunication service provider as it appeared to an equipment manufacturer? An open communications network, economists have pointed out, shares many features with a public good, including the possibility of free riding (Katz & Shapiro, 1994, pp. 102–103), but the radio network, which used the airwaves for connection, could never be truly closed. Company executives sought a solution somewhere between an open and a closed network configuration. During the next few years, Marconi executives were busy fitting radiotelegraphy into the conceptual framework used to manage wired networks, and they began to deploy the non-intercommunication policy as a way to fortify a technology that was difficult to monopolize.

Foremost among the conceptual tools company executives relied on was natural monopoly theory, an economic theory that had been developing at the time to address the problems of the railroad industry and was being extended to understand the features of wired communications networks. Hall was on well-trodden ground when he pointed a finger at the considerable upfront costs of establishing the network itself. In the railroad industry, for example, the acquisition of land and laying down the tracks were responsible for the lion's share of the costs (Hovenkamp, 1991, p. 142). Upfront costs were fixed, meaning they varied little with the amount of traffic, while the marginal cost of serving an additional user was minuscule. This was especially the case with communications networks, where messages flowed without causing any wear and tear.[36] Natural monopoly theory warned against a duplication of facilities, because competition would lower prices to the level of marginal costs, which would not be enough to cover fixed costs (Hovenkamp, 1991, p. 111).[37]

Marketing radiotelegraphy as a complete system was a direct result of understanding radiotelegraphy as a type of telegraphy when in fact the technology resisted the classification. Importantly, technological compatibility allows users and consumers to mix and match the components from different systems (Katz & Shapiro, 1994, p. 109). Provided all stations used a spark set, there was no technological barrier to connectivity in radiotelegraphy. Even the British Admiralty conceded privately that it was "physically possible" to receive messages from other systems.[38] When the Marconi organization marketed wireless as a complete system, however, it claimed that its transmitters and receivers were incompatible with those of other systems (Douglas, 1989, pp. 68–71).

Since connectivity was the norm in the radio industry, it was solely the corporate strategy of non-intercommunication policy that produced the effect of incompatibility. In just a quarter century, mixing and matching instruments would become the norm in the radio industry. Under the advertising-supported model of radio broadcasting, which offered programs to foster a large consumer market for receivers, both equipment sales and station operations could be profitable. Under the point-to-point framework, however, mixing and matching would have left the cost of shore stations to the Marconi organization.

During the first decade of the twentieth century, Hall expended a great deal of energy to convince policymakers that the wireless network was essentially the same as wired networks. He repeatedly drew parallels between the Marconi organization and wired networks, pointing out that, as infrastructure providers, companies in these industries faced unique problems. The presence of fixed costs, the undesirability of duplication,[39] and the value of centralization as a customary way to manage these industries were all prominent in Hall's arguments.[40] "It would be considered most inequitable," he wrote to the Post Office, "if legislation enabled anyone to secure for his own benefit subscriptions to a telephone service already established by someone else at an enormous outlay."[41] It was hardly possible to recoup the cost of shore stations, the company contended, if any other company could use these stations without paying its share of the costs.[42]

Framing radiotelegraphy as a kind of wired network helped company executives assert that intercommunication was technically difficult and that converting the company's facilities to accept messages from different systems would entail substantial costs.[43] Unlike in the submarine cable industry, however, in radiotelegraphy it was actually easy to establish a connection. In response, the Marconi organization promoted a conception of wavelengths as the equivalent of wires used by a telephone company or cable company. Hall repeatedly asserted that the non-intercommunication policy was the equivalent of the cable company refusing to allow anybody "to connect instruments with their systems."[44] Perhaps to bolster the effectiveness of the non-intercommunication policy, the Marconi organization also sought to keep the wavelengths it used secret, which immediately caught the attention of the German government.[45] This strategy, however, was also born out of weakness. It was the direct result of the fact that the Marconi organization could not make its wavelengths "private," as in unavailable to its competitors. They could only make them secret, as in unknown to others.

In the short term, the Marconi Company seemed to be successful. The non-intercommunication policy provided the company with end-to-end control over its network, which, because of the hold of the Marconi organization over shore stations, became synonymous with global connectivity via radio. Company executives boasted early on that two ocean liners registered in Germany but under contract to the Marconi organization could not communicate without the company's permission.[46] Yet, several problems lay dormant. First, end-to-end control over *intracompany* traffic was of limited value: without a domestic distribution arrangement with the Post Office, Marconi stations could not carry public correspondence, only the correspondence of their institutional subscribers. Unlike sending telegrams via cable, individuals could not simply walk into any post office to send a Marconigram. Therefore, for an aspiring global infrastructure provider, a closed system was not the pinnacle of monopoly capitalism but was instead an organizational dead end. Second, the non-intercommunication policy immediately ran into resistance from states around the world. Perhaps Marconi executives imagined the world economy as a unified economic space, where they would be free to conduct business (Aitken, 1985, p. 252), but it was also a divided political space, where countries jealously eyed threats to their sovereignty. A global service provider was dependent on the use of various countries' territories, which led the company into tangled relationships with both its home state and the various host states it sought to enter.

On the one hand, the Marconi Company asked Britain to welcome a potential replacement to the cable network, an idea that met with a lukewarm reception. This was a bad sign because Britain was central to the company's success. Shore stations were the point of connection between ships and the economies of countries around the world, and the importance of specific stations depended on *where* they were. On the other hand, company executives were asking Britain's geopolitical rivals (countries that might actually have welcomed an alternative to the cable network) to allow another British firm to offer the service. Beyond this goal, the company sought global expansion via private contracts, which effectively placed a fence around its stations in the territories of other countries. American naval officers, in particular, would soon perceive these Marconi-owned stations as threats to national sovereignty. Whether the non-intercommunication policy and a potential worldwide Marconi monopoly served Britain's geopolitical interests would be a persistent question for policymakers in the years to come—in Britain as well as abroad.

On the Road to the 1903 Conference: German, American, and British Policies

At the turn of the twentieth century, economic changes led to a general realignment in world affairs. The United States became the world's lead economy in the 1880s, as American wares flooded other countries (Lake,

1988, pp. 120–121). When a new conception of national security emerged, emphasizing colonies, overseas naval bases, and spheres of influence, military policy became central in determining foreign policy (Iriye, 1965, p. 5). The treatises of Admiral Alfred Thayer Mahan guided the transformation of America's strategic priority from land power to sea power, and naval policymakers began to focus on the ability to use the sea and to deny its use to the country's enemies (Hannigan, 2002, p. 19; Ross, 2009, p. 48).

In the wake of the Spanish-American War of 1898, the British Admiralty concluded that the United States was on its way to commanding the Caribbean Sea and American waters on the Pacific Coast (Friedberg, 1988, p. 169). In response, Britain made a series of one-sided concessions and retreated from the Western Hemisphere (Kennedy, 1987, p. 251). The American foreign policy executive, convinced by the Boer War in South Africa that the British had "lost all skill in fighting," correctly identified these concessions for what they were (cited in Beale, 1956, p. 87; Bönker, 2012, p. 70). Therefore, in the short term, British dominance on the high seas and in the Eastern Hemisphere complemented American control of the Western Hemisphere, and both countries came to identify Germany as the most important security threat (Baer, 1994, p. 39; Hannigan, 2002, pp. 187–190). As early as 1903, the General Board's fleet design was aimed at overmatching the expected size of the German Navy by 1919 (Kuehn, 2017, p. 54).

Though British policymakers were giving way, the country's decline was uneven. Britain retained its supremacy in finance, shipping, and global communications (Hannigan, 2002, p. 201; Hugill, 1999; Zakaria, 2008). Communications security for Britain and surveillance of others' communications were the British government's objectives. It was developing an "all-red" network, a designation based on the color of British territories on turn-of-the-century maps, which would connect all parts of the Empire without ever touching foreign soil (Kennedy, 1971, p. 731). Meanwhile, the commercial submarine cable network, operated by cartels, provided the country with worldwide communications hegemony. The Anglo-American Telegraph Company, part of the Eastern and Associated Telegraph Companies, held the dominant position on the transatlantic route, operating most of the twelve functioning Atlantic cables.[47] (Western Union and the Commercial Cable companies, both registered in the United States, were participants in a different cartel.) In 1898, policymakers at the Post Office stressed "the importance to Great Britain of retaining in the hands of British Companies the main cable communications of the world" (cited in Headrick, 1991, p. 87). Eastern's network was an invaluable asset for surveillance. If the company treaded lightly, letting the messages of neutrals and even the private messages of inhabitants of hostile countries pass undisturbed, nobody would suspect that the British government monitored and suppressed the official communications of hostile nations in wartime.

The cable and radio policies of the challengers were developed in the context of Britain's communications hegemony. By this time, Britain's unquestioned "intellectual and moral leadership" was a thing of the past; no longer did countries trust that companies headquartered in Britain respected their interests (Arrighi, 2010, p. 29). Concerned about their country's dependence on British cables, German policymakers sought the ability to communicate by subsidizing a German-owned cable to connect the country to the United States. The first such cable, inaugurated in 1900, diverted most of the German traffic from Eastern's network (Headrick, 1991, p. 106).[48] Though in the long term the United States would benefit from decentering Britain, in radio policy the German government was the first to propose measures on the structural level of network control and was the quickest to experiment with the tactical level in the interim. Both the idea of free intercommunication and the recommendation to use control over territory as leverage originated in Berlin. Two weeks before the 1903 conference, and under government pressure, the wireless subsidiaries of AEG and Siemens-Halske merged to create the Gesellschaft für Drahtlose Telegraphie, better known as Telefunken, to represent German radio interests (Kurylo & Susskind, 1981, p. 153).

American policymakers, in turn, realized their country's dependence on Eastern's cables during the Spanish-American War of 1898, when it became apparent that the U.S. Navy needed Eastern's collaboration to make contact with Washington and the Philippines (Hills, 2002, p. 143). Central to both cable and radio policy was the Bureau of Equipment, a supplies division of the Navy Department. Foreign countries were laying cables "in order to control the messages that pass over them," Admiral Royal B. Bradford, the chief of the Bureau, explained to Congress, "and to be independent of cables operated by foreign companies."[49] Since the United States did not have a state monopoly on telegraphy, the U.S. Post Office played a less important role in communications policy than its counterparts in other countries did. The State Department repeatedly expressed no independent interest in wireless policy and acted as a conduit for the wishes of the other government departments.[50] Thus, the American delegation to the 1903 conference was dominated by military interests, including a retired officer, Francis Barber, Bradford's former classmate at the Naval Academy.

In late 1901, Bradford received letters from Barber and from the American ambassador to Germany warning of the Lloyd's contract as a step toward reinforcing Britain's communications hegemony and urging steps to prevent a possible British monopoly over wireless traffic.[51] A wireless monopoly "will be worse than the English submarine cable monopolies which all Europe is groaning under," Barber wrote, adding, "and I hope the Navy Dept of the U.S. will not be caught in its meshes."[52] In chapter 3, I analyze the development of American policy in detail. Suffice it to say here that American policymakers viewed radiotelegraphy in the context of the submarine cable network and attributed a geopolitical purpose to the non-intercommunication policy. They found it necessary to act, even though the Lloyd's contract did not cover the insurance organization's stations in the United States.[53] Other Marconi stations, including the installation on Nantucket Island contracted to the *New York Herald*, observed the non-intercommunication policy, which remained relevant even after the Lloyd's contract unraveled.

That the German proposal for an international conference was a direct attack on the Marconi Company's exclusivity policy was not lost on the British government. "There [was] reason to believe," policymakers in the Post Office wrote to the Foreign Office, "that [the conference was] mainly directed against the proceedings of the companies interested in the Marconi system."[54] Under ordinary conditions, the Post Office went on, the British government would approve of the antimonopoly thrust of the German proposal. But these were far from ordinary conditions: the British government was itself "practically a party" to the Lloyd's contract.[55]

The British negotiating position was hammered out between the Admiralty, the Post Office, and the Committee of Imperial Defence (C.I.D.), the voice of strategic thinking, which became central in the preparations for the 1906 conference. These departments periodically took their opinions before the interdepartmental Cables Landing Rights Committee, which issued recommendations. This was because wireless was a new technology in an international communications environment dominated by the submarine cable. The interests of the Marconi Company had to be weighed alongside the interests of the existing communications network and the position of the country in global communications. The central proponent of this perspective was the

British Post Office, which pursued a version of the national interest in which the cable network was paramount (cf. Hugill, 1999, pp. 88, 96).

The strong position in which long-distance radiotelegraphy had placed the Marconi Company goes a long way toward explaining why Britain went to the conference defending some of the company's interests. Captain Henry Jackson, assistant director of naval operations, predicted that the company's Poldhu station, in Cornwall, was likely to obtain complete control over all wireless sea communication from the Straits of Dover to the Isle of Man, aiding in the defense of the British Isles.[56] Protecting the transatlantic trade route would also be much easier with the help of high-power radio, which would allow instantaneous dissemination of intelligence to cruisers over a thousand miles away—something that previously would have taken three to four days.[57]

During internal negotiations that are beyond the scope of this chapter, company executives deftly played on naval policymakers' hopes and fears. What the Admiralty wanted, first and foremost, was to persuade the Marconi Company not to erect long-distance wireless stations in any foreign country or on any foreign ship.[58] The so-called long-distance commitment, they hoped, would prevent foreign governments from setting up their own networks. Their attempt, however, foundered on the company's apparent interest "to make [its] apparatus available for all nations on equal and favourable terms."[59] Honoring the Admiralty's request would have meant that the company's prior efforts to establish foreign subsidiaries would simply have been a waste of time and effort; the Marconi Company could not operate as a multinational corporation. Marconi executives even threatened at one point to remove the Poldhu station from Britain and shift the European center of wireless to Italy, while downplaying the advantage that access to British territory could provide to the company (Raboy, 2016, p. 207).[60] The Admiralty fell for Marconi's bluff. They assumed that other countries were lining up to adopt the company's innovation, which could not have been further from the truth, and never stopped to ask why the Marconi organization picked Britain, rather than Italy, for its place of registration at the outset.

In July 1903, less than two weeks before the conference, the Admiralty signed a restrictive contract with the Marconi organization that would influence the British government's negotiating position during both radio conferences. Naval policymakers locked in the full use of all the Marconi Company's patented inventions and the use of any improvements in those inventions for the next eleven years, but the nonmonetary concessions bound Britain the most.[61] The contract committed the Admiralty to the non-intercommunication policy, making an exception only for warships and ships in distress, and promised compensation if Britain imposed an obligation to exchange messages with other systems.[62] The British government could decide to accept free intercommunication, but not at the company's expense. Even so, naval policymakers were unable to secure the long-distance commitment. This "would seem to be an extraordinary document for any Navy Dept to have signed," a naval officer in the American delegation scoffed later.[63]

Although the Admiralty agreed to support the non-intercommunication policy at the 1903 conference, the British delegation did not pursue end-to-end control over wireless. The Post Office had advised the Cables Landing Rights Committee against entering into active competition "with the great Cable Companies which provide communication with America and distant parts of the world,"[64] and it recommended adherence to an international convention. Policymakers were willing to consider a national security justification for siding with the Marconi Company, but Marconi executives had not yet hit upon the way to connect the company's interests to the interests of the British Empire (cf. Tomlinson, 1948, p. 294).[65] The Admiralty advised that there was no national security reason to support the non-intercommunication policy and that the question "should be considered from a commercial standpoint."[66] When the Cables Landing Rights Committee endorsed free intercommunication, British delegates went to Berlin to adopt "an attitude of reserve" and made only one condition for Britain's participation in an international agreement: that it should protect "the legitimate commercial interests of patent holders."[67]

The 1903 Conference

Delegates from nine maritime states (Germany, Spain, Britain, the United States, France, Italy, Russia, Austria, and Hungary) presented themselves for the conference opening on August 4, 1903.[68] Most of the delegates were post office experts on telegraphy who had recently finished a six-week international conference that updated the regulations applicable to that technology. "Wireless telegraphy was not, properly speaking, a new organization for the exchange of correspondence," a French delegate would soon declare, but was merely "an extension of the existing means of transmission."[69] The second most important constituency among the delegates was naval officers, who took an interest in wireless telegraphy as a way to improve the coordination of men-of-war. Though the conference's focus on ship-to-shore and ship-to-ship communication was well suited to this objective, the potential of radiotelegraphy as a form of shore-to-shore telegraph communication and a substitute for the submarine cables was also apparent by this time. Nevertheless, long-distance radiotelegraphy fell outside the scope of these early negotiations.[70] The use of radiotelegraphy for shore-to-shore communication did raise issues of a given country's "territorial atmosphere," analogous to territorial waters, but it would take until 1912 for an international conference to reach *this* matter (cf. Douglas, 1989, p. 106; Hills, 2002, p. 114).[71] Individual uses of the technology for contacting distant peers or broadcasting music were not even mentioned. This conference was clearly convened to regulate a kind of telegraphy where regulatory objectives and arguments drew on a mixture of legal, military, and geopolitical considerations. At issue were the very principles underlying the management of an emerging global network.

M. Sydow of the German Post Office, presiding, explained, "The object aimed at is, then, *in the first place*, to prevent the creation of a monopoly in favour of a single system, and, in the second place, to avoid disturbances of the different systems between themselves" [emphasis added].[72] This was a change from the German invitation, which had only recognized the non-intercommunication policy as a problem, but the agenda the German government had prepared still prioritized the issue of a pending world monopoly. Sydow then explained that the arrangements between the Marconi Company and Lloyd's constituted an aspiration toward such a monopoly. "The British Lloyd Co.," the German invitation to the conference had pointed out, "is forwarding most of the ship news and is therefore of extreme importance to all Navigation companies."[73] When Lloyd's agreed to the non-intercommunication policy, its stations refused to reply to calls from ships furnished with other systems, diminishing the general utility of radiotelegraphy.[74]

The questions the non-intercommunication policy had prompted did not address coordinating the use of the global commons. Rather, they were the questions of a regulatory framework designed to identify and regulate public service industries. What if the most important network to carry messages related to ship movements did not take one's calls? Would shippers equipped with Marconi sets be able to signal their arrival to Britain several hours ahead, while others would arrive unannounced? Would ships equipped with wireless from a different manufacturer sink without being able to ask for help just miles away from Marconi stations? Would the ships of Germany, the United States, and other countries resisting a Marconi monopoly simply be excluded from global commerce? Was radiotelegraphy the kind of industry where such discrimination was to be condoned? Marconi stations commanded the main lines of ocean traffic. They had been erected at the most advantageous spots for ship wireless traffic, and many of them touched British territory.[75] By providing access to trade routes, Marconi shore stations were vital for participation in global trade; they became an essential facility of global shipping. Therefore, at stake at the first international radio conference was not access to the spectrum but access to these shore stations and, through them, access to the coasts of Britain.

That policymakers sought to apply the interconnection principle familiar from telegraph regulation to wireless telegraphy is apparent from the core of the German draft protocol. Article 1 endorsed the principle of free intercommunication, stating: "Radio-telegrams originating from and destined for ships shall be received and forwarded without regard to the system employed." "This is the only really important matter before the conference," Barber marked on the side of the copy that he sent to the Bureau of Equipment.[76] Significantly, however, Article 1 was not a provision about "the right to transmit," meaning the unrestricted use of the airwaves. Rather, it was about the right to have one's messages handled.

Obligations to "receive and forward" goods and messages without discrimination had long formed part of the obligations of private companies in public service industries. "Gentlemen, what would you have said, at the time when the conferences were being held to frame telegraphic conventions," a Romanian delegate would ask in a 1906 session, if a country had proposed to sign the convention but reserved the right that "[its] telegraph offices may refuse to answer the calls of offices which are not equipped with apparatus coming from such or such a manufactory?"[77] International interconnection agreements had existed from the earliest days of telecommunications, and there was no precedent for sanctioning the kind of discrimination that the Marconi Company had instituted. Even the submarine cables observed the regulations of the International Telegraph Union, which compelled them to accept messages from everybody.[78]

Since the non-intercommunication policy was the only thing that allowed the Marconi Company to monetize the use of its network, delegates to the 1903 conference vied to convince each other about the nature of the regulatory problem. Whereas the German delegation identified the non-intercommunication policy as a tool of centralization and defined centralized control as a problem, the Italian delegation presented the position of the Marconi Company, highlighting centralization as the solution to the interference that had plagued early radio transmissions. A few months before the conference, Italian policymakers had also signed on to the non-intercommunication policy. Since Italy received the use of Marconi patents for free, they found it inequitable to force the company to connect its instruments with those of the company's competitors (Balbi, 2012, p. 4).

At the conference, Lieutenant Luigi Solari, who was a childhood friend of Guglielmo Marconi, and Commander Bonomo del Casale, took pains to describe the difficulties resulting from interference and advocated the adoption of the "best" system, defining quality by the range of the communication, the development of the international service, and the efficiency of organizing the service.[79] Hall had already stressed in Britain that the best system was the one developed by the Marconi Company.[80] Perhaps the Italian delegates did not know, but they certainly did not say, that what caused most of the interference was the spark technology the Marconi Company was championing. Instead of one radio wave, a spark transmitter generated a large number of waves, and it contaminated frequencies far removed from those being used to carry the message (Aitken, 1985, pp. 5–6). Either way, the delegates from the other countries listened, quietly pitying their Italian counterparts who were tied to the Marconi Company by contract.[81]

The Marconi Company's vision included a single system, one international tune, a prohibition on nonsyntonized apparatuses (the company had just patented tuning), and uniform organization and instruction of staff.[82] Uniform apparatuses were necessary to establish a public telegraph service, because, according to Marconi executives, interference was caused by the fact that *different* systems were communicating.[83] It was desirable, an Italian delegate noted, to employ apparatuses "of the same system at each end."[84] This was precisely the second instance when the spectrum came up at the conference. The first reference had appeared in the German draft proposal, which responded to the Marconi organization's strategy of keeping its wavelengths secret by recommending that organizations involved in ship-to-shore telegraphy make their wavelengths public.[85]

The Marconi Company sought to be accepted as an international public utility, the sole provider of all commercial and even military wireless services that it could imagine, all of which were point-to-point. Even vessels of war would use the single system, the same way they did the international system of signals.[86] "All public services involved the principle of centralized control," the company complained later, "whereas the Convention was based on co-operation and competition, which were irreconcilable."[87] Under the company's plans for end-to-end control, the operations of all stations around the world, whether under government or private control, would be governed by a private contract. In effect, the Marconi organization used contracts to aggregate control over territory worldwide.[88] Marconi executives not only wanted the non-intercommunication policy sanctioned on the international level but also sought an exclusive license to conduct radiotelegraphy in Britain. Taken together, this meant that British Marconi would roam the earth without interconnecting with any other firm, while no company established outside Britain could enter the territory of the British Empire. Marconi executives proposed a global network under the control of a single company—a communications system operating above the interstate system.

Though interference was a technological fact of life for maritime countries of the period, it did not proscribe particular policy choices. The Marconi Company's proposal for an international public utility offered a solution to the global coordination problem, to be sure, but it was an unacceptable solution to a problem policymakers were barely aware of. Perhaps the international nature of radiotelegraphy would have resulted in a radio conference sooner or later, as members of the American delegation believed,[89] but, as the events unfolded, interference did not explain either the impetus to regulate radiotelegraphy, the timing of legislation in any given country, or the particular provisions of regulations. When policymakers in different countries picked up or debated the company's talking points, interference became *an argument* whose significance cannot be understood without also understanding the policy environment of the rising and the declining hegemons in which it was deployed. Instead of interference, "interference plus" shaped policy. In British policy, as I will shortly show, the treatment of interference was inseparable from the assessment of the value of radiotelegraphy in relation to the submarine cables.

The 1903 conference itself did not come to a decision on interference in the end. Though the British Post Office had considered minimizing interference a desirable outcome of international coordination,[90] when the conference reached the matter, the British delegation protested that it was not on the agenda and that they were not prepared to discuss it.[91]

Germany may have been the chief rival in a future war for both the United States and Britain, but, in the field of radiotelegraphy, American policymakers found common ground with their German counterparts. The U.S. delegation had received guidance from the Department of Justice and went into the conference convinced that their government had absolute power over wireless.[92] Policymakers understood radiotelegraphy as similar enough to the submarine cables for regulatory purposes and felt prepared to apply American common carrier precedents to radiotelegraphy. The principle of nondiscrimination, among others, was a central aspect of American common carrier law, which regulated communications networks as being essential to interstate and foreign commerce. Thus, both Germany and the United States supported free intercommunication, while Italy and Britain supported the Marconi Company's position, but only Italy expressed full support for a single system.

There was certainly no technological reason for centralization. By this time, both the American and the French navies had experimented with wireless, and both delegations would soon go on the record to show that different systems worked well together.[93] There was no universal system in place, a German delegate offered, and were one to accept a single system today, "a better system might be invented tomorrow."[94] As a result, the delegates quickly ruled out the idea of a single system. But what did free intercommunication mean in practice?

One possible course of action would be to require the Marconi Company to open its stations—hitherto available only for intracompany traffic—to public correspondence. Mandatory access and sharing would soon be a familiar principle in common carrier law, which was focused on firms' responsibilities to serve the public interest. In the American legal context, for example, the legal equivalent of natural monopoly was the "essential facilities" doctrine (Lipsky & Sidak, 1999, p. 1187). In industries where a single firm can provide a product or a service most efficiently, the situation requires some type of remedy if three conditions are present: the industry is deemed to be naturally monopolistic; there is no substitute for the service; *and* it is impracticable to duplicate the facilities offered by the company (Lipsky & Sidak, 1999, pp. 1211, 1213). In the domestic context, policymakers had to be careful, however, lest an interconnection requirement be construed as an unlawful taking of company property. Both the British and the American legal systems recognized room for compensation in such instances, and the Admiralty had already agreed to it in the July 1903 contract.

When policymakers at the British Post Office explored the matter, they offered to help the Marconi Company recoup the expense of setting up its network by requiring ships and shore stations communicating with a Marconi installation to pay a surcharge.[95] The Marconi Company welcomed the suggestion. A "very substantial compensation" would be in order, Hall wrote to an American delegate, because intercommunication was technically difficult and converting the company's facilities to accept messages from different systems would entail substantial costs (cited in Feldman, 1975, p. 23). This was a mistake at best and a lie at worst, but it reflected a consistent theme in the company's position, that wireless was just like telephony, where receivers and exchanges were connected by wires.

British policymakers thus put the additional rate on the agenda, suggesting that Marconi's coastal stations be permitted to charge 50 percent of the normal rate as a surtax.[96] Since the idea of the single system received little support, most of the discussions in 1903 revolved around the possibility, the nature, and the extent of compensation to be paid to the Marconi Company. Why, the Americans asked, would governments compensate companies that erected stations without authorization (Waterbury, 1903, p. 666)?[97] Whose fault was it, a French delegate pressed, if the company chose to restrict the number of organizations with which it did business?[98] Marconi representatives, on the other hand, would soon reject the German argument that an infrastructure provider was fairly compensated by the increased traffic that went its way.[99] The American delegation was privately stunned at the stance of British policymakers, and only after receiving a copy of the 1903 Admiralty-Marconi agreement were they able to make sense of it. In the absence of the agreement, it simply seemed "quite unaccountable" for government officials to be driven by corporate demands in such obvious ways.[100]

On August 13, the participants, with the exception of Britain and Italy, signed a protocol that endorsed the principle of free intercommunication and agreed to hold a second conference, with the purpose of securing an international agreement on the free interchange of messages (Douglas,

1989, p. 122). Though contemporary press accounts and researchers tend to dismiss the 1903 conference, pointing out that both the Marconi Company and the British government ignored its resolutions, the conference revealed general support for the principle of free intercommunication (Harlow, 1971, p. 449; Headrick, 1991, p. 120).[101] The final version of Article 1, section 2, read: "Coast stations are obliged to receive and transmit telegrams going to or returning from ships without distinction as to the systems of wireless telegraphy employed by the ships."[102]

Even though Germany succeeded in convincing the other countries about the harmful effects of a Marconi monopoly, international law could not compel the Marconi Company to do anything. Mandated sharing required domestic legislation and, in Britain's case, some kind of incentive to get the Marconi Company to agree to it. Thus, the delegates left mandated sharing and the thorny problem of an additional rate to the next conference.

Beneath the surface, the fact that a company headquartered in Britain volunteered to run the network made a difference. Company executives' attempt to have the Marconi system accepted as dominant was the opening salvo in the struggle for network control on the structural level. Who would define the configuration of, and the rules applicable to, the emerging network? Could an international public utility truly be devoid of national loyalties? Since radiotelegraphy was an emerging global industry at a time of declining British hegemony, a geopolitical dimension to interconnectivity was emerging. The only reason the delegates did not agree on a treaty then and there, the British Post Office commented, was because of the opposition of the Marconi Company.[103]

Following the geopolitical significance of radio technology thus sheds light on the impetus behind the first international radio conferences. The global coordination of the spectrum was more of a bonus at this time than a requirement for an international agreement. Nor did countries need an international convention to exclude the Marconi Company from their own territories and erect stations in their place, as the Nantucket controversy in the United States would soon reveal. Rather, policymakers needed an international convention to get Britain to agree to open access to *its* territory. Years later, when the ratification of the 1906 convention was being debated worldwide, it was still commonly held that "if England refused to ratify, the Convention becomes a dead letter."[104] In the wake of the Marconi Company's efforts to highlight interference as a problem, however, the issue was expected to return during a future conference. Policymakers had well-established precedents for dealing with networks but had yet to consider the unique features of a network that relied on the airwaves for connection.

The Nantucket Controversy: Network Control on the Tactical Level

Soon after the conference, the State Department received a complaint from the German embassy that American Marconi's station at Nantucket Island, under contract to the *New York Herald*, did not take calls from German ships. The German complaint pointed to the statement of the American delegation at the 1903 conference that American shore stations were "bound under the 'common carrier law'" to receive messages from every sender regardless of the system used, and the Germans requested that the United States remove the Marconi station from the lightship.[105] This suggestion was rooted in the conviction that the company's reliance on the service of lighthouses, a type of public property, put it in a vulnerable position.[106] As if to lead by example, the German government put pressure on shipping lines operating under the German flag to either persuade the Marconi Company to relax its conditions or face the removal of the Marconi station from the lightship on the island of Borkum. When the company refused, the German Post Office removed the station and replaced it with a Telefunken installation. They also forbade the Marconi Company from communicating with the German coast.[107] Germany showed both the Marconi organization and the world what was possible when a state used control over its territory as leverage in the struggle for network control.

The extent to which common carrier law was applicable to wireless telegraphy in the United States, however, was unresolved. Despite the American delegation's confident pronouncement at the conference, the staff at the Department of Commerce and Labor found no law "requiring a station to receive messages according to the German wireless telegraphy system."[108] For the moment, American Marconi indignantly refused to comply with the request, threatening to remove its station from the light vessel instead.[109] Chapter 3 recounts American policymakers' approach in detail, but the Navy's action on the tactical level is worth mentioning here.

American Marconi's defiance did not mean that the company acted as an agent of the British government or even that it enjoyed that government's support. Hall certainly sought to convince both the Post Office and the Foreign Office that U.S. common carrier law did not require a company to provide access to its *competitors*.[110] British policymakers, however, expressed little interest in the fine points of American common carrier law and were not about to challenge American sovereignty. The Post Office wrote to Hall that both the German and the American governments were well within their rights to impose any conditions they pleased on the ships sailing under their flags and the stations operating on their soils.[111] Policymakers even informed the American delegation that the British government declined assistance to the company.[112]

Little did Hall know that the Post Office also doubted American Marconi's ties to Britain. "Although the English Company claim to have a predominating interest [in American Marconi]," Postmaster General Lord Stanley warned, "it is really a United States company incorporated under the laws of New Jersey."[113] This view would have come as a surprise to the Marconi Company, which asserted absolute control over its subsidiaries.[114] Company executives had accepted the Admiralty's request to employ only British subjects at its stations, which meant that merchant ships registered in foreign countries traveled with operators tailored to the requirements of the Royal Navy.[115] This was at a time when the loyalty of operators was widely considered to be the key to secure communications.[116] Yet, the Post Office discounted British Marconi's assertions of absolute control via stock ownership and emphasized American Marconi's place of incorporation.[117] Diplomatic intervention, the Foreign Office informed the Marconi Company, would hardly be appropriate under these conditions.[118] While policymakers around the world were beginning to identify British Marconi as a corporation in a symbiotic relationship with its home state, policymakers at the Post Office questioned the parent company's power over its subsidiaries and the British government's power to force its will on the latter.[119]

That a corporation headquartered in Britain inserted itself between the United States, its ships, and ships registered in foreign countries was duly noted in Washington. Henry Manney, the chief of the Bureau of Equipment during the 1906 conference, testified years later that the Marconi Company had always refused to allow ships equipped with Marconi sets to communicate with vessels equipped with other instruments "entirely regardless of the nationality of the vessels."[120] In the wake of the company's refusal to change its policy, the Navy Department requested the use of the Nantucket light vessel for its own wireless station, announcing that the naval station shortly to be erected would communicate with everyone.[121] Marconi technology was not indispensable, and naval policymakers gave notice that British Marconi would not decide the terms of American participation in a global radio network. However, territorial control was not a permanent solution, and legislation on the structural level would soon attempt to reconfigure the relationship between the company and its host state. In the interim, the Navy Department's stations operated under the rules laid down in a document titled "Special Notice to Mariners, No. 47a," which mandated free intercommunication.[122] So did the department's contract with the DeForest Company for a long-distance network.[123] Though the interconnection principle had yet to be cemented in legislation, in practical terms the replacement of the Marconi installation meant that ships approaching the U.S. coast had an alternative to Marconi shore stations.

Network Control on the Structural Level: The 1906 Convention

On October 3, 1906, thirty states began negotiations in Berlin. Both the final protocol adopted at the 1903 conference and tactical-level measures on the part of Germany and the United States had sent a message that the centralization of the network under Marconi control was unacceptable. Now, the delegates would turn their attention to how to ensure global connectivity for ships—even without the Marconi system, if necessary. Although spectrum management would enter the negotiations for the first time, countries picked up where the previous conference left off. "Coastal stations and shipboard stations are bound to exchange radio-telegrams reciprocally without distinction of the radio-telegraphic system adopted by those stations," read Article 3 of the proposed convention.[124] This was the most essential part of the convention, the president of the conference announced.[125] Had the delegates failed to "break down for once and for all" the practice of one system refusing intercommunication with any other system, the conference would have failed.[126] Since the Admiralty-Marconi contract committed the Royal Navy, in the words of an American delegate, "not to permit other systems to be established on the shores of Great Britain," the success of the conference hinged on opening British territory to the ships of other countries.[127]

During the second session in Berlin, the British delegation announced that Britain was in favor of free intercommunication, provided adequate regulations could be drawn up to prevent interference and that each country would be allowed to exempt certain stations from the obligation of intercommunication (Raboy, 2016, p. 278).[128] Assistant Director of Naval Operations Captain Alexander Bethell and Hall spoke with one voice when stressing the importance of regulations "which should suffice to prevent disturbances and interferences."[129] What started as a framing device on the part of the Marconi Company to justify its monopoly became essential to Britain's adherence to a telegraph conference. The management of the spectrum was now everybody's problem.

The British negotiating stance reflected a protracted debate between the Post Office, whose position remained consistent, and the national security community, which now lined up behind the Marconi Company. British policy discussions during the first decade of the twentieth century revolved around four topics: the long-distance commitment, British diplomatic support for the non-intercommunication policy, an exclusive license to the Marconi organization for the territory of the British Empire, and domestic distribution facilities to connect with the inland telegraph system managed by the Post Office. In December 1903, the Admiralty, which sought to keep long-distance radiotelegraphy in British hands, broke with the recommendation of the Cables Landing Rights Committee and announced its support for Marconi's exclusivity policy.[130] In return, they sought the long-distance commitment.[131] By 1904, it was possible to send messages to stations 1,700 miles away, and at such distances the Marconi Company had no rival.[132] "The exclusive possession of a means of communication at this great range must be highly advantageous to this country," naval policymakers pointed out, "even if the advantage could not be permanently held."[133] The Admiralty's decision was a significant victory for British Marconi. "They cannot afford to drive the business out of the country," Hall wrote to Marconi triumphantly after the Admiralty reversed course (cited in Raboy, 2016, p. 263).

The Post Office, on the other hand, focused on getting the Marconi Company to give up the non-intercommunication policy, which would allow the British government to adhere to the proposed convention. Policymakers made it clear that standing outside was not an option.[134] Germany could get the majority of countries to "form a Union," analogous to telegraph and postal unions, which would exclude Britain.[135] If the British government was to adhere to the convention, an agreement with the Marconi organization was necessary.[136] In return for releasing the Admiralty from its 1903 contract, and opening access to British territory, Hall wanted an exclusive license to conduct radiotelegraphy in the Empire as well as diplomatic support for the non-intercommunication policy around the world. If the Marconi Company had its way, it would secure an exclusive license for both ship-to-shore and shore-to-shore work, incorporate the non-intercommunication policy into all of its contracts, and not allow any ships unaffiliated with the Marconi system to communicate with the Empire.

In spring 1904, policymakers arrived at the so-called Heads of Agreement, which paved the way for the Wireless Telegraphy Act later that year.[137] The Act subjected radio stations to licensing requirements and secured for the government the ability to refuse an application.[138] Yet, the Marconi Company and the Post Office did not see eye-to-eye on shore-to-shore communication, and the company did not receive distribution facilities for such work. As a result, the four demands that played a central role in any bargain would remain in flux until the 1906 conference.

The fact that the Admiralty regarded leadership in wireless telegraphy as inseparable from the Marconi Company testifies to the company's success in cementing the links between the non-intercommunication policy and the interests of the British Empire. With the victory of the Liberal Party in the 1906 general elections, a new Board of Admiralty took the helm. These Lords Commissioners were especially receptive to the ideas of the Marconi Company and found an ally in the C.I.D., which had recently acquired a secretariat and had begun to claim a larger role in the coordination of imperial strategy (Beloff, 1970, p. 120).

What naval policymakers were aiming at by mid-decade was less a network used for surveillance, though the idea did present itself, and more the ability to communicate.[139] Radiotelegraphy was a unique technology without a substitute, which, given similar fighting forces, would decide the course of war.[140] To the goal of keeping the use of the Marconi system from foreign countries, the C.I.D. now added the idea of a commercially self-supporting system that could be integrated into the British communications system in wartime.[141] Sir George Clarke, the first secretary of the C.I.D., did not simply consider the advantages of radio technology in isolation but rather thought in terms of a network that would serve as "an alternative to or as a substitute for" cables.[142] Clarke saw no reason why the all-British network then under development had to consist of cables alone when the advantage of treating wireless and cable as complementary technologies was so great. In order to facilitate a commercially self-supporting system, the Admiralty would have granted the Marconi organization's wish for an exclusive license for the territory of the Empire.[143]

The Marconi Company, the C.I.D., and the Admiralty spoke with one voice, the voice of the world leader. They agreed that, as "the greatest sea Power in the world," no other power had the same need as the British Empire for an efficient system of wireless telegraphy.[144] A Marconi monopoly in the Empire was a building block of world monopoly and would give Britain a position in wireless, in the words of naval policymakers, "as strong and commanding as she now holds with regard to the cable communication throughout the world."[145] By contrast, if the policy of free intercommunication was accepted, the company informed policymakers, "the actual control of a number of connections would pass into the hands of foreigners" and the value of the Marconi system "as a weapon" would decline.[146]

Leadership in radio communications was designed to shore up a Royal Navy whose dominance was fading. On the eve of the second radiotelegraph conference, Britain was still the first-ranked naval power in the world, as measured by the number of capital ships, but the United States had caught up significantly, improving its position from twelfth to second in a space of fifteen years (Baer, 1994, pp. 9, 40). Aware of the massive geopolitical transformation, British policymakers had quietly given up preparing for war with the United States and sought a soft landing. "To the west," First Lord of the Admiralty the Earl of Selborne wrote the cabinet in 1904, "the United States are forming a navy the power and size of which will be limited only by the amount of money which the American people choose to spend on it" (cited in Friedberg, 1988, p. 134). The Admiralty was anxiously eyeing the development of the U.S. Navy at a time when, in the words of Selborne, the Royal Navy included slow, aged vessels that could "neither fight nor run away" (cited in Friedberg, 1988, p. 137).

Since the British government considered Germany to be the primary security threat, it had recently entered into an alliance with France—the Entente Cordiale—to avoid "a selfish isolation which would lead to a combination of all Europe against us under the dictatorship of Germany" (cited in Gooch, 1994, p. 295). The simple fact that the German emperor was moving heaven and earth to defeat "the Admiralty view," First Sea Lord Sir John Fisher now declared in connection with the non-intercommunication policy, was enough reason to hold firm in supporting the Marconi Company: "The Post Office know nothing and the Foreign Office less as to our fighting necessities."[147] The Admiralty's support for centralized control over radiotelegraphy therefore was not aimed at the United States, though it would have affected it.

Policymakers at the Post Office, however, were far from convinced that another communications monopoly was in Britain's interest. Underneath the two departments' differing positions lay different assumptions about the relative values of cables and radio. When radiotelegraphy emerged, there were two central ways to understand its relationship to the cable network: either as *complementary* to the cables, working as a backup without threatening the viability of the cable network, or as a *substitute* that threatened to replace long-distance cable links completely (for a theoretical treatment, see Sawhney, 2012). The Admiralty held the former view, the Post Office the latter. If radio technology was a success, J. M. Gavey, the engineer-in-chief of the Post Office, warned, radiotelegraphy would drive the cables out of business, destroying a private industry "on which the State might be very largely dependent for communication in the event of a general or a European war."[148] The logical outcome of Post Office concerns was a merger, which would not be realized until the 1928 establishment of Cable & Wireless.

To develop an inferior network just so it could destroy the more valuable one seemed to be the height of folly for the Post Office. Policymakers saw radiotelegraphy as a weak technology because it needed the cooperation of other countries to work. The Post Office had long considered interference a form of leverage, and policymakers were convinced that Britain's rivals enjoyed greater powers of retaliation in radiotelegraphy than was the case in the submarine cable industry.[149] The Post Office had little interest in the Admiralty's plans to retaliate via jamming in wartime, since most of the uses of the radio network would take place in peacetime.[150] "Foreigners will not submit to a Marconi monopoly and a Marconi operator on board of their ships," the Post Office stressed repeatedly.[151] Interference was not the only source of leverage foreign countries possessed. They could also boycott ships equipped with Marconi sets, as Germany already had done.[152] An absolute monopoly of radiotelegraphy was therefore out of the question; the fight to support the interests of the Marconi Company was not worth fighting and could not be won.[153] Despite the Admiralty's recommendation, the Post Office refused to grant the Marconi Company an exclusive license for shore-to-shore wireless, which left the door open for cable companies to enter the field.[154]

By summer 1906, policymakers at the Post Office had concluded that both the Marconi Company and the Admiralty were simply using interference as an argument to justify their opposition.[155] The British delegation was divided to such an extent that their draft instructions contemplated rejecting free intercommunication or referring the matter home. Shortly before the conference, the Admiralty finally agreed to British participation in the convention but acquired a veto power based on the adequacy of the regulations that would serve as a substitute for centralized Marconi control.[156] Because of the conflict within the British delegation, the country's negotiating stance would appear confused to observers (Raboy, 2016, p. 279).[157]

The key to understanding the 1906 convention is the pattern of compromises that undergirded Britain's adherence. Mandated sharing of Marconi facilities would not be possible without a surcharge, but who should foot the bill? Wireless was a luxury, Henry Babington Smith, the head of the British delegation, explained, "and the public which makes use of it could well afford to pay an extra rate."[158] Both the American and the French delegations rejected the surtax, which, Manney explained to the Navy Department, was "plainly intended to make parties to the conference generally assist in the payment of such royalties as might be due the Marconi Company."[159] The 1903 Admiralty-Marconi contract guaranteed compensation to the company, and the British government wanted other states to pick up the tab. Anticipating that they could not convince their counterparts to pay higher rates, British policymakers had already agreed that the British government would compensate the company, a fact that the American delegation was well aware of.[160]

Hall made the work of the British contingency especially difficult by participating in the 1906 conference as the representative from Montenegro. This was necessary because the Post Office refused to include him in the British delegation.[161] Hall pointed out that the Marconi Company did the exact same thing as the cable companies when it refused a direct physical connection to its stations.[162] By this time, however, the technological features of radiotelegraphy were better understood. Only Montenegro opposed the German proposal, and policymakers were aware that the unique features of the network required a new approach. "The delegates will find it a great deal easier to break the Marconi monopoly," Barber wrote to the Navy Department, "than to discern an efficient substitute for it."[163]

When the conference accepted Article 3 without an additional rate, the British delegation pushed to exempt the Marconi Company from the obligation to exchange messages with its competitors. Post Office policymakers made it clear that Britain would need to withdraw if their request wasn't granted,[164] so the other participants agreed to the exemption. "The article was solely for the purpose of letting Great Britain keep to her contracts with the Marconi Company," Manney informed the Navy Department.[165] When Britain eventually adhered to the convention, the ability to exempt stations was recorded as a reservation.

If Marconi stations were exempt, however, how would shippers communicate with Britain's coasts? Britain had no intention of reserving all of its stations for the use of one system, British delegates declared early on, "so as to close our coasts to other systems."[166] The delegates' response underscores that—scholarly attention to territory as a metaphor for the spectrum notwithstanding—these early conferences focused on access to actual territory. The answer to the question was duplication of stations. The British government now undertook to provide stations for general public correspondence "side by side with the reserved stations."[167] In contrast to Britain, Italy did not agree to establish stations for the general service, but that did not stop the conference.[168] The objective of the conference was not access to the coasts of any country but only access to *Britain's* coasts.

Behind the scenes, naval policymakers continued to back the Marconi Company. Though the Post Office had been preoccupied with the possibility that foreign countries would boycott ships equipped with Marconi sets, the Admiralty expressed no concern. "The principal shipping routes of the world are commanded by British territory," Marconi executives pointed out, "and it is of no consequence to us, if, for example, France refuses to accept messages from ships equipped with our apparatus."[169] The company that had threatened to leave Britain for brighter prospects now declared its home state indispensable to the global economy. Since its hopes for a world monopoly depended on denying access to the territory of the British Empire, the Marconi organization asked Britain to risk retaliation. Britain had so many stations, Captain Bethell said, echoing the company, "that the foreigners [could not] do without us."[170]

Policymakers at the Post Office were getting increasingly frustrated with the company, which, in addition to an inferior technology, seemed to have a self-serving understanding of the interests of the Empire. Britain did indeed lie on the transatlantic trade route, or "the great highway to Europe," Chief Engineer Gavey explained.[171] This simply meant, however, that other countries would be "as keen to develop wireless communication as they have shown themselves anxious to open up independent cable communication."[172] Germany and France, the two countries where enough transatlantic traffic originated to make sense setting up a station, refused to use the Marconi Company, and the latter's government was putting up its own stations.[173] Both the removal of the Marconi station from the island of Borkum and the Nantucket controversy had made it clear that the Marconi Company was not indispensable. If the company sabotaged the convention, Gavey warned, it would cut ships equipped with Marconi's apparatus from communication with the adhering countries, "including, it is feared, the United States."[174]

Pieces of land, the Post Office quickly grasped, had no value in isolation. Countries acquire value in the world system not simply because of their size or location but primarily because of their economic position. By the early twentieth century, the value of access to British territory had declined as the fulcrum of the world economy shifted to the United States. The transatlantic trade route, the Marconi Company seems to have missed, had two ends, and countries around the world were clamoring to connect to the United States. "It would not be the first time that a strong man like the Company's representative has over-rated his strength," Gavey concluded, "and if some of the foregoing views were ultimately realised the result would in the end not only be fatal to the Marconi Company but this Country might be placed in an undesirable position."[175] British shippers would lose out if they could not get land communication with the United States. And would the Marconi Company really want a global network that did not include the United States?

When the negotiations ended, the first radio convention incorporated eleven articles from the 1875 St. Petersburg Telegraph Convention, though it modified certain aspects to fit the new industry.[176] The participants recognized the centrality of shore stations and agreed to a division of rates that favored the Marconi organization. Section 12 of the service regulations allowed coastal stations to charge 11.6 cents per message while setting the shipboard rate at 7.7 cents.[177] Even though the convention provided for a maximum rate for wireless messages, to be fixed in the future, Article 10 allowed countries to authorize higher rates "in the case of stations of ranges exceeding 800 kilometers" or of stations whose work was exceptionally difficult because of physical conditions. Thus, British Marconi would benefit from the receipts from the long-distance wireless that it was pioneering. When Parliament ratified the convention, the Marconi Company received a three-year compensation for any losses it might suffer as a result of the convention entering into force.[178] Once the three years ended, the British government would buy the Marconi Company's coastal stations. By 1909, the company was out of the ship-to-shore business in Britain and could focus on its long-standing objective of developing high-power stations for transoceanic traffic (Hills, 2002, p. 107).

Duplication, important as it was to free intercommunication, exacerbated interference. The task before the conference now was to find "adequate regulations" that would satisfy the Admiralty, which had since realized that standing outside would be inimical to naval interests. A visit to German stations at Norddeich and Nauen demonstrated that they could disturb signaling in the English Channel, and Britain's nonadherence would only increase the desire to erect more stations in foreign countries. Moreover, the delegates attended a demonstration of the Poulsen system, which was rumored to be "better than anything yet invented."[179] The chance that the Marconi system would keep its technological lead was dimming.

During the debate about the ratification of the 1906 convention in Britain, policymakers at the Post Office and the Admiralty finally spoke with one voice about the value of radiotelegraphy. "For military and naval purposes, the importance of the invention cannot be overestimated," the parliamentary Select Committee concluded, "especially to Great Britain in time of war, when the cables might be cut."[180] The cable network was the backbone of imperial communications, as the Post Office had long asserted, and wireless was better left as a backup. The idea of an independent commercial radio network, parallel to the cable links, was losing support, as radio technology was now officially pushed to second place. Though American policymakers would cite British support for the Marconi Company as evidence for collaboration between the firm and its home state, British policymakers were moving away from the company's grand plans.

Treating the service regulations separately from the main text, as has been customary, misses that spectrum management became crucial to the success of a telegraph convention, which in turn enhanced the position of the United States in global communications. In fact, the first wavelength allocations emerged from the British Post Office, where officials had long been convinced that international law could successfully address the problem of interference.[181] Captain Bethell linked access to British territory and wavelength allocation for the first time at the 1906 conference in a proposal for "a modified method of intercommunication."[182] Now that mandated sharing had been replaced by duplication, interference would become a central issue in "congested places," such as ports, where it was not possible to separate stations in space. If at these locations a station that was open only to limited public service (i.e., it was equipped with a Marconi set) used its own wavelength, "it would be possible," Bethell advised, "to permit the establishment of another station in the vicinity which would use the international wavelength."[183] International regulations, the Post Office added, could focus on the use of different wavelengths and the order of precedence in signaling, and require users to obtain licenses of competence.[184] These rules would be enforced nationally: infractions would be punished, and if a ship persistently violated the rules, it would lose its license.[185] Rather than separating stations in space, policymakers were now drawing lines in the sky.

When the convention was finalized, section 2 of the service regulations authorized the wavelengths 300 and 600 meters for general public service and reserved those between 600 and 1,600 meters for governmental use.[186] Shipboard stations were expected to use the 300-meter wavelength, but governments could use any wavelength.[187] Long waves were set aside for shore-to-shore communication, paving the way for the state-to-state model of radiotelegraphy (Hills, 2002, p. 106). Given that longer wavelengths were considered more valuable in the early twentieth century, governments reserved access to the better part of the spectrum for themselves (Douglas, 1989, p. 140). The Admiralty was completely satisfied with the regulations.[188]

The regulations of the 1906 convention were designed for ship-to-shore traffic. British policymakers kept the regulation of ship-to-ship communication out of the convention, although the American delegation understood free intercommunication to cover ship-to-ship and shore-to-shore traffic as well.[189] When Britain threatened to withdraw for the second time over the ship-to-ship provision, the delegates made accommodations again, helping the British delegation make what seemed like difficult decisions. Ship-to-ship interconnection was included as a "supplementary article," but its significance was symbolic at best.[190] Britain was not bound by the article, and countries such as the United States committed themselves to something that did not require an international convention: regulating how ships registered in their own countries used radio.[191]

After all the service regulations were hashed out, states agreed to give priority to distress signals and undertook to operate radiotelegraph service in a way that would diminish interference.[192] The regulations also provided for setting up an International Wireless Bureau, which maintained the list of all wireless stations, together with the call letters, system, and wavelengths used by each station.[193] Though geopolitical rivalry lay at the heart of the first radio conference, the measures aimed at coordinating the use of the spectrum were in the interest of all states. Since enforcement would take place via national legislation, the delegates agreed to propose to their respective legislatures "the measures necessary to insure the execution of the present Convention."[194]

Importantly, the convention did not assign discrete, narrow channels to parties who had the exclusive right to transmit (cf. Benkler, 1998, p. 291). Since competition over the number and type of wavelengths was not yet a source of geopolitical rivalry, American ascendancy in radiotelegraphy began with the principle of free intercommunication (cf. Douglas, 1989, p. 140; cf. Hugill, 1999, pp. 92–94). The delegates signed the treaty on November 3, 1906, with eight countries, including Britain, reserving the right to exempt certain stations from the provisions of the convention.[195] The service regulations of this convention constitute the first international regulation of the radio spectrum. They have since been revised numerous times under the auspices of the International Telecommunication Union and are now known as the Radio Regulations.[196]

The 1906 convention made pure end-to-end control without interconnection impossible for wireless telegraphy. British policymakers now settled on wartime control as the central strategic objective.[197] The British Parliament ratified the treaty by a single vote in 1907, and it went into force in 1908. Once states accepted free intercommunication, the Marconi Company would no longer be able to determine network development via private contracts. Had centralization prevailed, on the other hand, the United States would have found it much more difficult to establish a sovereign commercial radio network.

Though Britain's geopolitical rivals prevented the country from denying access to its territory, the 1906 conference did not mandate opening British territory to companies registered abroad. American wireless companies were still in their infancy and could not get anything more than permission to establish experimental stations in Britain.[198] For now, British government stations handled messages arriving from ships, and British Marconi would be responsible for long-distance work. It would take forty years before American companies could establish direct communication with the territory of the British Empire.

After the conference, the American delegation attributed their country's clout to the purity of their country's motives. The United States alone was able to consider the broader public interest, because the country did not own or operate a telegraph network, nor was it restricted by contracts with private service providers.[199] The influence of the United States was indeed substantial, but it is best understood in the context of the contemporary geopolitical transformation. The very fact that the German government succeeded in calling an international conference testifies to Britain's diminishing power. If Britain had been powerful, as it was when the first submarine cables were laid, the principles for the management of the emerging global radio network would not have gotten on the agenda. If Britain had been simply weak, a British-headquartered company could not have raised the specter of commercial and strategic isolation. Instead of simply being powerful or weak, Britain was in transition. Its decline was registered both in British inner circles and abroad, and it influenced the positions of all parties to the conference.

The United States advanced, in large part, because Britain was a reluctant hegemon in radiotelegraphy. British policymakers recalibrated their interests based on two important considerations: Britain's declining economic position and the weakness of radio technology. Radiotelegraphy was ill suited to the conceptual framework of wired networks, which produced the Marconi Company's competitive and geopolitical problems and provided opportunities to Britain's rivals. German and American policymakers' actions on the tactical level of network control put Britain on notice, and policymakers at the Post Office were keenly aware of the leverage other countries derived from the weakness of radio technology. America's clout depended on its increasing economic and naval power, which made British policymakers eager for a lucrative long-term relationship. The importance of the United States, apparent when British Marconi was unwilling to withdraw long-distance rights from its American contracts, was reinforced by the Admiralty's lack of concern about the spread of radio technology to the United States and from Britain's decision to shoulder the costs of opening access to its territory.[200] In recalibrating Britain's interests to match its declining position, the Post Office took potential disruption in economic relations with the United States into account and gave way.

The 1906 convention was a product of state power and registered the underlying changes in the relative power position of the British Empire. It represents a bargain between a declining hegemon unwilling and unable to centralize control over radio communications and its challengers eager to establish independence. It was not simply the case that a multinational corporation backed by a declining home state was unable to expand; rather, its own home state held it back. For the next two decades, however, fears of integration into a global network serving the interests of the British government would be a central theme in U.S. radio policy as policymakers sought to extricate both radio technology and American territory from the control of British Marconi. It is to the origins and final passage of the first licensing requirements that we turn in chapter 3.

3 Licensing: Incorporating Radio into the American Common Carrier Regulatory Framework, 1899–1912

In late 1901, American Marconi's decision to bar officers of the U.S. Navy from entering its long-distance station on Cape Cod set off a decade-long effort to bring radio stations under American jurisdiction. British Marconi executives opposed this move by relying on the nineteenth-century framework for private property, where the ownership of patents undergirded corporate control over stations. Nothing prevented inward foreign direct investment (FDI), and the company's American subsidiary fiercely defended its right to decide the placement and use of its stations. Eventually, the Radio Act of 1912 situated "wireless telegraphy" in the common carrier regulatory framework, addressing the use and operation of radio stations under the Commerce Clause of the U.S. Constitution. What happened during these early years is essential to understanding American ascendancy in global communications. The Radio Act of 1912 was telegraph legislation, whose geopolitical significance lay in three provisions: licensing, interconnection, and citizenship regulations.

Licensing functioned on the structural level of network control to loosen British Marconi's control over stations on American territory and constituted a key step in achieving autonomy of communications. These early radio policies were defensive and were aimed at securing for the United States the ability to communicate. By the time the Radio Act of 1912 passed, licensing requirements had become the mechanism for enforcing the provisions of the 1906 Berlin convention, including free intercommunication. Once the licensing requirement weakened the legal protections for private property, British Marconi no longer had full control over its property on U.S. territory, and America's position in radiotelegraphy improved.

Taking into account that radio licensing was designed for a point-to-point medium and that a foreign corporation was instrumental in the emergence of radio technology, we must dispense with the customary link between this licensing regime and those implemented for the content industries, such as press licensing (cf. Pool, 1983, p. 3). Arguments that look to the interests of the regulated industries to explain the origins of licensing must also be laid to rest (cf. Benkler, 1998, p. 59; Douglas, 1989, p. 216). Finally, we must trace how the spectrum emerged as a relevant concept for policymakers in the first place. Since radiotelegraphy was understood as a type of telegraphy, American ascendancy in radio communications in these early years was intertwined with the applicability of the common carrier framework for the new technology. Rather than being a management tool for the prevention of radio interference, licensing proposals targeted radio *stations* themselves, and the separation of licensing and the airwaves was a key feature of radio regulation in these years. It would take a while before policymakers realized that this new public utility relied on a public resource, and the Radio Act of 1912 would not fully address the problem of the spectrum. Of the four regulatory measures used in spectrum management, the Act would include only two: allocation and service rules.

Toward Technological Sovereignty: From the Composite System to the Navy's Network

In fall 1901, the Navy Department sent an officer to inspect the wireless apparatus on several lightships. However, when Lieutenant Beecher tried to enter the Marconi station at South Wellfleet, Massachusetts, Chief Engineer Richard Vyvyan denied that there was even a station there. When he overcame his surprise at the officer's visit, Vyvyan told Beecher that, according to company policy, he was not allowed to explain or show the apparatus to anybody "not properly accredited from the office of the Marconi Co. in London."[1] The South Wellfleet station was unique because it was "intended for the transmission of long distance wireless messages."[2] As noted in chapter 2, the Marconi organization saw long-distance wireless as its future, and it would establish the first high-power experimental transatlantic connection just a month after Beecher's visit.

American Marconi's most immediate plans included connecting the United States and Cuba, followed by a link to the Philippines.[3] As company executives pursued commercial and naval clients, they took into account the expansion of the American sphere of influence. In the aftermath of the

Spanish-American War, the United States acquired possessions in the Caribbean, including the Panama Canal, Puerto Rico, and Cuba, as well as in the Far East, including Hawaii, Guam, and the Philippines. The company's long-distance links would follow a pioneering ship-to-shore wireless service, which was fast becoming essential for the safety of life at sea. While the Marconi organization marketed its ship wireless service as being complementary to the cable system, its proposed long-distance links competed with them.[4]

By Marconi standards, Vyvyan's secretive behavior was nothing out of the ordinary. The company had long fretted about its innovations being copied by its competitors, and the ability to offer long-distance communication could turn out to be its most valuable asset. Indeed, Managing Director Cuthbert Hall allowed Kaiser Wilhelm II to pay a visit only on the condition that he leave his advisers behind (Raboy, 2016, p. 266). From a network control perspective, such strict rules were possible because control over technology, capital, and territory in the U.S. market favored the Marconi interests.

Patents provided American Marconi with control over its pioneering technology. Incorporated in 1899, the Marconi Wireless Telegraph Company of America operated via a patent-sharing agreement with its British parent, which gave it exclusive rights to the entire United States, its newly acquired possessions, and its protectorates. In addition to the Philippines and Hawaii, Cuba, Puerto Rico, and the Danish West Indies belonged to American Marconi.[5] Though the "ether," as the spectrum was called then, was indeed unowned, the first decade of the twentieth century was far from the years of nonmarket relations in the radio industry (cf. Benkler, 1998, p. 296). Patents were a form of intellectual property, and the American legal system protected the company's right to decide how its equipment was used.

Control over capital, in turn, was in the hands of British Marconi. In spring 1902, American Marconi underwent a corporate reorganization through which E. Rollins Morse and Bro., representing the Morgan banking interests, secured the American rights to the Marconi patents.[6] However, British Marconi kept the controlling interest in its subsidiary via stock ownership, which meant that major policy and marketing decisions had to be cleared with the London office first (Douglas, 1989, p. 73).[7] The connection was so close, Hall would declare later, that the subsidiaries were "no more than branches of our English business."[8]

Finally, as soon as American Marconi purchased real estate and asked permission from individual states to erect its stations, it laid claim to parts of American territory. Presenting Marconi technology as a complete system was central to the company's objective of end-to-end control, highlighting the way the patented components worked together, whether in the individual apparatus or in the network as a whole. However, the stations at various parts of the network were in different countries, and there was no security agreement in place that would have required the company to provide the host states with access to its stations on short notice.[9] When American Marconi solicited the first orders from the Navy Department in the United States, naval policymakers were favorably disposed, but their enthusiasm would soon dissipate.[10]

The decision whether to adopt radio technology for the use of the U.S. Navy fell to the Bureau of Equipment, a procurement and supplies division, which provided ships with signaling apparatus (Douglas, 1989, p. 109). These same officers, more surprisingly perhaps, would also be responsible for devising communications policy, considering problems such as free intercommunication, the desirability of a commercial radio industry, and the national identity of leading companies. Policymakers at the Bureau were keenly aware that the British Admiralty was ahead in working with the new form of signaling, while they were still stuck with homing pigeons.[11] With its improving range of transmission, the new technology would be decisive in future wars, the head of the Bureau pointed out in 1904, saying, "This nation cannot afford to risk being behind other nations in this respect."[12] Control over radio technology would be the foundation for control over the radio network of the future.

As the Navy tested the sets provided by inventors, policymakers viewed the new technology in the context of the existing submarine cable network and reasoned from the mind-set of a challenger nation. The most pressing issue in cable communications at the time of Beecher's visit was the proposed Pacific cable that would link the west coast of the United States to Hawaii and then on to the Philippines. In the course of the Spanish-American War, American policymakers had found out that the exclusive concessions held by the Eastern group effectively barred access to the Far East (Headrick, 1991, p. 101; Headrick & Griset, 2001, p. 563). The control of global communications was part of the larger struggle for world leadership. A cable connecting the country to its newly acquired possessions, an officer noted in the publication of the United States Naval Institute, was one of the three most urgent questions for national advancement (Hood, 1900, p. 481).

No one understood the importance of autonomy of communications better than Admiral Royal B. Bradford, the chief of the Bureau of Equipment, who had spent the better part of his career thinking about the use of submarine cables in wartime.[13] Like foreign countries, the United States needed an independent cable system to control the messages that passed over it, Bradford concluded.[14] An officer spelled out the purpose of network control early on, stating that a nation deprived of "the means of gaining its own information and interrupting that of the enemy" would find itself at a disadvantage in wartime (Hood, 1900, p. 486). Like many other observers, congressmen predicted that radio links would replace the submarine cables, and legislators would soon consider this prediction in arguing against government funding for the Pacific cable.[15]

The decision about whether wireless was a "system" marked a Navy victory on the road to autonomy in radio communications. Though Bradford considered adopting Marconi's apparatus, naval policymakers never planned to entrust naval wireless *service* to the company. The central purpose of such service was preparation for wartime, and outsourcing it would have left enlisted men without training.[16] Policymakers quickly took aim at the system designation. "There is no such thing as a system of Wireless Telegraphy, which is patentable," Commander Francis Barber observed in late 1901.[17] The Navy Department placed an order for twenty sets of the Slaby-Arco system, manufactured by a subsidiary of the German Allgemeine Elektrizitäts Gesellschaft (AEG) (Douglas, 1989, p. 117). Electricians mixed and matched Slaby-Arco components with those provided by other inventors to arrive at the technology they were most comfortable with. This "composite system" was an assemblage of distinct parts that nevertheless worked together (Douglas, 1989, p. 131). A composite system prevented the Marconi Company from gaining influence based on its exclusive control over a coveted technology.

Alarmed to find out that the Bureau of Equipment was not interested in its technology, American Marconi sought to convince the higher echelons of the Navy to change their minds. E. Rollins Morse, a Wall Street banker, approached Secretary of the Navy William H. Moody, a personal acquaintance. In a series of letters, Morse hammered home the American identity of the corporation, especially in contrast with Slaby-Arco.[18] The company's place of incorporation, the nationality of its managers, the use of American labor, and the possession of American letters patent all signaled that this company had subjected itself to the American legal system.[19] While British

Marconi executives at home waxed about the complete control they had over subsidiaries, Morse downplayed the importance of stock ownership. "Although a large block of our stock is held by the English Company," he explained, "it is so held simply in place of royalty, carrying out the theory of the Telephone Company, that the parent company should be so far in control of the sub-companies that they cannot be bought up and utilized to the benefit of others."[20] Morse did not dispute the link between ownership and control but explained the admittedly large equity investment as a defensive move in corporate competition.

This was not the first time policymakers had heard such arguments. Foreign ownership had played a prominent role in debates about the Pacific cable during the previous three congresses. In 1902, policymakers openly questioned whether the new company offering to lay the cable connecting the United States to the Philippines served American interests or simply integrated the country into Eastern's network.[21] Some versions of the Pacific cable bill included foreign ownership regulations both for individuals and for corporations.[22]

Discussions about the Pacific cable also covered the nationality of operators, an aspect of corporate nationality unique to early communications networks. Policymakers worried about operators sending sensitive information to the enemy, a breach of security protocols that intensified with radiotelegraphy, since messages could be easily intercepted. When Lieutenant Beecher observed Marconi installations along the East Coast, he made note of the number of American operators.[23] Naval policymakers were well aware of the Royal Navy's requirement that cable companies only employ English subjects, and they pushed for American operators in U.S.-based companies (Hood, 1900, p. 485). On this point, however, Morse was silent, precisely because contracting with the Marconi companies meant leasing, and leasing involved company-supplied operators, who were British subjects. Just as the British Post Office had predicted, foreign governments were bound to object to this aspect of company policy.

The existence of concerns about corporate nationality in cable and radio communications alike underscores the challenge the multinational corporation posed for the American legal system. Central to the emergence of the multinational corporation (MNC) was the possibility that companies could own shares in another firm and own enough of them to acquire "a controlling interest" (Vagts, 1970, p. 742). This was a recent development in American law. During the nineteenth century, companies incorporated in another state were considered "foreign" corporations, and states barred them from building plants or purchasing real estate in their territories (Hovenkamp, 1991, pp. 258–259). That changed in 1889, when New Jersey permitted companies to hold stock in other firms, and "the holding company" emerged (Hovenkamp, 1991, p. 257). When the formation of a national market opened the door to companies registered in another state, the door also opened to companies registered outside the United States. Meanwhile, the legal system continued to identify a company's place of incorporation as the key to its nationality, treating American-organized subsidiaries of MNCs headquartered elsewhere as essentially American (Vagts, 1961, pp. 1528–1529). As a result, some foreign direct investment in the American economy went unrecognized, which was advantageous for British Marconi. Had the company succeeded in convincing policymakers around the world about the value of its service, it would have organized a global network in line with its own priorities—as if borders did not exist and the state system did not matter.

Though the concept of the multinational corporation was unavailable to naval policymakers at this time, they quickly concluded that American Marconi was unlike other companies with which they were familiar. "The American Company is probably controlled by the British parent company," noted an officer as early as 1899, suggesting that American Marconi was not going to cut a better deal, because it didn't make independent decisions on pricing.[24] In July 1902, Commander Barber noted that 55 percent of the American stock was owned by the British Company, which "can therefore control it in very serious matters like patent suits."[25] Bradford took the information to his superiors, pointing out "that the majority and controlling interest in the branch company is still held by the English parent company."[26] Since naval policymakers were faced with an industry they saw as naturally monopolistic and in foreign hands, corporate nationality formed a central point of contention on the structural level of network control from the very beginning, but it would not shape legislative proposals until the following decade.

In 1904, the Nantucket controversy brought the problem of end-to-end control by the Marconi organization to the fore. When, in 1901, American Marconi contracted with the *New York Herald* to provide news of ship arrivals, the company decided to locate its station on the lightship at Nantucket Island. The island was the first landfall of North Atlantic ocean liners and was "more favorably located than other stations for ship-to-shore traffic."[27]

As a result, the *Herald* was able to announce a steamer's arrival eight hours earlier than under its previous arrangement.[28] Since the lightship stood at the gateway of commerce, naval policymakers predicted that vessels that wanted reporting from Nantucket would gravitate toward the Marconi apparatus.[29] This, however, was not only because of the technology but also because of the station's favorable location on the coast, which would soon provide naval policymakers with leverage.

When, in February 1904, naval policymakers considered a German complaint that the Marconi station refused to take calls from ships not equipped with Marconi sets, it became apparent that the company used the policy to regulate land communication with the United States. Unlike in the case of the South Wellfleet station, however, direct control over American territory provided policymakers with leverage. At South Wellfleet, the station was erected on real estate the company had purchased, while the lighthouse was a public vessel. The Marconi Company's demand for a place on the lightship, naval policymakers pointed out, was about as reasonable as a claim for a place in a customhouse or on a man-of-war.[30]

By this time, competing claims to authority over radio on the part of the Departments of Navy, Army, and Agriculture had resulted in the appointment of an interdepartmental board to study wireless, the so-called Roosevelt Board, whose decisions I will examine in more detail in the following section. In June 1904, President Roosevelt asked the Board to provide an assessment of the Nantucket incident. American Marconi had long sought orders from the Navy Department and now, relying on assumptions of natural monopoly, advocated "a departmental combination" between itself and the Navy. No other private company would be allowed in the radio industry, and the Navy would receive the company's services in time of war.[31] The company deferred to territorial sovereignty: stations could be taken over, and the subsidiary would serve the host state in time of war.

Significantly, however, the Marconi organization had heeded a request from the British Admiralty to limit the range of the company's instruments on offer to 240 miles at a time when officers in the U.S. Navy sought installations that could communicate to upward of 1,000 miles.[32] In addition to royalty payments, Marconi executives asked for exclusive privilege of the Nantucket lightship, which, the Board concluded, would "go a long way toward helping them establish a monopoly of the wireless business."[33] Fully aware that the U.S. government had supported the policy of free intercommunication at the 1903 conference, company executives now proposed that the Navy, like the Admiralty before it, sign on to the non-intercommunication policy.[34]

Had the Navy Department agreed to the company's terms, the territory of the United States would have been closed off to ships equipped with apparatus from the company's rivals. The Roosevelt Board, however, concluded that there could be only one station on the lightship. Policymakers rejected the company's terms and made plans to replace the Marconi station with an installation made by a different manufacturer.[35] The Bureau of Equipment considered ordering from the National Electric Signaling Company (NESCO), registered in the United States, and even advised inventor Reginald Fessenden, himself originally from Canada, not to give any information about its apparatus to foreign governments, precisely the way the Admiralty had done with British Marconi.[36] For now, however, naval policymakers settled for the composite system, which established independence both from American Marconi and domestic suppliers for experimental purposes, and ordered its apparatus for the Nantucket lightship from Telefunken. The fact that the Navy had a choice of technology proved to be important for the resolution of the Nantucket controversy. Without a different apparatus to put in place of the Marconi installation, the removal of the Marconi station from the lightship could have left the American coast without a wireless connection.

The Navy did not, as researchers have noted, pursue a policy of building up American equipment manufacturers. Naval policymakers effectively undercut them at times and were not averse to buying from a German company (Aitken, 1985, p. 255; Douglas, 1989, p. 119). This does not mean, however, that nationalism did not matter in these early years; it simply means that the national identity of equipment manufacturers was ultimately less important to the Navy Department than the fact that naval personnel operated the stations.

In July 1904, the Roosevelt Board recommended that the Navy Department install a complete coastwise wireless telegraph network and supported the licensing of commercial stations (Douglas, 1989, p. 124).[37] Naval policymakers sought to connect the fleet and the country's newly acquired possessions to the mainland, which required long-distance stations. The Navy ordered five shore stations, some of which were to have "a scope of more than 1,000 miles."[38] Three of the five stations, in Puerto Rico (San Juan), Cuba (Guantanamo), and the Panama Canal Zone (Colon), were to communicate with men-of-war in the West Indies (Douglas, 1989, p. 132).[39] Information security proper was also essential to the Navy's plans. In 1906, for example, naval policymakers received rumors that the British Imperial Naval Station at Bermuda, equipped with the Marconi system, "tuned the instruments" in such a manner that they were able to intercept messages from American vessels and stations.[40]

During the first decade of the twentieth century, as this section has revealed, the Navy Department did not press for a commercial radio network. Rather, officials imagined autonomy of communication in terms of the Navy's own network, and independence from the Marconi organization was an important building block of autonomy. The Navy's network, extending from Maine to Unalaska, with "branch lines" to Hawaii, Guam, and the Philippines, was to guard against a private monopoly.[41] Just who would run the external commercial communications of American protectorates was unclear at this time, and cable companies registered in the United States advised the Navy Department to claim exclusive jurisdiction over international telegraphy linking these territories to the outside world.[42]

The American legal system of the early twentieth century was permissive enough to allow British Marconi to establish a subsidiary, and newspaper companies entered into contracts with American Marconi. Though the company did not receive any orders from the Navy Department and was ordered to remove its station from a public lightship, most of American Marconi's stations were off limits to the government. The first draft of what would become the Radio Act of 1912 can be traced to concerns about the extent of American control over commercial stations on U.S. territory.

The Origins of Licensing: Submarine Cable Licensing, Government Ownership, and the Administration's 1905 Bill

Radio regulation originated from the Bureau of Equipment in the wake of Lieutenant Beecher's visit to the South Wellfleet Marconi station. In January 1902, Admiral Bradford complained to the Navy Department about the interference caused by the station and recommended bringing wireless under government control.[43] But interference, as a political argument, worked in connection with another policy objective: "interference plus" influenced radio policy. While, in Britain, concerns about interference were intertwined with policymakers' worries about integrating a radio network with the submarine cable system, in the United States, such concerns were insepa-rable from concerns about the subsidiary of British Marconi. In February, the Navy Department contacted the governor of Massachusetts for authority to inspect the South Wellfleet station.[44] The station was erected by "a foreign corporation," Bradford wrote, and the agent of the Marconi Company who established it "was known by an assumed name."[45] The company, he added a month later, had established a very extensive wireless telegraph station "with no authority whatever from the Government."[46] When the Navy Depart-ment realized that Massachusetts did not have authority to compel the Mar-coni station to permit access to the Navy, the problem reached the cabinet.[47] In their search for authority to regulate the technology, policymakers sought to fit radiotelegraphy into the common carrier framework.

During these early years, policymakers considered three distinct prob-lems, which often blended into one another: control over the physical infrastructure, control over the airwaves, and control over information. A global commercial radio system required control over property at the choicest locations in countries around the world, and, as seen in chapter 2, access to American territory was vital for the viability of British Marconi. Beecher's unsuccessful visit, however, set off alarm bells about the extent of Marconi's control over its stations. Could the owner's right to exclude others from the use of their property, naval policymakers began to wonder, extend to *excluding the United States from its own territory*? The alarm bells about end-to-end control only rang louder with the development of the conflict over the non-intercommunication policy. "The operations of all these stations," the Bureau of Equipment would comment before Congress in connection with stations erected for foreign governments, "although under Government control, are limited by the nature of the contract."[48]

Control over the airwaves in these years was often inseparable from con-trol over stations. The ability to communicate via a network connected by the airwaves meant uninterrupted use of the latter. The Navy found it difficult to get its messages through because operators controlling a powerful transmitter could "prevent reception of a message within the radius of their influence."[49] The idea of wavelength allocations still lay in the future, so the most appar-ent way to avoid unintentional interference was to place stations far apart. The choicest locations for ship-to-shore communications, such as Nantucket Island, served as chokepoints, necessary for both a naval network and a viable company in a naturally monopolistic industry.

Naval policymakers first predicted and then observed that private stations claimed the best locations for themselves, especially in congested ports, such as New York.[50] Bradford wrote to the Navy Department that it was not advisable to let companies establish stations on the coasts without control by the government, since these stations "monopolize the air."[51] Complaints about interference were about lack of access to the airwaves, which would have raised concerns even if all instruments in the early radio field had been unquestionably under American control. The solution to this problem at this time was a restriction on the number of stations, domestic or foreign, which meant a restriction on the use of American territory. During much of the decade, the Bureau of Equipment would seek to secure a "priority of right," not in the air but in the most desirable locations on the coast.[52] Perhaps not surprisingly, American Marconi consistently objected to licensing requirements, which specified the location of stations, advocating wartime takeover instead.[53] "We would be unable to put down stations where we require them," executives would tell Congress later, adding, "We wish to have perfect freedom to put them where we choose."[54]

Finally, policymakers sought to make sure that their messages got to their intended recipients and no one else. In wartime, Bradford pointed out, the government would be forced to take control of the stations "in order not only to communicate with its ships but to prevent the transmission of wireless telegraph messages to irresponsible private parties both afloat and ashore."[55] Control over confidential information could be achieved by the use of codes, which the Navy Department would perfect during World War I, or, naval policymakers were convinced at this time, by ensuring that operators were trustworthy. As chapter 2 has documented, commercial interests, which were the first to erect radio stations, were interested mostly in the problem of the airwaves. Thus, the idea that policy reflected the interests of the regulated industries paints with too broad a brush (cf. Benkler, 1998, p. 59; cf. Douglas, 1989, p. 216). Control over the physical infrastructure and over confidential information were the Navy's problems, so the Navy Department's outsized role in radio regulation is hardly surprising.

The cabinet took up the problem of radio regulation on March 14. Attorney General Philander Knox advised that the president had the constitutional authority "to control the location of" radio stations, but Knox recommended including such a section in the Pacific cable bill under consideration before Congress.[56] This had been Bradford's first idea as well. The

State Department had always exercised supervision over submarine cables landing on American territory, he pointed out in January, and the Marconi station "would seem to require quite as much if not more control on the part of the government."[57] After all, long-distance wireless was just around the corner, and the Bureau of Equipment had already received Barber's letter in December about the Lloyd's contract, which drew a parallel between a global Marconi monopoly and the monopoly established by the English cable companies. The German government's invitation to the 1903 conference arrived shortly after the cabinet meeting, and the Bureau of Equipment was asked to offer its views on the non-intercommunication policy. In April, Bradford declared a future Marconi monopoly in traffic handling to be "injurious to the best interests of the country," and he reinforced his call for legislative action.[58]

The general thrust of the U.S. negotiating stance at the 1903 conference as well as the basis for legislation were formulated in August 1902, when Acting Attorney General James Beck proposed to regulate radio analogously to submarine cables, which were considered to be a public utility.[59] Based on Beck's recommendation, the American delegation took the position in 1903 that the U.S. government had absolute authority to impose conditions on the operation of any wireless system used for interstate and foreign communication. Beck identified radiotelegraphy as a means of commercial intercourse but dismissed the fact that this network used the airwaves for connection. What mattered for federal authority was that radio transmission was commerce.[60] This was, at best, a partial application of common carrier precedents to the new technology.

Since policymakers set out to regulate a public utility rather than a public resource, they drew on the Commerce Clause of the U.S. Constitution to reach the necessary regulatory precedents (cf. Douglas, 1989, p. 217). Under public service liberalism, judges and lawmakers sought to facilitate the circulation of goods and services. Companies that "devoted [their] property to a use in which the public [had] an interest" were considered both common carriers and public utilities (Bowman, 1996, p. 56). Common carriers were required to provide adequate facilities at reasonable charges and serve all without discrimination, while public utilities had the additional duty to extend facilities (Cherry, 2008, p. 276; Horwitz, 1989, p. 13; Stone, 1991, pp. 30–34). Communications networks, in particular, were seen as both common carriers and public utilities, occupying the same relation to commerce as carriers of messages that railroads did as carriers of goods (Cox & Byrnes, 1989, p. 27). Since each transportation or communications network had unique features, fitting radiotelegraphy into the common carrier framework would be the challenge of the decade.

The cable analogy signaled that radiotelegraphy was a global industry, that radio policy was foreign policy, and that the federal government had authority over it. But submarine cables formed a wired infrastructure where companies exercised end-to-end physical control over circuits. The power of the government to impose conditions on the landing of cables rested primarily on its obligation "to preserve the territorial integrity" of the United States.[61] No one had the right to establish "a physical connection" to the United States without the permission of its government, Attorney General Joseph McKenna had written a few years earlier.[62] The danger of unauthorized physical connections is apparent from the comparison between a submarine cable and a bridge. Bridges could facilitate the invasion of ground troops between the United States and a hostile foreign power, a policymaker would note later.[63] By erasing the border, physical connections provided free access to an invading force, whether in the form of troops or messages. The first time the United States imposed conditions on the landing of submarine cables was in 1875, and these are generally seen as the first instance of regulating FDI in a communications industry (Hills, 2002).

In the end, Congress did not address whether the cable analogy was in fact appropriate for a network that did not establish a physical connection with another country. By summer 1902, it had become apparent that the bill authorizing a government-owned Pacific cable—one that the Bureau of Equipment also favored—would not pass, and the possibility of simply adding a radio section to an existing bill vanished. The Commercial Cable Company had secretly agreed with the Eastern group to enter its territory in the Pacific, and American policymakers privately acquiesced to U.S. participation in the British-dominated cable pool (Rogers, 1922a, p. 18). The implications of this arrangement for the autonomy of cable communications were far-reaching. That a British company still had an important role in connecting the United States to Asia would not become public until 1921 (Headrick, 1991, pp. 100–101, 179).

When regulation analogous to submarine cable licensing fell through, the Bureau of Equipment settled on government ownership as the next viable strategy. Though control over the network, the airwaves, and information were distinct problems, government ownership of the network had a lot to recommend it, since it solved all of them at once. A clear alternative—working with a single commercial organization—had appeared desirable to the Admiralty and would again seem so to the U.S. Navy in another twenty years. The Bureau, however, was unwilling to work with what policymakers saw as a foreign corporation. Naval policymakers repeatedly rejected American Marconi's proposition for "a departmental combination," and the Bureau used the Nantucket incident as an argument for abolishing private stations on the coast.[64]

Not all of the Bureau's reasons were geopolitical: policymakers viewed the profit motive with particular suspicion.[65] The Spanish-American War had taught some officers to consider it "suicidal" to trust private enterprise with managing the country's links to the outside world (Hood, 1900, p. 487). The idea that commercial stations were "freebies" to be taken over in wartime, widely held among British policymakers, would not be accepted until the 1920s.[66]

If the Bureau of Equipment had its way, private wireless stations would have gone the way of private mail carriers, and the European state-to-state model would have governed radiotelegraphy.[67] Policymakers sought information about international best practices, which revolved around extending telegraph statutes to cover the new industry.[68] Government ownership of telegraphy meant public ownership of the network and a monopoly over traffic handling. Because the radio network used the airwaves for connection, government ownership would, of necessity, sweep up the airwaves. Newspapers immediately protested, commenting that the government should not own "the entire ether as well as the earth beneath" (cited in Douglas, 1989, p. 126).

The most important objection, however, came from the General Board of the Navy, which had coordinated strategic planning since 1900 (O'Brien, 1998, p. 16; Kuehn, 2017, p. 41) and was far less concerned about British control than the Bureau of Equipment was. These retired admirals judged the use of the Marconi system on the Great Lakes to be a "convenience" since this was a location where "only ourselves and the British [were] concerned."[69] In May 1904, the General Board advised against a naval monopoly but recommended that the Navy receive a priority of right to the placement of stations. In addition, it delegated the authority over licensing wireless companies to the Department of Commerce and Labor.[70]

Table 3.1
Hypothetical and actual ownership structures in radiotelegraphy.

		Type of station		
		Naval stations	Coastal commercial	High-power
	1. Foreign	British Marconi	British Marconi	British Marconi
Ownership	2. Domestic or foreign (?)	American Marconi	American Marconi	American Marconi
	3. 1904 Roosevelt Board	U.S. Navy	American Marconi in competition with other private companies	American Marconi in competition with other private companies

In July, the Roosevelt Board took the advice of the General Board and recommended licensing. Table 3.1 outlines possible ownership structures of radio stations on American territory in the wake of the Roosevelt Board's decision. Although naval policymakers would later exaggerate that, in the United States, the field for foreigners was "more open than in any other country," the American telecommunications environment never reached the low level of sovereignty that characterized national control in peripheral countries.[71] At no point did such an undeniably foreign corporation as British Marconi own and operate all coastal commercial and all high-power stations. Moreover, American Marconi itself was subject to competition by NESCO and the various DeForest companies.

In the wake of the Roosevelt Board's decision, the Bureau of Equipment drafted the first stand-alone wireless bill. The October 1904 draft bill included several elements of telecommunications legislation that are with us today. It mandated free intercommunication, outlawed the transmission of false messages, and provided the federal government with emergency powers to either close stations or operate them in wartime.[72] Naval policymakers pushed for "a national policy" to guide the American delegation at the upcoming Berlin conference while submitting the draft bill to the Department of Commerce and Labor for review.[73] A brief comparison of the Bureau's draft and the January 1905 substitute drafted by the Department of Commerce and Labor proves instructive.

Since naval policymakers' refusal to adopt the Marconi system and their recommendation to support free intercommunication were developed in the context of pursuing autonomy in cable communications, the Navy Department continued to seek powers to control, and even prohibit, the establishment of stations. They drew on the British Wireless Telegraph Act of 1904, which required a license for the erection of stations.[74] By contrast, the Commerce draft brought the regulation in line with Congress's constitutional authority to regulate interstate commerce and required a license only for using or operating a station "as a means of commercial intercourse."[75] When the Navy Department agreed to these revisions, policymakers forwent the opportunity to reject requests for the erection of new stations, which remained under the authority of individual states. But this was not immediately recognized.

Second, the Bureau of Equipment's draft required every licensed wireless station to transmit and receive messages "without respect to the systems in use," bringing U.S. law in line with the proposals discussed at Berlin.[76] Had the Navy's version passed, American Marconi would have been forced to abandon the non-intercommunication policy or risk losing its license. After consultation with the representatives of commercial companies, however, the Department of Commerce and Labor weakened the free intercommunication provision. In its draft, stations were required to receive and forward messages and signals "tendered for transmission to any other neighboring or connecting apparatus."[77] Neighboring apparatuses could have been stations close by, such as a ship in distress. But what was "a connecting apparatus" in a network that required no physical connection? Perhaps it was one whose owner had a contract with the Marconi organization. Contractual relationships between the Bell System and noncompeting independents, for example, allowed connections to Bell's long-distance lines, while noncompeting independents were refused such connections (Mueller, 1997, p. 101n24). This version did not have the same bite as the one that decision makers in Berlin had come up with.

The cabinet met and approved the bill, whereupon naval policymakers accepted the changes.[78] Policymakers hoped that intensifying interference would prompt Congress to take up the bill, but opposition by the War and Treasury Departments thwarted their hopes.[79] In the absence of legislation, Special Notice to Mariners, No. 47a, issued in November 1904, controlled the operation of naval wireless stations, mandating free intercommunication.[80] Thus, licensing and interconnection, two of the three geopolitically important features of the future Radio Act of 1912, were in place by 1905.

Though the nationality of operators was a central issue for those interested in the security of information, citizenship requirements had yet to find their way into legislative proposals.

Given these developments in legislation, the United States entered the second international radio conference in a position remarkably similar to the one Britain would adopt after the conference. Neither country was able to force the Marconi Company to change its non-intercommunication policy, and both opted for duplicating Marconi stations with government stations that would accept messages from every wireless system. When the American delegation signed on to the 1906 conference's recommendations, policymakers referred to the Commerce draft as an appropriate measure to ensure that the recommendations of the convention were adopted.[81] Under the administration's proposals, radiotelegraphy would be considered a public service industry, though the exact provisions remained in flux. However, American Marconi had yet to weigh in on the matter in any considerable manner.

By summer 1906, the Marconi Company was teetering on the verge of bankruptcy, which made naval policymakers wonder whether they even needed the Berlin conference to settle the monopoly problem.[82] Since only the transatlantic trade route covered the cost of shore stations, the future, the Bureau of Equipment asserted, was a question of the survival of the fittest. There was room for one company "with capital not inflated."[83] That the Marconi organization could not be the fittest, however, was also apparent to policymakers, since it carried a very small number of messages "for a company with such a large capitalization."[84] When Hall failed to sabotage the Berlin conference, the Bureau concluded that there would shortly be "but one company maintaining wireless communication for public service," and it recommended collaborating with that company (Raboy, 2016, p. 279).[85]

The Bureau of Equipment's willingness to consider an informal arrangement with a private company made it clear that interference, on its own, was not sufficient for licensing. When the threat of a foreign company subsided, so did the Navy's interest in legislation. Naval policymakers on both sides of the Atlantic had a clear preference for working with one commercial company, but, in the United States at least, the identity of that company was not yet clear. "The best and most economical system will replace the others," Henry Manney, the chief of the Bureau of Equipment, informed Congress in 1908.[86] Naval policymakers had already contracted with the DeForest Company for the delivery of long-distance stations but were burned when the company supplied poor stations. The company now rose again in the form of the United Wireless Corporation (Douglas, 1989, p. 133). Under serious consideration were the Fessenden and the Poulsen systems, which offered the new, "continuous wave" transmission, which promised to reduce interference. In early 1907, naval policymakers predicted that the Poulsen system would "probably supersede all other systems of wireless telegraphy now in use."[87]

While waiting for the right company to emerge, President Theodore Roosevelt's administration secured emergency powers over radio stations via an executive order in April 1907.[88] Now the United States had the authority to take over stations in wartime and integrate them into the network the Navy was developing. The legal status of commercial companies would receive attention yet again in early 1908, when the Senate considered the ratification of the Berlin convention. It was during these hearings that policymakers confronted the unique technological properties of radio for the first time.

Radiotelegraphy as a Public Service Industry

Though policymakers were just grappling with the new corporate form, the United States was a host state to an aspiring MNC headquartered abroad. Radiotelegraphy was a global, strategically significant industry at the cusp of developing a shore-to-shore network. In October 1907, British Marconi opened its first transatlantic circuit, which linked Clifden, Ireland, and Glace Bay, Nova Scotia (Jacobsen, 2010, p. 236). By charging half the cable rate, the company was poised to challenge the dominance of the existing cartels over message handling. American Marconi's stations in the United States did not have transatlantic connections at this point, but it was just a matter of time. As British Marconi was developing its operations worldwide, it was quickly confronted by states with differing interests and legal traditions. At issue in the United States, in particular, was whether Congress would sanction interconnection as the foundational principle governing the operation of the global radio network. In terms of developing a sovereign commercial network in the future, this option would be preferable to sanctioning centralized control via the Marconi organization. Though the Bureau of Equipment had already identified American Marconi as a foreign corporation, the arguments company executives or policymakers came up with also had to make sense under American legal precedents. The 1908 hearings before the

Senate Foreign Relations Committee provided the opportunity for both policymakers and company executives to present their views.

No one was better suited to represent the Marconi Company's interests than John Griggs, the president of American Marconi, who had been trained as a corporate lawyer and had previously served as attorney general. Since the Berlin treaty was in the nature of a contract, Griggs told Congress, the United States would need "some kind of a license" to enforce it.[89] The Commerce and Labor Department's licensing bill would soon be introduced in the Senate as bill S. 5949.[90] Company executives had already been alerted to the necessity of legal arguments in 1903, when the American delegation announced to the world that the common carrier framework mandated that companies accept messages from anyone. When word of the 1905 draft bill got out, Cuthbert Hall invited Griggs to London to coordinate legislative strategy.[91] The details of these meetings are yet to be revealed, but the result is available for analysis.

During the 1908 hearings, the Navy and War Departments both supported ratification, but the legal justification for the government's position fell to the Department of Commerce and Labor.[92] One memorandum, written by Charles Earl, the solicitor for the Department of Commerce and Labor, represents the first sustained attempt to spell out the status of radiotelegraphy as a common carrier. It was submitted to the Senate by President Theodore Roosevelt as the best explanation of the executive branch's support for the ratification of the 1906 convention.[93] Over the course of the hearings, lawmakers, career professionals in government departments, and company executives considered four interrelated questions. Was radiotelegraphy a public service industry? To what extent, if any, was this industry best run under central control? Did the nondiscrimination principle in common carrier law require radiotelegraph companies to carry their competitors' traffic? Finally, did compulsory intercommunication amount to a taking of private property? Applying the interconnection requirement from telegraph legislation to the new technology, however, brought a long-simmering problem to the fore: what exactly did it mean to establish a connection in radiotelegraphy?

Both American Marconi and the representatives of the government agreed that radiotelegraphy was a public service industry. Under public service liberalism, industries cloaked with the public interest provided infrastructures "essential to the nation" (Cherry, 2008, p. 274). By the turn of the century, the telephone had become a public necessity, just like the steamboat, railroad, and telegraph before it (Speta, 2001, p. 262). American Marconi situated radiotelegraphy in this line of thinking when its executives testified that passengers would not cross the ocean on ships unless they were equipped with wireless. "It is a necessity just as much as it is a necessity to have a dining room," Griggs explained to Congress.[94] The Earl memorandum also acknowledged that radiotelegraphy was "a public employment," and it asked that four types of interests in the technology be satisfied: the naval and military requirements of the several nations involved, the needs of the government with respect to international correspondence, the necessities of ships in distress, and the rights of the public.[95]

British Marconi could not exercise end-to-end control over a global radio network without a policy consensus worldwide that radiotelegraphy was best run under central control. At the international conferences, however, American policymakers rejected this idea, and the Earl memorandum now sided with the British Post Office in suggesting that international regulations could provide the same uniformity of operation as a monopoly.[96] The policy of compulsory intercommunication had a "strong prima facie claim of recognition," policymakers asserted.[97] Under international law standards, this meant that a rule had to be just if most countries agreed that it was so. Since only Italy supported centralized control, international agreement was beyond dispute. That most countries were all too eager to avoid another British communications monopoly, or that the majority opinion in the British government sought to protect the country's cable industry from wireless, fell outside the bounds of legal reasoning.

The Earl memorandum pointed out that "the rights of the general public require that wireless telegraph companies should serve all customers alike, without discrimination."[98] Today, nondiscriminatory access to a common carrier's facilities means that carriers are mandated to accept interconnection from each other (U.S.C. 47, §§201(a) and 251; Horwitz, 1989, p. 12). In the first decade of the twentieth century, however, American Marconi was fully prepared to provide shipping companies with access to its network but sought to reserve the right to treat its competitors differently. At issue was whether the nondiscrimination requirement applied to provider-to-provider relationships, meaning to the relationship between competitors.

Griggs made his case by comparing radiotelegraphy to telephony, where the idea that competitors deserved to be treated differently from subscribers was well accepted. "We have established [our shore stations] there to do business with our ship stations, and it is just exactly the same as though a telephone exchange is established in a town to do business with its subscribers," he explained.[99] Perhaps the Marconi organization identified wireless telegraphy as a type of telephony in order to cement the perception of the radio network as an expensive infrastructure.[100] Griggs, however, studiously avoided any legal comparison to the submarine cables, whose landing required government approval. While British Marconi emphasized the advantages of a mixed network at home, downplaying the threat that radio posed to the submarine cable industry, Griggs presented the radio network to Congress as "the unquestioned rival of the ocean cables."[101] Griggs told lawmakers that the regulation the administration was pushing for was "different from any method [under which] any company in the United States has ever been regulated before."[102]

Common carrier law, Marconi executives emphasized, did not compel one company "to connect its lines to those of another" or, to put it another way, it did not mandate "actual physical contact" between the lines of two rival companies.[103] Naval policymakers watched in disbelief as Griggs sought to dismantle the legal advice that had guided the American delegation during both conferences. It was "pretty absurd," Barber wrote to the Bureau of Equipment, that British Marconi asked Griggs, a former attorney general, "to go for the decisions of the present Atty General."[104] British Marconi's arguments against free intercommunication were, however, easily transferable to the United States, perhaps because the Bell System had already treated policymakers to the exact same points. In 1895, an internal Bell memorandum made what can be termed "the system builder argument" against compulsory interconnection: the company had invested a lot of money in constructing its system, and if competitors had also been able to connect to it, they would not have needed to assume the burdens of building a network (Mueller, 1997, p. 50). Interconnection facilitated cream skimming, the practice whereby competitors made money by linking customers to profitable network segments, leaving the development of unprofitable connections to the system builder. In response, Bell executives allowed only noncompeting independents to access the company's network (Mueller, 1997, p. 77).

The telephone analogy directed policymakers' attention to the relevant railroad precedents that provided protection against the policy of compulsory intercommunication.[105] The courts were guided by the landmark

Express Cases (1885), which arose from a conflict between a railroad and a package delivery company. "Express" companies received and forwarded items of great value or goods requiring careful handling over the lines of a railroad company.[106] The conditions for the use of such "through-line facilities" were laid down in a contract. When certain railroad companies terminated their contracts, express companies asked the court to grant them the same facilities on a nondiscriminatory basis. If common carrier obligations trumped contract law, railroads would need to carry another common carrier's shipments and serve as "common carriers of common carriers." The railroads objected because such a requirement would have prevented them from prioritizing passenger traffic. In a significant victory for the railroads, however, the *Express Cases* spelled out that common carrier obligations did not extend to competitors.

The public service designation removed the commercial use of radio stations from the purview of private property law, but American Marconi continued to press for the right to determine who could connect to its network. Under the liberal concept of private property, ownership carries six rights, the most important of which are "use" and "exclusion" (Raymond, 2003, p. 17). "The owner can button his patent up in his pocket and say no one shall use it except on my terms. That is his right," Griggs declared.[107] Common carrier regulations requiring interconnection transferred part of the owner's property to the public, a development that American Marconi contested. In doing so, the company protected its right to use its patents and did not claim a legal right to the airwaves.[108] The value of a patent was in its use, Griggs told Congress, and the Berlin convention required the company "to give the use of those shore stations to people against [its] will."[109] By making the process of receiving and forwarding messages mandatory, the convention asked a radio company to do "just what the telegraph and railroad companies [did] by agreement between themselves."[110] Compulsory connections allowed one company's property to be used for the commercial benefit of another and were best understood as a form of confiscation.[111]

This argument was directly in line with that of the *Express Cases*, which had rejected compulsory connections as nothing more than a "taking" of private property. A taking, in turn, was a violation of the Fifth Amendment of the Constitution, which prohibited the government from taking private property for "public use" without offering compensation. As long as the railroad precedent controlled the regulation of communications networks and as long as wireless telegraphy was judged to be sufficiently similar to the telephone, American Marconi had a case.

Whether compulsory intercommunication amounted to a taking of private property was significant because, unlike their counterparts in Britain, American policymakers had no interest in compensating the Marconi organization (Waterbury, 1903).[112] Policymakers affirmed the general principle that private property could not be taken for public use without compensation. If the injury to property rights was "an accidental consequence of a lawful exercise of government power," however, the courts did not find it to be a taking.[113]

American Marconi would take issue with these arguments. Rather than allowing the public use requirement to eviscerate its property rights, the company was more likely to contest either the lawful exercise of government power—a line of inquiry that went to the definition of public use—or whether the interconnection requirement was in fact "an accidental consequence" of the exercise of government power. The potential for a constitutional argument pitting private property rights against the common carrier regulatory framework would delay legislation about free intercommunication until 1912.

Given that common carrier precedents likely favored American Marconi, arguments supporting free intercommunication had to distinguish radiotelegraphy from telephony. Congress had been moving toward provider-to-provider interconnection, as the 1887 Interstate Commerce Act reveals. Just two years after the *Express Cases*, Congress mandated interconnection for the railroad and related industries (Cox & Byrnes, 1989, p. 27). To take advantage of this framework, the government would have needed to extend the Act to radiotelegraphy. However, legislation to this effect would not develop until the 1910 Mann-Elkins Act.[114] Until then, policymakers foregrounded the different technological features of the two networks.

The distinction policymakers were advancing hinged on addressing what constituted a connection in different network industries. Telephone connections were not quite the same as railroad connections, and the "ether" would be something else altogether. Marconi executives seemed to be saying that if the shore station was the equivalent of a telephone exchange, the wavelengths were the company's wires. Yet, the telephone analogy, the Earl memorandum quickly pointed out, was "more apparent than real."[115] Earl noted that "each system is sensitive to the waves emanating from the apparatus of every other known system" and that "this mutual sensitiveness makes interference possible and also permits intercommunication between stations regardless of systems."[116] In radiotelegraphy, as contemporaries had already observed, connection was the default, and the only thing that stood in the way was corporate policy. The Marconi organization itself reinforced this conclusion when it exempted distress signals from the non-intercommunication policy.[117] "Under any conditions where humanity requires it we have nothing to say," Griggs declared.[118]

The idea of the airwaves as a public resource was first introduced into policy discussions as government officials grasped for a legal argument against existing interconnection precedents. Accepting that the earth's atmosphere was to a wireless system "precisely what wires and conduits, and poles and rights of way" were to the telephone network meant accepting that the new technology was much cheaper.[119] But there was more. While wired networks relied on a physical infrastructure along with franchises and rights of way, the plants of radio companies included isolated stations relying on a connecting medium: "the ether of the earth's atmosphere, *the common property of all*" [emphasis added].[120] Policymakers seized on the airwaves to show that a radio network could not be fully private.

It was in these discussions that the first glimpse of radio as a unique medium for regulatory purposes emerged. Currently, the dominant understanding of radio policy during the first decade of the twentieth century is that it was focused on the problem of the airwaves. But this was not how policymakers thought about the problem. Rather than making an intellectual leap from the intangible ether to a consideration of property rights, they had been thinking about property relations in connection with stations and found themselves faced with the issue of the airwaves (cf. Douglas, 1989, p. 218).

Because securing the ability to communicate involved the problem of the station, the airwaves, and information, the metaphors policymakers relied on would multiply. Stations, as we have seen, had been compared to switchboards and lighthouse plants. In a 1908 memorandum, John I. Waterbury, an American delegate to both international conferences, did not so much as mention telephony or the railroads. Instead, he compared the atmosphere to "a common highway" or the high seas.[121] Attention to the difference between wired networks and radio opened the conceptual domain of a "natural resource," which would require a rethinking of common carrier precedents in the long run.

All of this was geopolitically significant because American Marconi's exclusive focus on private property—radio *stations*—had reinforced the control of an early MNC headquartered outside the United States over parts of American territory. Though the spectrum had just emerged as a relevant concept for policy deliberations, it still formed a small part of radio policy. Policymakers now identified the airwaves as the commons, but they proposed no language to regulate it. Instead, conceptualizing airwaves as a public resource helped loosen assumptions about property rights that had hitherto influenced the discussion and strengthened the case for common carrier rules. As policymakers inserted the public airwaves between the Marconi Company and its own stations, they cemented the public service classification while drawing a clear distinction between radiotelegraphy and telephony.

American Marconi and the land telegraph companies fought the ratification of the 1906 convention, while United Wireless, the latest company to work the DeForest patents, and American Marconi's most important competitor, supported ratification.[122] United executives complained to the Navy that American Marconi enjoyed "all the privileges of American institutions without assuming any responsibilities."[123] However, lawmakers felt that the bill raised many questions that they were unprepared to address (Douglas, 1989, p. 217). According to later accounts, American Marconi succeeded in killing action in 1908.[124] In the end, the Senate Committee on Foreign Relations never reported on the treaty, and the Committee on Naval Affairs took no action on S. 5949.

Therefore, by spring 1908, the third attempt at radio regulation had failed. There was no provision included in the 1902 Pacific cable bill, the first general wireless bill, in 1905, did not have the support of the entire administration, and now licensing became intertwined with the ratification of the 1906 convention, which failed to secure congressional support. Yet, radiotelegraphy as a public service industry had been cemented, and future regulatory efforts would focus on regulating the use and operation of radio stations, not their establishment. Significantly, S. 5949 was the last licensing bill whose only purpose was the regulation of private companies. During the next four years, policymakers would grapple with the problems posed by the amateurs, a new force in American radio.

The Geopolitical Significance of the Radio Act of 1912

In late 1911, the Department of Commerce and Labor issued its annual report, which called for government ownership of radiotelegraphy. The ether was "common property," Commissioner of Navigation Eugene Chamberlain explained, which had to be brought under government control lest "unrestrained trivial messages" create Babel.[125] Control over stations was in turn necessary, Chamberlain spelled out, because control over wireless messages was possible "only by the most searching and complete surveillance of government."[126] By the end of the following year, Congress would pass the Radio Act of 1912, a piece of telegraph legislation aimed at regulating station use, which nevertheless touched on control over both the airwaves and information.

The Department of Commerce and Labor's recommendation was of recent origin. Just a year earlier, when the secretary of the Navy expressed his preference for government ownership, the Department of Commerce and Labor was not convinced.[127] Since the Navy was building its own network, Chamberlain noted, no private company could have a monopoly.[128] Lawmakers showed no concern about the expansion of the Marconi organization, given that a House committee had declared in 1910 that there were plenty of American wireless companies in the market.[129] In just a year, they would change their minds.

The most ardent supporter of government ownership had long been the Bureau of Equipment, which, after a brief period of optimism with regard to working with a commercial monopoly, renewed its support for the policy in 1909.[130] Naval policymakers would continue their support even after a 1910 reorganization that placed wireless under the Bureau of Steam Engineering. Under the direction of Lieutenant Commander David W. Todd, its Radio Division would play a central role in the development of legislation (Todd, 1911).

Policymakers across the government now saw the United States as a naval power of the first class, though it had yet to develop a network connecting the country with its outlying possessions.[131] The Navy Department credited the emergence of U.S.-based inventors with the attainment of technological sovereignty, which made it possible to equip the fleet without buying from the Marconi Company.[132] Experiments with the Fessenden and the Poulsen arc systems revealed that the future lay with continuous-wave radio. Naval policymakers expected stations at Puerto Rico, Hawaii, Panama, and the Philippines to connect the United States to its possessions and help the Navy Department control the fleet at sea.[133] Yet, the Navy Department's annual reports for the next several years showed delays caused by limited funds and by the failure of contractors to make deliveries on time.[134]

By contrast, American Marconi was emerging from a period of retrenchment. It was locked in competition with United Wireless, a company that, its executives liked to point out, resisted the expansion of "a hostile foreign corporation" (Douglas, 1989, pp. 181–182).[135] The precise contours of the Navy Department's relationship with United Wireless are for future researchers to explore. Perhaps some hoped that the company would become the market leader that the Navy could collaborate with, while others suspected early on that company executives were most interested in selling stock.[136] Meanwhile, American Marconi's British parent was expanding under the leadership of its new managing director, Godfrey Isaacs. In January 1911, Isaacs came to an agreement with Telefunken, established in 1903 in the wake of a merger between Siemens-Halske and AEG in Germany, to set up a jointly owned subsidiary and stay out of each other's markets in marine communications (Hills, 2002, p. 112). British Marconi now had nine subsidiaries, with American Marconi holding an unrivaled position in the United States (Maclaurin, 1949, p. 43). When, in May 1911, the directors of United Wireless were found guilty of mail fraud and the company was placed in receivership, American Marconi initiated a patent suit against the company (Douglas, 1989, p. 184). With a resurgent American Marconi, government ownership would be considered in the context of a potential private monopoly.

The Department of Commerce and Labor's reasoning, laid out in its annual report, hints at a possible relationship among three parts of radio communications that policymakers hoped to control: information, the physical infrastructure, and the airwaves. Information, which was very difficult to control, lay at the top of a metaphorical ladder and could not be reached without climbing several other steps first. Both control over stations and control over the airwaves would facilitate control over information, while the former would also reinstate some of the control that the U.S. government seemed to have ceded to a corporation headquartered abroad. Control over stations represented the middle rung, but, as the 1908 hearings revealed, stations were harder to control than it appeared, protected as they were by patents and a broader system of private property rights. The airwaves, at the bottom of the ladder, seemed to be perhaps the easiest to reach. Policymakers had already declared them a public resource, and access to the airwaves had recently emerged as an important part of policy discussions. Now, it appeared that government control over the airwaves would help pave the way to public ownership of the network, which in turn would help the government control the flow of information.

The perception that "none of the present bills [were] broad enough" had already seeped into newspaper editorials ("Government regulation of wireless telegraphy," 1908). The most common response was to extend the earlier radio bills, aimed at stations operated for public service, to individuals, which would soon result in the classification of "amateur" stations. In the wake of several months of conferences between the Navy, War, and Treasury departments, Representative William Greene and Senator Chauncey Depew introduced the bills that regulated station use from a common carrier framework, laying the direct foundation for the Radio Act of 1912. A particularly controversial provision in these bills was section 4, which empowered the president to designate wavelengths—an option that the Navy also favored.[137] Meanwhile, the most ambitious approach to regulating "the air" came out of the Committee on Naval Affairs, chaired by Representative Ernest Roberts, who asserted, "It has always been understood that a man owning real estate owned to the center of the earth and the heavens above and controlled everything above and below the surface of the piece of land that he happened to own."[138]

The way Roberts formulated the problem foreshadowed a conceptual transformation at the heart of radio regulation that would not be resolved for another fifteen years. At stake was the concept of property. All previous discussion had assumed that lawmakers were deciding about property rights in relation to the station, the physical embodiment of intellectual property law. But what if the property right in question no longer concerned the use of the station but rather the use of the airwaves? Thinking about the air as a type of real estate highlighted private ownership of land as a model, which clashed with the ocean and highway metaphors that policymakers used during the 1908 hearings.[139] The latter two metaphors conjured up global and nationwide forms of common property resources, respectively. The Department of Commerce and Labor, in its argument for government ownership, compared the airwaves to natural resources that defied "the boundary lines of nations" (cited in Dorsey, 1995, p. 407).[140]

Nowhere was the clash of metaphors more apparent than in the proposals for wavelength allocations. The Berlin conference had assigned broad tracts of frequencies (e.g., 300–600 meters) for commercial traffic, rather than particular wavelengths. NESCO representatives compared the 300-meter assignment to "a party line for all maritime business" (cited in Douglas, 1989, p. 222). Party lines, familiar from telephony, meant that several users shared a line. Inventor Reginald Fessenden told Congress that the party line was a mistake, and he recommended dividing "the ether" into fifty wavelengths, separated by a band of 10 percent.[141]

While thinking about the air as a piece of real estate meant the extension of property rights vertically, wavelength allocations focused on dividing the airwaves into distinct channels—a horizontal division. Even if policymakers abandoned the common carrier framework, which recognized the use of stations as a property right, and agreed to view the airwaves as a common property resource, and even if they agreed on the appropriate metaphor for the resource, how could they reconcile these two ways of creating *exclusive rights* in that resource? And could the government create wavelengths without asserting sovereign control over the airwaves above the territory of the entire country? Since the Roberts bill foundered on the opposition of the Department of Commerce and Labor and the Marconi interests while Congress refused to grant the president the power to determine frequency assignments, these questions did not need to be answered.[142]

The activities of amateur stations may have revitalized interest in radio regulation, but they did not influence most of the provisions that would be enacted. The regulation of the air proved to be beyond reach, and the expansion of the Marconi organization only reinforced policymakers' concerns. In 1912, British Marconi had control over capital and maintained access to the territory of the United States, though it was weakening on the technological front with the emergence of continuous-wave radio. In February 1912, the company announced its plan to encircle the globe with wireless—the future Imperial Chain, which would connect the country to the world via radio.[143] The following month, United Wireless agreed to a merger, prompting Marconi executives in the United States to predict that the company would "control all the wireless in America" (cited in Douglas, 1989, p. 185). Perhaps the fortunes of American Marconi ebbed and flowed, but these were good times: its American identity was largely assumed, and it could help scuttle legislation. End-to-end control over the transatlantic circuit seemed to be within reach when in April the British government approved the parent company's bid for the Imperial Chain (Headrick, 1991, p. 131). How policymakers ensured that the chain would not threaten the viability of the cable network is yet to be documented. During the following month, American Marconi requested permission to erect stations in Panama and the Philippines, precisely the territories the Navy was hoping to link to the mainland. The United States was faced with being integrated into a radio network controlled by a foreign corporation.

International considerations would prove to be as relevant to the passage of the Radio Act of 1912 as they were to the first draft bills. Since Congress failed to ratify the Berlin convention, the United States was invited to attend the 1912 international radio conference in London but would not have been able to vote.[144] The final version of the Radio Act of 1912, Senate Bill 6412, emerged in the wake of the Senate's ratification of the Berlin convention on April 3,[145] and applied to shore stations that undertook "to carry on general public business"—in other words, to common carriers.[146] It included the requirement for the compulsory interchange of messages for the first time since 1908.[147] The bill was drafted by the Senate Committee on Commerce and reflected lawmakers' conviction that previous bills gave too much power to the military and naval stations, especially in the matter of designating wavelengths (Aitken, 1994, p. 700).[148]

By this time, the prevention of a Marconi monopoly had become first among the goals of radio legislation. The attempt to establish such a monopoly led to the 1906 convention, the Committee on Merchant Marine and Fisheries noted in April 1912, and there was "reason to apprehend that an attempt to establish such a monopoly [was] at least contemplated in the United States."[149] On May 2, the Commerce Committee favorably reported the bill, whose stated purpose was "to carry into effect the basic provisions of the Berlin convention."[150] Since wavelength allocations had been rejected, the Radio Act of 1912 would remain a piece of telegraph legislation, closer to the Interstate Commerce Act in some ways than to the Radio Act of 1927. The geopolitical significance of this legislation lies in three provisions: licensing, interconnection, and citizenship regulations.

Licensing

The separation of licensing from the airwaves was a central aspect of radio regulation in the first decade of the twentieth century. Of the four steps involved in spectrum management—allocation, service rules, assignment, and enforcement—lawmakers only took the first two. Allocation establishes the types of use allowed for a block of spectrum, while service rules outline the parameters for offering the service, including transmitter power (White, 2000, p. 8). Under the first service regulation, stations were required to designate a wavelength between 600 and 1,600 meters.[151] This was still the "party-line" setup of broad tracts that the Berlin convention had recommended, which transferred what was considered the best part of the spectrum to the military. The only significant change the Act introduced in terms of spectrum allocation lay in the fifteenth service regulation, which confined amateur users to wavelengths of 200 meters or less.[152] Several sections of the Act worked together to regulate interference, without resorting to frequency assignment. Division of time, restrictions on the amount of power a station could use, and the requirement to use "pure" (i.e., continuous) waves were all important. Spectrum management ended at this point. There were no channels: no person had the exclusive right to transmit on a narrow slice of the spectrum. The Radio Act of 1912 did not envision property rights in the ether (cf. Benkler, 1998, p. 291).

Instead, the Act situated radiotelegraphy in the common carrier regulatory framework, addressing the use and operation of radio stations under the Commerce Clause of the Constitution (table 3.2).[153] Section 1 of the Act stated that "a person, company, or corporation ... shall not use or operate any apparatus for radio communication as a means of commercial intercourse,"

Table 3.2
Regulatory options for station use and station ownership.

| | | Station | | Airwaves | |
		Ownership	Use	Ownership	Use
Private		Commercial radiotelegraphy		N/A	Radio Act of 1927
Public	Government ownership	Radio Act of 1912		Government ownership	

interstate or foreign, except in accordance with a license, "revocable for cause."[154] The licensing language, first drafted in 1905, had been finalized in the 1910 Greene and Depew bills. With the exception of replacing "wireless telegraphy" with "radio communication" in 1912, the language laid out here was included in the Radio Act of 1912 word for word.[155]

Licensing functioned on the structural level of network control by overriding the privileges afforded by patent law. The imposition of the common carrier framework extended public service liberalism to the radio industry and loosened the existing framework for property relations, which had delivered radio stations into the hands of an aspiring foreign monopolist. The Radio Act of 1912 required companies to ask the government for permission for something they had hitherto taken for granted: the use of their own stations. Policymakers made it clear that the license was for the purpose of "control and regulation" and would be withheld from companies unwilling to comply with the new rules.[156] Thus, the Department of Commerce and Labor did not make a selection from a pool of applicants,[157] but it could revoke a license if, for example, a company failed to exchange messages with other carriers. After American policymakers removed radio stations from the nineteenth-century protections for private property, public utility MNCs like British Marconi no longer had full control over their property on U.S. territory, and America's position in radiotelegraphy improved.

The Commerce Clause, however, was not strong enough to give the federal government the authority to decide about the erection of stations. Yet, the Navy Department consistently operated under the assumption that a license would cover the erection of radio stations, not simply their operation.[158] The failure of the Navy Department to secure control over the establishment of stations revealed both that naval policymakers didn't exactly understand what they gave up when they moved away from regulating on the basis of submarine licensing and that the early twentieth-century American legal framework was ill suited to the demands of a rising power. Geopolitical objectives had to be translated into legally cognizable claims even as they were being reformulated. An important transformation for network control in later decades would be the emergence of wavelength allocations as a terrain for geopolitical struggle. The importance of wavelength allocations, which we will only touch on later, likely played a role in policymakers' decision that public regulation of private use of stations was insufficient; the property itself had to become public. Not until 1927 would the United States nationalize the spectrum.

Interconnection

By the 1910s, a shift in the American regulatory environment in favor of interconnection among competing communications networks had taken place. This meant a growing separation in legal reasoning between communications and transportation as courts distinguished the *Express Cases* precedent, which allowed discrimination against competitors. The 6th Circuit Court in Ohio referred specifically to the different physical properties of a railroad and a telephone network when in 1909 it ruled that subscribers and competitors had to be treated the same way.[159] There was clearly a physical difficulty when one railroad company tried to run its cars over another company's lines, but a telephone exchange could connect a subscriber to a competing long-distance network as easily as it could connect subscribers to each other.[160] Between 1911 and 1913, twenty-one states passed laws authorizing some form of compulsory physical interconnection between telephones (Mueller, 1997, p. 114). However, the adoption of interconnection as the default principle took a very different form in telephony, which was primarily a domestic industry at this time, and in radiotelegraphy, which was a global industry.

In telephony, interconnection paved the way to monopoly. The federal government's suit against AT&T ended in the 1913 Kingsbury Commitment, in which the Bell System agreed to allow independent exchanges to connect to its long-distance lines. If an independent wanted to interconnect with the Bell System, it had to build its own lines to the nearest Bell exchange and pay a ten-cent surcharge on every call handled (Mueller, 1997, p. 131). This was clearly advantageous for the Bell System, which maintained the most extensive long-distance links. Significantly, both Theodore Vail, the president of the Bell Telephone Company, and executives at the Marconi organization recited natural monopoly arguments, but the latter were unsuccessful (for Vail's comments, see Wu, 2010, p. 55).

In radiotelegraphy, the common carrier designation was separated from an interconnection requirement until the Radio Act of 1912. This was not entirely intentional. Under the so-called Mann-Elkins Act, Congress extended the authority of the Interstate Commerce Commission (ICC) to wireless telegraphy (Cox & Byrnes, 1989, p. 28).[161] The Act was amended on the floor to include communications, and the Department of Commerce and Labor didn't realize what had happened until the next day. By passing one of the more comprehensive wireless bills, such as the Depew bill discussed earlier, Congress could create a conflict of jurisdiction between the secretary of commerce and labor and the Interstate Commerce Commission over wireless.[162] Thus, wireless became a common carrier, but the legislation left out the interconnection obligation, and the ICC had no authority to compel physical connection (Cox & Byrnes, 1989, p. 42).

Lawmakers did include an interconnection provision in the Wireless Ship Act of 1910, which passed a week later and required all ships carrying at least fifty passengers and traveling at least two hundred miles to carry a wireless set and employ an operator.[163] This legislation advanced safety at sea but did little to solve the thorny problems of radio regulation. The House Committee on the Merchant Marine and Fisheries seemed receptive to the arguments of American Marconi that Griggs had put forward in 1908. Lawmakers rejected a provision on the compulsory interchange of messages, a staple of earlier radio bills, for fear that it would raise the constitutional question of "deprivation of property without due process of law and lead to debate on patent rights."[164]

Instead, the Wireless Ship Act required that ships calling at U.S. ports be equipped with "efficient apparatus."[165] Installations would only be considered efficient if the shipping company contracted in writing to exchange messages with all systems. Whether an exchange was physically possible was left to the master of the ship.[166] Instead of mandating access to the facilities of the Marconi organization, Congress used access to the country's territory to incentivize shippers doing business with the United States to pressure the company to change its policy.

Though American Marconi continued to oppose any requirement mandating the interchange of messages, the requirement for the compulsory interchange of messages was included in radio bills yet again after the Senate had ratified the Berlin convention.[167] Whereas the Wireless Ship Act had left it to the master of the ship to decide whether physical connections were feasible, section 11 of the Radio Act took away this discretion and imposed the obligation to receive and forward traffic on radio stations, regardless of the system used. Just as in telephony, the principle of nondiscrimination translated to mandated sharing in radiotelegraphy. However, an interconnection requirement could easily ruin the network with the largest scope, which is why the British government pressed for, and later paid, a surcharge to British Marconi and why independents were required to pay a surcharge to connect to the Bell System.

What was possible in a domestic industry was not possible in a global one, which is why the conventional wisdom, that the Radio Act of 1912 treated corporate interests favorably, is incomplete (cf. Streeter, 1996, p. 224; cf. Winseck & Pike, 2009, p. 35). American Marconi did ward off the requirement for free intercommunication three times—in 1905, 1908, and 1910. But now, far from receiving pride of place in the spectrum, the company had to shoulder the cost of developing its network on its own without having so much as an exclusive wavelength at its disposal. As policymakers around the world turned a deaf ear to natural monopoly arguments, they settled on fragmentation—via the policy of free intercommunication—as an alternative to centralization and monopoly. Faced with being excluded from an international convention that others had ratified, the U.S. government finally agreed to adhere to it.

Citizenship Requirements

Naval policymakers identified American Marconi as a foreign corporation early on, but they did not translate their knowledge into legal action. The first suggestion for imposing restrictions on licensees on the basis of nationality originated during congressional hearings in 1912, and they constitute the earliest form of foreign ownership regulations in the radio industry (cf. Sidak, 1997, p. 10; Zajácz, 2004). Todd of the Bureau of Steam Engineering recommended to Congress that license holders and operators of radio stations should both be American citizens.[168] These rules were necessary, Todd pointed out, to "keep aliens out of shore stations," as the powerful transmitters operated by foreigners "might send a message across the ocean inimical to the United States Government."[169]

Though a debate about citizenship requirements as a form of protectionist trade measure emerged in Congress, naval policymakers themselves had little interest in opening foreign markets for American companies (for the trade angle, see Douglas, 1989, p. 235; Hills, 2002, p. 116; Sidak, 1997, p. 28).[170] The Radio Division specifically designed citizenship requirements for long-distance commercial communications (Todd, 1911). The Navy Department was grappling with the possibility of operators acting as spies and attempted to control access to the network in order to control the flow of confidential information.

Lawmakers would later connect citizenship requirements to the regulation of merchant shipping, which required owners and officers of American vessels to be American citizens, but concerns about the activities of alien operators also dovetailed with the long-standing precedent in British cable regulation that required operators to be British subjects.[171] British Marconi's practice of supplying operators to their customers had long prompted suspicions about the company's attempt to exercise end-to-end control over its network. Recall that Lieutenant Beecher's visit to the Marconi station included a record of the number of English and American operators.[172] At that time, policymakers were pursuing autonomy of communications in the cable industry and viewed citizenship requirements as a bulwark against a "betrayal of trust" on the part of both operators and station owners (Hood, 1900, p. 485).

When the final version of the radio bill came before the Senate, lawmakers approved citizenship requirements for both owners and operators.[173] Because of opposition in the House, however, the Act passed with the citizenship requirements for license holders intact, but the regulation did not extend to operators.[174] Section 2 of the Radio Act of 1912 specified that licenses could be issued only to citizens of the United States or to companies "incorporated under the laws of some state of the United States."[175] Though lawmakers didn't give the Navy everything it wanted, citizenship requirements worked alongside other policies aimed at incorporating radiotelegraphy into a nationalist framework. The policy of free intercommunication thwarted British Marconi's attempt at centralization, licensing overrode property rights, and technological sovereignty formed the backbone of the Navy's own network. None of this happened at the behest of industry players. When the dominant corporation does not enjoy policymakers' trust, conventional assumptions about business-government relations are easily upended.

The Radio Act of 1912 left at least two problems unsolved. First, it regulated station use but provided no authority to prevent the erection of stations and thus did not bar access to American territory. This was in contrast to the British Wireless Telegraphy Act of 1904, whose proponents at the Post Office viewed the right to reject an application as the cornerstone of effective regulation.[176] Second, the Navy Department failed to secure control over the identity of operators, which policymakers would find crucial when the possibility of the Marconi organization erecting high-power stations on both British and American territory raised the specter of asymmetric end-to-end control over the transatlantic *circuit*. As American policymakers started loosening British Marconi's grasp on stations in the United States, they would zoom in on corporate nationality. It was at that point that the nineteenth-century legal framework, whose place of incorporation test was based on state law, proved unsuitable for a rising power. Fears that the United States would be integrated into a British-dominated wireless network would drive U.S. policy in relation to radiotelegraphy during the next two decades, and policymakers would begin to work out solutions at the federal level.

4 American Control at Home: From Government Ownership to Direct Foreign Ownership Regulations, 1912–1919

> Efficient radio communication requires effective control; effective control of radio requires a monopoly; and the Government should exercise such control.
> —The General Board of the Navy, June 1915

By mandating interconnection and requiring that all radio stations be licensed, the Radio Act of 1912 extended U.S. territorial control at the expense of the Marconi Wireless Telegraph Company of America, the most powerful player in the industry. Autonomy of communications, which these earlier measures had also furthered, now emerged as an explicit policy objective: the external communications of the United States had to be under American control. Just what exactly qualified as "American control" would be worked out on two fronts: domestic legislation and policies designed for international expansion. The theme of the 1910s was national ownership, as policymakers turned their attention to controlling the companies that established radio links with the outside world. This chapter follows the competing definitions of national ownership in domestic legislative proposals in order to show how the principle became tied to a geopolitical purpose.

My central claim here is that policymakers pursued national ownership—defined as either government ownership or direct foreign ownership regulations—as a general policy principle on the structural level of network control. These policies were aimed at advancing the position of the United States in global communications by loosening British control over the circuits connecting the country to the outside world. They did so by edging the American subsidiaries of foreign multinationals out of the U.S. market or by bringing them under U.S. control, respectively. In order to consider this claim on its merits, two existing interpretations of radio policy require a closer look: that the distinction between domestic and foreign companies was irrelevant, as the corporate liberal thesis assumes, and that foreign ownership regulations were passed for national security, rather than broad geopolitical, reasons (cf. Sidak, 1997; cf. Streeter, 1996).

An understanding of American control as national ownership, and of national ownership as a government monopoly, placed technology, territory, and capital in the hands of the U.S. government. But the Navy Department's proposal for government ownership during the 1910s ran parallel with the development of foreign ownership regulations, which provided an alternative to it. Analyzing the development of direct foreign ownership regulations, which tightened accepted definitions of corporate nationality, shows that policy measures promoting geopolitical interests were built on a genuine attempt to understand the multinational corporation, a new force in the global economy. Debates around corporate nationality, in turn, reveal key fixtures in the scaffolding of nationalist thought—how autonomy of communications came to be associated with purity, and how purity became measurable—which are indispensable for understanding the creation of the "100 percent American" Radio Corporation of America (RCA). Because of the global dimension of high-power radio and the geopolitical significance of the network, policymakers were less concerned about American Marconi's claim to monopoly status than about delivering radio into the hands of a *foreign* monopolist.

How American policymakers realized the limits of territorial control and came to agree on an independently financed, brand new, "100 percent American" company cannot be understood without linking developments in domestic legislation to policies for international expansion that took place at the same time. If this chapter is the story of how American policymakers loosened British control over the U.S. end of the transatlantic circuit connecting the country to Europe, chapter 5 examines simultaneous attempts to establish U.S. control over the circuit connecting the country to Latin America. The connections forged by the General Board, laid out in the opening quotation, between efficient communication, control, monopoly, and government ownership, for example, were transferred word for word into the U.S. Navy's proposal for an intergovernmental regional network in the Western Hemisphere.

Paving the Way for Government Ownership

In the tense years before World War I, the activities of a high-power radio station at Sayville, Long Island, owned by the Atlantic Communications Company, called attention to the inadequacy of government control over radio. Just days before President Taft signed the Radio Act of 1912 into law, the Atlantic Company, a subsidiary of the German firm Telefunken, requested permission to upgrade its Sayville spark station on Long Island to continuous-wave technology so that it could communicate with the recently upgraded Telefunken station at Nauen, Germany. In response, the Navy and Commerce Departments sought—frantically, but in vain—to block the installation of the new transmitter.[1] Less than a year later, a report by Fleet Radio Officer Lieutenant Stanford C. Hooper reached the General Board. The report's claim that Sayville intercepted traffic between the Navy Department and ships of the U.S. Fleet prompted an extended discussion.[2]

Sayville's planned upgrade immediately pointed up two significant changes in the industry. First, the spark technology pioneered by the Marconi Company was being phased out as technological innovation shifted to the United States. Of the three known methods of generating continuous high-frequency radio waves, the arc and the alternator were developed for commercial use by American companies—Federal Telegraph and General Electric, respectively—and the vacuum tube was still in its infancy (Aitken, 1985, p. 250). Second, the most dynamic part of the radio industry now lay in the establishment of high-power stations for long-distance, trans-oceanic communications—precisely the long-term objective of the Marconi companies. After buying out its largest competitor and contracting with Western Union for the domestic distribution of its telegrams, American Marconi carried about 90 percent of short-haul (ship-to-shore and ship-to-ship) messages (Douglas, 1989, p. 253; Headrick, 1991, p. 126; Maclaurin, 1949, p. 41; Wilkins, 1989, p. 521). For the time being, however, the most powerful company in marine telegraphy did not have a high-power station on U.S. soil. Commercial wireless messages intended for the United States via the Marconi system were still received at the company's Canadian station at Glace Bay, Nova Scotia. Therefore, in 1912, only two high-power radio stations connected the United States to the outside world: Sayville, the first commercial station to operate in the country, and the naval station at Arlington, Virginia. During the balance of the decade, explicit geopolitical interest would surround only the *high-power* stations for long-distance communication.

Between May 1913 and April 1914, when the Navy's first draft legislation was formulated, naval policymakers were primarily concerned with Sayville's ability to collect intelligence and pass it on to the German government.[3] This early emphasis on spying provides the best example of the national security purpose, identified by legal scholar J. Gregory Sidak, behind the administration's revision of radio legislation in general and the introduction of foreign ownership regulations in particular: "control of the transmission to unfriendly recipients of information vital to U.S. interests, particularly in time of war" (Sidak,1997, p. 10). Yet, this concern cannot explain legislative proposals whose central features would not be finalized until 1916 and that would not pass into law until 1927. As I will show, by the time the administration bill reached Congress, these initial fears about information security in preparation for war had given way to broader geopolitical concerns, and policymakers' attention would be fixed on American Marconi.

The long-term significance of the Sayville installation for foreign ownership regulations lay less in the station's ability to relay confidential information than in the attention it drew to the definition of corporate nationality (cf. Sidak, 1997, p. 36). In the wake of allegations that the station was owned by "a dummy company" controlled abroad, the Department of Commerce and Labor turned to the Justice Department.[4] Could the United States refuse to grant a license to the Atlantic Communications Company, incorporated in New York, "on the ground that the capital of the corporation [was] German capital?"[5] What prompted the spying, policymakers concluded, was the allegiance of the station to Germany, which in turn was possible because the company that owned it was insufficiently anchored in the United States. "The statute," Attorney General George Wickersham pointed out in reply, "does not undertake to exclude from its benefits *domestic corporations whose stock is owned or controlled by foreigners*" [emphasis added].[6]

A seemingly narrow national security problem, affecting one particular German station, thus immediately exposed a gaping hole in the fabric of American law. Although large corporations, the driving force in early twentieth-century American capitalism, quickly became large *multinational* corporations, established legal measures of corporate nationality had not yet adjusted to the transformation. The most widely accepted metric of the nationality of a corporation throughout the previous century was its place of incorporation, not equity ownership (Vagts, 1961, pp. 1527–1528). In publicly held corporations, stock ownership was commonly associated with a say in the formulation of corporate strategy, as in the concept of "a controlling interest," but foreign ownership of stock apparently did not make the corporation any less American. The Radio Act inadequately specified *who* could operate a station: its citizenship requirements only covered individuals and failed to protect against firms with foreign ties. This was not, however, a mere "loophole" that any corporate lawyer worth his salt could easily recognize (cf. Sidak, 1997, p. 28). In the early twentieth century, corporate law simply did not make a distinction between "foreign" and "domestic" corporations beyond their place of incorporation. As chapter 3 showed, before the widespread expansion of multinational corporations (MNCs), companies registered in a different state were understood to be foreign corporations.

Worries about Sayville's loyalty thus prefigured the main thrust of discussions about foreign ownership in American radio, but they lacked a geopolitical dimension. Telefunken, Atlantic's parent company, owned several manufacturing subsidiaries but only one operating subsidiary. It was, at best, a proto-multinational, with no plans for a worldwide system until 1917 (for these plans, see Winkler, 2009). In a few years, however, high-power stations would multiply: the Hochfrequenz-Machinen Aktiengesellschaft für Drahtlose Telegraphie, commonly known as Homag, would build one at Tuckerton, New Jersey; the U.S.-headquartered Federal Telegraph would install two in California; and, most importantly, American Marconi would erect four in the United States to link up with the British Imperial Chain. The concern about corporate nationality that Sayville flagged in 1912 would return with a vengeance in four years and would be directly tied to concerns about British control over global communications.

On the eve of World War I, however, Anglo-American rivalry lay dormant. Clearly, both structural indicators of economic leadership and confidential government memoranda indicated a major realignment in world affairs. Britain's military prowess, measured in warship tonnage and ships built for the merchant marine, masked an underlying weakness (Friedberg, 1988, p. 163; O'Brien, 1998, p. 6). The U.S. economy had grown to twice the size of Britain's as industrial production soared and the new drivers of the world economy, including steel, chemicals, and machine tools, came to be dominated by the challengers (Kennedy, 1987, pp. 210–211; Zakaria, 2008). The most conservative predictions had the United States surpassing Britain as the world's lead economy by 1926, not anticipating, of course, a global war that would propel the country to first place by 1919 (Kennedy, 1987).

Though policymakers on both sides of the Atlantic had converged on Germany as the most immediate security threat, they never stopped to regard Britain as a rival and viewed the country's withdrawal from the Western Hemisphere with suspicion (Baer, 1994, p. 39; Bönker, 2012, p. 74; Thompson, 2000, p. 202). The Navy's official 1913 war plan against Germany, for instance, warned that a war between the United States and Germany would enable the British Empire to enhance its position (Bönker, 2012, pp. 72, 84). Control over a global communications network would, of course, necessitate displacing Britain in the long term—regardless of either country's relationship to Germany—which is why wartime relations receive only minimal treatment in these pages (for an authoritative assessment, see Winkler, 2008).

Between May 1913 and October 1915, when the Navy's position on radio crystallized, policymakers quickly corrected the provision of the Radio Act that required a license to operate—but not to erect—a station. As chapter 3 showed, the Bureau of Equipment initially sought licensing powers in order to counter foreign investment in American radio. Congress, however, only put the aspects of radio communication related to interstate and foreign commerce under federal supervision and left the erection of stations under the jurisdiction of individual states. As a result, Attorney General Wickersham advised, the secretary of commerce and labor had no discretion as to granting licenses.[7] (This opinion would be confirmed in the famous broadcast license cases of the following decade.)[8] When, in March 1914, the General Board was finished with Hooper's report on Sayville's activities, it arrived at the same conclusion. Individual states grant franchises for the erection of stations, the frustrated admirals noted, and licensing "follows naturally from the existence of the station."[9] The government, as the very first revision of the Act explained, found it "absolutely necessary" that a license be required before a station could be erected.[10]

Therefore, the majority of the discussion in the Navy revolved around the three options for exerting stronger control over radio: introducing competition by opening naval stations to commercial business, government ownership, and wartime takeover. The first alternative originated in the Radio Division of the Bureau of Steam Engineering, which had drafted the early versions of the Radio Act of 1912 and still smarted from its losses.

Congress, influenced by natural monopoly theory, authorized naval stations to carry commercial traffic only at locations where commercial stations did not maintain a full schedule.[11] The Act positioned the Navy at the
fringes of the industry, which meant that the Navy's network did not run at
capacity and that its operators were less efficient than those of commercial
stations.[12] The Radio Division now pointed out that national security mandated the maintenance of naval stations, which would provide cheaper and
more efficient service than commercial stations did.[13]

Yet, the Bureau of Steam Engineering's proposal was not motivated
solely by efficiency and training operators. During the drafting stage of
the Radio Act, and for a while thereafter, naval policymakers tied the loyalty of radio stations to the nationality of their personnel, which led the
Bureau to push for citizenship requirements for operators. The requirement
targeted American Marconi, which, however, won a victory when House
lawmakers struck down the proposal "as a purely military feature of slight
importance."[14] If Congress were to approve Navy stations competing with
commercial ones for ship-to-shore traffic, policymakers now reasoned, all
but the largest commercial stations would have to be abandoned. The largest commercial stations were, of course, operated by proto- or full-fledged
MNCs. When the field had cleared, policymakers predicted, "Congress
would be more ready to grant the desired authority to restrict licenses to
operators of American citizenship."[15]

By contrast, the superintendent of the Naval Radio Service, Captain William H. G. Bullard, considered the opening of naval stations to commercial business to be simply a step toward "what must ultimately obtain" in
the United States: government ownership.[16] An 1886 graduate of the Naval
Academy, Bullard now managed the department's forty-five shore stations,
which covered the continental United States as well as the country's outlying possessions.[17] Bullard's vision for naval radio involved the creation of
what contemporary strategists would call a seamless military intranet. From
his perspective, commercial message handling was "an obstacle" to naval
communications, the purpose of which was to ensure "continuous, reliable,
and rapid communication of information" between the various units of the
fleet, its bases, and the center of government.[18]

Bullard's views, however, reflected the narrow understanding of autonomy of communications prevalent in the early 1910s, which would require
an overhaul before America could expand its influence in the radio field. The

United States, gushed Admiral John R. Edwards in May 1912, was "projecting a series of gigantic wireless towers that will not only unite the colonies with the homeland, but will join them in a manner absolutely independent of the cable and telegraph companies."[19] Edwards conjured this future on the basis of recent congressional appropriations for naval high-power stations that by 1919 would cover the outlying possessions of the United States.[20] Thus, even in these early years, autonomy was the goal: policymakers set radio apart from the cables, which still seemed to be under British control, but considered autonomy exclusively in the context of the Navy's own network. "This department is not vitally concerned with the establishment of radio communication between the United States and Germany," naval policymakers noted in 1914, recommending against taking over the recently completed station at Tuckerton, New Jersey, adding that "such communication would affect but slightly, if at all, the interests or needs of the Navy."[21]

Bullard's rejection of commercial companies' proposals to link the Philippine Islands to the United States illustrates both the advantages and the limits of network control on the tactical level, which involves state control over territory. The naval station at Cavite, just outside Manila, was one of three stations planned to link the United States to its outlying possessions, the others to be established at Darien in the Panama Canal Zone and at Pearl Harbor, Hawaii (Aitken, 1985, p. 284; Winkler, 2008, pp. 69, 71). These stations were to be equipped with Federal Telegraph's arc sets and erected on the naval bases themselves, which in turn contributed to American control over the Isthmus of Panama and the Pacific.[22]

Panama, Hawaii, and Manila were also key nodes in the Marconi Company's plans for a global network whose nine stations would serve as "the main artery" of a larger system with feeders in every country (figure 4.1).[23] In April 1912, just two weeks after the so-called British Imperial Chain was approved, American Marconi executives requested permission to erect stations both in Panama and in the Philippines (Headrick, 1991, p. 131).[24] The stations planned for these strategic locations were widely identified as "the American part" of a global British network.[25]

At the same time, Federal Telegraph, hoping to reimagine itself as a telecommunications service provider, underwent a reorganization: the Federal Telegraph Company of Palo Alto, California, the manufacturing arm of the company, had been separated from Federal Holdings Inc., based in New York, which had been set up to acquire concessions worldwide and operate

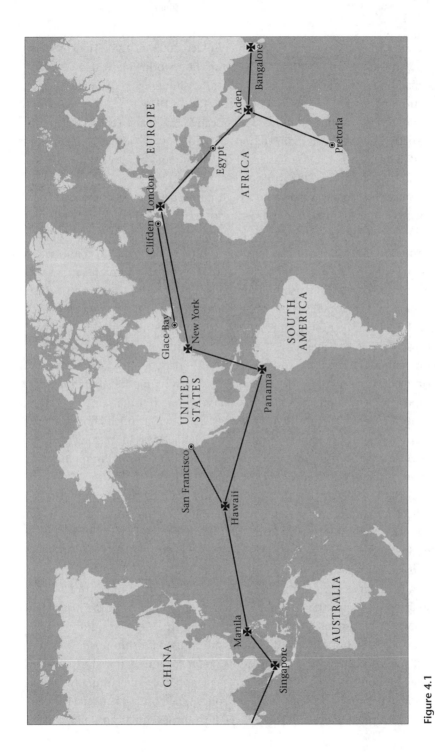

Figure 4.1
British Marconi's proposal for a global wireless network, September 1912.

the new stations it would establish (Winkler, 2008, p. 188). The company also envisioned the Philippines as a link in a worldwide wireless system, expanding from the west coast of the United States first to Asia and then to Latin America and Europe.[26] When, in 1912 and 1914, the Superintendent's Office received applications from American Marconi and Federal Telegraph, respectively, the naval radio stations existed only on paper.[27] Bullard now had to decide what role commercial stations should play in connecting the Philippines to the outside world.

Since the Navy was planning a high-power network of its own, the permissive policy of foreign investment was over, and Bullard quickly rejected American Marconi's application. "A single alien operator could put the entire installation out of commission ... if he so desired," he commented, giving voice to the prevalent view that the loyalty of station operations was best ensured by loyal personnel on the ground.[28] Federal Telegraph, which emphasized its American nationality and presented itself as a competitor to the submarine cables controlled in Britain, fared no better. Bullard narrowly defined the market as "international radiotelegraphy," rather than international telegraphy, and refused to authorize commercial operations.[29] He made it clear that ordering from Federal to equip naval stations and supporting the company's global expansion were not the same. American control over the Pacific did not need Federal, a self-certified chosen instrument of American radio communications. Bullard was in a strong position because naval control over the external radio links of the Philippines was directly tied to U.S. control over occupied territory.

Bullard's experience with naval radio in a colonial context provided the model for controlling the external radio links of the United States. Government ownership (in the form of a naval monopoly) would formalize territorial control as the country's radio policy. Rather than a necessary but undesirable measure, naval control would be "perfect," Bullard wrote in July 1914, "if all the coast stations were under government control."[30] This solution subsumed the problem of foreign control under the broader objective of displacing all private companies from the field and did not treat high-power stations differently from stations used for ship-to-shore traffic. But was government ownership also suitable for international expansion? The Philippines—a recently acquired, geographically and culturally remote colonial territory—occupied a unique conceptual position between the continental United States and the sovereign countries American policymakers hoped to reach via radio. Controlling circuits meant control over two stations: one on American territory and the other on foreign territory. U.S. government ownership of stations abroad would quickly raise uncomfortable questions about imperialism. If this solution were infeasible, as it indeed proved to be, how would the United States expand *in the absence of territorial control*? Chapter 5 takes up this problem.

If opening naval stations to commercial business was the second-best alternative to government ownership, wartime takeover had the least support in the Navy. Takeover was temporary government ownership, an unlimited but short-term solution that resorted to control over U.S. territory. Weeks before World War I broke out, Hooper, the future champion of American control via private corporations, recommended that the government "operate, not necessarily own, the entire radio service."[31] Naval policymakers, however, publicly refused to recognize takeover as a useful measure. It was too little, too late, Director of Naval Communications David W. Todd pointed out to Congress, as it only allowed the Navy to seal the doors of a station after it had already jeopardized American security.[32] The transition from a commercial radio industry to a wartime organization took time, which benefited no one but the enemy.[33] In the absence of government ownership, advisers briefed Secretary of the Navy Josephus Daniels, "[everything would] have to be done all over again should we have another war."[34] In the minds of naval policymakers, peace was the short interval between the last war and the next one, leaving barely enough time for training. When government ownership finally appeared on the congressional agenda, Daniels described it as "an ideal peacetime arrangement directly connected with instant readiness for war."[35] (Congress, it should be noted, was never swayed by arguments for government ownership and regularly used the option of wartime takeover to beat back stricter navy measures.)[36]

At the outbreak of the European war, takeover offered the most immediate solution. Naval officers quickly took control over Homag's station at Tuckerton and American Marconi's installation at Siasconset on Nantucket, but it would take almost another year to take over Sayville (Douglas, 1989, p. 270). The decision came in the wake of a German submarine attack on the *Lusitania*, a British ocean liner headed for New York, in May 1915, which claimed almost 1,200 lives. Rumors abounded that the German Admiralty had received information about the movements of the ship (Douglas, 1989, p. 272). Though the Navy Department did not have evidence that Sayville sent the information, policymakers blocked the Atlantic Communications Company's request for an upgrade.[37]

The sinking of the *Lusitania* may also have influenced the General Board's stance on government ownership. On previous occasions, in March and August 1914, respectively, the Board had identified Sayville as the outpost of the German government and recommended opening naval stations to commercial business as well as citizenship requirements for operators, but it regarded government ownership as "impracticable."[38] In June 1915, however, they accepted the interpretation of American control as government ownership. "Efficient radio communication requires effective control," the Board pointed out, adding that "effective control of radio requires a monopoly; and the Government should exercise such control."[39] The Navy took over Sayville the following month, and the draft bill, drawn up and revised in Bullard's office, received the Navy Department's official approval in October.[40] The exact words of the General Board would form the backbone of Bullard's proposal for an integrated hemispheric radio network in Latin America, which recommended government ownership as a regional policy (discussed in chapter 5).

From a geopolitical perspective, the early revisions to the Radio Act were in the form of modifications rather than radical new proposals. Policymakers did not separate out high-power stations for special treatment, nor did they consider the identity of a corporation apart from its personnel. Naval communications policy, especially in its most clearly articulated goal, government ownership, was defensive and U.S. focused: its primary goal was to link the country to its possessions, not to extend U.S. control over the country's external commercial links. In fact, government ownership had provided so much control over the country's internal and external communications, and was so unquestionably American, that it masked the fact that network control on the structural level also had a symbolic dimension. In other words, if private companies could also embody the principle of national ownership, what, if anything, made them "American"? Between October 1915 and December 1916, an interdepartmental committee would hammer out the version of the Navy's draft that would reach Congress in the form of H.R. 19350. It was during this process that percentage restrictions on foreign ownership received the most attention, laying the groundwork for the idea of a "100 percent American" corporation.

Americanizing the Corporation

Naval policymakers debating exactly how corporations should be removed from the field gave little thought to the definition of the corporation. As a result, the Navy's early drafts made no significant changes to section 2 of the Radio Act of 1912, which provided that only American citizens or corporations "incorporated under the laws of some state or Territory of the United States or Porto Rico [*sic*]" were eligible for a license.[41] Under this broad definition of corporate nationality, all companies established in the United States were American citizens. This would soon change with the development of percentage restrictions on foreign equity ownership. From a domestic perspective, the revision of section 2 would diminish the importance of state law and expand federal authority over corporations. From a geopolitical perspective, however, the revision of the section reveals how autonomy of communication became associated with corporate purity and how purity became measurable. This updated understanding of corporate nationality, in turn, would be essential for American expansion.

Changes to section 2 of the Radio Act of 1912 reflect a broader process whereby the American legal system came to terms with the multinational corporation. Metaphors and analogies serve as central conceptual tools aiding policymakers in deciding about unknown phenomena (Sawhney, 1996, p. 291). References to "the corporate alien" in legal research or to "the complete naturalization" of corporations as serving the national interest in radio policy were not a coincidence (Vagts, 1961).[42] Nor were the subtle connections based on family ties, which led policymakers to suspect that both immigrants and MNCs placed property in the name of their children and "daughter companies," respectively, in order to get around ownership restrictions (Gaines & Cho, 2004, pp. 275–276).[43] Though the precise connections between immigration policy and the revision of corporate law fall outside the scope of this book, the quick connections discussed here reveal that two were likely intertwined. The early twentieth century was an earlier period of globalization, which was also characterized by the free movement of labor and capital. Not until the 1980s would the world economy achieve a similar level of integration, credited, in part, to the MNC (Bairoch, 1996, pp. 180, 184).

As the population of the United States nearly doubled between 1880 and 1910, increasing mobility was accompanied by questions of nationality, citizenship, and loyalty. Perhaps not surprisingly, some of the policymakers most worried about assimilating the newly arrived immigrants also played a role in formulating ideas about the multinational corporation. Founded by Charles Warren, who would later advise the Navy on stock ownership restrictions, for example, The Immigration Restriction League came into being in 1894 with a mandate to protect the native culture and the white race from an onslaught of alien cultures. Influential members included Francis Walker, the superintendent of the 1870 and 1880 censuses, and Senator Henry Cabot Lodge, the author of the Lodge resolution, discussed later (Higham, 1955, pp. 141–142; Ngai, 2004, p. 30).

The earliest foreign ownership restrictions on corporations were tied to immigrant investors. The Alien Land Law of 1887 pioneered a 20 percent restriction on stock ownership in companies owned by aliens "ineligible for citizenship," a category that covered Chinese immigrants at the time (Higham, 1955, p. 42; Vagts, 1961, p. 1512). While the legislation reflected the growing emphasis on quantification in the late nineteenth century, it was otherwise one of a kind. Contemporary American law still used the term "citizen" to include American-organized corporations regardless of stock ownership (Ngai, 2004, p. 30; Vagts, 1961, p. 1514). A quarter century later, the ground was prepared for the narrow, quantifiable definition of corporate nationality in radio policy that the Alien Land Law had prefigured.

Just a couple of months before the Radio Act passed, Senator Lodge sought to thwart Japanese expansion in Mexico by denying a grant of any strategically valuable territory to a foreign corporation. The so-called Lodge resolution identified corporations headquartered outside the United States as appendages of their home states and identified foreign direct investment as a threat to territorial control (Bailey, 1933, p. 222). The administration, however, was unable to use the resolution to block the installation of Sayville's new transmitter because it targeted a corporation headquartered outside the United States doing business *outside* the United States.[44] Foreign ownership restrictions, it became apparent, covered both the immigrant investor ineligible for citizenship and the corporation headquartered outside the United States (via the Lodge resolution) but had nothing to say about the subsidiaries of multinationals incorporated in the United States.

The legal definition of corporate nationality, with its emphasis on the company's place of incorporation, was clearly out of sync with the assumptions of the foreign policy elite, a fact that came to light upon the outbreak of the European war. On the first day of the war, the Royal Navy severed all of Germany's Atlantic cables and destroyed German communications assets in Europe, Africa, and the Far East. As a result, radiotelegraphy remained the primary means of independent communication between the country and the outside world (Winkler, 2009, pp. 849–850). In an attempt to convince the neutral United States to censor Sayville and Tuckerton, British diplomats pointed to German stock ownership in Sayville in support of the claim that these stations were nothing more than "intelligence bureaux" for the German government.[45] Already convinced that Sayville was spying for Germany, few in the U.S. Navy needed more evidence.

Undeterred by byzantine corporate arrangements, naval policymakers saw clear lines of authority running upward from the Atlantic Communications Company, established in the United States, through Telefunken to Siemens-Halske, both registered in Germany, and from then on to the war room of Kaiser Wilhelm II himself. The German government did rely on a news agency, Transocean, to send news to Sayville, which was then distributed to American newspapers via the German embassy in Washington, D.C., and German representatives in New York (Tworek, 2019, chapter 2). Thus, the German government's involvement in the use of radio stations for propaganda purposes has been subject to analysis, but the ways, if any, in which Sayville shared information with the German military is yet to be documented.

At the heart of American policymakers' assumptions about the activities of the Atlantic Communications Company was equity ownership: each share of stock seemed to represent an alien with a say in corporate policy formation as well as awareness of and support for the policies of his home government.[46] There was hardly any American money in the Atlantic Company, Secretary Daniels told the *New York Times* on the eve of Sayville's takeover. Even naturalized citizens at the helm of the company owned only a few shares, just enough to qualify them to act as officers of the company.[47]

Radio policy was hardly unique. Stock ownership also emerged as a fixture of corporate nationality in shipping, mining, and aircraft as well. The regulation of the merchant marine, with its system of licenses and operators for merchant vessels, served as the most immediate model for radio legislation, though it, too, underwent a crucial transformation at the time.[48] Between 1914 and 1920, lawmakers considered proposals requiring American stockholding in shipping corporations for the first time. In 1920, Congress finally authorized a maximum of 25 percent foreign ownership, dismissing proposals for 51 percent and 100 percent American involvement (Vagts, 1961, p. 1506). In a seminal article titled "The Corporate Alien," written just before the "multinational corporation" became an accepted term in academic research, law professor Detlev Vagts made the connection between the patchwork of new legislation and the new, multinational corporate form. These regulatory attempts overlapped because "a partially foreign-owned company may seek oil on federal lands [and] need boats, aircraft and radios for conducting its far-flung operations" (Vagts, 1961, p. 1526).

Yet, legislative proposals drawn up in the Navy Department failed to reflect the emerging consensus about the link between stock ownership and corporate nationality. Early revisions to section 2 merely tweaked the law, precisely because they were too closely tied to its citizenship requirements. "No foreign company" should be allowed to erect or operate a sending or receiving station without permission from the federal government, the General Board recommended without defining what constituted a foreign company.[49] The Navy's first revision of the Radio Act, drafted a month later, failed to go beyond citizenship requirements for corporate officials and operators. The "principal point," policymakers pointed out, "is that all who have to do with the operation of shore stations must be bona fide citizens of the United States, either native born or naturalized."[50] Section 2 of the July and September 1915 draft bills retained the focus on individuals but tightened the requirements for proving the identity of those responsible for the management and operation of the station.[51] Section 3 of the December 1915 draft did the same, while section 7, developed under the assumption that licenses would be required to operate radio sets, introduced citizenship requirements for receiver licenses.[52]

The turning point came on January 5, 1916, when naval policymakers received comments on the draft bill from the Department of Justice. Assistant Attorney General Charles Warren suggested focusing attention on corporations, rather than on individuals, as they would be most likely to operate a radio station. Warren shattered any hope that the place of incorporation test, based as it was on state law, furnished an adequate safeguard against foreign control. A corporation may be organized in any given state, he warned, all but one of its shares may be owned "by foreigners residing in Europe," and every one of its officers, with the exception of the clerk, may be a foreigner residing in Europe.[53]

These were, perhaps not coincidentally, the facts of *Daimler Company v. Continental Tyre and Rubber Company*, a case that had been winding its way through the British legal system for the previous two years. Continental was incorporated in Britain and had done business there since before the war, but all except one of its shares were held by people residing in Germany. Its secretary was a British subject, but all of its directors lived in Germany (Sealy & Worthington, 2013, p. 57). The House of Lords' ruling was published just four days before Warren's comments on the draft radio bill.[54]

In what would become a widely cited precedent, the Law Lords modified the cornerstone of corporate law, the principle of separate corporate personality (Sealy & Worthington, 2013, p. 52). Under the "Fiction Theory" of the corporate form, full legal personality was among the five core characteristics of corporations, which also included limited liability for owners and managers and shared ownership by investors of capital (Hansmann & Kraakman, 2000, pp. 1–2). Both British and American courts in the nineteenth century recognized the corporation as a legal body independent from its owners, managers, and shareholders. Central precedents for this doctrine were laid down in the *Dartmouth College v. Woodward* decision in the United States and in the *Salomon v. Salomon & Co. Ltd.* case in the United Kingdom.[55] It was under the Fiction Theory that corporate nationality was tied to a company's place of incorporation. By contrast, proponents of the "Aggregate Theory" of the corporate form considered the doctrine of separate personhood a technicality and saw the corporation as simply the total number of individuals making its decisions (French, 1979, p. 209). At stake in the *Daimler* decision, therefore, was the strength of the Fiction Theory in the face of wartime pressures.

In *Daimler*, the House of Lords overruled the Court of Appeals, which held steadfastly to the undiluted Fiction Theory. The corporation was "a living thing," not a "technicality" to be swept aside. "Has the character of [Continental Tyre] changed," the Court of Appeals asked, "because on the outbreak of war all the shareholders and directors resided in a foreign country, and, therefore, became alien enemies?"[56] Just as a natural-born Englishman could acquire "an enemy character," the House of Lords countered, so could a corporation. The legal system must attempt to assess the character of a corporation by looking beyond its "artificial persona" to the character of its officers and shareholders.[57] If this sounded like the Aggregate Theory, the House of Lords certainly did not say so. In *legal* terms, the Law Lords created a national security exception to corporate personhood. The Fiction Theory survived, but, then as now, the courts could "pierce the corporate veil" to reach the natural persons acting for the corporation. The doctrine, it was plain to see, protected corporations only from legal actions emerging from civil society but was helpless in the face of state power. In *historical* terms, on the other hand, British courts and American policymakers across the ocean were grappling with the same problem: if a company's place of incorporation did not sufficiently capture its nationality, then what did?

The decision of the House of Lords seems to have come just at the right time. It relied on American precedent and provided a justification for the direction that American policymakers were heading toward. The extent to which Warren was aware of the Law Lords' decision requires additional research. However, if the British precedent mattered for any part of the U.S. government, it most likely was the Office of the Attorney General, which was well aware of the disconnect between the place of incorporation test and emerging worries about equity ownership. The Navy and State Departments, on the other hand, showed no awareness of the fine points of corporate law when they investigated the nationality of American Marconi in order to decide whether to support the company's expansion in Latin America during late 1915. Policymakers' decision, as chapter 5 reveals, hinged on equity ownership and patent licensing.[58] It was only after this investigation and Warren's advice that restrictions on stock ownership were incorporated into H.R. 19350, which would not eventually pass but would serve as the foundation of postwar radio regulation.[59] Thus, the core of contemporary foreign ownership regulations, widely applied to broadcasting, was first designed for companies in charge of a telecommunications network.

Though the modern corporation was accepted as an individual in the eyes of the law early on, it received the rights and obligations of citizenship piecemeal. The MNC emerged before there were words to describe it, so policymakers grasping for a way to understand this new entity turned for conceptual guidance to individuals who were similarly caught between two countries: the immigrants. This happened at a time, during World War I, when the discourse of "100 percent Americanism" challenged the melting pot model of American nationality, which had imagined the United States as an unfinished, cosmopolitan country, forever in the making with each new wave of immigration (Higham, 1955, pp. 159, 251). As policymakers dealing with the influx of immigrants thought about this new institutional form, the nationalist fear of divided loyalties engulfed the multinational corporation as well.

Perhaps some immigrants were torn between two countries, but the nationalist fear went further, assuming that they were agents of foreign states (Higham, 1955, p. 198). American nationalist discourse similarly positioned the multinational corporation as a "migrant subject" that is unable to leave its originary values behind (Honig, 2001, p. 66).[60] Both the immigrant and the multinational were limit cases for loyalty. Percentage restrictions on stock ownership were therefore a precursor to the "100 percent American" discourse as applied to corporations, which would hold the firm to the ideal of absolute purity during World War I. Thus, early twentieth-century policymakers independently arrived at the same conclusion that researchers would reach decades later: that corporate purity was a shortcut to loyalty and that corporate nationality was tied to the corporation's ownership and management (Lipson, 1985, p. 138; Vernon, 1971, p. 264). This stricter understanding of corporate nationality that both the Sayville incident and doubts about American Marconi facilitated would soon be hitched to U.S. geopolitical objectives.

British Control over America's External Communications as a Geopolitical Problem

By 1916, the Atlantic Communications Company had lost its importance as a catalyst for the development of radio legislation, and the Marconi companies were identified as "the real opponents of American governmental control."[61] The rapid expansion of American Marconi's high-power stations and the wartime impact of British control over the submarine cable network pushed geopolitical considerations to the forefront. Did the United States have control over its external communications if its high-power stations were simply links in a global British network? The ascendancy of "large institutions" at the expense of the amateurs seems central, and the Navy's proposal of government ownership appears to be a red herring only if we adopt an entirely domestic perspective and miss the single most important fact in radio policy at this time: private ownership meant foreign ownership (cf. Streeter, 1996, p. 69). However, it is hardly surprising that foreign ownership regulations seem "neither properly conceived nor well-tailored," in Sidak's words, for the purpose of controlling the transmission of confidential wartime information (Sidak, 1997, p. 10). For policymakers at the time, the narrow focus on national security during the early years receded into the background as radio was increasingly positioned as an important site in Anglo-American rivalry. Both foreign ownership regulations and government ownership (insofar as the latter concerned high-power stations) are best understood as structural-level attempts at network control. Policymakers pursued the objective of national ownership in order to wrest control over the U.S. end of the transatlantic circuit from American Marconi and to manage the participation of the United States in an emerging global radio network.

The excitement in the radio industry now was all about high-power stations, which held the potential for global connectivity. Edward J. Nally, the general manager of American Marconi, waxed about the virtues of participating in a global organization "covering the entire civilized world."[62] Marconi companies were already operating in ten different countries: in addition to the United States, Canada, England, and Italy, affiliates were established in France, Russia, Belgium, Australia, Argentina, and Spain.[63] The company also served as the equipment supplier for the British Imperial Chain, to be operated by the British Post Office. Now that the chain was under way, with a total of six stations planned for England, Egypt, East Africa, South Africa, India, and Southeast Asia, it was reasonable to assume that the first company to erect high-power stations in the United States would lock in the traffic agreements with the U.S. Post Office as well (Headrick, 1991, p. 131).

American Marconi was determined to secure these contracts. By 1914, when only the Cairo station of the chain was under construction, the company had erected two stations on U.S. territory, in Bolinas, California, and in Hawaii (Headrick, 1991, p. 131).[64] Two other stations on the Atlantic Coast were announced in 1913: the station at New Brunswick, New Jersey, would communicate with Britain, and a station in Marion, Massachusetts, would exchange messages with Norway.[65] Therefore, by the time the United States entered World War I, American Marconi operated all but three privately owned high-power transmitters in the United States.[66] The remaining three stations, in California, New Jersey, and New York, were owned by Federal Telegraph, Homag, and the Atlantic Communications Company, respectively.

By 1918, all of American Marconi's stations would be complete, though the Marion station would not yet be in operation.[67] Researchers have noted that the situation in radiotelegraphy mirrored that of submarine cables, where foreign companies connected the United States to the outside world (Wilkins, 1989, p. 521). Of course, historian Mira Wilkins's comment raises more questions than it answers. Who owned and who controlled the transatlantic cables? British policymakers and the U.S. Navy gave very different answers (see Aitken, 1985, p. 278, and chapter 7 in this book).

From a network control perspective, control over existing sources of leverage in the U.S. radio market was divided. As a telecommunications service provider, American Marconi had raised capital to cover the economically vital transatlantic circuit, via the New Brunswick and Marion stations, and part of the transpacific circuit, via its Hawaii installation. The company's position, however, was less secure than it looked, because it lacked access to up-to-date continuous-wave technology. It was just a matter of time before its weak technological position would also influence its ability to raise capital, let alone provide long-distance service. Thus, company executives quickly initiated negotiations with the U.S.-headquartered General Electric and Federal Telegraph, the respective holders of the Alexanderson alternator and the Poulsen arc patents (Aitken, 1985, p. 308; Winkler, 2008, p. 96). These companies, on the other hand, were primarily equipment manufacturers. Thus, the American radio industry was characterized by technological prowess and a weakness of commercial organization. For the time being, American Marconi also enjoyed access to the territory of the United States. Whether this situation would continue would depend on the Navy Department.

Naval policymakers did not need to wait for the final stages of negotiations about the alternator to fully realize the geopolitical significance of long-distance radio (cf. Aitken, 1985). As the case of the Philippines has revealed, that significance became apparent as soon as the American subsidiary of British Marconi sought to erect high-power stations in U.S. strategic space. As American Marconi was gradually filling out its network, the questions about corporate nationality that Sayville had prompted were coupled with geopolitical concerns about the United States being integrated into an emerging British radio network. Naval policymakers could no longer think of autonomy of communications exclusively in the context of the Navy's own network while ignoring America's commercial radio links with the outside world. The Navy turned to radio legislation in the wake of American Marconi's application, in November 1916, to use its high-power station at Oahu, Hawaii, to communicate with Japan.

By this time, the strategic importance of the Hawaiian Islands and their transition into the American sphere of interest had both been cemented. As the only habitable land of any size in almost a quarter of the entire Pacific

Ocean, Hawaii lies astride the trade route between North America and Australia. Its annexation provided the United States with a stopping point for the country's modern coal- and oil-fired fleet, allowing strategic planners to protect the country's west coast against, for example, a Japanese attack, and project power toward Asia (Bönker, 2012, p. 54; Morgon, 2011, p. 3). Not surprisingly, Hawaii therefore became a key node in the Navy's high-power radio network, which also included the Philippines and Panama. In contrast to the latter locations, however, American Marconi had already established a presence on the islands and even received permission from the United States to erect a high-power station.[68] Now, American Marconi planned to link the United States and Asia via wireless. In 1915, the company erected a high-power station near Tokyo, to be operated by the Japanese government, and company officials concluded a traffic agreement the following year to carry messages between San Francisco and Tokyo via Hawaii.[69] This was, of course, on the understanding that American Marconi operated the U.S. sections of the circuit, meaning both the California and the Hawaii stations. The company's request to link up to Hawaii reached the desk of Director of Naval Communications (DNC) David W. Todd as policymakers were putting the final touches on the first radio bill to be submitted to Congress.

Todd, the former head of the Radio Division, took over as DNC in the wake of a major reorganization that had made the Navy a more centralized and credible source of communications policy than the warring fiefdoms of the previous decade had been. The office of the chief of naval operations (CNO) took the place of the General Board as the key adviser to the secretary of the Navy (Roskill, 1968, p. 26). The naval communications districts and the commercial stations under Navy control were now managed from the Office of Naval Communications, the successor to the Naval Radio Service, which reported to the CNO (Douglas, 1989, pp. 266–267). Policymaking authority was shared between the DNC, heading up the Office of Naval Communications, and the Radio Division in the Bureau of Steam Engineering (Aitken, 1985, p. 290).

H.R. 19350, the first radio bill to amend the Radio Act of 1912, was the result of three years of negotiations within the Navy Department, followed by a year of coordinating the Navy's views with those of other government departments. Sections 5 and 6 formed the heart of the bill. They included the Bureau's proposal to open government radio stations to commercial business and authorized the Navy Department to purchase any coastal radio station that the owner desired to sell.[70] These sections were meant to be read together. After successful competition by the Navy, station owners would realize that their only remaining option was to sell out. At that point, the Navy Department would become the sole telecommunications service provider on the coasts, while commercial companies could still operate ship stations or concentrate on equipment manufacturing.

Naval policymakers wanted the bill to cover both coastal and high-power stations because they were worried that the United States was becoming a link in a global commercial network that served British strategic objectives. Whether such an outcome seemed likely, in turn, hinged on the nationality of American Marconi. "I doubt if it can be shown that the Marconi Company is a subsidiary of the English Marconi company," Todd worried privately, as he recalled the company's previous attempt to get into the Philippines, "although this is undoubtedly the case, and the Honolulu station is considered by the English part of their 'world-wide wireless chain.'"[71] There were two separate issues at stake in designating American Marconi as a subsidiary of British Marconi: first, the relationship between the parent company and its American subsidiary; and second, the chance that British Marconi might carry out the orders of the British government.

Naval policymakers conflated these two issues, just as they had in the case of the Atlantic Communications Company. Todd drew a tight connection between American Marconi and its British parent based on company annual reports, which presented the American stations as links in a future system encircling the earth, and emphasized British Marconi's participation in the American company through its "large share holdings."[72] Stock ownership, he concluded, allowed British Marconi to dictate the policies of American Marconi. In response, American Marconi went to great lengths to show that its relationship with British Marconi was arm's length. "We are not a subsidiary of any company," David Sarnoff, commercial manager of the company, would testify during hearings on H.R. 19350.[73] American Marconi was "an affiliated company"; its policies were decided in the United States. Affiliations with other companies, in turn, were central to global connections. "We must have an agreement with people abroad," Sarnoff asserted, "just the same as the United States Government would have to have an agreement abroad if it communicated internationally."[74]

Sarnoff conjured up the state-to-state model as the appropriate way to understand American Marconi's business. What took place between the two companies was the equivalent of a traffic agreement between two postal and telegraph administrations. By slotting American Marconi and a sovereign state in the same relation to British Marconi, company executives during the early twentieth century offered a view of a globalizing world in which corporations expanding abroad could remain national to precisely the same extent that governments could. Perhaps American Marconi did enjoy considerable autonomy as a result of its role in the U.S. market, as historian Hugh Aitken has suggested (Aitken, 1985, p. 356). Years later, however, Sarnoff informed researchers that the company had in fact been dominated by its British parent (and that he had been lying to Congress) (Archer, 1938, p. 63).

But did the foregoing mean that the two companies worked with the British government? Policymakers struggled to understand. Whatever future archival research may discover about the relationship between the parent company and its American subsidiary or about the relationship of either of these companies to the British government, the influence of those findings on policy analysis will be negligible. Though these factors may be important for students of political economy, policymakers used the pieces of information they found relevant at the time, while discounting the pieces that went against their assessment.

Nothing illustrates this tendency more clearly than the widely held conviction that the British government "has done everything possible to obtain a monopoly for the Marconi Company."[75] British government backing at international conferences, equipment purchases, and the contract for the Imperial Chain provided the necessary evidence. American Marconi executives certainly did not help matters when they threw in the threat of British retaliation during the debate on the administration's bill before Congress. England, Nally opined in the pages of the *New York Morning World*, could deny landing rights to Western Union and Commercial Cable companies if American Marconi lost control of its stations.[76]

The threat of reciprocal treatment, however, was a bluff: company executives knew full well that their hold on the support of the British government was tenuous. As the 1904 Nantucket controversy had revealed (see chapter 2), British policymakers provided no assistance, even at a time when Britain's position in the world system was more stable. Managing Director Godfrey Isaacs's attempt to secure a British subsidy for the purchase of Federal Telegraph in 1916, to be discussed in chapter 5, had also been rejected by this time (Winkler, 2008, p. 96). Policymakers may have been unaware that British Marconi had intended to operate the Imperial Chain for profit, though this is unlikely, which meant that the decision to entrust this task to the Post Office was a setback. However, they certainly knew that the Royal Navy was "tired of the company," yet they chose not to act on this information (Winkler, 2008, p. 201).[77]

Fears about British dominance of high-power radio fit neatly into a general climate of distrust about British intentions in the postwar world. Although the United States entered World War I on the side of Britain, the relationship between the two countries was characterized by a mixture of cooperation and rivalry. British policymakers shared important organizational tips about running efficient intelligence operations, among other information, with their American counterparts, but were convinced that the Americans were getting a free ride from Britain's efforts to uphold a world order that clearly benefited the United States. American policymakers, on the other hand, suspected that Britain would use American assistance in the war to hold onto its primacy (Beloff, 1970, p. 331; Hannigan, 2002, p. 253).

British control over the global submarine cable network received a great deal of attention in this context as awareness about the commercial consequences of British surveillance spread. How could American commerce expand if companies were unable to close a deal because their British rivals found out about confidential commercial messages before they did (Winkler, 2008, p. 127)? This was merely the tip of the iceberg. The Americans were similarly unaware that British intelligence was reading U.S. diplomatic traffic and that such choice bits as the Zimmermann telegram, which the German government used to invite Mexico to join the war against the United States, reached them only as the outcome of careful British planning (Winkler, 2008, pp. 103–104).

British intentions could not help but figure prominently in policymakers' concerns about the postwar world. American naval strategists, in particular, shared the emphasis of world systems analysts on historical succession. Competition for trade led to war, and the United States was merely the last in a long line of challengers to British power. "Four great powers have arisen in the world to compete with Great Britain for commercial supremacy on the seas—Spain, Holland, France and Germany," policymakers noted in 1913, adding, "Each one of these in succession has been defeated by Great Britain and her fugitive allies" (cited in Bönker, 2012, p. 70; see also p. 71).

While Britain had already given up preparing for war with the United States, American policymakers did not discount the possibility. Before the United States entered World War I, the General Board took the view that the country had to be prepared to fight *either* victor of the war. Thus, the 1915 and the 1916 naval war games on the Atlantic simulated a war with Britain (Bönker, 2012, p. 70).

The General Board's 1915 recommendation that the United States should build "a navy second to none" jettisoned the previous goal of parity in naval construction with Britain and signaled an explicit challenge (Roskill, 1968, p. 20). President Woodrow Wilson backed the plan. "Let us build a bigger navy than [Britain's]," he wrote to an adviser, "and do what we please!" (cited in Hannigan, 2002, p. 255). Congress passed the Naval Act of 1916, a building program that would make the U.S. Navy nearly the equivalent of the Royal Navy within three years (Hannigan, 2002, p. 255). Anxiously eyeing these developments, the British Admiralty estimated that the United States spent more money on new construction than the total British naval budget (O'Brien, 1998, p. 152).

Outbuilding the British Navy was one of many things on the American to do list, which would soon include outbuilding the British cable network. In the meantime, however, naval policymakers identified the obstacle that prevented them from fully exercising control over the American end of radio circuits. "There is no provision of law by which the erection of these high-powered stations can be prevented," Todd reported to his superiors in fall 1916, commenting on American Marconi's request to connect Hawaii to Japan.[78] The United States had nowhere near the strong hold over Hawaii that the War Department had on the insular government of the Philippines.[79] The former had been designated as an "organized, incorporated territory," where the Constitution applied in its entirety, while the latter had been classified as an "unincorporated territory," where the Constitution only partially applied and the military wielded disproportionate influence (Kramer, 2006, pp. 162–165). Indeed, American Marconi's transpacific circuit began operations in November 1916.

Control over territory, as the hand-wringing over American Marconi's application has revealed, was a powerful but limited tool. Its usefulness was influenced by the particular colonial arrangement in place and required attention on a case-by-case basis. A more permanent solution would be in order. Naval policymakers' proposals for government ownership and their attempts at pinning down corporate nationality now converged on a geopolitical objective. Radio was a site of geopolitical rivalry, and legislation was inseparable from advancing the position of the United States in global communications.

The Navy had to contend with internal opposition, since the Department of Commerce was pressing for an "equal voice" in the preparation of the administration bill.[80] After two attempts at redrafting the bill, the two departments reached a compromise at the end of 1916: H.R. 19350 would cover only the sale of coastal stations, not those of the high-power stations that could be integrated into a global network.[81] Foreign ownership regulations took the place of the Navy's most desired objective. Of the thirty-one sections of the bill, three sought to ensure local control by restricting the operations of MNCs. Section 7 declared American subsidiaries of foreign corporations ineligible for a license if more than one-third of their directors were aliens or more than one-third of their capital stock was owned abroad.[82] By setting the limit at 30 percent, the president of American Marconi would later complain to Congress, the bill targeted his firm as if it were "the bull's eye at which they were shooting."[83] Further, section 8 ordered corporate applicants to provide information regarding the percentage of stock held by aliens and report the place of birth and citizenship of each director and officer. Finally, section 12 imposed citizenship requirements on operators. No longer were American-organized subsidiaries of MNCs automatically American citizens; the conditions on their citizenship multiplied. Section 7 of H.R. 19350, with the modifications discussed in chapter 7, would be enacted as section 12 of the Radio Act of 1927. Its restrictions on stock ownership are known as direct foreign ownership regulations and are still good law today (47 U.S.C. §310).

"This draft represents the utmost that could be obtained by the Inter-Departmental Committee of 14 members," Todd reported to his superiors in December 1916.[84] The Navy had secured the support of the Departments of War, State, Treasury, and Commerce (Aitken, 1985, p. 281; Morrow, 2011, pp. 24–25). Nevertheless, the compromise was a victory for Commerce, Todd concluded. After all, the bill "[did not] force any commercial enterprises out of business."[85] Policymakers at the Commerce Department did indeed find the final version to be "a great improvement" over the Navy's 1915 draft, and H.R. 19350, more widely known as the first Alexander bill, after its sponsor, Representative Joshua W. Alexander, was introduced a week later.[86] The compromise was also agreeable to the Marconi interests, which were most worried about losing the company's high-power stations.[87] Company executives deliberately ignored the bill's foreign ownership provisions. They did not apply to American Marconi, because it was an American corporation.[88] Whether the compromise would succeed would depend on whether each party held up its side of the bargain.

The Pitfalls of Natural Monopoly: American Marconi and the Navy Department before Congress

Between January 1917 and January 1919, Congress considered three bills asking for government ownership of radio: H.R. 19350 focused on coastal stations alone and sought government ownership indirectly; H.R. 2573, introduced in April 1917, granted temporary wartime authority over radio; and H.R. 13159, introduced in November 1918, provided the president with authority "to take permanent possession of" commercial stations.[89] The latter two bills covered high-power stations as well. The first set of hearings were held just three weeks after H.R. 19350 was introduced. Yet the likelihood of U.S. entry into World War I had quickly increased, and Todd seized the moment by recommending that government ownership be extended to high-power stations as well.[90]

To many in the Navy Department, the foreign ownership provisions of H.R. 19350 had never been satisfactory. Ensign J. C. Cooper expressed the common view that foreign governments would exercise control over radio stations via "dummy directors and dummy stockholders ... no matter how strictly the law may seek to prevent foreign ownership."[91] In opposition was American Marconi, which sought to keep control over its high-power stations. After Todd's request, all congressional hearings covered both coastal and high-power stations. Executives at American Marconi and naval policymakers both built their arguments on natural monopoly theory, but the theory, as this section reveals, proved to be equally difficult ideological terrain to navigate for both parties.

The administration bills changed the ownership structure of the radio industry cemented by the Roosevelt Board in 1904. H.R. 19350, as it was originally approved, threatened American Marconi's coastal stations, while H.R. 13159 threatened its high-power stations as well. The latter bill reconfigured America's radio communications on the European state-to-state

Table 4.1

Hypothetical and actual ownership alternatives in radiotelegraphy by the 1910s.

		Type of station		
		Naval stations	Coastal commercial	High-power
Ownership alternatives	1. Foreign	British Marconi	British Marconi	British Marconi
	2. Domestic or foreign?	American Marconi	American Marconi	American Marconi
	3. 1904 Roosevelt Board	U.S. Navy	American Marconi in competition with other private companies	American Marconi in competition with other private companies
	4. The Navy's 1916 proposal (H.R. 19350)	U.S. Navy	U.S. Navy	American Marconi in competition with other private companies
	5. The Navy's government ownership proposal (H.R. 13159)	U.S. Navy	U.S. Navy	U.S. Navy

model in which a government agency exchanged traffic with another government agency at the other end of the circuit (table 4.1).[92] Reasoning from natural monopoly theory, both the Navy Department and American Marconi emphasized centralization and uniformity as valuable goals that inevitably pointed to control by a single organization. Both organizations operated "systems" that included ship and coastal stations, but only one system could survive. Congress was now asked to pick the winner.

American Marconi's sustained references to telephony had long formed the centerpiece of its symbolic strategy of framing radiotelegraphy in terms of domestic industries. Now that debates about government ownership of public utilities were front and center, the 1913 Kingsbury commitment made the telephone industry an even more desirable source domain for analogies. The agreement between AT&T and the Justice Department recognized telephony as a natural monopoly and left it to private industry, ignoring the Post Office, which had sought nationalization (Janson & Yoo, 2013, pp. 991, 1003; John, 2010, p. 360). By contrast, the recently nationalized British telephone industry seemed to be but a shadow of the Bell System.[93]

American Marconi's emphasis on the similarities between the two industries kept radiotelegraphy squarely within the purview of domestic economic arguments, where concepts such as "waste" and "innovation" played a central role.

Comparisons to the telephone industry *were* advantageous for American Marconi, even though opponents of the Bell System sought to associate private ownership with waste (John, 2010, pp. 368–369). The domestic focus, however, allowed Nally to tap into a cornucopia of well-worn arguments. He could extol the virtues of competition in free enterprise—the mother of innovation—even though he was arguing for a monopoly. He could associate government ownership with technical backwardness while privately scrambling to acquire continuous-wave technology in order to keep his company afloat.[94] By inviting attention to a successful commercial model, the telephone analogy did double duty. It deflected attention from corporate nationality while mitigating the key weakness of natural monopoly theory: that it failed to exclude a natural *government* monopoly.

The idea of a natural government monopoly, however, was hardly sufficient for the Navy Department, because the U.S. Post Office had long sought to consolidate message handling under its own authority (Janson & Yoo, 2013, p. 991). Postmaster General Albert S. Burleson agreed with American Marconi that radiotelegraphy and telephony were similar, but he pointed out that the transmission of intelligence, whether in physical or electronic form, was in fact "a distinctly postal function" (cited in Aitken, 1985, p. 254). "Beyond making this declaration and asking us for data, they have made no move," Todd would inform his superiors in 1919.[95] Nevertheless, when naval policymakers showed Congress that 68 percent of all wireless shore stations in the world were government owned, they were quick to ignore the fact that "the government" in all of these countries meant the Post Office.[96]

Naval policymakers therefore drew a distinction between the two technologies while acknowledging their essential similarity as natural monopolies. For the Post Office, all messages were alike. The Navy, by contrast, handled unique messages—those vital for national security—and naval radio served as the model for organizing radio communications in the United States. Bullard's conviction that the Navy's network was necessary to maintain "direct and independent" government communication with the fleet was relayed to Congress.[97] Thus, when commercial companies invested in network development, they built facilities that the government had to build anyway. Natural monopoly theory coupled with the imperative of national security undergirded the argument that commercial stations were a "needless duplication of capital."[98]

The pride of place interference received in naval arguments can also be traced to the desire to draw a distinction between wired and wireless technologies. Policymakers had long argued that radio was not like the cables in that duplication would simply destroy the ability of stations to carry messages.[99] Yet, interference no longer posed the serious threat that it had during the previous decade. With proper government regulation of matters such as location, power, and wavelengths, Hooper advised privately in 1917, interference "can be absolutely controlled" (Douglas, 1989, p. 107).[100] Nevertheless, during the December 1918 hearings, naval policymakers continued to present naval monopoly as a solution to interference.[101] It wasn't only American Marconi that misled Congress.

While national security arguments had conjured up at least a breach of neutrality or even a British enemy, the administration's geopolitical arguments presented America's external communications as subject to British control.[102] This was the line of reasoning that identified American Marconi as a subsidiary of British Marconi, as discussed in the previous section, and the latter company as subordinate to the British government. Government ownership, Secretary of State Robert Lansing pointed out, would prevent "the extension of foreign-government-controlled high-power stations to American territory."[103] Admiral William Shephard Benson, the highest-ranking career officer in the Navy, identified naval monopoly as "the best way to exclude British domination of worldwide communication" (cited in Aitken, 1985, p. 386). In his subsequent calls for government ownership, Secretary Daniels continued to present the policy as furthering "the best interests of the United States in its international relations."[104]

As the geopolitical arguments mounted, company executives were unable to contain an international industry within the framework of a domestic debate, paving the way for the exit of American Marconi from the market. In radiotelegraphy, policymakers did not accommodate the rise of the large corporation, nor did they simply oppose a monopoly. Radio policy was foreign policy: the fact that American Marconi sought a monopoly mattered because policymakers feared a monopoly under foreign control. Natural monopoly theory was therefore inseparable from American ascendancy. The only question that remained was whether the Navy Department would have enough ammunition to install itself as the network manager and bring about the state-to-state model in radiotelegraphy.

The Fate of the Government Ownership Bill: De Facto Naval Monopoly over Coastal Stations

In April 1917, shortly after the hearings on H.R. 19350, President Wilson granted the Navy operational control of all radio stations on American territory.[105] Commercial stations were either closed or were integrated into the naval communications network, and new stations were constructed to meet the wartime demand for increased traffic. As a result, the United States finished the war with the most expansive radio network of any power (Winkler, 2008, p. 251). Naval policymakers marveled at the amount of control the Navy Department had achieved. "We are, in fact, in absolute control of the radio situation ashore and afloat," Commander Todd commented privately, quite in contrast to the inadequacy of wartime takeover he had been drilling into Congress.[106] U.S. control extended to the mainland, the country's outlying territories, and to ships of all kinds, with the exception of War Department stations.

Naval policymakers expected to continue "nearly all" of the wartime activities of the Naval Communication Service after the war.[107] Their best hope was H.R. 13159, the government ownership bill introduced in November 1918, which would have also eliminated the amateurs from the airwaves. Though the territory-technology nexus of network control falls outside the scope of this book, it is worth mentioning that amateurs' active interest in the bill helped them withstand the Navy's efforts to oust them from the field.[108] The Navy, however, started from a weak position, because the benefits of takeover had decreased its chances for more extensive authority over radio. Todd informed his superiors that lawmakers found the Radio Act of 1912 quite adequate for war purposes.[109] As an alternative, naval policymakers hoped to purchase "as many of the present commercial stations as [could] be bought."[110] In May 1918, the Navy bought Federal Telegraph's stations and patents and made an offer for American Marconi's coastal stations (Aitken, 1985, p. 295).[111] Rear Admiral Robert Griffin, the new head of the Bureau of Steam Engineering, commented that the deal was satisfactory since "the Navy [could] rightfully claim interest only in coastal stations."[112] Less than two weeks after H.R. 13159 was introduced,

American Marconi sold its coastal stations to the Navy.[113] With the largest private company out of the field, the bill now targeted only high-power stations for government ownership.

Why, then, didn't Congress accept the Navy's bid for government monopoly? Researchers have contextualized the failure of H.R. 13159 in broader political processes, such as the Republican victory during the 1918 midterm elections, as well as the public's negative wartime experience with other public utilities (Douglas, 1989, pp. 280–285; Howeth, 1963, p. 317; John, 2010, p. 403; Sidak, 1997, p. 46). Yet, internal factors deserve a lot more attention than they have hitherto received. Most important, by the time Congress took up H.R. 13159, the bill had lost the support of the War Department, which weakened the national security rationale behind the measure. During the war years, the Army became interested in plane-to-ground communication and began to cooperate with the U.S. Post Office on the recently established Air Mail. Now Army pilots carried the mail in order to gain flying experience, while the Post Office Department took advantage of planes that were in short supply because of the war (Smith, 1942, p. 57). It may have been the potential for an inland use of radio, well before the emergence of broadcasting, that prompted the Army Signal Corps to recommend against naval monopoly of radio.[114] (Todd, who had judged the Signal Corps to be too "apathetic" to put up any opposition, was in for a surprise.)[115] Secretary of War Newton Baker thus reversed course, telling Congress that naval control endangered the autonomy of the Army.[116] At the same time, the civilian support that Todd had expected never materialized. Todd counted on the press, the steamship lines, the cable companies, and even radio companies like United Fruit to support the Navy's proposal. All declined. They were largely concerned about similar government proposals for their own businesses either at home or abroad.[117] Faced with such internal opposition, the House Committee on the Merchant Marine and Fisheries unanimously tabled the bill in January 1919 (Douglas, 1989, p. 283).

By May 1919, the possibility of a concerted government action was waning as executives at General Electric and American Marconi sat down for their first business lunch, a meeting that would be followed by many others until September, when the two companies agreed on the formation of RCA (Aitken, 1985, p. 402).[118] Naval policymakers were unable to convince the War Department about the compatibility of the two departments' interests, and the Department of Commerce also gave up its long-standing support for naval monopoly, instead urging support for a private company that would operate "in silent partnership" with the U.S. government.[119] The focus of this collaboration would be more ambitious than ever before, providing "purely American wireless communications throughout the world."[120] Foreign ownership regulations had tightened the screws on recognizing companies as "American." Once policymakers pinned down the MNC as a disloyal migrant subject, companies headquartered outside the United States had little future in the radio industry.

On July 11, 1919, after the conclusion of a substantial part of the Versailles Peace Conference and after negotiations about RCA were well under way, President Wilson approved the return of radio stations to their owners. Yet, wartime takeovers had permanent consequences for the industries involved in global communications. Domestic industries such as the telephone and the railroads were returned to their owners, in 1918 and 1920, respectively. By contrast, American Marconi never regained its stations, and U.S.-headquartered companies participating in the submarine cable industry would soon be subject to stringent licensing requirements.[121]

In the following decade, coastal and commercial high-power stations would be operated under a different authority. The Navy Department had secured a de facto monopoly over coastal stations, the only stations that some officers believed the Navy could rightfully claim interest in. In 1920, Congress authorized the Navy to transmit and receive private commercial messages at locations that lacked adequate commercial facilities (Howeth, 1963, p. 318). Yet, this was no return to 1912. Because the Navy had already acquired all but sixteen private stations, nearly all locations lacked adequate commercial facilities. Four of the remaining sixteen were American Marconi's high-power stations, which would soon be transferred to the newly established RCA. Five of the remaining installations were low-power stations for local traffic. Thus, only seven coastal stations of any significance were left outside Navy ownership (Aitken, 1985, p. 287).[122] Moreover, the Navy continued to operate its own high-power stations, which connected the continental United States to its outlying possessions and ships of the fleet.

American control over commercial high-power radio, in turn, was built on the foundations that the overhaul of corporate law provided. Attention had shifted from ensuring the loyalty of the station to ensuring the loyalty of the *corporation* via foreign ownership regulations. The evidence outlined in this chapter has identified the geopolitical objectives underlying the development of foreign ownership regulations. These rules emerged from a country in transition. They were the product of a United States that had transformed itself from a host state of foreign communications multinationals into a home state with its own homegrown MNCs. The rise of the United States as a world power in radio required several conceptual adjustments. In the 1910s, naval policymakers' conception of autonomy of communications had to expand to include control over the country's commercial radio links rather than just the Navy's own network. Policymakers had to concede that American control could in fact be achieved by private companies. Only after these conceptual changes could naval policymakers, in particular, understand "American control" as separate from control over U.S. territory.

The conceptualization of "American control" as "a 100 percent American" corporation, however, cannot be understood without grasping how American policymakers tried to implement the General Board's link between effective control and government monopoly *abroad*. Could the policy of government ownership, originally designed for a colonial relationship, be transferred to U.S. radio links with Latin America as well? Or, more broadly, what types of state-centered and commercial options were best suited for international expansion? Because expansion was at stake, there were no two ways about it. An independent American company signaled autonomy of communications only on the transatlantic circuit connecting the United States to Europe. This relationship was the closest to the arm's-length state-to-state model: the future RCA would conclude traffic agreements but would refrain from foreign direct investment. In Latin America, however, governments would not erect their own stations but would bristle at the thought of foreign control over their territories and airwaves. We turn to this dilemma in chapter 5.

II Expansion

5 "A Monroe Doctrine for Radio": The Development of U.S. Radio Policy in Latin America, 1912–1919

In the 1910s, policymakers pursuing the twin goals of network control—the ability to communicate and to deny the same to America's opponents—looked beyond American colonial holdings for the first time. They sought control over the radio circuits connecting the United States and Latin America, a region where private corporations and foreign governments held the property rights. Foremost among the foreign powers was Britain, whose lingering influence in its erstwhile informal empire dwarfed its formal property rights. As British Marconi sought to link the region to the United States, naval policymakers identified American control over radio communication in the Western Hemisphere—the "Monroe Doctrine for radio"—as the central foreign policy objective.[1]

"American control," however, required interpretation in the international context as much as it did in the domestic one. Naval policymakers would spend the decade working with the State Department to block the Marconi Company's expansion country by country. Denying the ability to communicate to a perceived opponent, however, was insufficient. The United States also needed to secure the ability to communicate for itself. Thus, policymakers aspiring to regional preeminence in radio faced the following question: what was the best way for the United States to expand? Just how they realized the limits of control over territory and decided that the key to U.S. advancement was control over the identities and loyalties of the commercial companies deploying the network is the story of this chapter.

By the end of the decade, American policymakers arrived at the idea of an independently financed, brand-new, "100 percent American" corporation—soon to be incorporated as the Radio Corporation of America (RCA)—as the only possible avenue for expansion. It is not that they lacked alternatives. Natural monopoly theory was compatible with both state-centered and commercial policy options. All policy alternatives, as I will show, were a response to the fact that a U.S. Navy monopoly of radio stations encountered opposition both at home and abroad. The proliferation of alternatives, in turn, reflects a fundamental uncertainty in policymakers' minds with regard to the amount of control they could secure via commercial expansion.

The resulting RCA was tasked with managing the external commercial communications of the United States, which included the U.S.–Latin American circuits. Those circuits, however, also comprised the external communications links of *other countries*, which raises questions about the relationship between autonomy and expansion. Exactly how did the United States transform itself from a country subject to media imperialism to a media imperialist in its own right? The answer to this question requires understanding both the different forms of expansion available and policymakers' attempts to ensure that the commercial networks served American interests. In the latter respect, RCA had been a long time in the making. Its structure, imposing a 20 percent limit on foreign ownership, is inseparable from the update of corporate law, discussed in chapter 4, which tightened the definition of American corporate nationality. The company, "100 percent American" only in rhetoric, represents policymakers' efforts to adjust to the less certain form of control that reliance on a commercial company entailed. This conceptual step would be central to the expansionist vision of an aspiring world leader.

The idea of an independently financed, brand-new company to manage America's external commercial communications did not arise in domestic policy as a way to keep American technology out of the hands of the Marconi interests. The key to U.S. ascendancy was control over the network, but technology is only one element of network control and can be deployed by several different organizations. From the start, RCA was envisioned as an operating company, not an equipment manufacturer, whose role was to carry traffic between the United States and other countries. Nor was the creation of the company simply a defensive move to save American communications from British control after government ownership failed to gain traction, even though RCA did perform that role for the transatlantic circuit, which connected the United States to Britain. Rather, the company was a tool of expansion. The idea emerged only after other commercial routes for expansion in Latin America—via American Marconi, United

Fruit, Federal Telegraph, and the proposed Pan American joint venture—had been exhausted (see also Winkler, 2008, p. 256).

From a network control perspective, RCA was a stepping-stone rather than an end point, whose purpose was institutional but whose impact was therapeutic. As an institutional development, RCA was a historically contingent embodiment of "national ownership," a general policy principle on the structural level of network control, which ensured that the external commercial communications of the United States no longer went through service providers that policymakers had come to identify as foreign. But it also did something far less tangible and far more important: the company, hedged by foreign ownership regulations, reassured American policymakers that control over global capital was possible.

Radio in Latin America in the Context of American Ascendancy in the World System

Naval policymakers' extension of the Monroe Doctrine to radio came in the wake of its gradual extension to the economic realm, but it cannot be understood without sketching the uneasy mixture of collaboration and rivalry that characterized Anglo-American relations in the 1910s. Originally promulgated as a defense against European reconquest of the Americas, the Monroe Doctrine had gradually been transformed from a yearning for influence to an ever-expanding expression of U.S. power to be reckoned with (Major, 1993, p. 22). As the United States strove for regional preeminence in its backyard, American efforts to integrate Latin America into the U.S. sphere of influence sparked rivalry with Britain. By the turn of the century, the United States had gained ground. British policymakers gave up preparing for war with the United States and made such major concessions as giving it the right to unilaterally control a proposed canal across the Isthmus of Panama (Bönker, 2012, p. 41; Hannigan, 2002, p. 188; Kennedy, 1987, p. 251; Thompson, 2000, pp. 190, 202).

While it may seem like Britain gave way graciously, naval rivalry marred the relationship. Pro-British and anti-British factions divided the U.S. Navy. The former envisioned joint use of naval power to guarantee peace, while the latter sought naval supremacy and distrusted British intentions (Beloff, 1970, p. 267). Chief of Naval Operations Admiral William S. Benson, an important participant in radio policy, was convinced even during World War I that the United States "would as soon fight the British as the Germans" (Beloff, 1970, p. 331). Even though American planners identified Germany as the central threat to the Monroe Doctrine, concern about the resurgence of British power never disappeared, and it would continue to influence radio policy well into the 1930s (Bönker, 2012, pp. 30–31, 36, 51; Thompson, 2000, p. 202).

Benevolent neutrality toward Britain under President Woodrow Wilson's administration and subsequent wartime cooperation proceeded alongside American efforts to relieve Britain of its imperial burden in South America. In the early 1910s, the United States controlled the largest single share of Latin American trade—30 percent—and improved banking, transportation, and communication facilities appeared to be essential for further trade expansion (Gilderhus, 1986, pp. 10, 27). The scope of the Monroe Doctrine expanded simultaneously from the territorial control embodied by the 1904 "Roosevelt corollary," justifying U.S. military interventions, to economic forms of control via foreign direct investment, as the Lodge resolution, discussed in chapter 4, shows, and to portfolio investment, which involved control over countries' public debt (Bailey, 1933, p. 222; Gilderhus, 1986, p. 35; Hannigan, 2002, p. 31).

As the Monroe Doctrine had become déclassé, given its association with American imperialism, U.S. statements with regard to Latin America would be suffused with a new sentiment. Pan-Americanism, the centerpiece of President Wilson's policy toward the region, highlighted an equitable system of association and partnership, whereas imperialism connoted deception and disguise (Gilderhus, 1986, pp. x, 7, 25; Hannigan, 2002, pp. 83–84). Striving for regional integration under U.S. leadership, American policymakers emphasized natural harmonies among the countries of the Western Hemisphere while downplaying racial and cultural divisions (Gilderhus, 1986, pp. x–xi, 11; Schoultz, 1998, p. 76). Out of the nineteen countries on the continent, American policymakers worked to enlist the help of Argentina, Brazil, and Chile in policing the region and advocated such concrete proposals as collective self-defense (Gilderhus, 1986, pp. 20, 8; Hannigan, 2002, p. 84). Therefore, for both economic and military reasons, control over radio communications became essential to American efforts to reorient regional ties toward the United States.

In radio communications, a joint British and American effort neutralized Telefunken's plans for expansion (Winkler, 2008, pp. 167–170), which left British Marconi the target of the Navy's efforts to extend the Monroe

Doctrine to radio. The links between the Caribbean, Latin America, and the United States were integral to the Marconi Company's vision of end-to-end control over a global communications network. Such a network required investment abroad, so the company followed the strategy of horizontal integration characteristic of early multinational corporations (MNCs) involved in the service industries. As seen in chapters 2 and 3, British Marconi had set up subsidiaries or invested in wireless companies similar to the parent company throughout Europe and in the United States (Headrick, 1991, p. 130; Hugill, 1999, p. 98). During the 1910s, expansion to the Western Hemisphere would pick up. British Marconi's widely advertised "girdle" around the earth, reproduced in chapter 4, envisioned a crucial node in Panama, and the company also began scouting for concessions with the hope of connecting Latin America to the United States and Europe.

In 1915, the field of Latin American radio was still wide open. British Marconi had not acted on its previous concessions, and earlier American attempts at expansion had been unsuccessful (Schwoch, 1990, pp. 19, 38).[2] The central weakness of the Marconi Company at this time was technology. Its pioneering spark system was now obsolete, but two kinds of continuous-wave technology—the arc and the alternator—were being developed in the United States. Patents are central to intercorporate competition at the intersection of technology and capital, which means that piecing together a global network would have been a challenge even without taking into consideration home and host states' control over territory or their influence over capital markets. British Marconi executives, for example, claimed the rights to the Poulsen arc patents for the British Empire and South America, but patent rights for North and Central America were in the hands of the U.S.-based Federal Telegraph (Aitken, 1985, p. 289). Thus British Marconi contemplated acquiring Federal outright in order to cover parts of the Western Hemisphere, while American Marconi initiated negotiations with General Electric to secure an alternative to the arc system in case it became necessary (Aitken, 1985, p. 308).

Pure end-to-end control over a global network without interconnection, as laid out by policy researcher Jill Hills, was no longer possible after the 1906 convention, but executives at British Marconi planned to keep control over shore stations on both ends of each circuit. If marine communications during the previous decade posed a challenge to existing frameworks of network management and regulation, the emerging radio network of the 1910s was readily understood along the lines of its wired alternatives. Companies acquired "concessions," permission from states to establish facilities on their territories, which in turn required foreign direct investment. End-to-end control over a circuit by a commercial organization was the direct opposite of the state-to-state model of network management, whereby telegraph administrations concluded "traffic agreements" for the exchange of messages.

For now, the Marconi Company seemed to have an advantage. Assuming the support of the British government in excluding competitors from operating long-distance stations on British territory, its executives could secure "the Western Union model" of network regulation, a type of asymmetrical end-to-end control that involves foreign direct investment but protects the domestic market from the intrusion of foreign companies (Hills, 2007, pp. 11–12). Even then, however, the company faced some challenges. First, the managerial control over assets that was the hallmark of FDI could quickly be understood as a form of imperialism in the countries British Marconi sought to enter. Second, when British Marconi pursued concessions in Latin America, it faced *two* host states in any one transaction: the local government and the regional heavyweight, the United States, which sought to block its access to the territories of other states as a strategic move to improve its position in the world system. The Marconi organization targeted Brazil and Argentina early on because they accounted for three-quarters of the communication business of the region.[3] Both the business potential and regional importance of these countries attracted the attention of American policymakers and made them a central point of contention in geopolitical rivalry.

For the United States, the Marconi Company's expansion to the Caribbean and Latin America raised the problem of hemispheric network control. Should radio stations in Latin America be integrated into the Marconi Company's worldwide system or belong to the U.S. sphere of influence? Success in the U.S.–Latin America circuit would continue to decenter Britain, a process that began when American policymakers used the 1906 international conference and domestic licensing requirements to seek to establish autonomy of communications. While protecting American radio stations from foreign influence at home can be interpreted as a defensive move, any attempt to "save" a radio circuit from British influence in the Western Hemisphere was immediately expansionist. The form of expansion, however, was undecided. In the 1910s, policymakers considered two state-centered alternatives, direct rule and the integrated hemispheric radio network, alongside support for some of the following companies: American Marconi, United Fruit, Federal Telegraph, and a proposed joint venture, the Pan American Telegraph and Telephone Corporation.

Direct Rule: Control over Radio in Panama

The first challenge to U.S. aspirations to network control would be the easiest to block. In 1912, a couple of weeks after the British government had approved British Marconi's proposal for the Imperial Wireless Chain, American Marconi submitted an application to erect a high-power station in the Republic of Panama.[4] The application covered both Panama and the Philippines, which were to serve as nodes in the company's global network. The Navy Department was bound to take a strong interest in the application, because of the strategic importance of the future Panama Canal. When the decisions were made, the U.S. Navy secured all three elements of network control for the first time *outside* U.S. colonial territory. Direct rule over Panamanian stations marked the first step in U.S. global expansion in radiotelegraphy: control over a radio circuit would be separate from American territorial control.

The population of Panama was not yet half a million, and its only sizable export was bananas, yet the small country became indispensable to the United States after it seceded from Colombia and came to control the site of a proposed interocean canal—the future linchpin of U.S. economic and strategic influence in the Western Hemisphere (Major, 2003, pp. 128, 144). The Panama Canal—under construction between 1904 and 1914 and fully available to ships in 1920—promised eastern merchants access to markets in the Pacific and the transfer of warships between the two oceans (Major, 2003, p. 161). The isthmus was the shortest route between the Atlantic and Pacific Oceans and would become particularly important for radiotelegraphy. A wireless station erected there could simultaneously communicate with ships on both oceans (Schwoch, 1990, p. 40). When Britain withdrew from the region, the State Department negotiated treaties to secure the unilateral control over the site of the canal that it had been pursuing for fifty years (Major, 2003, pp. 10, 34–42).

Territorial control exercised in foreign countries is the most obvious form of imperialism, and the Panama Canal Zone was an unmistakable example. The 1903 Hay-Bunau Varilla convention provided the United States with perpetual ownership of the canal and ten miles of territory on each side of it, which became the Canal Zone (Major, 2003, pp. 43–44). The United States exercised direct rule in the Canal Zone, setting itself up as sovereign over a foreign territory and its people (Major, 2003, p. 47). The Republic of Panama, in turn, became a protectorate: it retained its sovereignty, but the United States guaranteed its independence against a foreign aggressor. As a result, the canal treaty authorized American intervention in its internal affairs (Major, 2003, p. 116). In time of war, the country's highways, railroads, air defense, and communications would all serve America's security objectives (Major, 2003, p. 5).

In radiotelegraphy, the United States would negotiate terms even more favorable: direct rule over the airwaves both in the Canal Zone and in the Republic of Panama. American Marconi's application anticipated the reconfiguration of trade routes in the wake of the construction of the Panama Canal. If wireless during the previous decade primarily provided continuous radio service to ships on the North Atlantic run (Aitken, 1976, p. 244), ships would now cross the canal on their way to Asia and would benefit from continuous communication along the way. As trade picked up, shore-to-shore traffic would also increase, first linking business communities and then the general public. Naval policymakers, on the other hand, saw the isthmus as a fortified zone serving as the first line of defense in a war against the United States, which meant that the country needed even greater control of radio there than on its sovereign territory.[5] When, in 1911, the Navy secured a monopoly over radio communications in the Canal Zone, policymakers obtained all three aspects of network control (Major, 1993, p. 165). The United States controlled the territory, and the Navy Department selected the equipment and paid for it. Federal Telegraph served as an equipment manufacturer, supplying, in 1913, the transmitter for the Darien high-power station, the future center of the integrated hemispheric radio network, discussed later in this chapter (Hugill, 1999, p. 111).

The Republic of Panama, by contrast, had both naval and private stations until naval policymakers concluded an informal agreement with United Fruit, the operator of the latter. During the first decade of the twentieth century, United Fruit invested in a fleet of banana ships and erected radio stations to keep in touch with these ships in order to solve the central problem of the banana trade: getting the fruit to customers before it rotted (Schwoch, 1990, p. 21). The company's Bocas del Toro station went up in 1905, the same year that the naval station did. In 1910 and again in 1913, executives secured new concessions to establish stations in the Republic of Panama.[6] Since radiotelegraphy was an auxiliary to the firm's main line of business, stations were financed from the firm's operating revenues. This was the case even after the 1913 establishment of a wholly owned subsidiary, the Tropical Radio Telegraph Company (TRT), which contracted with Federal Telegraph to erect stations in Central America (Howeth, 1963, pp. 361–363; Winkler, 2008, p. 81). Commercial plans for expansion, however, would soon be subordinated to naval planning. Under pressure from the Navy, company executives agreed to erect no additional stations until the United States reevaluated the threat of war to the region.[7]

If naval policymakers could neutralize the U.S.-headquartered Federal Telegraph in the Philippines and United Fruit in Panama informally, the rejection of American Marconi's application prompted negotiations for a formal agreement extending the Navy's monopoly to the Republic of Panama.[8] Company assurances that it would employ naval reservists as operators and recognize U.S. government control in wartime were seen as insufficient safeguards of American control.[9] Incoming secretary of the Navy Josephus Daniels emphasized the importance to the United States of having "actual physical control" of all radio stations in Panama, while the War Department pressed for a prohibition of private wireless installations on the territory of the Republic of Panama (Winkler, 2008, p. 86).[10]

Despite internal divisions, the U.S. government presented a united front to Panamanian policymakers in demanding "absolute and permanent control" over every type of wireless communication in the Republic of Panama.[11] When the talks ended, the Panamanian decree of 1914 gave Washington the absolute and permanent control it had requested in return for the U.S. Navy setting up three radio stations in the Republic of Panama at locations suitable for both countries.[12] With this measure, the expansionist plans of the Marconi Company were thwarted. The United States secured the equivalent of direct rule over radio for the first time outside U.S. colonial territory, which enabled it to assert end-to-end control over the U.S.-Panama circuit.

Direct rule meant that government ownership, the policy the Navy Department would fail to attain at home, was realized abroad. Naval policymakers would presumably implement the state-to-state model of network management. If foreign telegraph administrations wanted to connect to Panama, they would deal with the U.S. Navy, not with the Post Office, let alone anybody in Panama. Though Panama's sovereignty remained intact in the eyes of the law, the entire episode was closely watched in the region, in part because, under the doctrine of extraterritorial jurisdiction, the grounds on which the stations were established turned into U.S. territory.[13]

For naval policymakers, the decree of 1914 represented the high-water mark of control against which all other concessions in the Western Hemisphere

were measured. Controlling stations in foreign countries in wartime, Superintendent of the Naval Radio Service Admiral William H. G. Bullard asserted in
1916, "simply extends our lines of communication ... with the added feeling
of security that they never could be used to our own disadvantage" (cited in
Winkler, 2008, p. 90). The State Department prepared draft treaties for negotiations with Guatemala, El Salvador, Honduras, Nicaragua, and Costa Rica,
which provided for U.S. control over the radio operations in those countries
(Winkler, 2008, p. 97). The Navy pushed for a similar concession from Haiti.[14]
Counting on the inability of the smaller republics to set up their own radio
stations, Assistant Secretary of the Navy Franklin D. Roosevelt suggested that
the United States might be invited to provide the service (Winkler, 2008,
p. 90). If they weren't, the United States might invite itself, as happened in
the Dominican Republic, when it extended sovereignty over radio as part of
its military occupation (Atkins, 1998, p. 48; Winkler, 2008, p. 91).

Direct rule was the preferred policy for radiotelegraphy in Central America, but what was possible in a few protectorates did not work in others, let
alone in other countries in the region. Thus, all policy options in Latin American radio were alternatives to direct rule. In the following years, the United
States would experiment with both commercial and state-centered policy
options, none of which had room for significant participation by the countries on whose territories the stations would be erected. Pan-Americanism
was an ideal, not a policy. When it came to the regional heavyweights, such
as Brazil or Argentina, naval policymakers would encounter even greater
challenges to America's territorial aspirations and less satisfactory solutions.

Expansion via Existing Companies: American Marconi's "American" Character Investigated

Because Latin American countries had yet to assert legislative control over
radio via licensing, the fate of concessions would be decided informally
between the U.S. and British governments, the local government, and the
interested companies. Three companies emerged as possible conduits of
American geopolitical aspirations in the region: United Fruit, Federal Telegraph, and American Marconi. In 1915, the Navy approached United Fruit
to erect a station in Mexico, and the State Department supported Federal's
entry into Brazil. American Marconi, however, would receive no support.
Instead, policymakers conducted a full-blown "corporate loyalty check" of

the company, and the conclusions of this investigation would influence the incorporation of the stock ownership criterion into H.R. 19350.

Naval policymakers preferred United Fruit. During the period of neutrality and thereafter, the company's stations were integrated into the Navy's network in wartime to such an extent that officers described the company as "a branch of the Naval Communication Service" and its stations as the equivalent of government stations (Winkler, 2008, p. 92).[15] There was just one hurdle. United Fruit did not imagine itself as an operating company. The company ran a private network, and its stations were not open to public correspondence. The difficulty with this became apparent during the Mexican Revolution in 1915, when the Navy needed better communication with ships in Mexican waters but the company's commercial interests did not demand a station in the area.[16] In response, Bullard recommended a government subsidy, which grew out of the recognition that it would be impossible to obtain a site for a U.S. government radio station on Mexican soil.[17] This incident revealed not only the difficulty of obtaining subsidies for commercial companies but also an important mental roadblock to American ascendancy.

The General Board rejected Bullard's alternative to direct rule, reasoning that the subsidy would establish "an inconsistent precedent."[18] The U.S. government, Admiral George Dewey pointed out, could not back an attempt to impose American control via commercial companies when the United States was fighting precisely such attempts by foreign powers on its own territory.[19] Though the Board was writing during a tense period, the admirals' conviction that the United States should hold to the same principles it expected from others is nevertheless striking. This was far from the attitude of the confident hegemon, who, as political scientist Michael Cox commented in another context, "set the rules and punished those who broke them" (Cox, 2004, p. 586). Instead, it reflected the defensive mindset of a challenger, which would need to be abandoned before the United States could advance.

While the General Board was considering subsidies for United Fruit, the State Department sought to support Federal Telegraph's expansion in Latin America. If Panama was the strategic chokepoint of the region, Argentina and Brazil were both the largest markets and the keys to regional military collaboration, which made them desirable targets for corporate expansion. Federal Telegraph underwent a reorganization for precisely this purpose, entrusting the Federal Holdings Company with acquiring concessions in South and Central America.[20] Betting on Federal's ability to transform itself into an operating company, the State Department instructed its diplomats in Latin America to provide assistance.[21] In 1915, however, British Marconi also renewed its effort at expanding into Latin America and asked the U.S. government for help in securing a concession from the Brazilian government.[22]

Before American policymakers could make a decision about various types of commercial expansion, they had to get a handle on who exactly was expanding. Which country, the United States or Britain, benefited from the expansion of American Marconi in Brazil? Hills's Western Union model of network development would not prompt this question, because it conceptualizes an interaction between two states at the expense of a systemic view. Under the Western Union model, for example, an American company could enter the Brazilian market, but Brazilian radio firms would be denied entry. This assumes that there are Brazilian radio firms and ignores the possibility that a country's external communications could be in the hands of companies headquartered outside the country or even outside the continent. The model further assumes that the American nationality of companies is settled, but in the 1910s, corporate nationality was subject to negotiations both within the government and between American policymakers and corporate executives. Both Federal Telegraph and American Marconi were registered in the United States, but were they equally "American"?

As concerns about American Marconi's national identity mounted, in domestic and external radio policy alike, the company encountered a crisis of organizational legitimacy. Multinational corporations regularly face the challenge of establishing and maintaining their legitimacy in multiple host environments (Kostova & Zaheer, 1999, p. 64). A corporation's organizational image—how the public sees the organization—is key to organizational legitimacy, defined as the acceptance of an organization by its environment (Gioia, Schultz, & Corley, 2000, p. 63; Kostova & Zaheer, 1999, p. 67). Given the importance of the United States in the Western Hemisphere, what American policymakers thought about American Marconi was a matter of survival or ruin, which prompted executives to actively manage the company's image.

Edward Nally, the general manager of American Marconi, supported his company's application before the State Department by promising an increase in facilities between the United States and Latin America and a one-third reduction in rates while reassuring the U.S. government that control of the stations would remain in American hands.[23] Policymakers, however, rejected these assurances. When, in October 1915, the State Department informed American Marconi that the United States preferred to support "undivided American interests" abroad, a flurry of letters and conferences followed, all probing the identity of the company.[24]

Between October and December 1915, American policymakers critically examined American Marconi's written statements and collected evidence from various sources with a single goal in mind: to decide where company policy was made. While in the domestic context stock ownership was the central element of corporate nationality, in the international context a full-blown loyalty check was in order. After investigating American Marconi's nationality and actions, policymakers came to the conclusion that the company could not help but serve the interests of Britain, given the interlocking directorates among the several Marconi companies worldwide and such sources of control over subsidiary policy as stock ownership and patent licensing.

Guglielmo Marconi and Managing Director Godfrey Isaacs, naval policymakers now pointed out, served on the boards of the other Marconi companies, which meant that "policy might well be dictated by the so-called affiliated companies and particularly the parent company."[25] The emphasis on interlocking directorates placed authority over company policy in top management rather than exclusively in the owner, which shows an awareness of the bureaucratic transformation of the corporation in the early twentieth century (Streeter, 1996, pp. 35–36).

By contrast, Alvey Adee, a senior policymaker in the State Department, pointed out that the various Marconi companies were the embodiment of Guglielmo Marconi himself. The "Marconi" name was present in most subsidiaries, associating the company with the achievements of its founder, but Adee went further. "The several corporations may be separable," he offered in an internal memorandum, "but they are not national in any one country." "The so-called parent company in London is not English any more than the American company is American," he continued, "Marconi is It everywhere."[26] Unique among the perspectives presented here, Adee found the very exercise of assigning a national identity to corporations futile.

Both the emphasis on top management and Adee's attention to the identity of the founder identified the corporation with living people, pointing to the influence of the "Aggregate Theory" of the corporate form, which ties corporate nationality to natural persons. Even though policymakers were well versed in the law, they did not give any serious consideration to the doctrine of corporate personhood in these decisions. The United States "recognized the American corporate character of the company," Secretary of State Robert Lansing, an authority on international law and former counselor to the State Department, pointed out. He went on to inform American Marconi about U.S. support for undivided American interests as evidenced by the identities of officers and managers.[27] The corporation as a legal subject was perhaps a consideration for Congress when drafting radio legislation, but in international radio policy, it was simply bypassed.

American Marconi fought "the migrant subject" frame, one whose loyalty would be forever tied to Britain, as if in a trial run for hearings before Congress. As we saw in chapter 4, the company highlighted that its arm's-length relationship to its British parent was the equivalent of a traffic agreement. Executives directly countered Adee's views, informing the State Department that "the connection of Dr. Marconi with the American company [was] a[n] honorary one," but they could not adequately address the problem of interlocking directorates.[28] Instead, American Marconi sought to alleviate policymakers' anxieties by playing up not only the American citizenship but also the patriotism of its prominent executives, such as former governor of New Jersey and former attorney general John W. Griggs, who served as the company's president.[29]

If the relationship between the two companies was akin to a traffic agreement, policymakers wondered, then why did British Marconi own stock in the company? Just as during the previous decade, American Marconi downplayed the importance of stock ownership in general and of British Marconi's investment in particular. Stock ownership entitled British Marconi to dividends but conferred no authority to dictate corporate policy, company executives asserted at a time when the link between stock ownership and policy decisions was well accepted in corporate circles (Stone, 1991, p. 173).[30] British Marconi owned just 10 percent of the total number of shares, Nally offered, which meant that American Marconi was "wholly independent."[31] Policymakers, in turn, took the Marconi Company's arguments to mean that it wanted to be seen as "a truly real American company" and disputed the veracity of this statement.[32] They pointed out that 566,826 of the company's shares—approximately 25 percent of the total—were owned by British Marconi.[33] They were not worried about foreign stock holding per se, as their lack of attention to the influence of Brazilian capital reveals (Schwoch, 1990, p. 51). Instead, they were concerned about the control that companies based in geopolitical rivals could exercise via voting shares, a fear that would influence policy-makers' approach to all future commercial alternatives for expansion.

Patent licensing, as evidenced by control over equipment manufacturing, was not quantifiable like stock ownership, but it deserved attention.[34] Even if the concessions were awarded to American Marconi, British Marconi retained the right to build stations in Latin America, which testifies to a common strategy employed by MNCs to keep local branches dependent on the parent company in order to ward off nationalization (Lipson, 1985, p. 23). Only British Marconi could make the kind of apparatus the company had installed, American Marconi asserted.[35] Perhaps executives were referring to the outdated spark installations that the company was negotiating to replace. Otherwise, both Federal Telegraph's arc and GE's alternator were clear alternatives. American policymakers quickly identified American Marconi's inability to provide such an apparatus as a sign of dependence on the parent company. "Such a requirement presupposes some arrangement with regard to patent issues that might tend to give the English company too great a control over the American Company," Assistant Secretary of the Navy Franklin D. Roosevelt wrote.[36]

Information obtained indirectly reinforced the centrality of patents and showed policymakers' interest in corporate actions, which included both past behavior and anticipated decisions. The diplomats gathered, for example, that patent negotiations had to be "submitted to England for final approval," which provided evidence that British interests had the final say in corporate decisions.[37] The State Department also picked up on cues that the company did not mean to offer. After a visit by a Marconi representative, the diplomats recorded that the representative did not know which state the company was incorporated in.[38]

The only question that American Marconi could satisfactorily answer in the course of this exchange had to do with wartime operations. Nally reminded the State Department that the company had already offered to provide free service to the United States during the Mexican crisis in 1914 and that it did not challenge U.S. control over Latin American radio in wartime. He vouched for the loyalty of the company's American staff of 1,100 and assured the U.S. government that it could supervise wireless stations in wartime.[39]

Although American policymakers believed that the company was claiming an American national identity, executives were faced with a more difficult challenge: presenting the company as a loyal American *and* a global organization at the same time. American Marconi sought to develop a global communications network, and company executives were hard-pressed to see the organizational innovations this objective required as anything but an achievement. Nally proudly listed the company's stations erected for transatlantic and transpacific communications and detailed the company's future plans to link both the east and the west coasts of Latin America to the United States.[40] "Radio communication, because of its very nature, must be international in its scope," he wrote to the State Department, "for it is only in this way that its greatest opportunities for expansion and development can be taken advantage of."[41] He trotted out the arguments for centralization and uniformity familiar from the previous decade, almost as if the company could not get past the fact that its offer for running the external commercial communications of the United States was unappealing to the U.S. government.[42]

American Marconi was not the only fledgling multinational challenged by policymakers at this time, but its attempt to claim an American identity testifies to its unique circumstances. Executives at U.S.-headquartered communications equipment maker Western Electric, for example, instructed an agent in Bangkok, Thailand, that company offices and factories in countries ranging from Germany to Japan provided evidence for an "international" identity (cited in Wilkins, 1970, p. 200). American Marconi, however, could not simply dispose of the issue in this manner because of the importance of the transatlantic circuit and the American market. The participation of the United States was essential to any attempt at building a global network. While Western Electric could distance itself from the United States without claiming to be Thai, American Marconi was under pressure to prove its American bona fides.

After this exchange, it became apparent that the arguments of American Marconi carried no more weight with the State Department than they had with naval officers. During the next twenty years, as the Navy's fine-grained metrics of corporate nationality would come to constrain the international expansion of *U.S.-headquartered* corporations, such discussions with the diplomats would become more contentious. For now, there was agreement. In a letter drafted by Admiral Bullard's office, Secretary Daniels asserted that American Marconi and British Marconi were "but one company with two names, or that American Marconi [was] but a branch of the parent company."[43] Policymakers in the U.S. government agreed that the company's efforts in Latin America should be thwarted, and they expressed support for the deployment of Federal Telegraph's arc throughout the region.[44] The decision was communicated to American Marconi in December 1915.

Perhaps some in the Navy preferred "an empire by standards rather than by companies," in the words of historian Jonathan Winkler (2008, p. 202), but this assertion deserves a closer look. Would the arc system be deployed by Federal Telegraph alone or in combination with other trusted companies? By an entirely different company, licensed by Federal Telegraph but rejected by the U.S. Navy? By foreign governments? Researchers who place the technology, rather than the company, front and center see private firms primarily as equipment manufacturers rather than as operating companies, but the scenario where foreign governments deployed the technology manufactured by trusted American companies was only one among several possibilities. Policymakers themselves would fully accept the importance of companies for American expansion only after the failure of their state-centered plans.

Whatever the wishes of the U.S. government about Federal Telegraph's expansion, they also had to be squared with the realities of international business. American Marconi had warned the diplomats at earlier points in the discussion that Federal's patents did not cover South America, and the significance of this piece of information now became apparent.[45] Even if the U.S. government favored Federal, it could not achieve its objectives without dismissing patent law worldwide. This meant either a return to state-centered alternatives or some kind of agreement with the Marconi companies. Naval policymakers first considered bypassing commercial companies altogether and floated the idea of intergovernmental cooperation in the Western Hemisphere.

The Proposal for an Integrated Hemispheric Radio Network

As policymakers sought to capitalize on the opportunities provided by the European war to reorient the communications traffic of the region, both economic and military interests in the United States lined up behind the idea of an integrated hemispheric radio network. The U.S. Chamber of Commerce, the Department of the Treasury, and the Navy Department all supported various plans that would help American financial and industrial expansion or foreground Pan-American defense collaboration in wartime.[46] The idea of a hemispheric network was suggested as an alternative to direct rule. "As the United States Government will probably be unable to establish radio stations in these countries," a former naval attaché to Argentina wrote in January 1915, it should focus on developing friendly relations with the countries and the companies in the region in order to develop a system of shared language and codes for wartime use.[47] The fleshed-out plan, drafted by Admiral Bullard's office, emerged in the wake of the recent difficulties of "non-governmental coordination," the problem raised by adjudicating between American Marconi and Federal Telegraph.[48] The Navy's plan inscribed contemporary political relations in network architecture, revealing the department's preferences both for direct rule and for the centrality of the United States in the Western Hemisphere.

The plan had Bullard's figurative signature. The integrated hemispheric network was informed by the conviction that radio was a natural monopoly, which meant that it had to be centrally organized to avoid duplication. Like the British Admiralty, Bullard preferred "one controlling administration" to manage the system, but that organization would be the U.S. Navy itself.[49] This plan was Bullard's solution to the dilemma that Federal Telegraph's application to the Philippines and United Fruit's need for a subsidy raised for the Navy: if control by private corporations was either undesirable or unworkable, how would the United States ever expand its influence?

In Bullard's mind, the radio network did not fulfill the needs of regional communicating publics but served instead as a tool for regional military collaboration under U.S. guidance. Coordination was necessary because "the problems to be solved in any military organization [were] naturally very much alike."[50] The loyalty of stations would be ensured by citizenship requirements: only citizens of the United States and those of local governments would work at radio stations.[51] The Navy's recommendations directly replicated the language used by the General Board in June 1915 to support government ownership in the United States: "Efficient radio communication requires effective control; effective control of radio requires a monopoly; and the Government should exercise such control."[52] In order to facilitate coordination among the parts of the network, Bullard proposed an inter-American committee to work on the regulations necessary to combine the radio services of the American republics into a homogeneous system.[53]

Whereas historians often see domestic radio legislation and policies for international expansion as separate matters, the proposal for the integrated network shows how intertwined domestic policy, colonial policy, and foreign policy were in the 1910s. Bullard's ideas were forged in 1914, in the context of colonial relations in the Philippines, and were applied to the radio industry of the United States via the General Board's recommendation a year later. While Bullard's office was finalizing the Navy's draft of H.R. 19350, it also drafted the proposal for the integrated network, which would extend the scope of the policy to the entire Western Hemisphere. The integrated network was state centered like direct rule, but American influence would be exercised indirectly, via South American governments. Government ownership of stations in the United States and in South America under American guidance worked in tandem. These policies would undergird a regional wireless network, which would compete with the British cable network and help integrate Latin America into the U.S. sphere of influence.

The American plan was finalized in the State Department, whose revisions left the door open to commercial companies.[54] Control over radio communication should realize "a broad and beneficent Pan-Americanism," the final version of the circular declared, whereby "the ownership and control [of radio] should rest in sympathetic hands and should not pass beyond this hemisphere."[55] The circular stressed that countries should not exclude "reputable American concerns," provided control over the stations was transferred to the government in wartime.[56] All governments were invited to discuss the U.S. plan in January 1916 (Winkler, 2008, p. 88).

Though researchers have consistently identified the presence of both commercial and state-centered options as mixed signals, which delayed American expansion in the region (Aitken, 1985; Winkler, 2008, pp. 269, 272), the alternatives seem clearly prioritized. Government ownership and wartime takeover were the main possibilities, just as in the United States, but, as Secretary Lansing wrote to the Treasury, private corporations would be allowed to operate only "when it [was] clear that the government concerned [did] not desire government ownership" (cited in Schwoch, 1990, p. 41). Policymakers looked to companies as equipment manufacturers first and as operating companies only in exceptional circumstances.

Bullard's blueprint for the design of the network's architecture (figure 5.1) was incorporated in the final version of the circular, which was distributed in March 1916. The integrated hemispheric network was modeled after the Navy's own network in the United States and assumed the use of American equipment,[57] but its very design, which included *other countries* as nodes, immediately signaled more than the superiority of the U.S. Navy's organizational skills. As other "logistical media," maps seem neutral. In the process of arranging objects in time and space, however, they reveal the order in the mind of the mapmaker (Peters, 2013, p. 41).

The selection of the network's topology is often the most important decision in its design (Hallberg, 2010, p. 38). Early communications networks

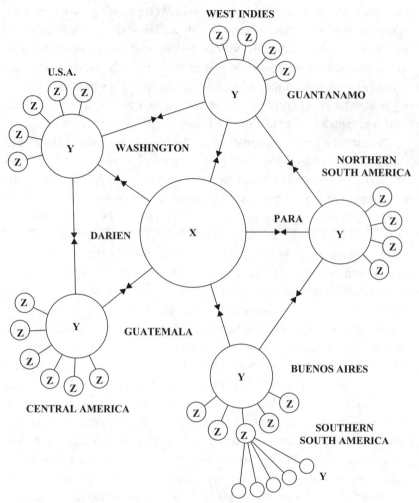

X   Main Station (1).
Y   Zone Center Stations (5).
Z   Government Center Stations (distributing stations).
V   Local stations necessary for each country.

Figure 5.1
The Navy Department's plan for an integrated hemispheric radio network, 1916.
Source: Navy Department, January 1916 memorandum, Circular, March 11, 1916,
Foreign Relations of the United States, Vol. 1, 1916.

were modeled after the architecture of transportation networks because of common economic and physical properties, such as high and distance-sensitive capital costs and unreliability (Neuman, McKnight, & Solomon, 1997, p. 59). The Navy's radio network was configured as a double star; that is, it connected *multiple* central stations and their nodes. This design is more expensive and more reliable than a single-star configuration, which connects a central station to several nodes, and it has a key security advantage: if any single connection is damaged, only that connection is affected. A double-star configuration, however, is both less expensive and less reliable than a distributed, or "mesh," network, where every node is connected to every other node. Because of the expense involved, mesh networks are generally used when there are high traffic levels between exchanges (Hallberg, 2010, pp. 41–44).

All variations of the star configuration involve centralization and hierarchy—a good fit with the organizational roots of communications networks in military line-and-staff command and control (Neuman, McKnight, & Solomon, 1997, p. 78). The final nodes are less important than the intermediary nodes—the zone centers in figure 5.1—which in turn are less important than the center. The implications are wide-ranging. Capital invested in physical infrastructure constitutes the built environment for production and consumption and "form[s] the physical core to what a region is all about" (Harvey, 2003, pp. 109–110). Transportation and physical infrastructures help constitute social, economic, and cultural life, effectively redrawing the heart of a region (Morley, 2010, p. 751). Links that reinforce the connectedness of northeastern centers, as in David Morley's example of the European railway system, also reinforce the relative exclusion of all outlying regions (Morley, 2010, p. 751). Thus, the design of communications networks on the international level contributes to the production of regionality while providing insights into the aspirations of the designers and the relative value accorded to participating and nonparticipating countries.

In addition to its center-periphery structure, which replicates the organization of world communications on a smaller scale, the most obvious feature of the Navy's plan is its limited nature. Instead of replacing Britain at the center of global communications, the plan redraws the heart of the Western Hemisphere. Eastern's cables connected the Atlantic coast of South America to Britain, and even messages intended for the United States were routed to go through Britain (in figure 5.2, Eastern's network is indicated

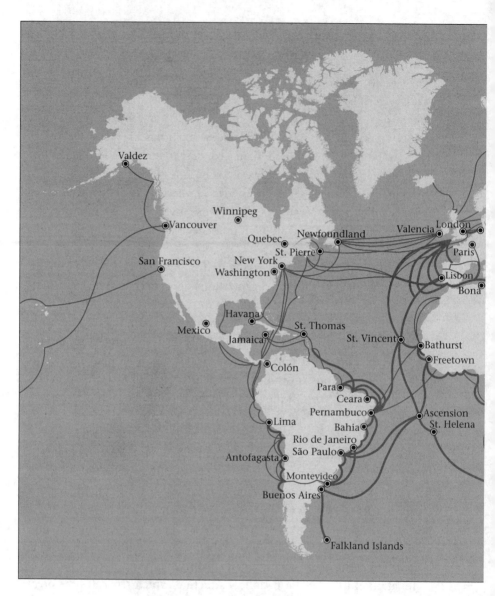

Figure 5.2
The network of The Eastern and Associated Telegraph Companies, 1922.
Source: Modified from http://atlantic-cable.com/CableCos/EATC/1922/1922.htm.

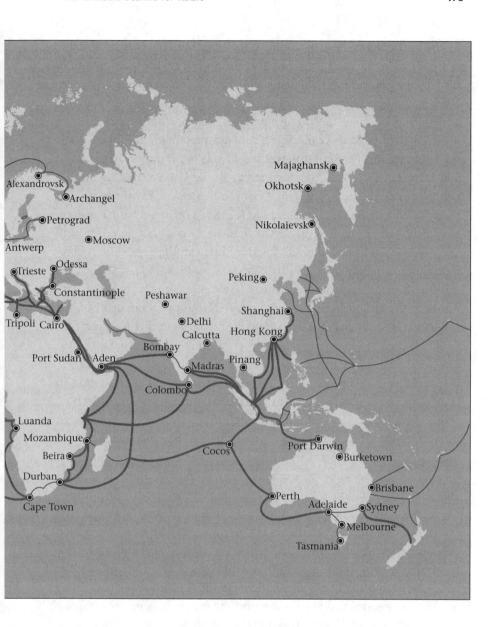

by the heavy black lines). By contrast, the Navy's plan orients radio traffic toward the United States, bypassing Britain altogether. The main station in the Panama Canal Zone, Bullard explained, was "located in as nearly a central position geographically, with reference to all the American Republics, as may be practicable."[58] What would have been practicable had the plan been designed to connect the South American republics to *each other* was not explored. Wresting control over the circuits between the United States and Latin American countries, as the fate of the U.S.-Panama circuit prefigured, would be the first step in American expansion. Expansion to Asia would follow in the 1920s, alongside RCA's negotiations with telegraph administrations in Europe, while the final step would not be taken until the 1940s, when Britain allowed American interests to provide direct communication with parts of the British Empire (Headrick, 1991, p. 266).

Instead of an "equitable system of association" at the heart of Pan-Americanism, the integrated network thus reveals the aspirations of the United States for a central role in the region and the Navy's preference for direct rule. Rather than connecting every station to every other one, as in a mesh structure, local stations are connected via five zone centers—Washington, D.C., Guantanamo, Para, Buenos Aires, and Guatemala—to the main station in Darien, Panama Canal Zone. Of the six stations, three, including the center, would be under American territorial control. The United States was sovereign in Washington, D.C., and in the Canal Zone and administered a protectorate in Cuba, the site of the Guantanamo station. In terms of location, three of six stations would be erected in Central America, one in the United States, and two stations—Para in Brazil and Buenos Aires in Argentina— would distribute traffic to the nineteen countries of South America. The only real lateral link, one that does not go through either the main station or a zone center under direct U.S. control, connects Brazil and Argentina, the most powerful countries in Latin America, whose help the United States was actively courting in managing the region. The absence of a lateral link between Guatemala and Buenos Aires on the map is striking only because they are drawn next to each other, but there is no lateral link between Guatemala and Para or Guatemala and Guantanamo either, which means that either they had to communicate through the main center or messages had to be relayed via several other zone centers.

For all of its military advantages, Bullard's plan assigned value to countries. Under an economic logic, larger markets would have been connected first, leaving either Guatemala or Cuba behind such options as Chile or Colombia for the location of zone centers. Chile, the third country whose help the United States had enlisted to police the region, predictably raised an eyebrow. While it was generally enthusiastic about the plan, it quickly asked for "a principal autonomous station" on its territory.[59] In the absence of designating Chile as a zone center, traffic originating in the country had to be routed through its more important neighbors. Not only did this subject Chilean traffic to monitoring, but the zone center designation seemed to indicate a country's status in the region. For both practical and symbolic reasons, Chile had to ask for its own station.

The idea of the integrated network would be received with little enthusiasm in Latin America. First, information from Brazil, the largest market in the region, indicated early on that government officials expected to rely on foreign capital for erecting its radio stations.[60] Soon after the circular was distributed, it became apparent that most Latin American governments preferred private companies to finance the construction of stations and repay the foreign concessionaire from operating revenues (Winkler, 2008, p. 174). Because of this underlying structural feature of Latin American radio, the appeal of the state-to-state model was limited, even though, as Winkler notes, the American proposal had the potential to solve spectrum-sharing problems (Winkler, 2008, p. 85). Second, Latin American countries were far from confused by the twin possibilities of private and governmental control. They were worried that the plan for the integrated hemispheric radio network simply meant U.S. government ownership of stations on their territories.[61] If the Navy Department sought to capitalize on Latin American countries' desire for connectivity, their solution had to take into account both these countries' lack of interest in building their own networks and their fears of U.S. control of radio communications.

The Proposal for the Pan American Wireless Telegraph and Telephone Company

Given the general lack of enthusiasm for the integrated network and the fact that control over technology, territory, and capital was distributed between American Marconi and Federal Telegraph, some type of arrangement with the Marconi interests seemed necessary. However, imperialism was intertwined with geopolitics in Latin American radio policy, and concerns about lingering British control divided the Navy. Just as the measures policymakers developed to ensure the American national identity of MNCs in domestic legislation were built on an internal and intellectual assessment of the new corporate form, the struggles over the identities of such hybrid business arrangements abroad as joint ventures and cartels were structural-level attempts at network control, which had to grapple with the same problem first: was the proposed joint venture "us" or "them"? In this section, I show that a joint venture between Federal Telegraph and the Marconi companies foundered on American policymakers' concerns about the nationality of the undertaking.

A joint venture between the Marconi companies and Federal Telegraph was nobody's first choice. In the United States, the idea emerged in summer 1917 from the Bureau of Steam Engineering as a response to the unsolved problem of the Brazilian and Argentine concessions and as an alternative to the integrated hemispheric network.[62] With the change of management at Federal, there was now little doubt about the "purely American" identity of the company, but it was a weak contender for connecting the United States to Latin America on its own.[63]

An assessment of control over technology, territory, and capital on the tactical level of network control reveals that the three forms of leverage were distributed relatively evenly between Federal Telegraph and American Marconi. In Latin American radiotelegraphy, both companies had weaknesses in technology. Federal built superior arc transmitters, but British Marconi claimed the patent rights to the deployment of the arc system in Latin America and could exclude Federal from the region. Federal's executives would later assure American Marconi that they wanted to avoid a patent suit and would allow the latter to dictate the terms of the proposed combination (Winkler, 2008, p. 188). Control over territory favored Federal, but only in the long run. While both companies obtained concessions from Latin American countries, Federal was more likely to gain access to the territory of the United States. In the 1910s, however, naval policymakers' drive for government ownership threatened the U.S. stations of both companies. Finally, both firms had difficulty obtaining financing. Federal had long-standing, widely known problems raising capital, while the Marconi companies now ran into novel difficulties (Aitken, 1985, p. 290). On the one hand, Wall Street financiers tied their investment to a commitment that the firm carrying out the operations be "American" (Winkler, 2008, pp. 174, 187), which could pose a problem for American Marconi. On the other hand, the British government denied British Marconi's request for a loan for buying out Federal. Policymakers in Britain concluded that the U.S. government would not allow foreign firms to control its radio industry and did not budge even after Managing Director Godfrey Isaacs predicted that his company would be forced to spin off its American subsidiary and would lose any chance at control over radio in Latin America (Winkler, 2008, pp. 96, 176).

In fact, wartime collaboration with the United States masked such a readjustment of geopolitical relations that the British government would have found it difficult to help out. As the United States emerged as a major creditor, Britain sank into debtor status, becoming dependent on American supplies and loans. The lesson was not lost on policymakers on either side of the Atlantic (Beloff, 1970, p. 235; Hannigan, 2002, p. 252; Schake, 2017, p. 219). When British Marconi asked for British government subsidies, it effectively asked the *U.S.* government to finance its expansion in Latin America. British control over Latin American radio was no longer possible. British Marconi was expanding from a hegemon in decline, which could not offer anything beyond diplomatic support. Yet, this did not mean that British Marconi gave up. By 1917, both companies realized the relative weaknesses of their positions and were ready for an agreement. A joint venture was on the table, and British Marconi executives would press on, with or without support from their government.

By October 1917, British Marconi and Federal Telegraph had reached an agreement that would soon create an internal rift in the Navy Department. The proposed Pan American Wireless Telegraph and Telephone Company would combine access to a superior technology with access to the territory of Latin America. On the technological front, the joint venture represented a patent-sharing arrangement: both companies would assign the new firm all of their patents and concessions. American policymakers were less concerned about keeping Federal's patents out of Marconi's hands than about American control of Pan American (Aitken, 1985, p. 292). Stock ownership, in turn, would serve as a proxy for American control, solving the problem revealed by the 1915 loyalty check: the presence of British voting shares in American Marconi.

On the suggestion of Frank Polk, the solicitor advising the State Department, the proposed arrangement specified that the stock owned outside the United States could not carry voting power (Winkler, 2008, pp. 191–192).[64]

After stocks and cash exchanged hands, the shares were distributed: Federal would own 25 percent of the new company, British Marconi 37.5 percent, all of which were nonvoting shares, and American Marconi 37.5 percent as well. The Pan American Wireless Telegraph and Telephone Company came into existence on October 15, 1917, and officials from both the State and Navy Departments approved the plan ten days later (Winkler, 2008, p. 193).[65] The exchange that followed not only shed light on naval policymakers' disagreement about the nationality of the joint venture but also raised the question of state control over capital in a globalizing world.

Was the new corporate structure "American"? That depended on two related factors: the nationality of American Marconi and policymakers' evaluation of the protection that nonvoting shares provided. Inside the Navy Department, the Bureau of Steam Engineering, Assistant Secretary Roosevelt, and Admiral Benson supported the joint venture. For them, both American Marconi and Pan American Wireless were American corporations, British stockholding in American Marconi notwithstanding. The 25 percent of stock owned by Federal combined with the 37.5 percent of stock owned by American Marconi added up to 62.5 percent (5/8) of the total.[66] In the eyes of these officials, Pan American Wireless represented the best of both worlds: the new company would have the foreigner's money without his ability to influence corporate strategy.

By contrast, the calculations of those opposing the joint venture, including Director of Naval Communications David W. Todd and Secretary Daniels, were entirely different. Because they considered American Marconi to be practically British, these policymakers added up the 37.5 percent of voting and nonvoting shares in the possession of the two Marconi companies. As a result, precisely 75 percent (6/8) of the proposed company seemed to be in British hands. Federal could easily be outvoted, Daniels found out, since "the American Marconi Company holds the majority of the remaining voting stock," which "leaves the control entirely with the Marconi interests."[67] The presence of nonvoting stock mattered little if American Marconi had more shares than Federal and simply followed the corporate policy set in Britain.

Finally, the very effectiveness of pinning down the maximum acceptable level of foreign stockholding also came under scrutiny. H.R. 19350, the revision of the Radio Act just introduced to Congress, specified a maximum of 33 percent of foreign stock investment in a radio company, whereas policymakers would have accepted 37.5 percent in the Pan American case. In H.R.

19350, a provision was under discussion to give the secretary of commerce the right to ascertain how the stock was owned, but the bill made no distinction between voting and nonvoting shares.[68] But what ensured that the percentages would remain stable in the future? "Who is to decide (and by what method) whether the controlling interest of a corporation was acquired by foreigners?," Polk now inquired.[69] Polk was doubtful. "No machinery is provided for determining the psychological moment when more than 3/8 of the Company's stock may be owned by others than citizens of the United States," he pointed out,[70] adding, "The changing of stock from one hand to another might in one business day kill the Company and revive it a dozen times."[71] Part of the reason why the legal system settled on the place of incorporation test as an indicator of corporate nationality was the difficulty of policing financial flows (Vagts, 1961, p. 1529). Precise calculations of stock ownership provided a false sense of security, Polk noted in the 1910s, when the extent of financial flows was nowhere near the proportions we are used to today, with automated stock exchanges and global capital flowing at speeds that threaten to destabilize the international monetary system.

This exchange points to a problem of contemporary relevance: could states exert meaningful control over publicly owned corporations operating internationally? Perhaps foreign ownership regulations worked less to constrain companies and more to make policymakers feel better in the face of a problem that went deep and with no solution in sight. For policymakers, amnesia would prove beneficial, as they continued on the now well-worn path. As chapter 7 explains, in 1934 the Navy Department would successfully introduce into law restrictions on indirect foreign ownership that limited foreign stockholding in the parent companies of radio license holders to 25 percent. That the United States, if it only had the right legal tools, could exercise control over global capital flows would no longer be questioned. Instead, policymakers at the State Department in particular would wonder whether such restrictions even served American interests. As the confident vision of an aspiring world leader gained ground, these earlier uncomfortable reminders about the limits of state power would recede into the background.

By early 1918, two important changes fueled the suspicion of those opposing the joint venture. On the one hand, Pan American's concession now covered communication with Europe, which meant that it could potentially control the Latin American end of both the U.S.–Latin America and the Latin America–Europe circuits. Naval policymakers worried that it would soon be integrated with British Marconi's high-power wireless system.[72] Moreover, Federal Telegraph was now turning toward manufacturing, and its negotiations with American Marconi threatened to put the Poulsen arc patents for the United States at the disposal of the Marconi companies. In response, the Navy bought out Federal's stations and patents (Aitken, 1985, p. 295; Winkler, 2008, pp. 195–197). Pan American's options were suddenly curtailed: it did modify its concession to allow the use of the Marconi spark equipment but reached the end of the road when Secretary Daniels required that the U.S. end of the circuit be a government station (Aitken, 1985, p. 292).

In the Pan American case, failure on the structural level of network control forced recourse to the tactical level as the United States continued to negotiate its participation in the thicket of emerging global radio connections. Because of the failure to ensure the American identity of the Pan American venture, American policymakers blocked the expansion of Pan American by using access to the territory of the United States as leverage. The decision had immediate ramifications for financing and for American Marconi's hopes of end-to-end control over the U.S.–Latin America circuit. Without U.S. approval, General Manager Nally complained, financiers would hesitate to invest in the venture.[73] Now the Marconi companies controlled an outdated technology but had no access to capital or to the territory of the United States. End-to-end control over a circuit seemed to be out of the question: without a corresponding station in the United States, it made no sense to build the station in Argentina (Winkler, 2008, p. 198). Executives must have wondered, could British Marconi retain any role in connecting Latin America to the United States?

The Pan American joint venture would have combined companies registered in different core countries to carry traffic between the United States, Europe, and the Western Hemisphere. A successful arrangement would have provided evidence of collaboration between two core states to control the flow of traffic between the Western Hemisphere and its two most important trading partners. However, the Pan American proposal foundered on the rocks of geopolitical rivalry. Though the British government seems to have left the negotiations to British Marconi, American policymakers assumed their guiding hand. As a result, the Pan American case taught naval policymakers that no amount of stock ownership by British Marconi was acceptable if they wanted a corporate arrangement to be widely recognized as "American." Because of the imperative of exclusive control over territory, dictated by natural monopoly theory, the arrangement envisioned for Pan American had far-reaching consequences. In just a couple of years, it would provide the blueprint for the division of the world that would take place between General Electric and British Marconi during the negotiations that would create RCA. Chapter 6 will analyze that arrangement.

A "100 Percent American" Corporation

The experiments with Federal Telegraph and Pan American were part of a larger trial-and-error process whereby naval policymakers worked out the right mixture of autonomy and expansion within the constraints of both the domestic legislative process and differing corporate objectives. Now that state-centered forms of expansion encountered pushback and commercial options relying on existing private companies seemed to be withering, the problem remained unsolved. Who would connect the United States to Latin America? Contrary to Daniels's hopes, that entity would not be the U.S. government station at Monroe, North Carolina (Winkler, 2008, p. 198). With the failure of the government ownership bill at home, the state-to-state model of network management was fading into the background. Instead, RCA became the future name of an idea: an independently financed, brand new, "100 percent American" corporation. This was the specific form of the Monroe Doctrine that eventually prevailed.

The idea emerged from the Bureau of Steam Engineering, where Stanford C. Hooper, now in charge of the Radio Division, looked to private corporations to "carry out the Monroe Doctrine as regards radio."[74] Foremost in Hooper's mind was the distinction between policies affecting coastal stations used for marine communications and those concerning high-power stations with global ties. "High power stations should be owned commercially," Hooper wrote in "Basis of Radio Organization, U.S.S. [sic] America," a key memorandum from 1917 that would form the basis of the Navy's negotiations with General Electric.[75] These stations served as alternatives to submarine cables and promised the United States the ability to communicate in terms of both confidential and public material. Private ownership of high-power stations, Hooper explained, will ensure "an open channel for [our] own operations in war time."[76]

Naval policymakers' newfound optimism about working with private corporations could be traced to their wartime experience with United Fruit. In terms of organizational image, United Fruit was the closest to the future RCA. Its American credentials were unquestionable, and its patriotic actions earned favor with the Navy Department. However, as in the case of the Mexican station in 1915, United Fruit's plans for expansion did not match those of the Navy. Nevertheless, the State Department now suggested that the company seek a concession in El Salvador to help prevent the expansion of Marconi interests.[77] The hope, the dream—the unfounded assumption—that private companies would be direct extensions of U.S. power was integral to policymakers' plans.

By 1918, the undeniable backlash against U.S. attempts at expansion in the Western Hemisphere had affected the state-centered options most adversely. "The attempt to get American government ownership even in Central America has failed," Benson was informed. "Considering the attitude of suspicion of our motives that prevails among a prominent class in South America any attempt to extend American sovereignty even over a radio station is not considered sound policy."[78] Direct rule hit a brick wall in what appeared to be the unlikeliest places—a communications industry in small, weak countries— paving the way for commercial expansion. Boaz Long of the State Department, echoing Admiral Bullard's earlier hopes, stated, "An American radio company could do many things in these countries that the American government could not" (cited in Schwoch, 1990, p. 53).

Long now focused on how the corporation could serve as a buffer zone between the interests of sovereign states, giving scant attention to the difficulties of expanding via private corporations. United Fruit's expansion to El Salvador quickly foundered, however, over the company's new request for subsidies. President Wilson rejected the idea of a federal subsidy on the grounds that the government had no business getting concessions for private companies. In the end, negotiations between TRT and El Salvador fell through and the U.S. did not make any progress in the country (Cronon, 1963, p. 290; Winkler, 2008, pp. 179–182). The failure of a subsidized chosen instrument paved the way for policymakers to view an independently financed company as the only possible avenue for American expansion.

Current interpretations link the immediate origins of the Radio Corporation of America to a deal in the works between General Electric and American Marconi. Central to the negotiations was the sale of the Alexanderson alternator, a type of continuous-wave generator, which would provide the Marconi interests with an alternative to the arc technology, whose patents were now in the hands of the U.S. Navy (Aitken, 1985, pp. 339, 363).

The negotiations that reopened in February 1919 granted the objective American Marconi had long pursued. The company was to have control over the operating end of the business, leaving GE to manufacture wireless equipment (Aitken, 1985, p. 308). On April 8, Hooper and Bullard met with executives at GE to dissuade them from selling the alternator to American Marconi, which prompted some journalists to label that day "the Fourth of July of American radio" (cited in Aitken, 1985, p. 338).

Yet the Navy's desire to keep the alternator from falling into foreign hands may not be sufficient to account for the immediate origins of RCA. An agreement between the Marconi interests and GE would have been inconvenient but far from a fatal blow to the aspirations of the United States in the radio field. After all, U.S. control over its own territory would have prevented British Marconi—with or without the alternator—from including the United States in any global network the company was planning. The participation of Latin American governments in a Marconi network in the face of U.S. opposition was also uncertain.

Just four days before Hooper and Admiral Bullard got on the train to meet executives at GE, Nally at the ailing Pan American requested permission to conclude a traffic agreement with British Marconi for the U.S.–Latin America circuit.[79] The ongoing problem was still unresolved. Even if American policymakers denied permission to Pan American, there was no company to take the place of the proposed joint venture. United Fruit needed subsidies to act as an operating company, and it had already become apparent that Federal Telegraph was ready to cut back so that it could focus solely on equipment manufacturing (Winkler, 2008, p. 191). Blocking the sale of the alternator therefore appears to have been part of a broader plan to arrange for an operating company that could run the external communications of the United States. The initial arrangement between GE and British Marconi represented a dead end. The future RCA, not American Marconi or Pan American, would conclude the traffic agreement with British Marconi and would carry the traffic between the two continents.

Hooper's proposal for a private company to operate high-power stations anticipated just one gap—foreign influence—between corporate interests and the national interest, and he solved it by requiring "100 percent American" stock ownership.[80] By taking the reliance on percentage measurements of nationality to its logical extreme, Hooper's proposal dovetailed with the wartime discourse of 100 percent Americanism, which, in the words of historian John Higham, altered "the whole texture of nationalist thought" (see Brewer, 2009, p. 69, for popular manifestations of the discourse; see also Higham, 1955, p. 204). As the connections forged by the General Board between efficient communication, control, monopoly, and government ownership unraveled, "American control" was translated into private ownership, whose loyalty was assured via restrictions on foreign shareholding. The "100 percent American" ideal shared in the wartime spirit but showed little awareness of the realities of international business, in which firms of varying levels of national purity made deals regularly to keep traffic moving.

Hooper's ideas came to fruition in the context of heightened attention to long-distance communications at Versailles. Three industries were understood to be central to world leadership in 1919: transportation, communication, and petroleum. International transportation meant shipping, where the British held the lead. The United States already dominated—or was "sufficiently independent," depending on the researcher's perspective—in the petroleum industry (Hugill, 1999, p. 120; Winkler, 2008, p. 256). The future of international communications, on the other hand, was undecided. Britain still led in cable communications, though, as chapter 6 will show, the American delegation to the peace conference sought to diminish their clout, while radio held the promise of evening out the balance. It was certainly just a promise at this point, because wartime radio capacity did not compare with that of the cable companies. Policymakers' push for a Monroe Doctrine for radio was part of America's drive for regional preeminence and was intended as a step toward leadership in international radio. Secretary Daniels and others negotiating at the Versailles Peace Conference, however, were left out of the negotiations at home between naval policymakers and GE, presumably because they were still committed to government ownership (Winkler, 2008, p. 257).

As executives at General Electric and British Marconi were negotiating about the creation of a new corporation, two of the topics they considered were immediately geopolitically significant: the identity of the new corporation and the contours of its expansion. Decisions about these matters formed part of both the Preliminary Agreement between GE and British Marconi, signed on September 5, 1919, and the Principal Agreement that RCA itself concluded with British Marconi on November 21 of that year, after it had received its charter (Aitken, 1985, p. 405). Since the problem of corporate nationality cuts across several chapters, I will touch on it here and in chapter 7, while leaving the analysis of the Principal Agreement, which outlined the division of the world between the two companies, to chapter 6.

The structure of the new corporation was selected from three alternatives. First, British Marconi pushed for a joint venture, with itself as a minority shareholder. By now, however, the presence of *any* British shares was a deal breaker, which left either American Marconi buying out its parent company and continuing as before or GE buying out the Marconi companies entirely (Aitken, 1985, pp. 371, 403). Under the last option, which would eventually prevail, top management came from GE, while American Marconi formed the operational core of RCA (Aitken, 1985, p. 372). But why was the proposal for an autonomous American Marconi also rejected? Chapter 7 will examine hitherto unexplored aspects of corporate nationality that informed policymakers' perspectives.

RCA's charter, issued by the state of Delaware in October 1919, demonstrates that conceptual developments cementing stock ownership at the heart of "American control" over companies were essential for both domestic legislation and for international expansion. RCA's bylaws contained citizenship requirements and incorporated the percentage measure of corporate nationality advanced by H.R. 19350 in 1916, though they reduced the acceptable level of foreign ownership to 20 percent (table 5.1).[81] The foreign shares could come from anywhere but British Marconi, which undertook not to acquire, prior to 1945, any shares or interest in RCA without the latter's written consent (Aitken, 1985, p. 405). In addition, the Navy also put an end to American Marconi's operations as an equipment supplier, and the U.S. Shipping Board, under the direction of Admiral Benson, proposed a requirement of 100 percent American ownership of all corporations in coastal shipping (Vagts, 1961, p. 1540; Winkler, 2008, p. 185).

Naval policymakers were elated at the success of their approach. Captain Todd, now at sea, expressed his hopes that working with "a strong, real American company" would provide the United States with a good chance to lead in the development and use of radiotelegraphy (Aitken, 1985, p. 428). RCA's stations in Europe, South America, and the Far East, he pointed out shortly after the company began operations, would be "of inestimable value both to American interests abroad, and to our military forces in the event of possible future hostilities."[82]

As the discussion in chapter 4 about the Navy's proposal for government ownership reveals, RCA came into being via a forced sale in the shadow of nationalization. In the strategically important radio industry, the Marconi

Table 5.1
Hypothetical and actual ownership alternatives up to the formation of RCA.

	Type of station		
	Naval stations	Coastal commercial	High-power
1. Foreign	British Marconi	British Marconi	British Marconi
2. Domestic or foreign?	American Marconi	American Marconi	American Marconi
3. 1904 Roosevelt Board	U.S. Navy	American Marconi in competition with other private companies	American Marconi in competition with other private companies
4. The Navy's 1916 proposal (H.R. 19350)	U.S. Navy	U.S. Navy	American Marconi in competition with other private compaies
5. The Navy's government ownership proposal (H.R. 13159)	U.S. Navy	U.S. Navy	U.S. Navy
6. Outcome in 1920	U.S. Navy	U.S. Navy—de facto control	Radio Corporation of America (20 percent maximum foreign ownership)

(left margin label: Ownership alternatives)

companies were disadvantaged as both domestic and foreign corporations. American Marconi did not receive the legal protections due the corporate citizen in the United States—foreign ownership regulations were tightened specifically to exclude the company from those protections. Meanwhile, British Marconi was deprived of the protections that were due foreign corporations. Under the recently established principle of national treatment, for example, countries were expected to give foreign investors the same rights they gave to domestic ones (Lipson, 1985, p. 4).

Whether the sale of shore stations would have qualified as expropriation under the legal standards of the 1910s requires further research, but under contemporary standards for foreign investment at least, the concept of expropriation covers not only obvious takings of property but also any interference with the use of property that has the effect of depriving the owner of the use of the property or of the benefits expected from its use

(Alvarez, 2009, p. 965). This matter never came up because the British government did not protest. British policymakers had already abandoned any hope of participating in the American radio industry when they refused to subsidize Isaacs's attempt to buy out Federal Telegraph. The structure of RCA therefore cemented a shift in power relations that had already taken place.

From a network control perspective, the creation of RCA was one of several steps on the road to American ascendancy in global communications. As the commercial embodiment of the principle of national ownership on the structural level of network control, the new corporation represented an institutional step in U.S. ascendancy, as important as interconnection and licensing. The newly formed RCA broke the Western Union model of network management in radio that had hitherto applied; namely, that Marconi stations had been erected on U.S. soil, while no comparable American stations had existed in Britain.

For policymakers thinking about a network that used the airwaves for connection, dependency on the network of a geopolitical rival was at least as important an issue as the freewheeling exploration of the airwaves by the experimenting public. Large institutions were far from unified in their interests. Some of the "large corporations" lumped together in revisionist histories, in particular, posed a problem for the state. In response, policymakers refined the distinction between domestic and foreign corporations, marginalizing American Marconi and setting the country on the path toward a media imperialist power in its own right.

That RCA itself straddled autonomy and expansion, in turn, is only apparent if we pay attention to both the identity of the company and its corporate agreements. Insofar as the transatlantic circuit was concerned, the United States achieved autonomy. Its external communications no longer went through service providers policymakers identified as foreign. RCA would conclude traffic agreements with European telegraph administrations, which financed the stations erected on their territories. Determining whose interests each circuit served requires an analysis of individual cases. On the U.S.–Latin America circuit, on the other hand, where governments did not finance stations on their territories, foreign direct investment was required. The creation of RCA, however, did not automatically transfer U.S. control over the U.S.–Latin America circuit. During the 1910s, the U.S. government was far more successful at blocking its geopolitical rivals abroad than at outright expansion, because it had expended so much effort sorting out the policy options it would accept as "American." This question would return in the context of expansion, engulfing RCA and other U.S.-headquartered MNCs during the following decade.

Whether direct foreign ownership regulations solved the problem of British influence would be debated until the Communications Act of 1934. While Hooper would wonder whether these rules made corporations truly American, a taste of a different set of doubts is apparent from a May 1919 exchange centering on a government charter for the future RCA. Both Admiral Benson and Walter Rogers at the Committee of Public Information pointed out that a radio company, however unquestionably American, could not be isolated from the global communications environment in which it would operate. A private corporation would sooner or later be handicapped by the British government, Benson commented, or it would be absorbed or influenced by British capital.[83] Rogers warned that radio would be enmeshed in the "intricate network of contractual relations" that characterized the cable industry, and he recommended safeguards such as that copies of any traffic agreement the new radio company entered into should be filed either with the Navy or the State Department.[84] "Unless some such publicity is required," he predicted, "any company, American or otherwise, will make a lot of deals which are not likely to be entirely advantageous to the American public."[85]

In addition to its role as a concrete step in ascendancy in radiotelegraphy, the creation of RCA also marks an important conceptual step toward the confident vision of the aspiring world leader. The very existence of the company signaled American policymakers' acceptance of the limitations of territorial control and the emerging conviction that controlling a communications network meant control over the identities and loyalties of the companies deploying it.

That adjustment to world leadership was a difficult and drawn-out process is hard to miss. Knowledge about the world system and knowledge about the corporation were linked, which shaped subsequent policy recommendations. Naval policymakers' defensive focus on autonomy, purity, and loyalty had prompted proposals for government ownership and 100 percent American capital ownership. By departing from the 100 percent ideal, however, the foreign ownership provisions of RCA's charter confirmed that purity was unworkable in practice. Global expansion invited capital investment, and some level of contamination was to be expected. Policymakers' willingness to rely on a private corporation for control over America's external radio links was, however, a small step toward a confident vision at this point because they held onto the idea that RCA would act as an unproblematic extension of the national interest.

In the radio industry of the 1910s, there was little evidence for the possibility that American policymakers sought to attach themselves to the power of capital in order to facilitate the country's rise in global communications. Federal Telegraph, which had a hard time securing financing, and United Fruit, which needed subsidies, serve as poor examples for the thesis that the state served the interests of capital. Would GE and RCA be different in this regard? The relationship between policymakers in the Navy and State Departments on the one hand and RCA on the other would gain center stage during the following decade as policymakers formulated a new goal for the United States: to make the country the center of world communications. Far from an unproblematic extension of the national interest, the newly established RCA quickly sought to exploit fissures in the government and demanded a central role in shaping both domestic and global communications policy. Could corporate executives set the contours of American expansion in radiotelegraphy? Would policymakers recognize their attempts at expansion, however successful, as the successes of the United States? These would be the vexing questions of the 1920s.

6   Strategies of Expansion: Type Competition, Cartels, and Limited Foreign Direct Investment, 1919–1929

As World War I was drawing to a close, there was general agreement that "most of the world [was] to be made over" and that opportunities for the United States abounded.[1] The economic and political transformation of the country into a key challenger to British power during the previous quarter century was reflected in communications policy. Policymakers now appreciated the importance of radio not only for military maneuvers but also for the position of the country in the world system. Just how best to transform the country into the center of world communications would be decided in the halls of the State, War, and Navy building where naval policymakers and diplomats vied for policymaking authority. Before policymakers could translate their newfound wartime clout into peacetime preeminence, a central decision had to be made on the structural level of network control: what form of expansion best suited the national interest?

During the 1920s, naval policymakers and the State Department offered competing visions for improving America's position. Taken together, these visions attest to a prolonged process of accommodation between the U.S. government and early multinational communications corporations with regard to appropriate forms of global expansion. Synchronizing the Navy's expansionist plans with those of the State Department and U.S.-headquartered multinational corporations (MNCs) would prove to be difficult, in part because the diplomats had a more optimistic view of U.S. power and because MNCs like the newly established RCA and International Telephone and Telegraph (ITT) sought to exploit fissures in the government and demanded a central role in policymaking. Opposition to the objectives of the United States by other states was certainly a major factor in delaying American expansion. However, as this chapter reveals, knowledge about America's role in the world system, about radio technology, and about the multinational corporation was still in flux, which also helped put a brake on policymakers' efforts to advance via commercial expansion (cf. Hugill, 2009, p. 274; cf. Winkler, 2008, p. 273).

Internationalizing the Submarine Cables

By the end of the war, industrial production, trade, and monetary relations had all been transformed to America's advantage. British steel output fell from one-third of the American output in 1913 to one-fifth in February 1919. The figures for coal production were similar. Even more striking, the tables were completely turned in ship construction for the merchant marine, where the United States now produced almost twice as many ships as its wartime ally (O'Brien, 1998, p. 151). As excess production found new markets, American foreign trade rose almost threefold between 1915 and 1921. In February 1919, America's exports surpassed its imports by more than two to one, transforming its balance of payments (O'Brien, 1998, pp. 150–151; Roskill, 1968, p. 22). Since the Allies could not fight without American financial assistance, New York had replaced London as the financial center of the world (Headrick, 1991, p. 173). The United States stood to collect an estimated £1 billion in war debt from Britain alone and rebuffed British overtures to have its debt forgiven (O'Brien, 1998, p. 151; Schake, 2017, p. 242).

Global communications presented some of the most important, and technologically most abstruse, policy issues. Of the three dominating factors in international relations—international transportation, international communication, and petroleum— naval policymakers were convinced that the United States had a good chance to advance in the second field (Howeth, 1963, p. 355). The centerpiece of national aspiration shared by the military departments, the State Department, and the Post Office was "direct communication," meaning communication free from foreign interference, or messages that did not go through British-controlled lines. "No more important problem confronts the American government than the establishment of direct communication with the principal countries of the world," Walter S. Rogers wrote in 1918, laying out a comprehensive plan for the reorganization of the world's cables.[2]

After serving as the editor of the *Washington Herald*, Rogers took up the position at the head of the Foreign Cables Division of the Committee on Public Information, the major U.S. wartime propaganda agency (Aitken,

1985, pp. 261–264). Rogers played a central role in shaping global communications policy during the Versailles Peace Conference and would negotiate for the United States at several postwar international communications conferences. In the course of these events, he became convinced that "after the war this country will occupy a much more conspicuous place in the life of the world than heretofore," and facilities commensurate with this larger role were required.[3] Rogers's vision foregrounded autonomy in cable communications, cheap news for communicating the perspective of the United States in world affairs, and a central role for governments in deciding about the fate of global communications networks. This perspective had to fail before Commander Stanford C. Hooper's vision for an independent global radio network, run by a 100 percent American corporation, could gain traction.

What stood in the way of direct communication with all parts of the world was the system of exclusive landing rights (Aitken, 1985, p. 263). Britain's domination of cable communications rested on multidecade monopolistic concessions granted to the Eastern group that barred companies registered around the world from accessing the territories of the countries where the group offered telegraph service. Without addressing the root of Britain's stranglehold on global communications, the United States could not advance, but by late 1919 it became apparent that neither the expertise nor the raw materials for an American cable manufacturing industry were in place (Winkler, 2008, pp. 230–234).[4] Unlike in general naval policy, where the large-scale construction authorized by the Naval Acts of 1916 and 1919 laid the groundwork for American ascendancy, outbuilding the British cable network was not an option.

At the Paris Peace Conference, such seemingly narrow topics as the disposition of the former German cables exposed major conflicts over global communications, many of which were directly tied to the future role of the United States in the field. Isolating Germany from its allies and supplies had been the first task of the Admiralty upon the outbreak of World War I. The Royal Navy had severed each of Germany's five Atlantic cables that passed through the English Channel and had the two cables cut that linked New York with the Portuguese islands of the Azores (Winkler, 2009, pp. 849–852). Britain and France had diverted the Atlantic cables and relaid them to be integrated with their networks, while Japan did the same with the German cable linking the island of Borkum to the island of Yap in contemporary Micronesia. As a result of the damage to the German cables, the United

States had lost all direct cable connections to Germany. American policymakers were convinced that U.S. allies had walked away with major gains and refused to recognize cables as part of the spoils of war.[5] When the Council of Ten, the heads of state and the foreign ministers of the five Allied and Associated Powers, gathered in January 1919 to determine the conditions that would end the state of war with Germany, they also considered the fate of the cable links that used to connect Germany to the outside world.

As the communications expert of the American Commission to Negotiate Peace, Rogers advised President Woodrow Wilson that the United States was most interested in the Pacific links of the German network. The Emden-Yap cable that Japan had diverted, Rogers suggested, should be "internationalized." Great Britain, Japan, China, and the United States would jointly own and operate the cable, displacing the British monopoly (cited in Baker, 1960, p. 440).[6] This was part of a larger plan. Rogers looked at communications networks from what he called "a comprehensive world viewpoint," which gave him the idea of "a world-wide network of communications operated on a public service basis" (cited in Baker, 1960, p. 433; Rogers, 1922b, p. 157). That cables were a public utility went without saying, but their global reach had made it possible to avoid government regulation (cited in Baker, 1960, p. 432).

The centerpiece of Wilson's liberal internationalist vision was the League of Nations, an intergovernmental organization designed to maintain world peace. The League represented the ideal of "a world of people acquainted with each other, cognizant of each other's needs and problems" (cited in Baker, 1960, p. 429; Winseck & Pike, 2007, p. 262). Rogers's vision for postwar global communications assumed the future existence of the League and brought communications regulation under its purview. The global community so desired could only be realized if the League supported the continued extension of facilities among members of the organization, nondiscrimination in rates and services, interconnection, and reciprocal landing rights (cited in Baker, 1960, p. 440). Operating the world's cables under an international trusteeship would help dismantle the barriers to communication that had divided the world (cited in Baker, 1960, p. 433; Rogers, 1922b, p. 144).

Rogers's central objective was to bring about a general flow of news "in all directions," which required adequate interconnecting facilities and low press rates (Rogers, 1922b, p. 147). Underneath this idea lay the well-accepted notion of communications networks as "highways of thought and commerce," which constituted "the world's neural system" (Rogers, 1922b, p. 144). Bringing the world together via improved communications, however, was the idealistic element of a plan that had an instrumental side. Rogers's newspaper experience and service with the propaganda agency positioned him to see communications networks, wired or otherwise, as the material underpinnings for the public dissemination of American ideas. Rather than making cable communications more responsive to the communication needs of the broad global public, "a world-wide freedom for news" would ease the constraints on American propaganda (cited in Baker, 1960, p. 429). With American communications dependent on British infrastructure and with British communications shored up by preferential treatment, spreading news from an American point of view had been expensive (Aitken, 1985, p. 264). Direct communication would fix the problem of exorbitant transmission rates for American news while reducing British control overall.

Liberal internationalist ideas therefore did not obscure American interests. While in public debates the multilateralism of the League was cast as the opposite of the national interest, it was simply an alternative approach to realizing it. President Wilson reassured the American public that the economic strength of the United States made it "the senior partner" in the organization (Brewer, 2009, p. 84). Similarly, the idea of an international trusteeship was not to disadvantage the United States, a rising world power. Instead of thwarting monopolies of any nationality, it was aimed squarely at weakening Britain's position (cf. Winseck & Pike, 2007). On the subject of decreasing British control, the State Department's liberal internationalist vision dovetailed with naval policymakers' brand of realism. It was the diplomats' approach to the specifics that naval policymakers would come to reject.

Rogers's views on American interests were most apparent from the clear distinction he made in his recommendations for cables under American sovereignty and those not subject to it. A closer analysis of Rogers's plan for the Pacific, based on his memoranda before, during, and after the Peace Conference, reveals that he preferred nationalization—government ownership of the cables—for ensuring direct communication between the United States and its possessions. To lay the groundwork for a larger role in the Pacific, Rogers recommended that the U.S. government purchase the Commercial Pacific Cable, which connected the United States with Hawaii, the Philippines, and continental Asia.[7] British cable companies were allegedly interested in the company—a suspicion that would later be confirmed—resulting in "extortionate" rates of over one dollar per word (cited in Baker, 1960, p. 439). Significantly, Rogers did not propose to "internationalize" *this* cable but instead wanted the U.S. government to buy it outright.

Rogers did not propose his trusteeship model for the privately owned transatlantic cable linking New York to the Portuguese islands of the Azores either. Instead, he emphasized America's claim to the portion of the cable lying within the territorial waters of the United States and sought to reverse Britain's decision integrating this cable into the British system. If the cable were returned to its original location, the United States could connect to it and lay its own cables to Europe. "For this latter purpose," Rogers wrote to Wilson, "it is required that the exclusive landing rights for the Azores held by a British company should be cancelled" (cited in Baker, 1960, p. 436). Exclusive landing rights essentially gave control over access to the Azores for cable communication purposes to Britain and locked this cable into the British system. For the United States to increase its influence on the transatlantic circuit, this had to change. Moreover, Rogers suggested, the British would need to agree "not to exercise any supervision or scrutiny over messages" (cited in Baker, 1960, p. 436). This was a clear reference to the concern of American businessmen that British surveillance deprived them of business opportunities and to the growing suspicion among American policymakers that even their own communications were not immune from prying eyes (Winkler, 2008, pp. 127–130).

Nationalization, however, did not work for cable communication with "the principal countries of the world" because, even in the best of circumstances, only one of a cable's two termini landed on American soil.[8] The former Emden-Yap cable that Japan had diverted proved to be especially challenging. Since Yap had been a German colony before the war and was now occupied by Japan, the United States had no territorial claim on either end of the cable. It was precisely for such cables that Rogers's framework of international trusteeship was designed. No matter how much it was twisted, a pure public service logic could not explain why the United States or Britain, separately or jointly, should participate in linking Asia to the outside world. The proposal for an international trusteeship worked on the structural level of network control, severing the connection between control over territory and control over the cables when control over territory did not favor the United States.

Rogers's recommendations about internationalizing the Emden-Yap cable fit into a broader vision for an expanded American presence in the Pacific. As American policymakers began to prioritize the Far East, the Open Door policy in 1900 declared China open to all powers, signaling an independent American role in East Asian politics (Herring, 2008, p. 334). Britain's decline had brought about a multipolar world with clearly delineated spheres of influence, which protected geopolitical rivals from each other. With only one ocean it needed to control, Japan was developing naval dominance in the Pacific (Andelman, 2007, p. 279). Japanese policymakers sought to turn Asia into their country's sphere of influence, calling for a Japanese Monroe Doctrine fashioned after the American concept (Andelman, 2007, pp. 281, 261). Meanwhile, Rogers envisioned the United States establishing connections to the Philippines and French Indochina, correcting the problem identified by Postmaster General Albert S. Burleson that the United States was connected to the world on one side only. At the same time, the Navy Department pressed for "a commanding superiority in the Pacific" to meet the challenge of Japanese expansion (cited in Bönker, 2012, p. 57).[9]

That the international trusteeship proposal was simply meant to ward off Japanese control over the Emden-Yap cable is apparent from the recommendations Rogers prepared in case joint ownership and operation was rejected at the conference. In the absence of joint ownership, the Yap cable should be turned over to the Netherlands. If this did not work, the conference should compel Japan "to grant cable landings on Japanese territory; to agree to exchange business with all cable and radio administrations on an equal basis and to cancel any exclusive landing rights or privileges that Japan may have in Continental Asia" (cited in Baker, 1960, p. 440). The alternative to internationalization was to force Japan to open access to its territory, a plan that Japanese policymakers were likely to resist.

The international trusteeship proposal may have had public service overtones, but when and how it was deployed points to a hierarchy of three policy principles that make the most sense in a geopolitical context. Government ownership of cables, the internationalization of cables, and reciprocal landing rights formed a continuum from the most desirable to the least desirable alternatives on the road to direct communication. Even though the ownership of a single cable or a group of cables was "not especially significant," Rogers wrote to President Wilson, British cable companies dominated the business (cited in Baker, 1960, p. 444). Control over the entire system of cables was no small matter, and the international trusteeship model was a step toward extricating the United States from this arrangement.

As the alternatives for postwar control over the Emden-Yap cable reveal, American policymakers resorted to the principle of reciprocal landing rights only when the international trusteeship model failed to gain any traction. Reciprocal landing rights referred to mutual access to the territory of the other country: a British company seeking to land a cable on the shores of the United States had to allow American companies to land cables on British-controlled territory. Reciprocity was the policy of the underdog and was certainly superior to exclusive landing rights in the hands of companies registered in a geopolitical rival, but it was inferior to the two other alternatives because it left the status quo intact. To advance under this arrangement, the United States needed its own strong and independent cable companies, which were in short supply. Continuing private management of the world's cables meant that most of them would still be controlled by British interests.

Thus, America's geopolitical interests and the global public interest converged in the liberal internationalist case against private ownership. The international trusteeship proposal was set up as an alternative to a commercial monopoly. Liberal internationalists attributed the "haphazard" development of the world's communications networks to the role that private interests had played in network development and argued that it had to be corrected in the interest of "the general good of humanity" (cited in Baker, 1960, p. 431).[10] "The practice of the United States—it can scarcely be called a policy—has been to leave the establishment and conduct of international communications services to private enterprise," Rogers noted derisively (Rogers, 1922b, p. 156). As a consequence, respect for private property rights thwarted intergovernmental actions "along broad and democratic lines."[11] International trusteeship, on the other hand, represented a strike against private ownership, and cable companies, regardless of their place of registration, opposed it.[12]

Between March and May 1919, American diplomats drew on Rogers's recommendations to challenge their allies' decision to keep the cables they had diverted and incorporated into their systems. The following fall and winter, between October 1920 and February 1921, the powers would gather for a Preliminary Conference to discuss setting up a Universal

Electrical Communications Union on the model of the Universal Postal Union. Months later, between November 1921 and February 1922, some of the same delegates would also participate in the Washington Disarmament Conference, which sought to bring about an agreement on naval building programs while addressing control over the external communications of China, among others. These early conferences were central to shaping the postwar order in global communications.

At Versailles, the other powers were quick to grasp the geopolitical significance of the trusteeship proposal. When President Wilson tried to put the matter on the agenda, Arthur Balfour, negotiating for Britain, suggested that the proposal would require such an extensive overhaul of the world's cable system that it would be best discussed at a later conference. The delegates then turned to the narrow question of whether the former German cables could be returned to Germany. The British delegation quickly rejected Wilson's recommendation of a temporary trusteeship of these cables by the five Allied and Associated Powers. All references to joint ownership and administration were deleted (Aitken, 1985, pp. 276–277). The cables were then, at least informally, part of the spoils of war and would remain the property of the powers that had taken control of them.

A few months later, the Committee of Imperial Defence (C.I.D.) instructed the British delegation to the 1920 Preliminary Conference to refuse to agree to anything in the nature of "internationalization" of cables if it meant more than "the joint ownership of any two Governments of cables connecting their respective territories."[13] At the conference, in turn, the other powers were unresponsive to the argument that America's selfless help during the war had brought nothing but disadvantage to it. When, in 1922, Rogers summarized the accomplishments of the conference, the powers that had diverted the cables were still in possession of them (Rogers, 1922b, p. 150).

Though the State Department's plan for a reorganization of the world's cables failed, diplomats were excited about the proposal for a Universal Electrical Communications Union, which would combine the existing telegraph and radiotelegraph conventions. As the Navy Department delved deeper and deeper into matters of foreign policy, however, its plans for global communications took a different direction.

Intermodal ("Type") Competition

The idea for a conference to consider all international aspects of communication by telegraphy, telephone, cable, wireless telegraphy, and wireless telephone emerged from the American delegation to the Inter-Allied Radiotelegraphic Commission and was incorporated in the EU-F-GB-I protocol, so named after the French abbreviations of the participating countries (Aitken, 1985, p. 331).[14] The objective of the conference was phrased in the language of telegraph regulation as "providing the entire world with adequate facilities for international communication on a fair and equitable basis."[15] During the sessions, the proposal by the British delegation for a joint convention for cables and radio would take center stage.

The British proposal would significantly affect the United States, since it had a mixed record on international conventions. The United States did not join any telegraph conventions, but it did ratify the 1906 and 1912 international radio conventions. The "amalgamation" of the radio and telegraph conventions would eventually take place in 1932 and would create the International Telecommunication Union. During the 1920s, however, commercial interests in the United States opposed a joint convention, while the State Department supported it, opening the way for naval policymakers to exercise their influence.

British policymakers sought a joint convention as a way to secure additional leverage for the Post Office when negotiating for British cable companies about domestic distribution facilities in the U.S. market.[16] Shortly before the conference, the C.I.D. suggested that the British delegation should "take any action that may be possible" to persuade the United States to essentially accept international telegraph regulations.[17] When the Inter-Allied Radiotelegraphic Commission approved the EU-F-GB-I protocol, RCA did not yet exist, and the United States went along. By the early 1920s, however, leading trade associations such as the National Foreign Trade Council and the U.S. Chamber of Commerce had sided with RCA, recommending that American delegations to international communication conferences should treat cable and radio as separate fields of activity (Schwoch, 1990, p. 62). In spring 1920, a broad conference of industry and government officials agreed, leading commercial interests to conclude that they had achieved an agreement on government policy in their favor.[18]

The Preliminary Conference opened on October 8 and adjourned in December, resuming in early 1921.[19] RCA's executives counted the company among the "American interests" the delegation was supposed to represent, but they privately worried that the British government's influence would prevail. They expected to be put in touch with the negotiations at a phase when they had a chance to influence them, wanted copies of drafts, and sought to convince the American delegation to present a separate radio telegraph convention or at least withdraw from consideration of the British draft.[20]

Rogers received the brunt of RCA's demands and responded by underscoring the importance of "a general working accord" among countries.[21] A joint convention, he hoped, would pave the way to the Universal Electrical Communications Union, which would handle all aspects of global communications under one roof. Bypassing the thorny problem of telegraph conventions, Rogers compared the contemporary communications landscape to the situation that existed before the adoption of the Universal Postal Convention, when the United States initiated policy coordination worldwide.[22] A twentieth-century universal convention combining visual, radio, cable, and landline matters would put in place uniform service regulations to govern messages passing through a number of different networks via numerous countries (Rogers, 1922b, p. 153).

In Rogers's mind, the primary relationships of the world took place between states that accommodated each other even as they competed for preeminence, while private companies were subordinate to them. After all, the world's telegraph and cable networks were largely government operated and did not look kindly on demands based on obvious self-interest (Rogers, 1922b, p. 157). The United States had to give way on some things, such as a joint cable and radio convention, to develop the influence to work on behalf of its companies in other situations.[23] Rogers now advised RCA to find its place within the web of relationships woven by state interests. Foremost among the foreign powers was Britain, who, Rogers noted, was "at once the financial and commercial center of the world, the cable center, and the principal news center" (Rogers, 1922b, p. 147).

Owen D. Young, the first chairman of RCA, couldn't have disagreed more. With false modesty, he offered his "perhaps amateurish" point of view on geopolitical matters, expressing support for a separate radio convention. However, Young pitched his argument at a more general level, setting out the recurrent theme in RCA's communications to policymakers during the balance of the decade—that the time was right for leadership in global communications. Far from acknowledging the primacy of London in the broad field, Young saw two centers. Perhaps Britain's dominance of the cables was not going to change any time soon, but in radio communications the United States was "the normal radio center of the world, or will be such." [24] This was because most European countries wanted "to get through by a direct route within their own control to America."[25] Radio, it was commonly held, had the potential to bypass British cable control. Sweden and Norway, in particular, intended to establish contact as soon as possible (Winkler, 2008, p. 250). Barely a year old, RCA wondered whether the United States was in fact serious about becoming the center of world communications rather than being content with its position as "an outlying link in foreign communication systems."[26] A separate radio convention, Young pointed out, was necessary for a central role.[27]

The Navy Department, under the guidance of Commander Hooper, held the same views. Josephus Daniels and William Benson, who had backed government ownership, left office in 1919, but Hooper gained an important ally in Admiral William Bullard, his former boss, who was appointed director of naval communications (DNC) that year. Between 1919 and 1923, Hooper took charge of the Radio Division in the Bureau of Steam Engineering and continued to rise to ever-greater decision-making authority. In 1928, he became DNC, which made him "the titular as well as the real head of communications."[28]

During the transitional years between British and American global leadership, naval policymakers on both sides of the Atlantic often compared the positions of the two countries in order to better understand their own standing. Size, either of the fleet or of the global network, was an important indicator of national power (O'Brien, 1998, p. 8). After World War I, the Royal Navy was still twice as large as the U.S. Navy, although the latter built more warships between the armistice and the 1921 Washington Disarmament Conference than the rest of the world combined (Beloff, 1970, pp. 331–333). From Britain's perspective, the United States was well on its way to naval superiority, and the only question was how long shrewd diplomacy could forestall this development.

Meanwhile, American naval policymakers were convinced that British policy was driven by its desire to preserve its dominant position in the world system (Challener, 1973, p. 17; Roskill, 1968, p. 24). "The present British policy," the General Board advised the Disarmament Conference, "is to control the markets, the fuel and the communications of the world so that the needs of the empire may always take precedence over the needs of all other political organizations of the world" (cited in O'Brien, 1998, p. 160). The Board also suspected that the British government would even initiate war with the United States to maintain Britain's position, but naval policymakers estimated in 1920 that, based on American capital ships already built or authorized by Congress, the U.S. Navy was already superior in battle forces over Britain and Japan (O'Brien, 1998, p. 155; Schake, 2017, p. 241). The immediate issue for the conference in 1921 was naval parity between the two countries. Britain wanted to achieve parity before the U.S. Navy finished its building program, while the General Board recommended that they finish building and then force Britain to grant parity (Beloff, 1970, p. 332; O'Brien, 1998, p. 160).

In global communications, the U.S. Navy was not this far ahead. An eight-clause communication policy, approved by Secretary of the Navy Edwin Denby in December 1922, directed the Navy "to watch and guard the radio and cable interests of the United States."[29] Naval policymakers considered radiotelegraphy in the context of the cable network and the geographical expansion of either network in relation to changing spheres of influence in the aftermath of the war. Radio was essential for fleet training in peacetime, providing the commander-in-chief with access to his sources of information and to distant detachments of his fleet, but the radio network was still a junior partner in an established system of communications, with submarine cables at its center.[30] American policymakers would have liked to match the size of the British cable network, but Britain's lead was substantial. In 1923, half of the total length of the world's cables was still British, and the United States was just approaching the 25 percent mark (Headrick, 1991, p. 195). Given the undesirably slow decrease of the British lead in cable communications, U.S. naval officers kept their focus on radiotelegraphy. The Navy Department operated 183 shore stations and identified 1921 as "the present approximate international equality in radio."[31] Policymakers now aimed at superiority in radio, which they saw as "a factor of the same order of importance as superiority in numbers, or types, or the trained efficiency of ships."[32]

While the State Department under Rogers set its sights on the cable network, the Navy Department was convinced that the road to autonomy in global communications went through radio. Policymakers in the two departments differed on what radio was for as well as on the relationship between the two networks. Whereas Rogers focused on the dissemination of public information, naval policymakers were looking for a facility to transmit confidential information and never stopped looking at radio as a future part of the Navy's network in wartime. Given the goal of securing the ability to communicate and denying the same to the country's enemies, Rogers's vision of the free flow of information fell short since it dwelt extensively on the former and did nothing for the latter. As for the relationship between cables and radio, Rogers and his circle saw them as complementary technologies. Each had "its own sphere and each will act as a feeder for the other" (cited in Baker, 1960, p. 431). This did not mean, however, that the two technologies were equal. Radio was a backup, "a very valuable additional means of connecting distant parties," Ernest Power, a policymaker in Rogers's circle, pointed out, but one that could not be regarded as a substitute for the cables.[33] The danger from radio was not so much that it would render the cables obsolete but that "hit-or-miss competition may cause capital to hesitate from financing cable extensions" (cited in Baker, 1960, p. 431). The advantage of government ownership, in turn, was that it would ensure the orderly development of each type of communications system (Baker, 1960, p. 432).[34]

Rogers's ideas were very much aligned with the conventional wisdom of the time, which considered radio unreliable because its signals were susceptible to interference, while the submarine cable was superior because of its secrecy (Aitken, 1985, p. 279).[35] Even President Wilson believed this was the case.[36] During the 1920s, however, the Navy Department developed the position that radio technology was superior to the cables, despite the fact that the only technological factor in radio's favor was that it could not be severed in time of war.[37] The security of cables, as the C.I.D. itself had asserted, depended on maritime supremacy, and the country that controlled the sea was able to maintain its own cable communications and interrupt those of its enemies (Headrick, 1994, p. 26). As long as the United States was uncertain about its maritime supremacy, American policymakers had to assume that the British cable system was inviolable.

Operating from a latecomer's position, the Navy Department presupposed an unequal relationship between the two technologies and ranked secrecy below availability. Under contemporary levels of technological development, it was radio that would serve as a feeder to the cable system and not the other way around. A global public utility with integrated cable and radio links could not help but disadvantage the independent development of radio. The buzzword in the 1920s Navy Department, therefore, was "type competition." It was Hooper's brainchild and was developed out of the conviction that any combination of the cable and radio industries would taint radio with undesirable British influence.[38] "The soundest principle you ever stuck to was that radio should be a competitor of cables and should not join up with them in transoceanic traffic handling," Hooper wrote to RCA, adding, "I've been with you first, last, and all the time on that, and as long as you stick it out we will never be far apart."[39] A few years later, section 17 of the Radio Act of 1927 codified type competition by prohibiting mergers between cable and wireless firms.[40]

Because of the importance naval policymakers accorded to type competition, the Navy Department opposed a joint cable and radio convention, which would reinforce the status of radio as inferior to the cables.[41] Under a joint convention, an officer objected, "radio is very liable to become an auxiliary means of communication, and will be greatly influenced by land wire and cable interests, even to the extent of retarding the development of radio for communication purposes."[42] RCA echoed this sentiment in November 1920, when, the company believed, the American delegation had agreed to an amalgamated convention.[43] In fact, American delegates put a reservation on the record that adherence by the United States would be conditional, depending on the reaction of private companies.[44]

RCA's attorneys received a draft convention for a Universal Electrical Communications Union in spring 1921 and prepared an analysis, which became the basis for the company's campaign before the incoming administration of President Warren G. Harding. Company executives quickly set up meetings with Secretary of Commerce Herbert Hoover and Secretary of State Charles Evans Hughes as soon as the new administration took over.[45] During these meetings, RCA underscored the importance of "a definite national policy" before a further conference was held, and it reiterated the separation of cables and radio as the basis of such a policy.[46] RCA told policymakers that the United States would dominate a radio convention, but it would be dominated by Britain in a joint convention, where the British would use their clout to prevent the development of a worldwide radio system. Executives repeated the point Young had stressed to Rogers, that America's influence in a radio convention was assured, given the desire of smaller countries to communicate directly with the United States.[47] Company executives were quick to deploy both the vocabulary of nationalism and the specific reservation that naval policymakers had about cables; namely, that they could be severed by the enemy.[48] Hoover also found out that Rogers had disregarded commercial interests and pushed for an international agreement "tending toward Government ownership of wires, cables and radio."[49]

RCA blasted the proposed Universal Electrical Communications Union as an example of internationalism and rejected Rogers's postal precedent as inapplicable to conditions in America, where facilities were under private control.[50] Company executives compared the proposed convention to telegraph conventions and the League of Nations.[51] In particular, the "super-commission" policymakers planned was strikingly similar to the Assembly of the League.[52] Because of these structural features, nationalism was completely subordinate to "what many believe to be utopian views of internationalism" in both organizations.[53]

Perhaps not surprisingly, Rogers was not impressed. The Radio Corporation's memorandum was "99.99/100% inane," he pointed out, scoffing at the purity of American nationalism manifest in the 100 percent American ideal. If American companies went out trying to "rape the world" instead of fitting into it, reprisals would quickly follow (cited in Winseck & Pike, 2007, p. 270). Not from the United States, of course, whose delegation Rogers regarded as little more than "spectators" at the conference, because of their lack of authority over private companies. Rather, the danger was that the four other powers could agree among themselves to the disadvantage of the United States (Rogers, 1922b, p. 152).

The connection RCA made to the League of Nations was a blunt, and ultimately successful, attempt to tie the proposal to a lost cause. By this time, the Senate Foreign Relations Committee had turned against the ratification of the Treaty of Versailles, largely because the League came to be perceived as the embodiment of universalist ideals. Campaigns against the organization predicted increased immigration or even a communist takeover as consequences of Wilson's super state (Brewer, 2009, p. 82; Herring, 2008, p. 430). In March 1920, the Senate voted against ratification, even with the American reservations that essentially gutted the treaty (Herring, 2008, p. 433). The League of Nations was thus set up without the United States, and the country concluded a separate peace with Germany during the summer of the following year.

By championing the cause of a separate cable and radio convention, RCA was riding a rising tide. During the new administration, government opinion began to crystallize around the idea that it would take a long time to offset Britain's superiority in the cable industry and that it would be best to emphasize radio. In early April 1921, Foreign Trade Advisor Prentiss Gilbert suggested exactly this course of action (Schwoch, 1990, p. 95).

RCA's memorandum soon found its way to President Harding's desk and was included in Harding's speech to a joint session of Congress. Harding called for active encouragement of the extension of American owned and operated radio services around the world and emphasized direct communication, free from foreign intermediation. The speech followed RCA's memo virtually word for word (Schwoch, 1990, pp. 65–66). Far from gaining control over the direction of radio policy, however, RCA was successful in its opposition to the joint convention because company executives aligned their vision with the Navy's definition of the national interest (cf. Schwoch, 1990). In the wake of widespread internal and external opposition to the State Department's plans, U.S. expansion in the 1920s would proceed via "a 100 percent American" corporation in radiotelegraphy.

Cartels

When RCA was incorporated, policymakers saw it as the solution to a long-standing problem. A few years later, the company would start to look like the problem itself, for two interrelated reasons. The first had to do with the identity of the company, which dovetailed with policymakers' continued interest in tying MNCs involved in international traffic handling to the United States. Second, policymakers wondered about RCA's plans for expansion: through what methods would RCA expand, and in what way, if any, did its arrangements with other companies further the interests of the United States?

As a private telecommunications service provider, RCA aimed at control over a share of the global radio traffic. In so doing, it went down the well-trodden path of cooperating with companies registered in other countries. In a "hard-core" international cartel, service providers from at least two different countries cooperate to control prices or allocate shares in world markets (Evenett, Levenstein, & Suslow, 2001, p. 1222). The vast majority of cartels collapse within a decade, in part because of the difficulty inherent in coordinating the behavior of cartel partners, preventing cheating, and blocking entry by noncartel firms (Levenstein & Suslow, 2006, p. 44). Yet, British cable cartels had survived for decades because control over traffic was undergirded by control over the network, which, in turn, required control over territory. Among others, cartels solved the problem of natural monopoly by dividing the world among companies that had secured exclusive landing rights.

That some arrangement would have to be made for radio had been apparent during the negotiations between General Electric, Marconi interests, and the Navy Department that led to the formation of RCA. Nally, the general manager of American Marconi, was anxious to find out whether the new company intended to establish stations in countries such as France or Belgium, where British Marconi had already set up stations.[54] Yes, that was the plan, policymakers replied. If so, was there any provision made for "taking care of" Marconi or Pan American?[55] When Nally discovered that there was no such plan, he told Young, then GE's chief counsel, that it would be difficult to establish stations in countries "where concessions had already been given to other companies."[56] RCA would need to find its place in the web of international corporate commitments that encircled the world.

The fact that American Marconi was part of a multinational corporation had shaped its strategy of expansion. Since the company had no rights to British Marconi's patents outside the United States, the parent and the subsidiary jointly controlled the transatlantic circuit until 1917, when the Navy Department imposed wartime control (Aitken, 1985, p. 424). Despite geographic proximity in the Western Hemisphere, American Marconi never sought to establish stations in Canada or Latin America. Canadian Marconi and the various Marconi concessionaires in Latin America, including Pan American (see chapter 5), were responsible for working the Marconi patents in the region. Had RCA simply taken over the existing rights of American Marconi, the position of the United States in global communications would have improved only via the transfer of company shares to American citizens.

RCA had both the technology and the capital to expand, but what would constitute acceptable forms of American control over parts of its network outside U.S. territory, and how much of it could be obtained, would be determined in the next few years. One avenue for expansion was to establish stations abroad, but the Navy Department ruled out this option. Instead, Hooper considered traffic agreements, or contracts with foreign companies and telegraph administrations, to be best suited for preserving the independence of national radio systems.[57] Hooper envisioned sovereign countries conducting their radio communications at arm's length, collecting traffic in their territory and handing it over at the border, so to speak, to a company from another country. The 1919 draft government charter between the Navy and GE, which would have authorized a commercial monopoly for RCA, specifically gave the Navy Department veto power over both the sale of company apparatus for longwave communications and over traffic agreements with foreign companies (Navy contract, in Aitken, 1985, pp. 565, 567). Naval policymakers therefore did not aspire to the Western Union model of control in all markets. Traffic agreements meant that American autonomy was safeguarded and foreign influence was minimized. In the early 1920s, the Navy Department asked both RCA and International Telephone and Telegraph (ITT) to stick to traffic agreements and refrain from direct investment. RCA obeyed, but ITT ignored the suggestion, laying the groundwork for a future clash with the Navy.[58] By working through RCA, however, the U.S. government subjected itself to the rules of transnational corporate expansion and would be forced to read national advancement from cartel structure.

The Principal Agreement, negotiated by RCA and British Marconi, divided the world into American, British, and "neutral" territories, as if companies in these two countries alone determined the fate of global communications. The world traffic agreement regulated the distribution of traffic and profits along certain routes, blocked entry on the part of nonmembers, and provided guarantees of exclusive territories.[59] This arrangement followed in the wake of the Versailles Peace Conference, where British delegates proposed that the world could be viewed as a series of Monroe Doctrines, where each of the main powers would be responsible for its own area of primary interest (Beloff, 1970, p. 269). Although American policymakers publicly condemned geopolitical spheres of influence, that was all everybody thought about.

The heart of the agreement was the exchange of patent rights for the territories of the United States and the British Empire. Patents were key to control over technology, but no company possessed enough of them to provide a complete system, domestically or around the world (Howeth, 1963, p. 360; Hughes, 1969, pp. 63–64).[60] Under the agreement, North America was classified as exclusive RCA territory, the British Empire and all its colonies belonged to British Marconi, and the rest of the world became neutral territory where both companies could compete for traffic. Yet, the exceptions are telling. Godfrey Isaacs, managing director of British Marconi, did not get the patent rights for the whole Empire that he wanted. The transatlantic circuit was unique. Canada, in the words of Albert Davis, GE's patent attorney, "was too close to the United States" and warranted special treatment.[61]

Canada, the part of the British Empire that shared the longest border with the United States, had long occupied a unique position in Anglo-American relations. At the beginning of the twentieth century, Britain effectively released Canada to the United States without informing its colony that it would not spend "one man or one pound" defending it (Friedberg, 1988, p. 198). In radio negotiations fifteen years later, however, British executives rejected GE's demands for "the whole Western Hemisphere," meaning transferring British Marconi's holdings in Canadian Marconi to GE.[62] Instead, GE received assurances that Canadian Marconi would not "invade the Radio Corporation's territory, nor solicit traffic to or from it."[63] The Canadian General Electric and RCA together were to acquire approximately half the shares British Marconi held in Canadian Marconi.[64] While localized traffic would prove untenable, RCA remained a major stockholder in Canadian Marconi, prompting the British government to open negotiations in 1927 about regaining British control.[65] As a result of its stock holdings, RCA therefore had a chance to influence the policies of Canadian Marconi, something American Marconi could never dream of. The Principal Agreement also transferred operating control over South American transoceanic communications to RCA,[66] and naval policymakers looked forward to the 1920s with optimism.[67]

The AEFG Consortium

For naval policymakers, controlling hemispheric communications—the Monroe Doctrine for radio—had long been a central objective.[68] Though Latin American countries pivoted toward the United States after World War I, American control over traffic between Latin America and the United States, let alone between Latin America and the outside world, would encounter practical difficulties. Importantly, the transatlantic circuit did not require investment by RCA on European soil. In Latin America and Asia, however, patent sharing would be complicated by the necessity of acquiring concessions on foreign territory. RCA quickly reopened the prewar American Marconi circuits with Britain and Japan and concluded traffic agreements with Norway, Germany, and France, all within a year, but it made no visible progress in Latin America.[69]

Under the Principal Agreement, RCA would have shared ownership with British Marconi in a soon to be established South American Communications Company (SACCO). RCA would have appointed five of the company's seven directors and would have owned half the shares in SACCO (Aitken, 1985, p. 406).[70] RCA's patents for Central America, in turn, went to United Fruit when that company joined the 1920 patent cross-licensing agreement between RCA, AT&T, and Westinghouse (Hughes, 1969, p. 110). That the Principal Agreement was largely inadequate, however, became apparent when Telefunken formed a subsidiary in Buenos Aires and erected a station in an attempt to build a chain of wireless stations across the Western Hemisphere (Winkler, 2009, p. 852). By 1921, RCA and British Marconi had broadened the tent to include Telefunken and a French corporation in the future AEFG consortium, so named after the French names of the participating countries. After various attempts on the part of participants to bypass each other, the stage was set for a four-party agreement (see Hughes, 1969, pp. 99–100).[71]

Under the cartel agreement, British Marconi, Telefunken, and the French Compagnie de Télégraphie Sans Fil pooled their concessions in the South American republics for communication with the outside world into a trusteeship that held the rights for the four parties in equal shares (Aitken, 1985, pp. 490–493). Duplication of stations would involve "a wasteful use of the relatively small number of bands of wavelengths available for wireless communications of the world," the AEFG traffic agreement announced, as well as an outlay "out of all proportion to the volume of traffic which can reasonably be expected."[72] The powers now shared control over a single company that would have national stations in particular countries. AEFG would take over the existing German station in Colombia and strip it of any markers of the Telefunken brand. All parts and equipment would now be marked "International Combined System," blending the efforts of the German company with those of the others.[73]

Analysis of the traffic agreement, however, reveals that the AEFG consortium was not simply an example of the collaborative model of empire, which emphasizes private regulation and collaboration among geopolitical rivals, but rather the *outcome* of geopolitical rivalry (cf. Hogan, 1991; cf. Hugill, 1999, p. 122; cf. Winseck & Pike, 2007, p. 104). With a concession in Argentina and a station on the ground in Colombia, Telefunken executives needed assurances that they would not be outvoted. These worries made it possible for Young to push for a neutral American as chairman, who would not be affiliated with the company (Hughes, 1969, p. 99).[74] Each company would appoint two officers to the board, but these officers did not have the same amount of influence over company policy. Both the two British trustees and the two German trustees had three votes, while the American and the French trustees had two votes each.[75] The American chairman would have no vote, but he could break a tie.

Most important, the votes were assigned *to maximize the chance of a tie*. If the British added their three votes to the two votes of the French against the two other parties with a similar combination of votes, the chairman would have to step in. More surprisingly, three plus three, as in the case of the British and the Germans voting together, also added up to five.[76] This was because the votes changed in value depending on whether the trustees from two different countries voted "in the same sense" or "in contrary senses." Thus, even the two firms with the largest number of votes could not avoid a decision by the chairman. Moreover, whenever any three companies outvoted a fourth, the minority could appeal to the chairman, who had the power to cancel the resolution agreed to.[77] This addressed Telefunken's concerns and enhanced the power of the chairman at the same time, which meant that RCA was gaining ground via the cartel arrangement. Meanwhile, Latin American countries were left without representation on the AEFG board, even though the consortium would have 60 percent ownership in the national companies that would conduct the external communications of their territories (Aitken, 1985, p. 491).[78]

As these negotiations went forward, the Navy was largely out of the loop. When Hooper paid a visit to RCA in September 1921, he found out that Young had sailed to Europe to meet with the representatives of the three other firms.[79] A few months earlier, RCA had taken an ownership interest in Westinghouse, its only competitor in manufacturing radio sets, without running the deal by the Navy. Hooper's advice that Young should "not get in too far on any of their big combination schemes" ignored the possibility that RCA would fully embrace these schemes as the best solution to the problem of natural monopoly.[80] Now Hooper began to look at RCA as "a wayward son" that may "thrive and make money, but it is nothing for us to be proud of."[81]

In an attempt to convince policymakers that the newly formed AEFG trusteeship realized the Monroe Doctrine, Young pointed to the power of the chairman.[82] He wrote to Admiral Bullard, "It is impossible for any action to be taken in South America without the approval either of the two

American members of the Board or the Chairman."[83] Young omitted that the consortium divided the total traffic between the four parties equally, even though most of the traffic was directed toward the United States.[84] In effect, RCA established itself in a region where it didn't even have a concession, let alone a station, but it gave up revenue in return (for perspectives on the consortium, see Aitken, 1985, p. 490; Howeth, 1963; Hughes, 1969, pp. 101, 103; Winseck & Pike, 2007, p. 289).

Naval policymakers, however, concluded that the AEFG trusteeship was not "a bona fide American interest" and did not deserve the assistance and protection of the United States.[85] Hooper took the view that the Germans led in South American radio, the French came second, and the British had dropped to third place.[86] What of the United States? "Apparently we are not in the class with our foreign rivals," Hooper commented bitterly.[87] By contrast, Assistant Secretary of Commerce Herbert Hoover favored government support for the consortium as the "best arrangement" that American interests could get (cited in Hogan, 1991, p. 144). Under Hoover's influence, the Navy eventually endorsed RCA's participation in the consortium, hoping that a bona fide American interest might develop in the future (Aitken, 1985, p. 493; Hogan, 1991, p. 145). Years later, Captain Hooper, serving as director of naval communications, would list the arrangement under "failures" because RCA had to share control of the region with foreign interests, saying, "the foreigners [have] sewed up the concessions."[88] The experience with the consortium taught policymakers that American expansion via commercial companies was far from government ownership in different institutional garb.[89] How best to understand the impact of international cartels on the geopolitical position of the United States had to be tackled head-on. RCA's attempt to conclude a similar cartel for the Pacific would provide policymakers with additional food for thought.

The Failure of the Pacific Consortium

Fresh from what then appeared to be the success of the AEFG consortium, Young advocated a similar arrangement for the Pacific. All nations with an interest in the Far East participated in the Washington Disarmament Conference, which took up the fate of China's external communications for the first time. By the end of the conference, the United States had widened its access to the region. Secretary of State Charles Evans Hughes tied the naval agreement to the abrogation of the 1902 Anglo-Japanese alliance, which had sanctioned Japanese expansion in Asia and secured Japan's undeviating support to Britain at Allied conferences (O'Brien, 1998, p. 169). The Navy Department was less than pleased, since the gain in the U.S. sphere of influence came at the expense of a suitable agreement on naval parity. The February 1922 naval agreement halted new capital ship construction, secured for the United States the right to equality with Great Britain in such ships, and replaced the Anglo-Japanese alliance with a toothless nonaggression pact (O'Brien, 1998, p. 169). In effect, debt-ridden Britain was forced to choose between the United States and its former ally because it saw no chance of winning an arms race against the United States (Schake, 2017, p. 251). British policymakers granted access to the Far East to the United States and secured naval parity *before* the U.S. Navy finished its building program (for different interpretations about the impact of the agreement, see Beloff, 1970, p. 335; O'Brien, 1998, pp. 171–172; Schake, 2017, pp. 248–253). The Navy Department was left in the dark about the State Department's plans until just before the conference opened (O'Brien, 1998, p. 161). In matters of global communications, it would take much longer for the United States to register any gains in the Far East.

RCA timed the opening of its powerful Long Island station for the week before the conference, pleading for the U.S. government's support of its plans for the Pacific. As President Harding's message calling for American owned and operated wireless service around the world circled the earth, Young's public speech reinforced what he had told Rogers in private. While Britain was the cable center, America was "the real center" of radio "because every country desires to get direct communication with the United States."[90] His plan, laid out in an open letter to James Sheffield, one of RCA's directors, recommended that the Americans, English, French, Germans, and Japanese should all transfer their concessions, rights, and property in and for China to a board of trustees.[91] Like the AEFG consortium, the proposed cartel was a solution to the problem of natural monopoly, Young would soon write to Admiral Bullard, adding that investment in China was bound to be precarious if "several stations [were] built where the capacity of only one [was] required to do the business."[92]

"Cartels, being secretive organizations, rarely announce their formation," economists note in reference to private cartels (Evenett, Levenstein, & Suslow, 2001, p. 1226), but the proposed Pacific consortium could not be fully private, because companies from other countries, most importantly from Britain and Japan, had preceded RCA in the market and the United States competed for influence in a region where the other powers were in a stronger position than in Latin America. Young called on Sheffield to use his letter "as will best serve the interests of the United States as those [were] the interests of the Radio Corporation of America."[93] The extent to which governments could set aside their differences would be central to the success of RCA's proposal.

That RCA positioned itself as the problem solver in a situation where it started with no rights whatsoever was hard to miss. When negotiating the Principal Agreement, company executives recognized the exclusive concession British Marconi had obtained and agreed that RCA would not compete in China.[94] If RCA was interested in anything, it was a monopoly over *the American end* of Chinese-American communications.[95] Politically, however, such a limited goal would be impossible. Executives soon got word that neither the U.S. government nor the U.S. Chamber of Commerce would tolerate it if American communications went through Japan.[96] Direct communications between the United States and Shanghai were required, which meant some authority over the Chinese end of the U.S.-China circuit as well.

If RCA seemed unwilling to compete, Federal Telegraph was a shell of a company, having sold its patents and stations to the Navy. Since the firm had effectively disbanded, it did not participate in the 1920 patent cross-licensing agreement and did not get a license to use RCA's patents (Hughes, 1969, p. 110), but the Federal arc was widely used in the Navy, and stations relying on that technology could readily establish connections. Federal's president came out of retirement to promise direct communication "without interference or aid of Japan or British interests."[97] By the time Young laid out his plan for a wireless cartel, it had become apparent that the United States had weak alternatives for expansion in the Pacific.

The State Department selected the Federal Telegraph contract as a test case for its Open Door policy, insisting on equal economic opportunity in China for all powers.[98] In January 1921, amid allegations of bribery, the Federal Telegraph Company of California received a concession from the Chinese government to connect China to the United States via wireless. The contract involved direct investment: Federal would build five stations, including the main station in Shanghai (Krysko, 2011, p. 17). Since Federal requested financing from the Chinese government, it had to show full title to the patents on all equipment installed. In spring 1921, the Navy agreed to return

Federal's patents to the company (Aitken, 1985, p. 299; Krysko, 2011, p. 22). Even though Federal was still negotiating to obtain financing, the State Department approved the contract in March 1921 (Hughes, 1969, p. 141). In September, Federal signed a supplement that made the January contract exclusive with regard to messages from China to the United States but not the other way around (Krysko, 2011, p. 25). Under this arrangement, Federal would handle traffic out of China, but American customers could file radiograms intended for China with RCA in the United States as well.

American control was now commonly understood as control in the hands of bona fide American companies, but the three aspects of network control on the tactical level were divided between RCA and Federal. Both companies controlled patents for their respective technologies, but Federal had a concession in China, while RCA's initial optimism with regard to obtaining one had quickly dissipated. RCA, on the other hand, was able to raise capital more successfully in the United States than could Federal, which had the reputation of setting up companies to sell them rather than actually work them.[99] This had become clear the previous March, when American bankers in a consortium set up to finance projects for the Pacific refused to market the Chinese government securities that Federal was planning to use to finance construction.[100] Since RCA's stations on the Pacific Coast did not work to capacity, the bankers doubted that the Federal venture would secure enough traffic to pay its way (cited in Rossi, 1985, p. 44). Under natural monopoly theory, the capital aspect of network control favored RCA.

Historians of American expansion established long ago that the United States was simultaneously opposed to spheres of influence while working to create one for itself. Policymakers relied on the Open Door policy to denounce monopolies in global communications only when the United States wanted to open a market (Rosenberg, 1982, p. 89). A central aspect of the Open Door policy was the principle of nondiscrimination, which the State Department applied to all industries across the board. When it came to control over global communications circuits, however, there was a wrinkle in this approach. The policy of the Open Door clashed with the emphasis of natural monopoly theory on a single station in a territory. Was the United States better served by treating its commercial radiotelegraph companies equally, which meant duplicate stations, or by supporting the monopoly of one?

Meanwhile, wrangling over wireless in the Pacific was shaping up to be "the biggest post-war drama in international communications" (Yang, 2010,

p. 64). The specifics of the negotiations, which would take up the entire decade, fall outside this chapter (see Winseck & Pike, 2007, pp. 299–303; Zajácz, 2015). Suffice it to say that both Britain and Japan, whose companies had already secured concessions, wanted a say in which company or combination of companies would conduct the external communications of China (Krysko, 2011, pp. 22–25). Their maneuvers took place against the backdrop of growing Japanese influence in the region. The fall of the Qing dynasty left China in internal disarray: warlords ruled its 400 million people, while its heads of state and cabinets changed rapidly. Japan annexed Korea and part of China, acquiring control over both the vital functions of the Chinese government and Chinese railroad lines at one point (Andelman, 2007, p. 256; Krysko, 2011, pp. 20–23). It was the Japanese government that operated the Chinese end of the cable connecting Nagasaki and Shanghai (Yang, 2010, pp. 235–236). A Japanese trading company received a concession to operate the Chinese end of the U.S.-China circuit with the understanding that the Japanese government could gain control over the company's station in China at any time (Hughes, 1969, p. 141; Yang, 2010, p. 65). The U.S. Navy viewed the concession to the Japanese company as a vehicle that granted a potential adversary "the control of the Pacific Ocean as regards radio communication" (cited in Hughes, 1969, p. 142). Thus, control over the Chinese end of the U.S.-China circuit was geopolitically important, but RCA had to tread lightly to avoid alienating the Japanese government. After all, the U.S.-Japanese circuit had been the first to be established on the Pacific, because the "the principal volume of communications across the Pacific" was with Japan, and this state of affairs was expected to continue.[101]

When the Washington Disarmament Conference took up the matter, the British and the French delegations were quick to accept Young's proposal (Hughes, 1969, p. 143). RCA, however, may have been too busy lining up support abroad to realize that its own government's support was far from certain. Both Rogers and Hooper, the latter now serving as technical adviser to the American delegation, recommended support for Federal, the only independent company they thought the United States could count on (Hughes, 1969, p. 145). This was quite in contrast to the Navy's unwavering support for RCA's monopoly during much of the decade.[102] Federal would watch American interests in China better than the Radio Corporation, Hooper told Senator Elihu Root, a senior American delegate, "because the Radio Corporation covered practically a world-wide field and naturally could give attention to no one locality as they would like to do so on account of the number of localities they had to cover."[103] As naval policymakers sought to align RCA's wide-ranging expansion with the American sphere of influence, they found it difficult to see how international cartel arrangements could benefit the United States.

Through the AEFG controversy and the proposed Pacific radio cartel, naval officers grappled with the influence of international expansion on the national interest. "In any international monopolistic combination," the Navy Department spelled out for RCA, "the interests of any one government must be compromised with those of the other governments, and whichever government is most efficient and aggressive for the moment gains important advantages above the others."[104] It did not help matters that RCA's share of ownership in the proposed consortium would be at most 25 percent (Hughes, 1969, p. 150).

Instead of the cartel route, Hooper recommended a division of spheres between Federal and RCA. Federal would get the west coast of the United States, South America, and the Far East, and RCA was free to compete everywhere else.[105] Between monopoly and duplication, the latter of which also seemed to provide insufficient control, Hooper supported the former, even as he was not necessarily wedded to RCA. Hooper's recommendations would soon surface as the Navy's policy toward radio (Howeth, 1963), testifying to the conviction that uncontested American control over a limited territory was worth more than murky control over a large territory. This approach, in turn, went against the recommendation of the interdepartmental task force that had prepared the instructions for the American delegation. Policymakers in that forum agreed to consolidation but limited the cartel to American members by recommending that the principal commercial radio interests would "jointly develop" high-power radio in China (Rossi, 1985, p. 42).

Not only would RCA be excluded from a joint venture with Federal under the Navy's plan, but naval policymakers would have made it very difficult for the company to expand (cf. Rossi, 1985, p. 39). Under Hooper's division of the world, Federal got the territories where the United States was gaining ground geopolitically, while RCA was forced into competition with its cartel partner, British Marconi. When RCA offered assistance to Federal on the condition that RCA would handle the American end of Chinese communication, Secretary of the Navy Edwin Denby swiftly warned them that under no circumstances should their agreement prevent competition in the United States for Chinese traffic.[106]

RCA's attitude toward international cartels signaled to officers familiar with radio policy that company executives did not share the Navy's goals. When Young announced that his main goal was to make the position of the United States in radio "equal to or superior to" that of any other country, naval policymakers cringed (Hughes, 1969, p. 149).[107] They had already achieved equality and were now striving for superiority. This was why the AEFG consortium was received with such disappointment and why the proposal for a Pacific cartel would soon be blocked. Rather than aiming at the "attainment of superiority over foreign companies," naval policymakers concluded, RCA accepted equality as an objective (cited in Rossi, 1985, p. 44).

Predictably, RCA immediately applied to the American delegates and Secretary Hughes to convince them that other countries were on board with the plan.[108] Focusing on America's external communications alone, Young asked that RCA be considered a public service monopoly regulated by the U.S. government, rather than by foreign governments, which was what competition produced. Young called attention to the recently enacted Webb-Pomerene Act, which exempted combinations in the export field from antitrust legislation, and he sought to convince the State Department that America's external communication was "an export product."[109] That the entire purpose of the Webb-Pomerene Act was to exempt combinations of *American* firms, not to encourage international strategic alliances in services vital for national security, was conveniently overlooked.

When the American delegation informed RCA that the conference would not pass on its proposal, the company held Hooper and Rogers responsible (Hughes, 1969, p. 151). "We feel very strongly," an executive wrote confidentially to a member of RCA's board, "that the American Commissioners are being advised by men who have not had any practical experience in the radio field, are not responsible for any of its investment and who have no particular interest in the economics of the position which American and Chinese communications find themselves in today."[110] Federal wasn't strong financially, which meant that it would not be able to execute its concession agreement. At the same time, duplication was a threat to both companies, and in the end RCA would be blamed for the failure of American aspirations.

RCA acquiesced and concluded a partnership with Federal in which RCA owned 70 percent of the stock and named the chairman of its board (Krysko, 2011, p. 27). As pro-American and pro-Japanese governments took turns in China, the following years witnessed the possibility of reviving the pool as well as rumors that RCA would drop Federal and conclude an agreement with the Japanese firm instead. In the course of these negotiations, Federal's longwave arc technology became obsolete. By the time the State Department agreed to give up support for Federal, the future lay with shortwave (Krysko, 2011, p. 38). In 1928, the Chinese Nationalist government canceled all existing contracts and concluded a new one with RCA (Yang, 2010, pp. 71–72).

As this section has revealed, RCA's traffic agreements did not duplicate the territories held by American Marconi or replicate the division of the world laid out in the Versailles Treaty. RCA gained ground because its traffic agreements divided the world in a way that favored the company. Because of disagreements on the structural level of network control, however, policymakers did not recognize the company's expansion via international cartels as the achievement of the United States. For policymakers who not that long ago had dreamed about government ownership, the cartel was an unsuitable strategy for expansion, because it tied companies registered in the United States to foreign firms. The debate about RCA's expansion reinvigorated the internal debate about the nature of corporations with international operations, which would reach its zenith during the behind-the-scenes negotiations about foreign ownership regulations.

Foreign Investment in "an American Communications Policy"

In January 1928, representatives of the Marconi Company and the Eastern group in Britain announced their intent to merge. The creation of Cable & Wireless, and the subsequent cabinet decision to unify all of Britain's external communications, led to frenzied fusion talks in American business circles. In February, RCA started a campaign to persuade Congress to unify America's international communications (Headrick, 1994, p. 28). The next month, just a few days after the official announcement of the British merger, International Telephone and Telegraph purchased the Mackay Companies, a company that owned both Federal Telegraph and Postal Telegraph. With the acquisition of Postal, the only competitor to Western Union in the transatlantic circuit, ITT became "an integrated record carrier" whose investments spanned telephony, submarine cables, and radio. The press described the acquisition as "an answer to the recent consolidation of radio and cable systems in the British Empire."[111]

In the meantime, RCA was actively seeking a buyer for its international radiotelegraph arm, RCA Communications Inc. In the wake of the broadcast boom discussed in chapter 7, RCA had developed other, more profitable lines of business, such as the sale of radio sets, but the company's problems in international radiotelegraphy resulted from its dependence on domestic distribution outlets. During the 1920s, Western Union refused to route transatlantic messages through RCA because, as a participant in the transatlantic cable business, it preferred to deliver that traffic to its own cables.[112] In response, RCA signed a contract with Postal Telegraph that allowed RCA to handle transatlantic messages collected in Postal's offices. When the acquisition of Federal provided the Mackay Companies with their own radio circuits, Mackay canceled Postal's contract, leaving RCA without pickup and delivery services for traffic to Europe.[113] RCA was now ready to abandon its international business. In March 1929, it found a serious buyer in ITT.[114]

Created in the 1920s to operate telephone companies in Cuba and Puerto Rico, ITT had grown by acquisition until it came into possession of nineteen radiotelegraph and telephone subsidiaries, which provided service in Latin America, Europe, and Asia.[115] The company branched out into manufacturing to supply its operating companies and acquired International Western Electric in 1925 (Wilkins, 1974, p. 71). Upon purchasing All America Cables in April 1927, ITT acquired its first property connecting the United States to other countries and sought further opportunities to expand in this field.[116] When it bought the Mackay Companies, it also acquired Federal Telegraph, which ran counter to the Navy's preference for type competition. As ITT and RCA were finalizing the details of the RCA Communications purchase, the two companies would tell Congress that only a merger of all international communications interests would present a challenge to the British merger. The companies then asked lawmakers to lift the ban on section 17 of the Radio Act of 1927, prohibiting cross-ownership of cable and radio businesses.[117] The Navy Department, which had pushed for codification of intermodal competition, in the form of section 17, took notice.

The day after the press ran the story of the ITT-Mackay merger, Hooper asked the Federal Radio Commission (FRC) to conduct a study of "questions of policy relating to the place of the United States in the field of international communications."[118] When the Commission showed insufficient interest, the Office of the Director of Naval Communications drafted "An American Communications Policy," which emerged from Navy officers' experience with budding American multinationals throughout the 1920s and sought to direct their expansion in line with the national interest. The policy was formulated in response to the British merger, planning the best for the nation's companies "with due regard for National Defense and good will among nations."[119]

The draft focused solely on point-to-point radio, expressing the Navy's conviction that international communications had to be considered "from an international and economic standpoint" and be quite disassociated from internal radio broadcast considerations.[120] Although the policy as a whole never received the sanction of the secretary of the Navy, it was a coherent expression of naval policymakers' approach to communications and would find its way into the Navy's congressional testimonies in the early 1930s. It was far from uncontroversial: even the chief signal officer of the Army disagreed with its assumptions and its alarmist tone.[121]

Naval policymakers' perspectives on Britain were colored by a mixture of admiration and fear. In Britain, "private enterprise [was] compelled to submerge its independence and operate to a common purpose," asserted Pacific Communication Officer Milton Davis, while American companies didn't even seek subsidies and wanted only "to be let alone."[122] The British were in control of the situation because the interests of the government, parent company, and subsidiary all combined to serve the national interest.[123] In the United States, by contrast, RCA was the sole island of hope.[124]

Not once did policymakers wonder why, after a quarter century of separate existence, the British cable and wireless interests suddenly decided to merge, nor did they reflect on Britain's postwar struggle to counter the economic and cultural influence of the United States. Just a year before the formation of Cable & Wireless, Parliament had passed legislation imposing quotas on American films, which were held responsible for the destruction of the British film industry and the decline of British customs and culture (Trumpbour, 2002, pp. 65–68). American advertising agencies spread everywhere that U.S.-based automobile manufacturers had gained ground, including the British Empire, and transformed advertising practices in their wake (de Grazia, 2005, p. 231). It was in this context that the British government considered ITT to be a tool of American expansion at the same time that ITT's three-year acquisition spree prompted journalists in the United States to comment on the company's size and speculate that only the British merger could compete with it (Hills, 2002, p. 19).[125] Though naval policymakers were aware of the improving position of the United States in global communications, they kept their focus on Britain's long-standing advantage.[126]

American companies' response to the British merger posed a real dilemma for the Navy. RCA seemed weakened and was ready to sell out precisely at the time when British companies pulled together, enjoying the full support of their government. Though ITT was emerging as the most powerful company in global communications, it was far less receptive to the Navy Department's guidance than RCA had been. Would following Britain's example, as the two companies advocated, further the national interest?[127] Hooper's draft policy favored an independent radio industry, a de facto monopoly, and stuck to the position that only a strong radio company could maintain its independence of the foreign-dominated cables.[128] Yet naval policymakers could imagine either intermodal competition between a radio company and a cable company or competition between two companies, each with its own radio and cable facilities. Their flexibility revealed that intermodal competition was a more important objective than a monopoly. Had the principle of an American monopoly been dominant, the Navy would have supported the proposed merger between ITT and RCA, even though the former owned cable properties.

Perhaps the most important aspect of the draft policy was section 3, which addressed foreign investment as a way to improve the position of the United States in global communications. "Should American companies own stations in foreign countries, and should foreign capital be permitted to own communications companies in the United States?," the section asked.[129] The draft policy answered both questions in the negative. Hooper recommended amending the Radio Act of 1927 to prohibit both "indirect foreign domination in United States territory [and] indirect domination of subsidiary radio companies by United States capital in foreign lands."[130] This section contains an early formulation of indirect foreign ownership rules, which would be enacted as part of the Communications Act of 1934.

The first part of the recommendation simply extended the foreign ownership requirements of the Radio Act of 1927 to holding companies. To operate in the United States, for example, both American Marconi and its parent would have to be predominantly U.S. owned. This was a new iteration of the principle of national ownership on the structural level of network control, aimed at decreasing the interest on the part of MNCs headquartered elsewhere to participate in the U.S. market. The second component of the proposed indirect foreign ownership rules, however, would raise eyebrows. It sought to prevent American holding companies from investing abroad as a way to prevent the growth of "a super nation in communication [and] a super company to dominate the subsidiary companies of the nations themselves."[131] "It is preferable, as an end to respecting sovereignty, that communication companies be owned by the capital of the country in which they are centered," Hooper wrote.[132] The Navy's recommendations were specifically aimed at holding companies like ITT, which refused to stick to traffic agreements and invested in subsidiaries abroad.

The acceptable level of American investment depended, in turn, on the target country's position in the world system. Hooper's draft distinguished minor powers "that [had] not sufficient initiative and wealth to provide their own radio stations" from important countries, and would have permitted temporary American investment in the former. It had been a customary arrangement for telegraph companies to pay for the erection of stations in various countries and repay the cost from the receipts of the service. The American company and the host country, Hooper now offered, could conclude an agreement that would, after a number of years sufficient to recover the cost of the stations, ensure the takeover of radio stations by the host state.[133]

Instead of expansion to small countries, naval policymakers were mainly concerned about foreign direct investment in the territory of other powerful countries. Reasoning from the experience of a host state, Hooper repeatedly drew on British investment in the United States to point out that foreign ownership led to "difficulties and jealousies between nations" and caused "ill feeling" in the military departments.[134] The United States, Hooper warned, had to remove "the seeds which might grow into unhealthy directions," resulting in "uncontrollable bad feeling, and war."[135] A major problem with international expansion, in Hooper's mind, was that it disrupted the delicate web of international arrangements. Trade advantage could not be the end of the calculation when commerce was a leading cause of war.

Upon receiving Hooper's draft, an alarmed David Sarnoff, vice president of RCA, warned the Navy that the new policy would require RCA to dispose of its radio stock holdings in South America and thwart the company's efforts to expand into China.[136] General J. G. Harbord, president of the company, pointed out that firm adherence to the ideal of national ownership would drive every customer into the arms of RCA's foreign competitors.

"Of course, power and leadership invite envy and unpopularity among nations," he lectured Hooper, "but what self-respecting nation … is swerved from the proper course because of such sentiments?"[137] Harbord saw no difference between radio and other industries in which America led, such as tramways, the power industry, and telephones. "I see nothing wrong with America being the super-nation in communications, as it is in other fields," he concluded.[138] The fault lines of U.S. expansion were becoming apparent: executives at RCA adopted the confident vision of an aspiring world leader, while naval policymakers continued to see the United States as inferior to Britain and preferred expansion only in the U.S. sphere of influence.

Hooper's final revision of the draft policy, in April 1929, scaled back the prescriptions of section 3. He now called restrictions on the expansion of American corporations "an altruistic policy" that would only work if the other powers also adopted a similar policy. The draft pressed for restricting foreign ownership in the United States alone and for the return of stations in small countries in due time.[139] Having failed to convince either the FRC or Congress, Hooper resigned himself to working with the companies as before. "No one can say that the I. T. & T. is not a good American company," he told a close associate. The company's directors and officers were "leaders in our nation's affairs and it is for them to make the country a success or a failure."[140] As U.S.-headquartered MNCs pushed back against the confines of the Navy's vision, however, further cracks appeared in the Navy-RCA alliance forged at the beginning of the decade. Was the Navy Department's guidance still relevant for a rising power? The ideas behind the first draft of the American Communications Policy would return to guide policymakers' actions in the early 1930s, when the Navy Department began to question whether ITT's international orientation prevented it from furthering the national interest.

7 National Ownership Revisited: The Development of Indirect Foreign Ownership Regulations, 1927–1934

The showdown over competing strategies for U.S. geopolitical advancement in general and the role of corporate nationality in particular came in the wake of a controversy over the application of All America Cables, a subsidiary of International Telephone and Telegraph (ITT), to operate radiotelephone stations for point-to-point voice traffic in the Republic of Panama. The domestic and international strands of the Navy's attempt to yoke the multinational corporation to the national interest were now intertwined in a case that ended with the enactment of indirect foreign ownership rules in the Communications Act of 1934. As naval policymakers sought to support intermodal ("type") competition outside the United States, they were faced with the difficulty of distinguishing between two early multinational corporations: United Fruit and ITT.

The various policy alternatives that emerged during the 1920s forced a consideration of the trade-offs between autonomy and expansion. The problem that prompted this line of discussion among policymakers in the Navy and State Departments was the fact that ITT, with subsidiaries in the cable industry, among others, was becoming the most powerful entity in point-to-point communications as RCA was exiting the international radio field. While the State Department was comfortable with ever more uncertain forms of control over the network, naval policymakers' defensive mind-set continued to influence what they considered the ideal extent of expansion for U.S.-headquartered multinational corporations (MNCs). During the previous decade, officers had been concerned about the activities of an MNC headquartered in Britain, but now they transferred their suspicion to companies registered within the United States. In the end, naval policymakers would be faced with a theoretical question: how did international expansion influence the identities and loyalties of American communications companies? In their answer, they would develop a nationalist critique of the multinational corporation well before there were words to describe the phenomenon.

As national ownership was refined as a general policy principle on the structural level of network control during this period, the unity of interest between the U.S. government and early MNCs was forged from a cauldron of clashing perspectives. By the early 1930s, naval policymakers' focus on autonomy had been sidelined in favor of a new attitude, which saw commercial companies taking the lead in advancing American interests.

The Codification of Foreign Policies in the Radio Act of 1927

By the time Captain Stanford C. Hooper drafted the American Communications Policy, which recommended no foreign investment in American radio, foreign ownership restrictions had become codified in section 12 of the Radio Act of 1927. Restrictions on foreign ownership of stock, as we will see in this section, carried over from the radio bills of the 1910s and RCA's charter to form a key pillar of naval policymakers' attempt to secure the loyalty of U.S.-headquartered corporations. Superiority in the radio field only seemed possible if the Navy Department could work with a thoroughly American corporation, which kept radiotelegraphy independent of the cables. Thus, the key principles the Navy would advance and refine throughout the 1920s would be national ownership and type competition, the future section 17 of the Radio Act of 1927.

In 1919, when RCA was formed, the Navy Department was primarily concerned about who the company was and where it expanded. In the background, some policymakers who supported government ownership were concerned that private companies' desire for profit made them untrustworthy. RCA's parent company, General Electric (GE), was particularly problematic, Admiral William S. Benson pointed out, since it "[came] nearer to being a British concern than probably any large concern in our country."[1] GE had been among the pioneering multinationals of the country, with a subsidiary in Britain by 1896. Just what exactly prompted this assessment is not clear, but Benson did not doubt the patriotism of Americans at the firm.[2]

When the Preliminary Agreement was being negotiated, executives at American Marconi believed that their company would, in the words of

historian Hugh Aitken, "continue to exist as a living and functioning organization" (Aitken, 1985, p. 409). Geoffrey Isaacs, the managing director of
British Marconi, had originally proposed keeping a minority share in the
new corporation, which would have held the exclusive transoceanic communication rights of both parties. The threat of government ownership
loomed large, and Owen D. Young, then general counsel of GE, understood
that no British stock holding would be approved. By insisting that GE sever
all existing ties with British Marconi, however, naval policymakers may
have inadvertently restricted RCA's territorial expansion. Arguably, RCA
could have persuaded Isaacs to concede more of the Western Hemisphere
if the British had been allowed to retain a certain amount of the new company's stock.[3] Fully aware that the new company was more likely to gain
government approval if they took out British interests, Young rejected the
proposal.[4] In the trade-off between autonomy and expansion, autonomy
won and the Navy's approval followed. The extent to which these initial
setbacks affected RCA's expansion is for future researchers to document.

By forcing British Marconi to divest its American subsidiary, the Navy
had successfully eliminated the most glaring manifestation of foreign control over the new company. Naval policymakers also successfully placed
an officer on the company's board who sought a say in corporate policy
formation and had the power to challenge the votes of any shareholder
if he suspected that the shareholder had voted them in the interests of foreigners.[5] The first (and last) officer to take this role was Admiral William
G. H. Bullard, but the Navy's attempt to transfer this provision into general foreign ownership regulations failed (Zajácz, 2004, p. 169). Yet RCA's
first years did not lack tension. Bullard immediately began relaying rumors
that the company's loyalty was in question. Some government officials, he
informed the president of GE, were concerned that the monopolistic features of RCA were being developed for cooperation with the British to attain
a worldwide monopoly.[6] Corporate executives referred to "Admiral Dullard"
in correspondence and resisted his influence.[7]

In this context, the selection of an appropriate president for RCA acquired
immense symbolic significance. In 1919, Edward Nally, general manager of
American Marconi, became RCA's president, but he did not enjoy the Navy's
confidence. Before being employed at American Marconi, Nally, an American citizen, had worked for Postal Telegraph for twenty-five years, gaining
extensive experience with British cable companies, to which his company

provided distribution outlets in the United States.[8] When Nally finally left for Europe to direct RCA's international operations, Hooper commented that this would enable him to be closer to "his master's voice" (cited in Aitken, 1985, p. 414). By contrast, General James Harbord, who became the new president in 1922, had no experience in international telegraphy but had distinguished himself in the Army (Garraty & Carnes, 1999). American citizenship was not enough for Nally to keep naval policymakers' approval; RCA now signaled its loyalty through its new president's former service in the country's interests.

On the assumption that the most important characteristic of private companies was their nationality, the Navy Department would spend most of the 1920s advocating for foreign ownership regulations.[9] The Office of the Director of Naval Communications lamented the fact that foreign capital could organize "a dummy company" and erect a high-power station without a license. "This inherent weakness in our national laws," policymakers pointed out, "threatens to place this country in a position of inferiority so far as international radio communication is concerned—with the consequent detrimental effect on the nation politically, economically and strategically."[10]

Postwar radio bills recommending a National Radio Commission tightened the screws on American subsidiaries of MNCs. Instead of the 30 percent foreign capital that the interdepartmental committee had approved in 1916, Senate bill 4038, introduced in 1920, permitted only 20 percent and gave the Commission discretionary powers to revoke the license.[11] Recall that RCA's bylaws had acknowledged that the 100 percent ideal was untenable, and the company had accepted contamination in place of national purity (for the development of foreign ownership legislation in the 1920s, see Zajácz, 2004). RCA now supported restrictions on foreign ownership, as they would provide the company with leverage to secure market access abroad, and it pressed lawmakers to include the provisions of the company's charter in the legislation.[12]

Meanwhile, broadcasting, a revolutionary new application of radio technology, transformed its lack of secrecy, which naval policymakers had long lamented, into the cornerstone of a new industry (Streeter, 1996, p. 61). The broadcast boom started with the decision of the Commerce Department to license "limited commercial stations" in 1921. The turning point came in December of that year, when Commerce licensed twenty-three stations, compared to five during the previous eleven months (Starr, 2004, p. 331). Receiver sales skyrocketed: by February 1922, 600,000 sets had been sold. By December 1922, the number had risen to two million.[13] In just a few years, a mass-market phenomenon conquered America, reconstituting the former users of radio technology as marginalized groups.

As a review of draft bills in the papers of Representative Wallace H. White and Senator Frank B. Kellogg, the most important sponsors of radio legislation, reveals, broadcasting would not affect foreign ownership regulations. Those rules reached their final form in 1921, with the introduction of H.R. 11964. Aside from tightening the wording of one sentence in 1924, the regulations would not change until 1934 (Zajácz, 2004). However, the controversy over the proposed purchase of Federal Telegraph by the Mackay Companies, discussed in chapter 6, demonstrates the continuing relevance of foreign ownership rules. Between 1921 and 1927, the Navy could have withdrawn support and Congress could have eliminated the future section 12 of the Radio Act of 1927.

Given the growing importance of broadcasting, provisions related to the new application led to the delay in passing the law. Once Congress found a compromise on monopolies, vested rights, and the appropriate regulatory body, the radio bill was signed into law on February 23, 1927. The Radio Act of 1927 vested licensing authority in the independent Federal Radio Commission (FRC), which was to operate for one year, after which all key functions would revert to the secretary of commerce.[14] Section 12 regulated foreign ownership, prohibiting the licensing of aliens, their representatives, foreign governments, and foreign corporations.[15] Section 17, in turn, codified type competition, the long-standing policy of the Navy Department that the worldwide radio system should be maintained independent of cable systems and should compete with them.[16] This was to avoid undesirable British influence, though it was still unclear how that influence would manifest itself. For example, how would a merger of a radio company headquartered in the United States and a cable company also registered in the United States result in a gain to British interests?

The difference between the Radio Act of 1912 and the new legislation was substantial. Both the Radio Act of 1927 and, later, the Communications Act of 1934 regulated the point-to-point application of radio technology alongside broadcasting. Both acts are best understood as hybrid legislation, embodying the simultaneous application of two different regulatory frameworks. A telegraphy framework, with its focus on natural monopoly, common carrier obligations, and geopolitical rivalry, now coexisted with a framework developed for the management of spectrum, in which licensing regulated access to the spectrum, a public resource, influencing the transmission of ideas. While radiotelegraphy was deployed as a *transnational* medium, broadcasting would develop as a *nation-based* enterprise during the next half century (Price, 1994, p. 17).

By the 1920s, lawmakers had come to view the ether as both a public resource and a scarce one, unlike the oceans, and formally insulated it from commercial exploitation (Aitken, 1994, p. 713). The United States extended sovereign control over the spectrum above the territory of the country and authorized a new regulatory agency to decide how it should be used. Now a license covered the right to operate a transmitter using a particular frequency, termed "station assignment" and informally practiced since 1921, and the ability to deny access to the spectrum was codified (Aitken, 1994, pp. 702, 689). Twenty years after the Marconi organization declared the radio network entirely private, the Radio Act of 1927 provided for the use of radio frequencies "but not the ownership thereof."[17] Political sentiment in the 1920s rejected private ownership of the electromagnetic spectrum, but radio regulation facilitated the commercial exploitation of the airwaves, in the form of a secondary market in stations cum frequencies (Aitken, 1994, p. 713).

Shortly after the Radio Act of 1927 passed, wavelengths became a site of geopolitical competition. Delegates at the 1927 International Radio Conference, meeting in Washington, D.C., divided the spectrum into bands to be devoted to the various kinds of services but did not allocate channels to countries.[18] Countries also retained autonomy over internal broadcasting as long as no mutual interference occurred, an arrangement that one analyst has called "globalization where necessary" (Gorman, 2010, p. 150). Two years later, however, when the United States, Newfoundland, Canada, and Cuba agreed on the regional spectrum allocation table (Mexico declined to send delegates), the conference distributed frequencies to individual stations. By this time, the goals of the United States had broadened considerably from the initial focus on confidential communications. As American companies were expanding, even officials at the Navy Department sought direct routes for them, especially in the Pacific, as a way to make sure that "Americans receive news direct."[19] The Americans took almost half the wavelengths for general communication services out of a total of 228, as well as 34 shared wavelengths (Stewart, 1929, p. 422). From this time on, geopolitical considerations would surround the distribution of frequencies both for point-to-point use and for broadcasting. At the 1932 Madrid conference, America's negotiating partners would fight for a larger share of the total.[20]

By the late 1920s, it had become apparent that the emergence of broadcasting had drastically transformed the regulation of radio technology. Radiotelegraphy did not disappear, but it was demoted from core use to a "fringe application." With the loss of its status as the largest user of radio's core application, the Navy also lost influence in the regulation of the technology, although its interests and aspirations for the United States had not changed. The case that drove the point home revolved around the decision of the Mackay Companies to purchase Federal Telegraph. After the August 1927 decision, Mackay executives planned to use Federal's facilities to introduce radio service on the Pacific Ocean that would parallel the Commercial Pacific Cable Company's cable to the Far East. The radio circuit would supplement the cable and relieve it of the cheaper classes of service.[21]

Commercial Pacific had been well known in naval circles ever since a 1921 congressional hearing revealed clandestine British investment in its facilities. Fifty percent of the company's stock was owned by the Eastern and Associated Companies outright, while 25 percent was in the hands of a company registered in Denmark, which was also thought to be British controlled. Thus, only one-fourth of the company that conducted almost all of the United States-Far East cable traffic was in fact in American hands.[22] In the eyes of naval policymakers, the part tarnished the whole. Milton S. Davis, Pacific communication officer and Hooper confidant, described Mackay as only "nominally American" and their decision to acquire Federal as aimed at putting RCA out of business.[23] Hooper quickly pointed out a violation of both sections 12 and 17 of the Radio Act of 1927 and recommended that the Mackay companies not receive transoceanic radio licenses unless they transferred their stock to American owners.[24]

When, in March 1928, International Telephone and Telegraph purchased the Mackay Companies, matters quickly deteriorated. The Mackay Companies now applied for licenses to operate shortwave radio circuits in competition with RCA. Their plan clashed with both of the Navy's objectives: to keep radio independent of cables and to operate international radio as a monopoly. Hooper, temporarily detailed to the FRC as technical adviser, campaigned to enforce both sections 12 and 17. By this time, however, RCA had become

an antitrust nightmare, deeply distrusted throughout the country for its business practices and natural monopoly arguments no longer cut it. Neither the
FRC nor the Justice Department found anything wrong with a competitor to
RCA and found no merit in the argument that the Mackay Companies were
influenced by British capital.[25] ITT agreed to spin off a wholly owned subsidiary, the Mackay Radio and Telegraph Company, which was involved only in
the radio industry and had no foreign investment, complying with the letter
of both sections 12 and 17 of the Radio Act of 1927.[26]

Yet policymakers' suspicions did not abate. The Navy Department complained that ITT violated the congressional intent behind the Radio Act—
through its "entangling ownership arrangements" with British cables and
because it employed two foreign directors—but did not introduce an amendment to the 1929 bill that would correct the problem.[27] Hooper's tenure as
technical adviser to the FRC, and his failure to attract commissioners' attention to problems of international communications, in particular, convinced
him that the FRC was largely useless and was only fit for handling broadcasting.[28] "They have missed the national viewpoint," Davis agreed whole-
heartedly.[29] From this point until the adoption of the Communications
Act of 1934, the Navy Department would repeatedly recommend that the
licensing of point-to-point radio, including international radiotelegraphy
and marine communications, should revert to the secretary of commerce as
it had been before the FRC was established.[30] The simmering conflict would
erupt as soon as a different ITT subsidiary sought radio licenses, this time in
Panama, the heart of U.S. strategic space.

Cracks in the Navy's Monopoly over Radio in Panama

Soon after the Radio Act of 1927 became law, a string of conflicts between
the Navy Department and ITT revealed naval policymakers' dissatisfaction
with its provisions on direct foreign ownership. By the early 1930s, ITT had
bought thirty-one manufacturing subsidiaries on five continents, which
made the company the largest multinational corporation involved in the
communications industry (Wilkins, 1974, p. 423).[31] After its purchase of
All America Cables, ITT connected the United States to other countries and
began to transform itself from an equipment manufacturer into an operating company.[32] Formerly known as the Central and South American Telegraph Company, All America Cables connected Latin America to the United

States in competition with the cartel between Western Union and Western Telegraph. With the acquisition of this company, ITT became the only competitor to RCA, the company the U.S. Navy trusted the most to carry out its vision for American superiority in international radio.[33] If RCA did not always follow the Navy's direction, Hooper got a taste of ITT's utter disregard for its views when the company acquired the Mackay Companies. During the 1930s, the company's strategies would challenge naval policymakers' plans outright.

In an attempt to bring ITT in line with the national interest, the Navy Department had asked the directors of the company to stick to traffic agreements and avoid ownership of radio stations in foreign countries while also minimizing the number of foreign directors.[34] When ITT ignored the Navy's advice with regard to traffic agreements and actually increased the number of foreigners on its directorate, the relationship quickly deteriorated.[35] The company seemed to be quite unaware how important the question of foreign ties was for naval policymakers, as evidenced by the nonchalant designation of a former British officer to negotiate with the Navy in Washington.[36] Meanwhile, ITT discreetly but firmly rebuffed the Navy's efforts to place its retired officers in its employ and recruited Army officers for its top government relations jobs.[37]

Naval policymakers' attempts to influence ITT's plans of expansion culminated in the pressure to keep the company out of the strategically important region of the Panama Canal. Ever since the 1901 Hay-Pauncefote treaty gave the United States a free hand in canal development, Britain had ceased to be a significant force in canal politics, and America's power over the Isthmus of Panama was undisputed (Beloff, 1970, p. 87). By the early 1930s, when All America Cables applied for a radio license to connect the isthmus to the outside world, all tangible aspects of British influence were gone. Yet the Navy's monopoly on radio in Panama had come under attack from several quarters, and the department was gradually losing the "absolute and permanent" control it had acquired in 1914.

The decree of 1914, carefully worded to "confirm" the rights of the United States under the canal treaty, was in fact the only authority for American control over radio in Panama.[38] For much of the 1920s, the Navy and the State Departments worked with the Army-heavy canal administration to maintain a complete monopoly over radio in both the Canal Zone and the Republic of Panama, ignoring Panama's protests in the process.[39] Section 35 of the Radio Act of 1927 formalized the division of authority between the two departments by exempting the Canal Zone from the jurisdiction of the FRC and giving authority over international radio matters to the secretary of state.[40] The State Department would issue radio licenses under the Radio Act of 1927 for the Canal Zone and under the 1914 decree for the Republic of Panama. By the 1930s, however, the diplomats had gradually departed from the Navy's policies and developed priorities that dictated a more lenient treatment of the Republic.

After the State Department convinced the Joint Board of the Army and the Navy to relax its blanket prohibition on private stations, provided the United States retained veto power, United Fruit secured a license for one of its subsidiaries in 1928.[41] When, during the following month, a different subsidiary of United Fruit, the Tropical Radio Telegraph Company (TRT), applied for a license, company executives were surprised to encounter pushback.[42] TRT requested permission to handle international point-to-point service—messages between Panama and the outside world—and commercial ship-to-shore service, the latter of which covered traffic not related to the operation and defense of the canal.[43]

By this time, however, Captain Hooper had been appointed director of naval communications, and he quickly decided that the Navy's permissiveness toward United Fruit in the earlier case had been unwise.[44] Relying on natural monopoly theory, naval policymakers had long been concerned that traffic in the region could not support two networks.[45] In addition, they hoped to avoid setting a precedent. If the Navy permitted a commercial company to enter the field, how could it deny licenses to other applicants?[46] Now that interference was "no longer a consideration," Hooper fretted, the Navy was left with concerns about equity as the only legitimate reason to deny future applications.[47] Indeed, the conflict between the company and naval policymakers over ship-to-shore traffic drove a wedge between the Navy and State Departments and would not be resolved until President Franklin Delano Roosevelt intervened during the run-up to the conclusion of the 1936 treaty between the United States and Panama (Zajácz, 2012).

On international commercial service, however, the Navy gave way. There were no geopolitical reasons to oppose TRT's application, and naval policymakers both on the ground and in Washington judged United Fruit "trustworthy."[48] When both the War Department and the canal administration recommended supporting the company's application, the Navy relented.[49] On the recommendation of the Joint Board, the total number of commercial radio stations in the area would not exceed two. "Beyond that number these stations are no longer a military asset but become a liability," the Board declared.[50] The State Department granted the permit to TRT in November 1929, and the company's station was placed into operation in May 1930.[51] From 1930, therefore, Panama's external communications were handled by subsidiaries of two MNCs headquartered in the United States. Panama's cable traffic went through the lines of All America Cables, a subsidiary of ITT, while its radio messages were carried by TRT, a subsidiary of United Fruit. The U.S. Navy continued to handle ship-to-shore and plane-to-ground messages, which constituted the bulk of radio traffic.

Meanwhile, the United States faced a challenge from the Republic of Panama itself. Panamanian policymakers had long resented the country's loss of sovereignty in radio matters and local businessmen were now constrained in their ability to develop broadcasting (Zajácz, 2012, p. 87). On December 29, 1930, the Panamanian government made the decision to abrogate the 1914 decree without informing the United States.[52] The only legal sanction of the U.S. Navy's radio monopoly was gone. Secretary of the Navy Charles Francis Adams quickly asked the State Department to initiate negotiations, with the objective of restoring American control.[53] The diplomats approached radio as they did any other area of U.S.-Panama relations, seeking to separate "the essential interests" of the United States from mere conveniences.[54] Wartime control was paramount: the United States needed authority to take over the stations or have them closed if they obstructed the operation or defense of the canal.[55] The War Department and the canal administration both agreed with State's assessment.[56]

Wartime control required Panama's assent, which meant that any decision on radio would take place in the context of treaty negotiations. Such negotiations to overhaul the commercial relations between the two countries began in 1920 and would go through several draft treaties until the Panama General Treaty of 1936 was finalized (Major, 2003, p. 107). The diplomats fully understood that a treaty required concessions, and they were unwilling to support the Navy's renewed drive for absolute and permanent control. "The complete control granted by the Panamanian Executive Decree of August 29, 1914, now abrogated," Allan Dawson of the Division of Latin American Affairs pointed out, "went beyond our needs … and as enforced retarded the development of commercial radio in Panama unreasonably."[57]

When, in fall 1931, the application of All America Cables reopened the matter, the considerable differences between the Navy and State Departments' positions were immediately revealed. After the Navy rejected the company's application out of hand, All America Cables first consulted the State Department and then went ahead to obtain permission from Panama.[58] If the Navy stood by its decision and turned the company away, the U.S. government would overrule the permission granted by Panama, a decision sure to be interpreted as an affront to the country's sovereignty.[59]

Hooper was taken aback at this turn of events. Instead of abandoning its plans to open a station on the isthmus, as RCA had done, ITT "worked around the matter."[60] "Certainly, this is the best possible evidence of the international character of their policies," Hooper would later vent in a fit of frustration, "when they will insist on having their way despite the U.S. Navy and despite Panama, or anyone else."[61] It was Hooper's understanding that only United Fruit could establish a station in Panama.[62] As the controversy showed no signs of abating, the Navy Department, as we will see, sought to put pressure on ITT by working with lawmakers to tighten restrictions on foreign ownership. By contrast, the State Department was willing to approve All America's application on the same terms as outlined in TRT's permission.[63]

On the broadest levels, the differences of opinion between the two departments came down to the fact that naval policymakers understood natural monopoly theory in the context of a systemic vision of global communications, while the diplomats viewed it in terms of the Open Door policy. Just as in the United States, naval policymakers pursued a monopoly for radiotelegraphy on the isthmus alongside competition between cable and radio. The Navy Department continued to place radiotelegraphy into the context of a global communications system in which the British-owned cable network was preeminent. Radio had become "the American opportunity," the technology of the future that would propel the United States to supremacy in global communications.[64] "The trend of the times is toward radio as a means of communications," Chief of Naval Operations Admiral William V. Pratt wrote.[65] In the medium term, the Navy would be vindicated. Western Union's revenue on the most profitable transatlantic route dropped from $10 million in 1930 to $4 million in 1938 despite its new loaded cables, while RCA's circuits prospered (Hills, 2002, p. 206).

However, as the merger of Eastern and the Marconi interests into Cable & Wireless had recently revealed, there were different ways to integrate cables and radio links into a network. Traffic could be directed to the cables, which were losing money, and radio could be used only for emergencies and over-loads.[66] Since the United States was dependent on radio for ascendancy in global communications, it could not afford having the technology rel-egated to backup status. Therefore, type competition overrode the principle of monopoly. Officers expressed concerns about "unfair" monopolies, such as a cable company that enters the radio business only to drive the radio company out and unify control of the two technologies.[67] ITT, the company that was widely perceived to be the embodiment of American expansion in Europe, seemed to be particularly threatening in this respect. By approving TRT's application and denying All America's, the Navy hoped to put type competition into practice and avoid the risk that radio would come under the dominance of the cables. Washington's emphasis on a commercial radio monopoly naturally disregarded the recommendation of policymakers in the Canal Zone who would have approved two stations.[68]

Whereas the Navy Department framed the license application as a ques-tion of national security, best decided by experts, the diplomats considered it a matter of general policy, in which all responsible departments had a say.[69] Ignoring the Navy's systemic framework, the diplomats focused their attention on the territory of the Republic of Panama and on radio technol-ogy alone. As a practical matter, if the State Department wanted to be able to offer Panama a compromise in treaty negotiations, it could not please the Navy in everything.[70] The United States, Undersecretary of State Wil-liam Castle pointed out, "had no right to dictate to any sovereign state whether or not it preferred one or two companies."[71] The diplomats, who saw the United States as about to take Britain's place in the world system, were scrupulously observing national sovereignty "in addressing one of the most minor of states."[72] The controversy over Panamanian radio, they were vexed to read in a January 1931 issue of the *Economist*, had already hurt America's reputation and prompted comparisons with the old days of the British Empire,[73] when Britain acted like a high-handed imperialist.

For the diplomats, radio was not part of an already constituted interna-tional communications system, where the cards were stacked against the United States. Rather, what mattered was competition in every industry and equal opportunity for as many American players as possible. This was in line with the nondiscrimination aspect of Open Door diplomacy, the framework for American foreign policy in the first half of the twentieth

century (Wetter, 1962, p. 277; Williams, 1972, p. 52). Given European opposition, American companies could only enter foreign markets if diplomatic
assistance was consistent across companies. The policy of the Open Door
protected American companies from their European rivals while shielding
them from the monopolistic tendencies of their compatriots. This feature
prompted observers to label it a brilliant strategic stroke in the service of
America's expansion (Williams, 1972, p. 52).

On the isthmus, the State Department only saw two companies facing
off, not a delicate geopolitical balancing act between two technologies. The
principle of nondiscrimination worked against monopolies at a time when
TRT asked to be protected from "unnecessary and ruinous competition."[74]
Significantly, natural monopoly theory had no place in the policy of the
Open Door, which pointed to a potential future difficulty as utility multinationals headquartered in the United States ventured abroad. For now,
however, the real problem was the Navy, whose support for United Fruit
interfered with the natural course of commercial competition.[75] Type competition may have made sense in the United States, the chief of the Latin
American Division commented, but the situation in Panama was not going
to result in a cable monopoly. "It took the Navy a long time to dig up this
argument," he added.[76] (Of course, given the position of All America Cables
in the cable industry, the State Department's support worked to stabilize the
position of the incumbent.)

Hoping to persuade the Navy against peacetime restrictions, the State
Department worked with All America Cables to offer the customary concessions: the company's station would not interfere with those of the Navy;
the United States could take it over in wartime; and the station would use
naval reservists as operators.[77] When the Navy Department offered no concessions in return, Secretary of State Henry Stimson bluntly informed the
officers that he could not imagine any more complete control than what
had already been conceded. The only thing left to do was to prohibit all
commercial radio companies from operating on the isthmus. However,
the Navy had already authorized a commercial company, evidently find-
ing no military reason to bar the Tropical Radio Telegraph Company from
operating.[78] Over in the east wing of the State, War, and Navy building,
naval policymakers realized that the decision to license TRT was a mistake.[79]
In the south wing, however, the diplomats were getting increasingly frustrated: what really was the difference between TRT and All America Cables?

A Question of General Policy: ITT as an International Company

As companies, both ITT and United Fruit were equally insubordinate for policymakers. United Fruit sought to monopolize ship-to-shore traffic, the bread and butter of the Navy's radio activity on the isthmus.[80] TRT's new station drowned out the naval station and reduced the Navy's revenue from ship-to-shore traffic by 80 percent.[81] Both United Fruit and All America Cables maintained a close relationship with politicians in Panama, which, naval policymakers feared, disadvantaged the Navy. The very idea of two commercial stations originated not from Panama, the Navy suspected, but from All America Cables.[82] Naval policymakers were also convinced that United Fruit had kept Panama stirred up about its communications and had prompted its president to abrogate the 1914 decree.[83]

While the Navy expressed no geopolitical concern about United Fruit, officers' amorphous suspicions about the activities of ITT had by now crystallized into the conclusion that the company was losing its American identity.[84] "The most important difficulty which this company now presents is ... in connection with its lack of a completely national character," Admiral Pratt would later inform the State Department.[85] As early as September 1931, the secretary of the Navy approved the department's approach to the applications of the two competitors, including the statement that TRT was "100% American," while ITT had several foreigners in its directorate and was backed by foreign capital.[86] Consequently, naval policymakers explained, "the policies of the latter company might easily conflict with American interests in Panama and the Canal Zone."[87] This was not simply the view in Washington. Admiral N. E. Irwin, the commandant of the 15th Naval District, concluded, "The nationality of the operators of All America Cables appears to indicate that the general character of this company in Central America is decidedly British."[88]

As these concerns reveal, policymakers in the Navy Department were now grappling with one of the vexing questions of contemporary international political economy: how did international expansion influence the identities and loyalties of American communications companies? In their answer, naval policymakers theorized how international expansion disrupted MNCs' ties to their home states, identifying the conditions that diminished home-state influence and resulted in the emergence of a new type of corporation. Specifically, they commented on the type of expansion companies engaged in, the worldwide flow of information among units of the multinational corporation, and, most important, the relative power of home and host states in the world system.

The linchpin of the Navy's theory was that foreign direct investment (FDI) exposed American companies to host-state influence. "Certainly no nation would permit the establishment of a foreign-owned fort within its borders," Hooper emphasized in a letter to RCA.[89] The fort metaphor revealed that Hooper thought of a radio company as the nation's secure outpost in a foreign land, but in order to operate abroad, international companies became dependent on "favors" from foreign countries and had to comply both with the laws of the countries where they were operating and with the wishes of the politicians favoring them.[90] The conduits of host-state influence were the company's foreign officials, who, in the interest of profit maximization, catered to the desires of their own government officials, whose interests did not necessarily coincide with those of the United States.[91] ITT appeared to be a harbinger of the changes that would affect every American company acquiring facilities abroad. "Each new absorption means the injection of more foreign capital into the organization and more foreign influence into its management," a memorandum prepared for Hooper explained, adding, "As the expansion of the company increases, its character becomes more and more international until it ceases to be American except possibly in name."[92]

As the American Communications Policy has already revealed, the areas of the world where U.S.-headquartered MNCs invested were of the essence. "The Navy Department would be less concerned with foreign personnel or foreign affiliations if such relations were only with the nations of Latin America," Admiral Pratt explained.[93] The expansion of communications MNCs to Europe or Asia, "where this country's potential enemies [were] located," was to be discouraged.[94] United Fruit obliged, investing only in smaller and weaker countries in the American sphere of influence. By contrast, ITT dominated radio "in nations everywhere, regardless of whether the nations [had] interests in common with the United States."[95] While host countries were expected to harbor resentments against American MNCs, the clout of the United States could shield companies from retaliation. Investments in the American sphere ran small risk of discriminatory legislation or outright expropriation.[96] By contrast, FDI in the territories of America's geopolitical rivals was a ticking time bomb because commerce was a potential cause of war (cf. Doyle, 1997, p. 283). Expansion by multinationals was only safe if confined within the purview of the home state's power; only a country with unlimited power could afford unlimited expansion. In the eyes of naval policymakers, however, the United States was not such a country.

ITT's apparent loss of stable American identity alarmed the Navy Department because it was a company's "character as to nationality" that "[determined] the degree of trust that [could] be placed in them."[97] Policymakers' efforts to guide companies toward traffic agreements reinforced the idea that the less direct contact an American radio company had with foreigners, the more loyal that company would be. Stable national identity and staunch loyalty laid the foundation for cooperative relations with the Navy Department. Naval policymakers expected commercial companies to defer to the Navy in matters of national security and counted on their cooperation in peacetime so that they could be seamlessly integrated into the communications network in wartime.[98] Quite in contrast to the military departments' views about private corporations in the first decade of the twentieth century, which emphasized their greed and unreliability, the idea that commercial stations were a dormant military asset was now widely held.[99]

ITT's public image seemed to confirm the Navy's conclusions. "The International Corporation was not organized with a single profit-making purpose to itself nor with the desire of imposing American practices in its foreign activities," navy officers read in *Electrical Communication*, the company's trade publication. "On the contrary, the International Corporation has always been ready and quick to adjust American practices to local conditions," it continued.[100] According to company historian Robert Sobel, ITT's subsidiaries did in fact enjoy a great deal of independence, as headquarters was never able to integrate them into a coherent whole (Sobel, 1982, pp. 50–51).

While the Navy Department was clearly not the intended audience for *Electrical Communication*, policymakers took what they read at face value. "By its own pronouncement, the company is thus clearly shown to be of a truly international character, rather than truly national," Commander Howard Lammers of Naval Operations wrote to the State Department.[101] The kind of corporate identity ITT imagined for itself and the extent to which its executives cultivated an image of multinationality as a defensive strategy at a time of rising nationalist sentiment is for corporate archives to reveal (Lipson, 1985, p. 138). Such information was not available to naval policymakers, who acted on their own interpretation.

In considering the dangers of FDI, naval policymakers focused on the flow of confidential information. First, as America took the lead in the development of radio technology, the Navy became increasingly jealous of confidential technological information. Policymakers in the early 1930s pointed to the frequent exchange of personnel between ITT's laboratories in the United States and abroad, citing the example of employing a former officer in the French Army Signal Corps as a danger inherent in such exchanges.[102] Second, the Navy Department was especially concerned that subsidiaries of U.S.-headquartered MNCs under obligation to foreign governments would enable their host states to gain access to sensitive military information in wartime.[103] If the United States was neutral, Secretary Adams wrote, international companies operating on U.S. territory "might even find it advantageous to perform unneutral service."[104] Cooperation with the radio and cable interests of the United States, the General Board advised, would be "impracticable" if one or more of the competitors comprised foreign personnel.[105]

From the vantage point of the Navy Department, the very fact of organizing operations on an international scale seemed to necessitate a worldwide flow of information within the company that inevitably hurt home-state interests. Companies with international links had to standardize their practices, which involved an interchange of information between their subsidiaries. "In that interchange any vital information given to the parent company can logically be expected to be transmitted to foreign governments through the foreign links," Hooper stated.[106] The Navy was unable to divulge its confidential plans to companies, Secretary Adams told Congress, "with even one foreigner on the board."[107]

From a less pessimistic perspective, of course, information from all over the world could flow into headquarters and through the headquarters to the home state, facilitating surveillance. After all, the parent must collect information from each of its subsidiaries to devise strategy, but it is rarely necessary to share all the information at the parent's disposal with each of the subsidiaries. Taking stock of the possibilities, the Office of the Director of Naval Communications believed that American communications companies abroad were likely to "keep American interests informed of matters, learned through handling communications, that would be commercially advantageous" and that the U.S. government would be able to use their facilities "for transmission of intelligence information and the dissemination of propaganda."[108] In fact, ITT itself was providing the State Department with useful information and even policy advice at the time of the Spanish civil war. Shortly before the Spanish government began to consider seizing the company's assets, Hernand Behn, the president of ITT, informed the Latin American Division that the Spanish insurgents would protect foreign investments, and he advised the United States to recognize the new regime.[109] Could the benefits that Britain had reaped from the expansion of its communications companies become available to the United States? Not yet. Naval policymakers dismissed these advantages as embarrassing for neutral states and believed they would result in a detrimental reaction against the United States.[110] Policymakers' primary goal was still the ability to communicate, rather than surveillance, and trust in the intermediaries managing the network was central to this objective.

The Navy's pessimistic approach rested on the conviction that information flow was not only a function of the company's organizational structure but was also influenced by the relative positions of the home state and the host state in the world system. Secretary Adams argued before Congress that "the creation of an international communication company that will serve all nations with the same degree of impartiality can never be possible until after the day that nationalism and national trade rivalries have ceased to exist."[111] If the United States could dominate such a company or all nations would share ownership in it, "we might not be too hard off," Hooper wrote in a letter to Roosevelt's private secretary, "but the President knows well enough that the British will control anything international in the end even if we start it."[112] The same sentiment was already present in the letters of Milton Davis, who was convinced five years earlier that private ownership without government assistance meant "eventual if not present British domination" of American communications.[113] In the international state system, the Navy concluded, no international company could exist: the country that dominated international relations would dominate international corporations.

The seemingly uncontrollable ITT was a case in point. Both the company's spin-off of the Mackay radio subsidiary and its effort to secure a radio license for All America Cables had demonstrated to the Navy that its executives saw laws as something to "work around."[114] Although the idea that expansion had transformed ITT into a British company outright was held by only a radical few, officers at the highest level were convinced that the British government had an influence on company policy. From the

Navy's perspective, American cable companies were hopelessly dependent on Britain for interconnection and access to key landing sites. According to Hooper, both All America Cables and the Postal Telegraph Company had to keep a "close liaison" with the British Cable Board.[115] However, when the U.S. Navy sought such a close liaison with ITT, it encountered difficulties because of foreign influence.[116] ITT's ties to its business partners in other countries and even to the British government were stronger than its ties to the United States, anxious observers in the Navy concluded.

Naval policymakers' consistent focus on the influence of one host state illuminates the type of multinational they imagined ITT to be. Even as British writers renewed their lament of the American invasion, for the U.S. Navy the ethnocentric (home country oriented) U.S.-headquartered multinational did not exist. RCA came closest, but it, too, was not free from doubt. The type of company naval policymakers were most concerned about was closest to Howard Perlmutter's (1969) geocentric corporation, given its propensity to invest without regard to informal understandings about spheres of influence. However, the firm-centered orientation of the business administration literature typically excludes consideration of systemic power relations, so it cannot illuminate the type of MNC naval policymakers identified. According to the Navy's theory, the internationalization of the communications industry brought into being a company loyal to the most powerful state: the hegemon-centric corporation.

By the early 1930s, the pessimism about the role of the United States in the world system still lingering in the Office of the Director of Naval Communications seemed out of step with developments in Anglo-American relations as well as with policymakers' own evaluation of the formidable British merger. Britain's attempt to regain its naval supremacy at the 1927 Geneva conference failed, and the 1930 London Naval Conference settled nearly all the outstanding naval issues between the two countries. The Admiralty came to the conclusion that Britain would be unable to resist a combined Japanese-German force, and it sought to strengthen the country's relationship with the United States (Roskill, 1968, p. 66). At the same time, American naval policymakers' fears of British naval power all but disappeared after 1929, when Congress authorized a navy of "modern, underage warships, second to none, on true and reasonable parity with the navies of rival maritime powers" (Roskill, 1968, p. 64). The same Admiral Pratt who had so convincingly presented Hooper's views to the State Department in the Panama case pointed out privately that only the combined naval power of Britain and the United States could restrain German and Japanese ambitions.[117] Similarly, naval policymakers saw British power weaken in matters of global communications. The merger between the Eastern group and Marconi interests reinforced Hooper's conviction that the United States had nothing to gain from imitating Britain. Because Imperial and International Communications Ltd. propped up its cables at the expense of radio, a combined cable-radio network was unable to show a profit.[118]

Even though the two countries settled their differences in general naval policy and the Office of the Director of Naval Communications saw no real danger in the British merger, the U.S. Navy's approach to communications in the early 1930s was still shaped by an increasingly anachronistic fear of British dominance. The Navy Department found ammunition for its argument against unlimited expansion in the controversy surrounding ITT's affiliate in Spain. Spanish opposition to foreign control of the country's telephone system culminated in the 1931 report of a Spanish parliamentary commission that recommended the annulment of ITT's monopoly concession.[119] For the Navy Department, this incident foreshadowed similar steps in the future by dissatisfied host states, which "might lead to war or at least to intervention by the United States."[120]

The State Department, however, had already encountered the problems arising from the internationalization of the communications industry in connection with the Spanish telephone system in 1924 (Little, 1979, p. 453). When the intervention they had predicted became necessary, the diplomats considered it in the context of U.S. investment worldwide (Little, 1979, p. 460). It was a test case closely watched in Latin America, a precedent that would determine the fate of all American investment abroad.[121] The diplomats were convinced that protecting American property with a firm hand was necessary to ensure future expansion. When the controversy reemerged in early 1933, President Roosevelt fully expected Spain to observe the terms of the original contract (Little, 1979, p. 465). The relationship between ITT and the Spanish government would be contentious until 1945, when the company sold its subsidiary back to Spain (Little, 1979, p. 471).

As both the Spanish incident and the example of All America Cables reveals, State Department officials encouraged worldwide expansion in every industry. During the 1930s, they went head-to-head with the Navy's systemic vision for communications technologies by decoupling radio from cables and situating it in the context of other industries. Communications was not unique, Undersecretary William Castle explained to Secretary Adams with regard to the Spanish crisis, stating that "the same trouble might happen to any American company carrying on any kind of business working in any foreign country."[122] Since the State Department was prepared to support unlimited international expansion, neither host-country retaliation nor American intervention on behalf of MNCs appeared to be anything out of the ordinary. For the diplomats, both were simply part of the price of being an expansionist great power. Cautiously limiting expansion to territories already secured was not a viable option, State repeatedly pointed out, because refraining from diplomatic support meant abandoning the playing field to foreign competitors (Little, 1979, p. 453).[123] Observing the limits of American power, as the Navy suggested, would merely perpetuate those limits.

Perhaps not surprisingly, the diplomats failed to entertain any "dreadful suspicion" about the influence of such expansion on the identities and loyalties of American multinationals.[124] When a naval officer informed the State Department that ITT's board of directors and its stockholders were "predominantly foreign," the diplomats were dumbfounded.[125] "I do not understand this," a confused Henry Fletcher in the Division of Latin American Affairs scribbled in the margin, adding, "The All American Cables is a subsid of the ITT. The ITT is an American corpn, mainly American owned, and mainly American directed tho in each foreign country it tries to bring in local interests & develop local executives."[126] Over in the Treaty Division, policymakers were far less certain. "If the ITT is not an American company," Undersecretary Castle commented dryly, "we have certainly spent a lot of wasted effort in promoting their interests the world over."[127] In an attempt to decide the matter for itself, the State Department began to investigate.

By late fall 1931, the investigation concerning ITT's national identity had turned up reassuring results. Former secretary of state Charles Evans Hughes, then attorney for the Mackay interests, provided up-to-date information. Of the company's thirty-seven officers, five were foreign nationals: two were citizens of Spain, one was a subject of Sweden, and two were from the British Empire.[128] Of the company's 85,000 stockholders, Hughes continued, more than 76,000 resided in the United States, and they possessed 6 million shares out of a total of 6,642,508.[129] ITT was able to show the State Department that a little over 10 percent of its stockholders were foreign nationals, who held a little less than 10 percent of the company's shares, and that 13.5 percent of the company's high-level executives were citizens of another country. Foreign earnings as a percentage of total earnings, however, did not figure into policymakers' calculations. After reviewing the information, the diplomats saw no reason for concern. In early November 1931, Irwin Stewart concluded that the company's statement established "beyond doubt that the International Telephone and Telegraph Corporation [was] controlled in this country."[130]

After the diplomats had satisfied themselves regarding ITT's national identity, they concluded that Navy Department officials "had shown a distinct bias" against the company.[131] They acknowledged that the company indeed had foreign directors, but they downplayed the importance of this fact. "The few figurehead foreign directors of ITT are a highly desirable asset for any American concern with foreign interests," Assistant Secretary Francis White asserted, adding, "Their effect on a station in the Republic of Panama could be disregarded."[132] Moreover, the State Department saw both FDI and a regular exchange of personnel between the company's laboratories worldwide as "evidence of a sound business judgment."[133] During the 1930s, therefore, the diplomats evaluated the concessions made by multinationals as the price of doing business, which would in no way affect where the true loyalties of these firms lay.

More than a year after All America Cables' application, the matter came up for final decision at the State Department. Hooper's immediate superior, Admiral Pratt, endorsed his approach and forcefully argued before the State Department that ITT officials "had evidenced a complete disregard of this department's views in matters affecting national defense, and a lack of willingness to cooperate."[134] Yet naval policymakers' approval of TRT's license undercut the Department's case because it made the arguments for military necessity sound hollow. When the application was considered as a matter of general policy, where the diplomats had the utmost authority, navy officers reiterated their arguments about ITT's international orientation and placed their hope in Secretary Stimson. It soon became apparent, however, that the Navy had failed to convince the State Department. "ITT is a loyal reliable American company, which is furthering the interests of this country in many parts of the world," Secretary Stimson asserted, "and ... it is entitled to the consideration and assistance which is customarily given by this Government to reputable American institutions."[135]

Naval policymakers made one final attempt at convincing their opposite numbers. In December, Secretary Adams himself met with Undersecretary Castle and went over the Navy's arguments. Castle refuted the arguments and finally offered an explanation that reduced the complexity of the case to a personality conflict. Either on his own or because of Captain Hooper's influence, Castle suggested, Adams distrusted the loyalty of Sosthenes Behn, the chairman of ITT.[136] Secretary Adams, a political appointee less familiar with the long history of foreign ownership regulations than navy officers were, agreed that this was the basis of the trouble. Castle defended Behn's reputation by pointing out that he had a first-class war record in the U.S. Army and that his foreign ventures worked to the advantage of the United States.[137] Since the company had been found to be thoroughly American, Castle pointed out, the State Department could not refuse a license based on an officer's suspicions.[138] Adams withdrew from further discussion of the matter, and Secretary Stimson gave the license the go-ahead.[139] Since the diplomats were already helping ITT in other parts of the world, including Spain, it was untenable to mount opposition only in Panama.[140]

The Revision of Foreign Ownership Regulations in Congress

Despite the similarities between United Fruit and ITT, it was the conflict with All America Cables that led to a revision of domestic legislation, because it provided a canvas on which the Navy's concerns about the internationalization of business were writ large. ITT's insubordination brought to the fore a problem with the Radio Act of 1927: its foreign ownership provisions only applied to operating companies and did not cover their parent companies. Hooper considered parent and subsidiary to be inextricably intertwined, the distinction between them a mere formality, just enough to help ITT circumvent the original intent of section 12 of the Radio Act.[141] "I contend that it was not the intention of Congress to permit such a set-up merely to get around the law," Hooper explained to his superiors, adding, "I have said nothing more about the matter as I did not consider it was any of the Navy's business, until the I.T. & T. made application for a radio station in Panama."[142] Undeterred by their failure to convince the State Department about the dangers of FDI, naval policymakers sought a broader audience in the U.S. Congress.

The revision of foreign ownership regulations would be taken up in the context of a multiyear debate about the reorganization of the American media and telecommunications industries. Between 1929 and 1934, several bills were introduced with the idea of merging the authority of the Interstate Commerce Commission, responsible for telegraphy and telephony, with that of the FRC, which spent most of its time on broadcasting. As I have shown, however, the FRC was in fact tasked with both broadcasting- and telecommunications-related functions. The foreign ownership provisions of the Radio Act of 1927 had never been aimed at a mass medium, and at stake in their revision now was the role that U.S.-headquartered communications MNCs would play in America's ascendancy.

The changing relationship between the cable and radio industries formed a crucial backdrop to the discussions, which spanned the Hoover and the Roosevelt administrations. The first hearings focusing on a Commission on Communications were held in 1929, shortly after the British merger that combined the Eastern and Marconi interests. Imperial and International Communications Ltd. was formed as a holding company, and Cable & Wireless became an operating company. Consolidation in British telecommunications and proposals for the same in the American context were responses to the threat that radio posed to the cable industry. Because a radio network was considerably cheaper than the cables, business logic dictated a mixed network. However, the realignment of business interests prompted by technological change resulted in a conflict with policymakers on both sides of the Atlantic.

In the United States, a mixed network went against the policy of type competition, and naval policymakers resisted ITT's entry into the wireless industry. In Britain, policymakers warned Cable & Wireless against abandoning many strategically important, but unprofitable, cables (Headrick, 1991, p. 212). British policymakers viewed ITT's expansion, in particular, with apprehension. Perhaps it was in response to this aspect of the "American invasion" that the British government set a limit of 25 percent on foreign investment in Imperial and International Communications Ltd. and stipulated that any stock in excess of this limit had to be sold back to British subjects.[143]

A major issue on the agenda during the 1929 hearings in Congress was ITT's purchase of RCA's telecommunications properties. When the Roosevelt administration took over, FDR appointed an interdepartmental committee to map out the communications landscape and consider the merger of all American communications systems. More far-reaching than the RCA-ITT combination, this proposal would have required a repeal of section 17 of the Radio Act of 1927.[144] The Roper Committee, named after Secretary of Commerce Daniel C. Roper, was assembled in fall 1933 and included representatives of the Navy, War, State, and Commerce Departments as well as the FRC and the U.S. Coast Guard (McChesney, 1993, p. 186). By this time, RCA's monopolistic practices in the sale of radio receivers had made it so unpopular that it had to settle an antitrust suit and seemed to have only one staunch proponent left: the Navy Department. Captain Hooper, the Navy's representative before Congress and the Roper Committee, continued to press for type competition and RCA's monopoly. Yet RCA was now far less enthusiastic about international radiotelegraphy than it had been a decade earlier. Company executives were focused on marketing radio receivers and overseeing the expansion of the National Broadcasting Company (Aitken, 1985). When ITT attacked the Navy's plans outright, RCA would do little to defend them.

The Navy Department did not suggest any changes to section 12 of the Radio Act of 1927 during the 1929 hearings, nor did it insert an amendment into the first radio bill of the new decade that Congress seriously considered, H.R. 11635, introduced in April 1930.[145] By the time the Senate commented on the bill, at the end of January 1931, the first version of indirect foreign ownership regulations had mysteriously found its way into it. H.R. 11635 simply extended section 12 to holding companies: it allowed no foreign directors or officers in the licensee's parent company and limited foreign investment to 20 percent of the parent company's capital stock.[146] Although naval policymakers denied that the Navy Department had been consulted about parts of the provision, they defended the amendment for years thereafter.[147] At first, the Navy used the proposal for the revision of foreign ownership regulations as leverage over ITT in the Panama controversy, while both the company and the Navy sought informal avenues of resolution.[148] When All America Cables received its license, naval policymakers were left with only the legislative avenue to keep the radio industry independent of the cables.

Navy officers did not forget the lesson the State Department was trying to impart: limiting companies' expansion would mean turning business over to competitors from other countries. "I am 100% for the I. T. & T.

in their efforts to own equipment and plants abroad," Hooper wrote to a colleague, "but as long as they are an international company, I do not believe they should own the Mackay Company in the U.S."[149] The Navy Department offered ITT a choice between eliminating its foreign connections or abandoning its radio licenses.[150] In the course of their debate before Congress, naval policymakers and ITT clashed over the broader importance of FDI for the national interest, and the precise contours of the final regulations, in section 310(b) of the Communications Act of 1934, would be shaped by a disagreement on three key factors: Should foreign officers and directors be permitted to serve on the boards of U.S.-headquartered MNCs at all? What percentage of foreign stockholding was permissible in holding companies? And how much, if any, discretion should the FRC have over companies with foreign ties?

Now that Hooper conceded the importance of American expansion, he recommended that indirect foreign ownership regulations should prohibit any American communications company from owning commercial facilities in foreign countries unless provided for by treaty.[151] "If [host countries] agree to a treaty they will do so with their eyes open," he commented, "whereas under the present scheme of things individuals sell out their own country without the people being aware of it."[152] The lesson Hooper seems to have drawn from the Panama controversy was that government officials in weaker countries were unable to defend the principle of national ownership against the wishes of powerful American MNCs and that their citizens were unaware of this fact. His solution would have exposed the terms of the MNCs' operation to more publicity than the contracts approved by the executive departments and would have given power of decision to the legislature in the host country, which was more attuned to societal pressures, such as the intensity of anti-American sentiment at any given time.

When pushing to eliminate ITT's foreign officers, the Navy Department clearly distinguished between headquarters and subsidiaries. The indirect foreign ownership provisions of the proposed legislation were to apply to the parent company alone, and existing board members would be grandfathered.[153] Hooper had resigned himself to local involvement in subsidiaries of MNCs, assuming that it was only a matter of time before every country nationalized its communications companies anyway.[154] Foreign management of subsidiaries, also a general practice at United Fruit, did not make a company any less American.[155]

Predictably, however, ITT did not want to remove its foreign executives, nor did it want to divest its radio holdings.[156] During congressional hearings in March and December 1932, it decided to make the case for the importance of FDI for the national interest and challenge the Navy Department's definition of control. Since RCA had already concluded exclusive traffic agreements with every important country, Vice President Frank Page testified, "the only way we could get in was to establish our own stations there."[157] Traffic agreements, Page pointed out, did not guarantee the security of confidential information. In fact, RCA itself provided information to foreign government administrations, as its contracts frequently called for an exchange of patents and other technical information.[158]

Far from putting the company under obligation to foreign governments, ITT executives pointed out, FDI protected American interests, because it ensured American control on both ends of the radio circuits.[159] ITT itself owned both ends of several circuits, including the circuit between the United States and Spain and the ones connecting the United States and the South American republics. These circuits provided competition to RCA, which operated its circuits jointly with the subsidiaries of foreign corporations, as the example of the AEFG consortium made clear.[160] ITT sought to be recognized for the preeminent telecommunications carrier that it was, pointing out that it wasn't RCA that wrested supremacy in communications from the British in South America.[161] With 60,000 miles of cable, ITT was now the second-largest international communications system in the world behind the merged British firm and, its executives repeatedly asserted, "the *only* really American international communications system" [emphasis in original].[162] They blamed RCA for turning a matter of commercial competition into a political question and charged them with trying to secure an unfair advantage.[163] The logic of ITT was the logic of end-to-end control over termini, which downplayed the leverage that control over territory provided governments and called attention to the amount of trust policymakers placed in the network manager. Type competition and end-to-end control sealed the network off from foreign influence in different ways. At issue was where exactly the imaginary borders protecting the United States should be placed. Even though ITT compared itself to the British merger, there was, perhaps not surprisingly, one thing it never addressed: the influence of cable holdings on its loyalty.

International expansion had no impact on national identity and loyalty, ITT stressed, ridiculing navy officers' fears about national security as "bugaboo."[164] From the vantage point of the company, FDI was no different from other forms of expansion, including international diplomacy. Company executives used the AEFG consortium to point out how tenuous RCA's loyalty was, and they brought up the 1920 controversy where the Navy had to dispatch destroyers to dissuade Western Union and its British cartel partner from landing a cable at Miami.[165] "If, as Captain Hooper has suggested, ... anyone who has any contact whatsoever with a foreigner is tainted," Behn declared, broadening his argument, "then I think that we ought to abolish our embassies and all legations throughout the world, and the State Department included since friendliness with foreigners makes one a suspicious American."[166] This was a more sarcastic version of the idea that American Marconi advanced during the previous decade: the relationship between parent and subsidiaries was arm's-length, and corporations expanding abroad could remain national to precisely the same extent that governments could.

Executives at ITT also downplayed the importance of both foreign executives and foreign stockholding. The two Spanish directors were put in "as a gesture of good will toward Spain," Vice President Page told the Senate Interstate Commerce Committee. A large part of ITT's stock held abroad, Behn pointed out, was owned by Americans living abroad, though he could not tell what percentage of the 9.35 percent of the stock owned by foreigners was actually held by Americans.[167] ITT, of course, would have preferred the elimination of foreign ownership rules from the bills, but it did not want to antagonize the Navy.[168] At the company's annual board meeting, just a couple of months after the spring 1932 hearing, ITT's Spanish directors were not reelected, and nobody was appointed to fill the place of the Swedish director, who had passed away.[169] Two years later, when senators grilled Behn on the subject, he would confidently testify that none of the senior officers at ITT were foreigners.[170]

When H.R. 11635 failed to pass the Senate, a practically identical bill, H.R. 7716, was introduced in the House, carrying over the same amendment to foreign ownership rules.[171] President Hoover vetoed the bill and left office, leaving the door open for language more advantageous under the new administration. In early February 1934, President Roosevelt reviewed the report of the Roper Committee submitted during the previous month as well as the recommendations of the Navy Department. He then received the vice president of All America Cables, John K. Roosevelt, a distant relative, to discuss the matter.[172] John Roosevelt quickly made the case against type competition, which the Roper Committee had also rejected.[173] The Navy's plan for disassociating the Mackay Radio Company from ITT's cable properties, the cable executive explained, "would result in throttling our program to strengthen and replace our cables with radio links."[174]

FDR assured John Roosevelt that he did not doubt the Americanism of ITT, but he recommended a few changes.[175] He asked, what if the limit on stock ownership was raised to 33 percent but foreign ownership regulations would be extended to the cable industry as well?[176] John Roosevelt requested an exception for the Commercial Pacific Cable Company, which was 75 percent foreign owned, and suggested that the future FCC be given discretionary powers to decide when foreign ownership was against the public interest.[177] The idea of discretionary powers for the regulatory agency thus originated with ITT, while the Navy Department favored an automatic revocation of the license if the foreign ownership provisions of the legislation were violated.

Shortly after the president's support for the committee report arrived, the revised communications bills were introduced in both houses of Congress. The indirect foreign ownership regulations contained in H.R. 8301 and in S. 2910 represented the changes agreed to after the 1932 hearings: instead of a complete ban, the bill put a 20 percent limit on the number of foreign directors and carried over the 20 percent limit on foreign investment.[178] Lawmakers accepted that national security was sufficiently safeguarded by the takeover provision of the bill. From March to May, hearings were held on both bills, and informal negotiations resumed between ITT and the executive departments.

By this time, the Navy Department had received additional ammunition in the form of a January 1934 Joint Board report. The Board defended the complete ban on foreign directors at the headquarters of American companies, reinforced the importance of the 20 percent limit, and recommended that the foreign-owned shares should not be entitled to voting privileges.[179] Vice President Frank Page immediately contacted the State Department for help, asking the diplomats to issue a clear statement of policy on the most important question: what was the U.S. government's position on international expansion?[180] The company's landing license for the controversial Commercial Pacific Cable would soon be up for renewal, and ITT was afraid that if the U.S. government adopted the Board's principles, the State Department would deny renewal of the license.[181]

The company had little reason to be concerned. The State Department still supported worldwide expansion. "The best interests of the United States may well be served," Irwin Stewart at the Treaty Division spelled out, "by an extension of the operation of American communications companies in foreign countries which invite such expansion, which may at times involve taking over of certain existing facilities."[182] While naval policymakers viewed the proposed foreign ownership regulations as a defensive measure against danger from abroad, the diplomats were in favor of lenient rules of market entry, as they hoped to secure the same for American companies abroad.[183] Since American MNCs were by now deeply involved in the economies of other countries, the United States had more to lose than to gain from such defensive legislation.

The cable industry was a case in point. If the United States passed stringent foreign ownership regulations, other countries could retaliate by revoking the landing licenses of cable companies headquartered in the United States.[184] End-to-end control, which overemphasized the capital aspect of network control, only went so far. There were only five foreign-owned cable lines touching the United States, while twenty-two American-owned cables connected the United States with various foreign countries.[185] In addition, three of the five foreign-owned cable lines were operated by what the diplomats (though not the Navy) considered American interests, Western Union and the controversial ITT subsidiary, the Commercial Pacific Cable Company.[186] The diplomats separated ownership and control, and when push came to shove, they found authority over operation to be the better indicator of American control. Policymakers' emphasis on operation as the location of control makes clear that—the importance of corporate nationality notwithstanding—network control in the cable industry must be analyzed in its own right.

The disagreement between the Navy and State Departments indicates a larger rift in the administration. From the perspective of the State Department, what appeared to stand in the way of U.S. expansion was the Navy Department. While the diplomats had come to realize the benefits of increasingly uncertain forms of control as the country's overall position in the world system improved, the Navy's insistence on autonomy continued to hinder the multinational corporation, the only source of expansion any country could rely on.[187] The diplomats were not alone. Senator Clarence Dill, the sponsor of S. 2910, warned Secretary Adams that it was not desirable "to become unduly fearful and handicap our own American capital in the development of communication service throughout the world."[188] Capital was still subject to nationalist discourse in the 1930s, but American policymakers were now divided on the central problem, whether a U.S.-headquartered MNC was one of "us" or one of "them." As early as 1934, State Department officials forwent policies appropriate for an underdog in favor of policies suitable for an aspiring world leader.

Lawmakers, well aware that ITT was the only company seriously affected by the foreign ownership provisions, were also sympathetic to the company's arguments.[189] U.S.-headquartered corporations were an alternative to government ownership of stations on the territories of other countries. The United States, they observed, could not carry on international communications without the consent of other countries.[190] Senators adopted the term "courtesy directors" from the company and questioned the dangers arising from such a small number of foreign executives.[191] From their vantage point, "practically the entire stock" of the company was owned in the United States.[192] "Language of this amendment would prevent licenses to these constituent companies," commented Senator Wallace White, who drafted the direct foreign ownership regulations in the 1920s, adding that it "would wreck this system and leave RCA supreme in field near *complete monopoly*" [emphasis in original].[193] In his view, the indirect foreign ownership amendment to Section 12 of the Radio Act was simply "nationalism run wild."[194] When ITT recommended raising the percentage limit, Senator Dill did wonder whether company executives would tolerate 30, 40, or even 50 percent foreign ownership, but he was satisfied with the company's recommendation of 25 percent, which would bring the company on par with the merged British company.[195]

In April 1934, Senator Dill introduced S. 3285, which made several changes based on the hearings. It increased the limit on foreign stockholding to 25 percent and made the section effective as of June 1935 to allow ITT the time to make the necessary changes.[196] After hearings during the following month, the bill raised the number of foreign directors to 25 percent of the total.[197] The Joint Board recommendation for denying voting privileges for stock held in foreign hands was raised during the hearings but was never incorporated into a draft bill.[198] The nationality of MNCs had long functioned as a geopolitical battlefield, and policymakers were now on their way to establish another symbolic border in global communications.

Now policymakers only had to consider the matter of Commission discretion in deciding whether foreign stockholding was against the public interest. Discretion by the FRC or any future Commission was ITT's preference; statutory guidelines were too rigid, and company executives much preferred to deal with the FRC on a case-by-case basis. Company executives were particularly opposed to the automatic revocation provision, pointing out that all the company's rivals had to do to get rid of the company was to buy a sufficient number of shares.[199] (Recall that in the 1910s it was the solicitor for the State Department who raised this possibility, wondering about the usefulness of foreign ownership regulations.) Keeping up the attack on the Navy's definition of foreign control, ITT pointed out that ownership was merely a stand-in for control, and not a very good one. If a percentage of the stock passed into foreign hands, it did not mean that foreigners exercised control.[200]

Hooper, who ever since the Mackay controversy had considered the FRC incompetent and disinterested in matters of international communications, opposed commission discretion and instead put his faith in specific legislative language.[201] "If the large companies in an industry wish to attain a common end," he articulated, employing an early version of the capture theory of regulation, "they will eventually succeed unless the laws passed by Congress are such as to provide adequate barriers."[202] The government was outmatched because of its "ever-changing personnel" and had little chance in the long run to resist pressure from companies with "clever executives and high-priced lawyers."[203] As a result, unlimited discretion should not be given to any regulating body on matters of broad policy.

When H.R. 8301, the bill that would become the Communications Act of 1934, went into conference, ITT relied on its Army connections to get the War Department to add the discretion clause, but the War Department refused.[204] Behn lobbied President Roosevelt and managed to secure the State Department's support.[205] When lawmakers agreed to the conference report, the discretion clause was already in the bill, and the Communications Act of 1934 passed with the clause intact.[206] According to section 310 (b)(4), "the station license ... shall not be granted to ... any corporation directly or indirectly controlled by any other corporation of which any officer or more than one fourth of the directors are aliens, or of which more than one fourth of the capital stock is owned of record or voted by aliens." The section also makes foreign governments and corporations organized under the laws of a foreign country ineligible for a license "if the Commission finds that the public interest will be served by the refusal or the revocation of such license." Only after the bill passed did naval policymakers find out that the State Department had weakened the rules and Congress had accepted the request for FRC discretion.[207]

The addition of FRC discretion vitiated the efforts of the service departments to retain control of American communications systems, the incoming chief of naval operations, Admiral William H. Standley, told Secretary of State Cordell Hull.[208] The source of all the trouble, according to Hooper, was the diplomats, specifically Francis White of the Latin American Division, who helped ITT so that he could gain employment with the company after his service for the government was up.[209] There was little love lost between Hooper and White, the latter having played a major role in the Panama controversy and having evaluated the Navy Department's actions as "highhanded, narrow-minded and arbitrary."[210] He blamed the Navy's intransigence on "one rather routine-minded individual," Captain Hooper.[211]

Naval policymakers could have influenced the first Federal Communications Commission, had Hooper's bid for membership been accepted. Citing the Joint Board's report for support, Hooper pushed for a seat for the military departments on the future FCC.[212] He made the president's short list, despite ITT's opposition, but did not get the nomination.[213] Irwin Stewart of the State Department, on the other hand, did gain enough support.[214] As a result, the vision of the State Department lived on in the new commission. Thus, the incorporation of the particular form of indirect foreign ownership regulations analyzed above in communications legislation has a broader significance. It marks the point where the confident vision of an aspiring world leader replaced the defensive stance of a challenger.

Until the end of his appointment as director of naval communications in late 1934, Hooper advocated continued vigilance against "the slightest trend toward an international company."[215] "I am absolutely appalled by the power of these corporations," he complained to former secretary of the Navy Josephus Daniels.[216] The future seemed uncertain, as Hooper's trust in the law was wearing thin. He speculated that ITT would work to eliminate foreign ownership rules. "Then," he predicted, "the British will buy the controlling stock and again dominate the rapid communications of the world as they did before radio."[217]

As this chapter has revealed, policymakers in the Navy and State Departments adopted markedly different positions available to a home state of MNCs, suggesting policies appropriate for the role they perceived for the United States. Naval policymakers, reasoning from the mind-set of an inferior power, challenged the State Department's optimistic perspective on international expansion. At the heart of the conflict over foreign investment lay the mutually exclusive visions of the government departments and ITT about the appropriate extent of the company's expansion. The basic tenet of the Navy's vision was the continued inferiority of the United States to Britain in global communications, even though cooperation between the two countries was increasing in general naval policy, and signs of growing American superiority were becoming evident in communications matters. The perceived inferiority of the United States shaped naval policymakers' theory about the internationalization of business. From whatever angle officers were looking at it, the United States stood to lose. Companies either expanded too far into other powers' spheres of influence, pulling the United States into a war it might not win, or their expansion ruffled no feathers, in which case it was reasonable to wonder why Britain, for instance, did not mind a U.S.-headquartered company encroaching on its sphere of influence.

Even though indirect foreign ownership regulations were included in the Communications Act of 1934, the section marked a defeat for the Navy Department. Decisions were not passed over naval policymakers' heads; their objections were duly heard and taken into account. ITT had an important say in shaping the legislation, but it did not gain the support of the State Department or Congress because all the diplomats or lawmakers were fishing for jobs at the company. Nor was the government powerless to deal with the company. Licensing, especially decision-making power about cable landing rights, was rooted in territorial control and provided significant leverage, which all participants were fully aware of. ITT prevailed because it was on the right side of the central rift in the U.S. government: its vision coincided with that of the majority of policymakers.

By 1934, the U.S. government as a whole had embraced the country's new role in global communications and sought to encourage the expansion of American multinationals. ITT's foreign investments were safe for now, though its provision of high-end communications equipment to Nazi Germany in the 1933–1945 period would test American officials' trust yet again. Control over the global network has not, however, passed to the United States with the Communications Act of 1934. Historians have pointed to 1945 and even the 1970s as the time of hegemonic transfer in communications (Headrick, 1991; Hugill, 1999). Future research would flesh out further when deeds truly sealed what had been known since 1934: that a new center was forming in global communications.

8 Conclusion

Ascendancy in the world system is tied to the extension of control over a communications network, which in turn is inseparable from territorial gains. For a rising power, both autonomy and expansion are important. Autonomy refers to the ability to assert control over parts of the network on the country's own territory. It is covered by the concept of jurisdiction, but jurisdiction is a national-level, legal category that is too limited to capture the goals of regional and global powers, which pursue control via both legal and extralegal means outside their territories. Instead, the network control framework laid out here explained what it would take to control a global communications network. In the preceding chapters, I identified the purpose of control, two levels of control, and three sites—technology, territory, and capital—of control. I then used this framework to trace the steps American policymakers took during the early twentieth century deploying their emerging knowledge about the world system, radiotelegraphy, and the multinational corporation (MNC) in order to shape a global network according to their geopolitical ambitions. Because of the countervailing influences introduced by control over technology, territory, and capital, complete control was beyond reach in the three decades under study, but policymakers were sometimes able to convince themselves that they were on the way to achieving it.

In their quest to secure the ability to communicate, states rely on policy on the structural level of network control. Policy mattered during the first part of the time period under analysis, when the autonomy of American wireless communications was intertwined with the applicability of a telegraph framework for the regulation of radiotelegraphy. As policymakers pursued interconnection, licensing, and national ownership, they adjusted aspects of the common carrier regulatory framework in response to both the inherent connectivity of radio technology and the possibility of centralized control via a British-headquartered early MNC. In addition, the place of incorporation test was supplemented first by citizenship requirements and then by foreign ownership regulations, in line with the transformation of corporate law in other industries. Whether radio was in fact a type of telegraph and what made companies "American" was never far from policymakers' minds as they pursued changes in the legal system to meet the demands of a rising power. Some of their solutions, most importantly direct and indirect foreign ownership regulations, are still good law today (47 U.S. Code, §310). On the tactical level of network control, the key to autonomy was control over territory, but expanding the available technological alternatives was also important. Naval policymakers were able to deny the use of American territory to American Marconi after the 1904 Nantucket controversy, and again in 1917, because they could replace the station with an alternative.

Dealing with the practical difficulties of squaring autonomy of radio communications with expanding the influence of the United States in global communications formed a central aspect of America's rise until policymakers became more comfortable with the multinational corporation as the vehicle for American ascendancy. American policymakers considered intermodal competition, cartels, and limited foreign direct investment to pursue expansion via corporations established in the country as the Navy Department continued to seek to seal off the radio network from the cable network and advocated limited geographical expansion. The United States was approaching a coherent position by the 1930s only because the State Department actively sought to marginalize the Navy in radio policy. When, in the wake of the Navy's marginalization, the United States finally accepted the joint treatment of the cable and radio networks, the road was open for American participation in the future International Telecommunication Union. Before addressing the significance of changes on the structural and tactical levels of network control for the rise of the United States in global communications, or for the framework proposed here to illuminate them, however, I will sketch changes in the conventional wisdom that should result from analyzing radio policy as a type of foreign policy aimed at an international telegraph network.

Radio History and Radio Policy

Broadcasting has cast a long shadow. Treating radiotelegraphy as the prehistory of broadcasting has foreclosed a thorough analysis of wireless as a critical infrastructure—a prehistory of the internet. Yet, central aspects of radio regulation were first enacted to regulate a point-to-point medium used for confidential, strategic communications rather than a mass medium. Because of the nature of radio technology, early radio regulation included provisions aimed at the network, the airwaves, and information. When government ownership of radiotelegraphy did not solve all of policymakers' problems at once, they developed different approaches for them over time, and this book has focused on policymakers' efforts to assert control over the physical infrastructure. As policymakers were figuring out what to do with a point-to-point medium, they also had to adjust to the emergence of broadcasting. If this was insufficiently complex, both radiotelegraphy and broadcasting were also geopolitically significant, which means that the development of all three pieces of major radio legislation in the early twentieth century must be understood in an international context. I will comment on domestic legislation before I address wavelengths and information in a geopolitical context.

By studying domestic regulation and policies for international expansion in relation to each other, this book has recovered the organization-organization (state-MNC) frame buried under the individual-organization frame that has dominated scholarship focused on the democratic potential of radio technology. Revisionist histories have largely bypassed the international aspects of radio policy, ignoring control over the network in favor of control over the airwaves. Prioritizing the airwaves over the network or over information has led to insightful analyses of the gradual elimination of alternative social visions for radio, but at the price of containing the story of radio in a domestic framework. In the domestic framework, the Radio Act of 1912 is seen as a watershed because of the curtailment of the individual exploration of the airwaves (Douglas, 1989, p. 236), but the amateurs, who played an important role in the technology-territory nexus of network control, came late to the regulation of radio and their role in radio policy during the 1920s has yet to be fleshed out, while the relationship between the state and the MNCs operating on its territory remained a constant feature during the first three decades of radio regulation. Thus, early radio policy was the site of several struggles that should be understood in relation to each other.

Much of the analytical difficulty stems from the fact that policymakers dealt with two different applications of radio technology. When the broadcasting boom began, with all of its utopian promise and quirky experimental programs, the point-to-point medium and the mass medium existed side by side. In the Radio Act of 1927, and then in the Communications Act of 1934, a telegraphy framework, with its focus on natural monopoly, common carrier obligations, and—because of the international nature of radiotelegraphy, geopolitical rivalry—coexisted with a nationally oriented broadcast framework focused on spectrum allocation and free expression in a democratic society. One consequence of the fact that researchers have not grappled with this issue head-on is the now ironclad legal treatment of foreign ownership regulations as associated with broadcasting and propaganda.

Radio policy in the early twentieth century represents a major challenge to the silo model of regulation, which assumed a one-to-one relationship between a medium and its use (Horwitz, 1989, p. 125). In Captain Hooper's mind, for example, the distinction between broadcasting and radiotelegraphy was so important that he favored reassigning radiotelegraphy from the FRC to the government departments.[1] Separating the licensing of a point-to-point station from that of a broadcast station would have quickly exposed the split between licensing under a common carrier regulatory regime and the evolving meaning of the concept relevant for spectrum allocation. Analyses interested in institutional choices with regard to spectrum management could trace the continuation of the common carrier regulatory framework into the broadcasting period with special attention to when and how the substance of the licensing framework was rethought for the new use of the technology.

The regulation of the airwaves looms large in a study of a global network that used them for connection, but exactly how lawmakers turned their attention to the spectrum is yet to be documented. In the early years, policymakers understood radio as a strategically significant telegraph service, whose regulation swept up the airwaves in the process. As chapters 2 and 3 have demonstrated, interference was a fact of life in these early years, but "interference plus" influenced radio policy. The debate about licensing in Britain was intertwined with discussions about the value of radiotelegraphy compared to the Empire's submarine cable network. In the United States, radio licensing in the Radio Act of 1912 was inseparable from policymakers' attempts to neutralize what appeared to be a foreign corporation.

These early chapters touched on the emergence of understanding the airwaves as a public resource but did not fully trace where this idea originated. For much of the first decade of the twentieth century, as chapters 2 and 3 document, licensing regulated station use, and spectrum management only gradually emerged as a separate concern. This analysis may help answer a question raised by legal scholar Yochai Benkler, who attributed the lack of mutualistic alternatives for spectrum management (i.e., multilateral coordination among numerous individuals) to the engineering assumptions underlying radio policy (Benkler, 1998, p. 314). It seems significant that governments and corporations took their seats at a table labeled "telegraph service regulation" well before anybody realized that they were going to decide the institutional framework for spectrum management. How can we talk about access to the spectrum as "the right of every citizen" in the early twentieth century when the spectrum itself was not the focus of early regulatory efforts (cf. Aitken, 1994)? To fully address this matter, future archival research must explore the relationship between the world of science and engineering and that of policymakers, the latter of which was informed by a legal framework for public utility regulation and a geopolitical framework for advancing the position of the country in the world system.

At the heart of understanding the spectrum as a legally significant concept is the idea of a public resource. Chapter 3 has addressed some of the ways American policymakers incorporated the idea into public utility regulation, but there seems to be a lot more work to be done. Researchers interested in the commodification of the airwaves, for example, have themselves termed the spectrum as a kind of real estate (Streeter, 1996, p. 230). During the early twentieth century, both the real estate metaphor and metaphors about common property resources circulated, and policymakers' use of metaphors in relation to each other is worth a closer look.[2]

In addition to the airwaves, I have also treated direct control over information in a cursory manner, focusing instead on the way control over the network stood in for control over information flows. It is apparent from the research presented, however, that explanations for licensing that start with the government's interest in the content of transmissions must be reconsidered (Bar & Sandvig, 2008; Pool, 1983; Streeter, 1996). Since licensing was initially aimed at station use in the common carrier framework, it was certainly not intended to be prior restraint; policymakers did not seek to stifle democratic debate. Insofar as naval policymakers were directly concerned with information flowing through the radio network, they used citizenship regulations to address the possibility of transmitting stolen information to the enemies of the United States. The ability to communicate and the ability to deny communication were first and foremost military requirements that focused on confidential information.

It is likely because of the origins of licensing in the common carrier framework that speakers before the Radio Act of 1927 did not have full First Amendment protections, but when and how did individual or corporate users of radio sets become "speakers" under the First Amendment? To answer this question, we must understand the legal status of the information that flowed through communications networks in the 1910s. In what way, if any, did the 1917 Espionage Act, which criminalized the delivery of information relating to national defense to a person who was not entitled to receive it, parse individual expression on a street corner, press traffic, and point-to-point communications for the purpose of regulation? How did the regulation of stolen confidential information develop into or alongside content regulation for a mass medium after the emergence of broadcasting? (For aspects of the story related to broadcasting, see Benjamin, 2001.) Research oriented toward such questions would uncover the way information changes shape under the different regulatory regimes.

Knowledge and Policy Decisions

Historical questions about the incorporation of radio technology in the American legal framework highlight the relationship between knowledge and action in policymaking. Currently, cultural analysts commenting on the policy process overemphasize the role of influential ideas and differ only on how immediately they influence policymaking. According to one position, there is "a very short step" between influential figures of speech, such as the ozone hole, for example, and an international treaty (Edwards, 2010, pp. 386–387; Hunter, 2003, p. 446). The problem with this perspective is the lack of one-to-one equivalence between knowledge and action: the same course of action may be consistent with different frames, and the same frame can lead to different courses of action (Rein & Schön, 1993, p. 151). A good example in media studies is "the discourse of the vast wasteland" in reference to broadcast television, which provided the context to two quite different policy outcomes: public service broadcasting, which sought to save television from the ills of commodification, and cable television, which did no such thing (McMurria, 2007; Ouellette, 2002).

The second perspective on how ideas influence policymaking, by contrast, describes discourse as a structural condition that sets the context for action but whose effects cannot be established in a linear sense (Streeter, 1987, p. 188). When a new discursive field opens up, it becomes possible to act in ways not explicable by simple self-interest (Streeter, 1987, p. 174). Governing ideas proscribe a range of alternatives but do not determine *which* one(s), if any, will win out. Social constructivist approaches generally study the early phases of technological change, offering insight into how culture appropriates new technologies (Edwards, 2003, p. 223). Such analyses stop at the point they call "interest group struggle," in effect leaving the minutiae of details to the policy analyst.

Given the underlying assumption that the state is simply one of the interest groups jockeying for power, these analyses tend to overlook the central role of the foreign policy executive, whose interests transcend the pressures of any societal group. Moreover, the neat separation of the "development of ideas" and the "interest group" struggle aspects of policymaking seems to suggest that bureaucratic bargaining has no impact on the ideas under consideration. Without fully understanding how policymakers approached the airwaves over the course of three decades—how and why they ended up with a particular way of seeing when several different options presented themselves—the following sketch is necessarily speculative and is intended simply to make the case for paying attention to the timing of policy developments in relation to the emergence of new metaphors in the long term. For such a study, the researcher will not be able to avoid the details of alternative proposals that are compatible with the same general idea, the juxtaposition of very different ideas supporting the same outcome, or even the analysis of how policy participants jockeyed for influence behind the scenes.

New technologies are "born nameless," being subject to multiple contradictory definitions (Altman, 2004, p. 19). Policymakers use metaphors and analogies to fill the void of understanding (Sawhney, 1996, p. 292). Such figures of speech are "creative," either bringing latent connections between ideas into view or creating those connections, depending on how influential the analyst deems them (Black, 1979, p. 39). In the case of radiotelegraphy, for example, the idea of the airwaves as a public resource emerged by 1908 and was incorporated into draft bills in 1910, but regulatory action relying on the idea would take another seventeen years. Why did the common carrier framework bind radiotelegraphy until 1927?

As with other studies of new technologies, radio policy raises questions about the relationship between policymakers' conscious intent and the use of figurative language to pursue their goals, the strength of the conceptual framework they rely on, and the unique properties of the technology itself. Policymakers identified radio as "wireless telegraphy" early on, and the analogy slotted the airwaves into the position of wires in a wired network. On this level of abstraction, the conceptual framework was so strong as to blind policymakers to the potential of broadcasting (Sawhney, 1996).

Perhaps the public resource metaphor emerged into an established, coherent way of seeing, fortified by related precedents, and it took time to cut a path through them. Policy is indeed a site for the production of new knowledge, but unique technological properties, various metaphors to make them intelligible, the legal frameworks housing these metaphors, and, in the case of strategic technologies, geopolitical interests, rub against each other via trial and error in a multidecade process until new knowledge is formed. Ideas may be transformative, but they are constrained every step of the way by established structures.

On a lower level of abstraction, policymakers and corporate executives thinking within the common carrier framework had several analogs at their disposal, such as telephony and submarine cables, and made conscious decisions to deploy them. The fact that early jurisdictional disputes about radiotelegraphy took place in a geopolitical context is difficult to avoid. However genuine the process of developing new knowledge is, at some point that knowledge is deployed to get results, and the policy researcher must be concerned at least as much with the differences in the ways various parties use an analogy as with the similarities. In chapters 3 and 5, I showed that policymakers used figurative language on the structural level of network control to further their geopolitical goals. American policymakers relied on the idea of the spectrum as a public resource to weaken the telephone analogy and on the idea of the corporation as a migrant subject for the imposition of foreign ownership regulations.

A quick comparison of the two problems leads to the hunch that policymakers found it more difficult to wrap their minds around a new technology than around a new corporate form. Though the first foreign ownership regulations were not enacted until 1927, the year the United States asserted ownership over the spectrum, they were conceptually in place by 1916. Naval policymakers were almost immediately suspicious of American Marconi's British ties, and some of them thought in terms of stock ownership as the manifestation of foreign influence as early as 1902. A nationalist framework was readily available; the difficulty lay in ongoing internal disagreements about how best to understand what made a corporation "American" and in adherence to the legal framework, which needed an overhaul. By contrast, even though the common carrier framework was readily available, policymakers ended up rejecting the submarine cable analogy, which they had originally preferred. Instead, they brought in a new metaphor, a public resource, which highlighted the role of the airwaves in the radio network but did not rely on the new metaphor for regulation. It was in the context of internal opposition to the Marconi organization's plans that the physical characteristics of radiotelegraphy came to the fore, prompting a rethinking of the common carrier framework that would not be completed until after the broadcast boom.

Network Control

By identifying the various facets of network control and examining the territory-capital nexus in detail, my work facilitates comparisons along three dimensions, either separately or in combination: the position of the country in the world system, the time period, and the network itself. The general world systems framework that informs this study presupposes that states' geopolitical interests are more similar than different over time and that a state's position in the system—as a hegemon or a challenger—overrides the other differences inherent in comparing very different time periods (for arguments against objectifying and utilizing the past, see Elton, 1967; O'Hara, 2010). It further presupposes that countries seek to hold onto their preeminence, or at least seek a soft landing, which makes the Trump presidency unique. (The words of an official from an Asian ally aptly capture a prevalent sentiment underlying contemporary geopolitical analyses: is this how a superpower commits suicide? [Heydarian, 2018, p. 11].) Thus, one could address the similarities and differences between British and American approaches to network control during the early twentieth century, but a different study might compare American approaches to network control at the beginning of the twentieth and twenty-first centuries. In the former example, different countries fill the roles of the hegemon and the challenger; in the latter, the same country fills two different roles.

Institutional Comparisons

Before we treat "Britain" and "the United States" as a single entity, the concept of the perceptual transitional lag, used to explain the disconnect between policies and the country's interests, needs to be examined on a more granular level. What accounts for the fact that naval policymakers, in particular, continued to reason from the mind-set of an inferior power even as the world was changing to America's advantage? Researchers have pointed out that the perceptual lag results from the pressures of institutions brought into being in an earlier stage of hegemonic transition (Krasner, 1995, p. 35).[3] However, those pressures may not have worked the same way in every context, and the clear differences among American policymakers in relation to the country's role in the world system deserve a closer look.

First, comparisons within the U.S. Navy between those responsible for radio policy and those responsible for general naval policy could prove instructive. In particular, to what extent, if any, was the transitional lag linked to the career trajectory of Captain Hooper, who became influential as fleet radio officer when the United States was still a host state to British Marconi and remained influential in naval communications through the end of the time period covered here? Did the defensiveness of radio policy develop independently of the main line of thinking in the Navy, or was Hooper's position indicative of the ideas held by a faction in the Navy? Second, as chapter 7 revealed, the Navy Department's perspective in the United States increasingly came in conflict with those of the diplomats. But what explains the State Department's optimism? Did the diplomats already encounter the issues resulting from the internationalization of business in other industries, as suggested in chapter 7, and did they resolve these issues to their satisfaction? If so, when and what theory did they develop about the internationalization of business in the context of America's rise?

Comparing the ideas of American and British policymakers, in turn, raises the question of imitation. World system theory posits that outstanding economic performance and the ability to project power globally are key characteristics of world leadership. It is because of their economic leadership that hegemons are seen as representing the future for other states (Gunder Frank, 1996, p. 20; Taylor, 1996, p. 5). As rivals start to copy the leading power, they catch up. In consequence, "high hegemony," when the hegemon is at its peak, is a relatively short period (Taylor, 1996, p. 3). Therefore, in this framework, imitation is the way to ascendancy, but are specific policies aimed at network control equally useful for world leaders and for challengers?

Though both British and American policymakers belonged to a transnational discursive community, it is striking that the latter often adopted policy solutions worked out in Britain (e.g., the importance of the nationality of operators for network security, the goal of "direct communication" with the principal powers of the world). In the 1920s, at the same time that the United States saw the potential to remake the international order (Schake, 2017, p. 252), American diplomats and naval policymakers came to think about the relationship between the radio networks and the cable networks quite differently. The diplomats still reasoned with the established way of thinking, which was tied to British perspectives, while naval policymakers were developing an approach that foregrounded the independence of the radio network. Was thinking about radio as a "backup" technology detrimental to the interests of the United States, as naval policymakers believed? Were the diplomats, perhaps even unbeknownst to them, too tied to British perspectives to effectively pave the way for American advancement? In more general terms, how does membership in a geopolitical discursive community influence a country's chances of getting ahead? It is only by following the development of the global radio and cable networks in relation to each other that we can begin to address such questions.

A comparison between the attitudes of hegemons and challengers toward either communications MNCs or toward intermediaries in general could also prove instructive because theories that are blind to the potential clash between nationalism and corporate expansion tend to overstate the commonality of interest between the state and large corporations, while nationalist accounts may overstate the commonality of interest between foreign governments and their MNCs, as the Navy Department did in the 1920s. The methodological challenge in this line of research is to harness nationalist thinking for analytical purposes while subjecting it to analysis when it is productive to do so. I incorporated the goal of the Navy Department with regard to communications networks into the theoretical framework to accomplish the first objective, and I aimed at the second one when analyzing how policymakers decided which companies deserved their support.

This book has revealed that cooperation between MNCs and their home states was far from preordained but was instead a historical development. In order to grasp the extent to which cooperation is tied to the position of the country in the world system, however, we must understand the relationship between MNCs and their home states in more detail. Arguably, the visions of world powers and global capital for organizing space run parallel, crossing paths only occasionally. Both need control over territory worldwide, but not always the same territories and certainly not for the same reasons. They may mutually use each other to their advantage, but both need to recalibrate as the position of the home state in the world economy changes. How have communications MNCs envisioned the global economy and their place in it? What did they think about the importance of their home states and that of the various host states they came into contact with? How did these ideas shape their corporate agreements? Without understanding how corporate visions informed strategies and combining their analysis with an analysis of policymakers' perspectives in both Britain and the United States, no comprehensive political economic explanation is possible.

During the early twentieth century, the relationship between multinational corporations and the governments they interacted with was the critical problem in the transition from British to American leadership in global communications. The commonsense realist perspective that "every government ... promotes the interests of its own national firms" does not explain the decades-long hand-wringing around the identities of companies with international operations (Gilpin, 2001, p. 299). Researchers of the multinational corporation who relied on "casual evidence ... gleaned from business histories" to comment on how easily MNCs acquire offspring and siblings also seem to have been mistaken (Vernon, 1971, p. 5; Vernon, 1974, p. 3). Such attempts have received intense scrutiny, as chapters 4, 6, and 7 have demonstrated. However, whether subsidiaries serve host states in time of war, as Raymond Vernon suggests, has yet to be documented with research about communications firms (Vernon, 1974, p. 3). Some of the questions pursued in this book dovetail with a general line of inquiry that has occupied American policymakers and researchers for the past half century. Were MNCs headquartered in the United States truly "US"? (Tyson, 1991). This question became central for network control because securing the ability to communicate and denying the same to one's opponent presupposes that policymakers working with private companies are able to identify companies as either friend or foe.

As I have shown, neither Britain nor the United States accepted British Marconi, with all of its subsidiaries, as theirs. Instead of the government and corporations acting together to create "a market for loyalties" targeting the general public (Price, 1994), in the early twentieth century the corporation itself became a subject of nationalist discourse. Corporations with international operations resisted the foreign-domestic binary that characterizes nationalist thought, but once locked into it, they were forced to accept the terms laid out by the state. American policymakers pushed back against the consequences of full legal personality to corporations and sought to reimpose a border breached by the expansion of MNCs. Foreign direct investment (FDI)—and, by extension, globalization—may not have shattered "the whole concept of nationality" but instead may have helped to bring it about (cf. Strange, 1996, p. 57). Just how MNCs in general and communications MNCs in particular evaluated and responded to this state of affairs requires a separate volume, one that would also incorporate the origins of the "multinational corporation" as an analytical concept. To what extent, if any, was this concept an ideological innovation linked to corporate executives' frustration with operating in a politically divided world economy? (For the idea that the term originated in IBM's PR division, see Strange, 1996, p. xiii.)

Further, the expansion of homegrown MNCs from a rising power raises questions for the theory of media imperialism. Foreign ownership of media outlets without a reciprocal presence in the owner's home state is identified as media imperialism (Lee, 1979). But how important is policymakers' support for corporate expansion in understanding whether any specific case is an example of media imperialism? During the first decade of the twentieth century, for example, the British Post Office pointed to interference with Marconi stations as justification for keeping out radio companies headquartered in the United States, making a reciprocal presence impossible.[4] This, however, was simply a convenient explanation from a government department that hindered the expansion of the very same company in the Empire and refused to support the company's non-intercommunication policy. Second, the general tendency to discount the difference between global and regional powers misses cases of layered media imperialism. Studies of FDI that position it as a threat to the sovereignty of host states have focused on the relationship between the company and one host state (Strange, 1996). In the

1910s, however, the decision about the presence of the Marconi Company in Latin America involved at least two host states of unequal power in any given instance. Brazil and the United States were both host states to British Marconi, but this did not stop the United States from seeking to influence the fate of the Brazilian concession. In what way, if any, does layered media imperialism affect the development of media industries in the countries subject to it?

While imperialism played an important role in American ascendancy, current conceptualizations of imperialism in communications and media studies are too focused on collaboration among core states to fully capture the dynamics at work. Corporate expansion in strategic industries is shaped by geopolitical rivalry. By ignoring who gave way and by how much, as the collaborative model of empire does, we are left with the perception that either equal control exists among core states or that no country in particular possesses control (see Hugill, 1999, p. 138, for the latter view; Winseck & Pike, 2007, p. 104). Perhaps the expansions of commercial radio and submarine cable companies are better understood as instances of "negotiated control," a concept that would treat imperialism and geopolitics as intertwined. Negotiated control refers to the mixture of cooperation and coercion among geopolitical rivals, the outcome of which serves as a barometer of advancement in the international pecking order. The 1906 convention discussed in chapter 2 serves as an example of negotiated control via international law, while the AEFG consortium, discussed in chapter 6, is an example of such control via corporate agreements. In the AEFG case, representatives from companies headquartered in core states divided up the communications traffic of peripheral regions, but the particular division of traffic was the outcome of geopolitical rivalry, which can be captured by analyzing corporate agreements over time. Successful instances of negotiated control often result after several failures.

Perhaps the broadest possible historical question related to the analysis developed in this book concerns the role of control over telecommunications networks for hegemonic transition as a whole. While American policymakers were setting their sights on network control in the radio industry, the United States itself was being transformed. This book has documented internal perspectives on America's rise in one particular industry, but structural theories of hegemonic transitions have long recognized that the position of a country in the world system does not change equally in every area of economic, political, and cultural life. Assessing the role of control over global communications networks requires researchers to grapple with conflicting theories about the order of transitions as well as with the interrelationships among the various aspects of a country's standing in the world. If world leadership is a package of leaderships in various fields, in what order did U.S. ascendancy take place, and how did preeminence in one area influence the others?

Based on the work of Immanuel Wallerstein, it is commonly accepted that world leadership rests on economic leadership, which is lost in the same order in which it was achieved: first in production, then in commerce, and finally in finance (Taylor, 1996, p. 32). Though the engine of the world economy had shifted to the United States by the 1880s, the country's financial preeminence would not be cemented until the 1920s. In concrete historical terms, the cultural influence of the American film industry followed the country's economic influence, but exactly how broader American cultural influence fits into the picture is inadequately understood. By 1923, Britain's share of its home market had dropped to 10 percent, with most of the exports arriving from Hollywood (Hills, 2002, p. 247). Military hegemony, in turn, followed economic and cultural power and reached a turning point during World War II (Headrick, 1991). Following the priorities of American policymakers, which focused on the oil industry, international transportation, and international communications, political geographer Peter Hugill argues that the United States enjoyed a definite advantage over Britain in the struggle over petroleum but failed to capitalize on its advantages in merchant shipping and did not achieve telecommunications hegemony until the 1970s (Hugill, 1999, p. 236; Hugill, 2014, p. 156). What's more, Hugill points out, British control over global communications explains Britain's continued dominance at the helm (Hugill, 1999, p. 236).

While the research presented here does not extend beyond the early 1930s, it appears that we cannot establish the importance of control over global communications for leadership without, first, separating communications networks from other strategic technologies and, second, theorizing their relationship to economic and military spheres of activity. When communications networks are used as auxiliaries of military and economic power, they must be linked to debates about various aspects of hegemonic transition, ranging from international finance to leading sectors and economic capabilities (Arrighi, 2010; Kennedy, 1987; Taylor, 1993; Thompson, 2000). Such links have been few and far between, in part because historical studies do not typically link up to the systemic level, while historical-structural researchers do not spend much time in archives. Studies linking historical and political science analyses can't avoid grappling with how policymakers' priorities at the turn of the century and the theoretical priorities of world systems analysis are related to each other.

Though this book has not reached the end of the transition, it has contributed to the literature on the transition between two very similar world leaders. The British and the American frameworks for understanding control over a global network could have been similar because the precepts of broadly similar legal systems mixed with the ideas of the geopolitical discursive community as policymakers were wrestling with the task of world leadership. If the next leader is not or is no longer a liberal democracy, will the assumptions of the transnational geopolitical community be fundamentally transformed? Country-specific comparisons will need to engage with this challenge as well.

In addition to its importance for geopolitics, a comparative study of communications multinationals may also be relevant for a study of globalization. That MNCs and globalization are intertwined is well accepted. Both structural researchers of international relations and historical sociologists are open to the possibility that part of the 1900–1934 period was characterized by globalization (Krasner, 1995, p. 30; Modelski and Thompson, 1996, p. xiv; Ohmae, 2000, p. 2; Strange, 1996, p. 43; Taylor, 1993, p. 8). This book has documented that the past was far from "a more stable and orderly world" in which corporate interests seamlessly mapped onto the national interest (cf. Sinclair, 2007, p. 139; cf. Strange, 1996, pp. 3–4). The communications industry, in turn, is crucial for both commerce and strategy, and its international expansion preceded the internationalization of production and finance. This book has contributed to our understanding of control over communications networks during an earlier period of globalization, when multinational public utilities were recognized as MNCs and became geopolitically significant. Since a direct corollary of the cyclical world systems framework is that globalization is a recurrent aspect of the system, historical comparisons make it possible to recognize what is truly new in globalization (Arrighi, 1998, p. 59; cf. Castells, 1997, p. 244).

If the policing of corporate nationality via ownership regulations presented serious problems in the early twentieth century, the problem is only compounded today, when a large number of stock transactions are conducted in automated "dark pools," and humans don't know what is happening (Faltesek, 2018, p. 107). This process increases speed and liquidity while making violations of concentration rules harder to detect. In fact, quantitative measures of corporate nationality have been in doubt for a long time (Gilpin, 1975, pp. 144–146; Teichova, 1986, p. 370; Vernon, 1971, p. 264). If contemporary markets are trending toward ever less transparency and public oversight, as communications researcher Daniel Faltesek notes, why are ownership restrictions still in place today (Faltesek, 2018, p. 107)? To what extent, if any, might the therapeutic function of policy (i.e., it reassures policymakers that something can be done about global capital flows) help explain its continued existence?

Though tracing the historical relationship between two countries in global communications requires years of work, researchers working with the world system framework are interested in a larger number of cases and would appreciate adding Dutch hegemony to the comparisons. In the context of global communications, such an analysis would mean leaving comparisons between electronic networks behind. Messages traveling via a communications network and mail delivered on a ship could be similar, but the mechanisms of control over sea-lanes proper and those of communications networks may be quite different. Would differences between a transportation and a communications network render a framework developed for control over the telecommunications infrastructure unsuitable for comparison with earlier empires, or could these differences be handled under "comparisons based on network properties," discussed in the following section?

Comparisons over time are even more complex than comparisons during the same historical period, because the issue of interest to the researcher is not the only one that changed. This factor will be central to any comparison between control over earlier global networks and the internet that I will discuss below. Today, for example, the United States is the incumbent world leader, haunted by fears of its own decline, as well as the infrastructural leader of global communications. U.S.-headquartered companies connect Europe to Asia, and even connect the countries of Latin America to each other. While America's military prowess is undisputed, the economic foundations of that military might have long been in doubt, as observers around the world have begun to monitor the rise of China.

Comparisons Based on Network Properties

It is tempting to imagine that a general theory of networks and power will help us understand everything there is to understand about the connection between the two. The most influential proponent of this thesis has been Manuel Castells, who posits, among other things, that the ability to exercise control "over others" depends, in part, on the ability to constitute and program networks (Castells, 2013, p. 45). Instead of control over the general public, my focus here has been on state control over telecommunications networks, a type of physical infrastructure. Control over such networks has been central to state power because of their promise as weapons of war. Social organization and interaction may constitute the true potential of telecommunications networks from the perspective of users, as Castells asserts, but "the programmers" often put them in place to facilitate their commercial and geopolitical objectives, which, as has already been demonstrated, are often in conflict (Castells, 2013, p. 24; Headrick, 1991).

Since the different characteristics of networks matter for geopolitical analysis, control over the network, the airwaves, and information must be treated as analytically separate in the case of radiotelegraphy. For an assessment of a country's attempt in controlling "global communications," these different aspects of control over a single network must first be examined separately and then connected back together. The analysis of the 1903 and 1906 international conferences in chapter 2 returns us to the geopolitical origins of spectrum management, which allowed Britain to accept free intercommunication as the principle governing the operation of a global radio network. However, the development of the spectrum as a site of geopolitical competition requires a far more extensive study, since wavelengths transformed a pair of stations into a traffic-handling circuit. Given that states did not set out to manage a global resource, how did they end up reconciling their common interests in coordinating the use of the resource with their drive to secure themselves a large number of frequencies?

If wavelength allocations for radio technology to different countries belong to the structural level of network control, jamming works on the tactical level. When the CID concluded that Britain, on account of its "territorial advantages," could deny the use of the airwaves to the country's enemies via jamming, they thought of the airwaves as a new domain of warfare.[5] By the 1930s, the system of changing frequencies in case of deliberate interference and the methods of radio deception (the attempt to thwart enemy efforts aimed at tracking the movements of the fleet based on the amount of traffic exchanged) had been accepted as consequential for wartime operations.[6] Tactical-level analyses would benefit from understanding how the airwaves were incorporated into military doctrine in either Britain or the United States, especially in relation to the development of other military uses of the air, such as for air attacks.

If citizenship requirements functioned to prevent the transmission of secrets to the enemies of the United States, control over information on the tactical level loomed large during World War I, as states navigated the norms regarding codes and ciphers. American policymakers may have changed their reserved approach to surveillance when they found out that their permission for Germany to use U.S. diplomatic facilities without giving up the key to coded messages had enabled German diplomats to make an offer to Mexico to enter the war against the United States (Winkler, 2008, p. 104). In what way, if any, did policymakers' reaction to this incident and other wartime experiences interact with their domestic concerns about aiding the enemy via information to influence their approach to control over information as separate from control over the network?

While the foregoing discussion concerned the radio network alone, the physical properties of communications networks present different challenges for control. The central feature of the wireless network, for example, was the fact that the termini on two ends of a circuit could be operated by different entities. Further, since stations did not require physical connections, a single station could communicate with a great many countries as long as the company operating them secured the necessary wavelengths. Given that natural monopoly theory made duplication undesirable, all communications networks were under a great deal of pressure to serve the national interest. In contrast to a radio circuit, however, both termini of an international cable were owned and operated by the same organization. Two immediate consequences for territorial control follow from this technological difference.

First, governments could be far more directly involved in the development of a radio network, since their decisions only affected stations under their own sovereignty. The Navy Department operated its own stations, credibly pursued government ownership as a general policy, planned an integrated hemispheric network for intergovernmental coordination, and placed an officer on the board of RCA. Second, a long-distance cable was made up of several smaller links, which made telegraph and undersea cables more closely tied to physical space. The circuit connecting Shanghai and London, for example, also connected many cities along the route, while the two wireless stations could only facilitate communications between the two cities (Jacobsen, 2010, p. 247). For undersea cables, small islands in the Atlantic and Pacific became particularly important because they broke up the route that long-distance cables had to cover. Control over these territories, in turn, became vital for network control.

The fact that the same company operated both termini of a cable, coupled with the importance of Britain in the world economy, allowed British policymakers the luxury of "free trade in landing rights." During the nineteenth century, the British government supported companies landing their cables on British territory. No matter who owned the cables, as long as one end landed on British territory, the government would be able to scrutinize the traffic going through them (Headrick, 1991, p. 102; Kennedy, 1971, p. 742). By the turn of the century, the system was breaking down, as companies sought landing points in Britain simply as stepping-stones to connect to the United States. In some instances, the British government refused landing rights (Headrick, 1991, p. 81). When and why the British government chose to deny access to Britain's territory would be central to a network control analysis of the cable industry.

When, in 1911, Western Union and Postal Telegraph transitioned into international traffic handling, they began to operate the Atlantic cables that were still owned by Eastern (Headrick & Griset, 2001, p. 556). The operation of cable termini was split off from their ownership, a central development that was at odds with what obtained in the radio industry and that could be the key to understanding network control in the cable industry. Despite the foregoing differences, naval policymakers shared a concern over corporate nationality in both industries. In the background lurked the fear of the hegemon-centric corporation, a company, as chapter 7 has explained, whose loyalty went to the most powerful state in the world system. When, in the 1920s, naval policymakers were comparing the size of British and American cable networks, they doubted the American character of Western Union to such an extent that they included six of the company's ten transatlantic cables, the cables Western Union leased from the Eastern group in 1911, under *Britain's* total.[7] The operation of these cables clearly mattered less than their ownership, and this early attempt at quantification was colored by distrust over whose interests companies served.

The Navy Department's reliance on radiotelegraphy raises the question of whether the United States could have achieved leadership in global communications based on radio alone. To answer this question, researchers would need to analyze developments on the tactical level of network control in both the radio and the cable industries to the point when U.S. control was finally achieved. This means analyzing actual territorial gains based on the expansion of U.S.-headquartered MNCs in addition to such network-specific features as the number of cable-laying ships in the case of the cable industry and control over wavelengths in the radio industry. This project would require an analysis of detailed negotiations on the model of the AEFG and the Pacific consortia in several parts of the world over time. In the end, however, cable and radio histories must be integrated to fully explain the transition to U.S. leadership in global communications.

Researchers interested in the geopolitics of networks have also shown an interest in political economist Harold Innis's distinction between space-biased and time-biased media (for different ways of classifying cable and radio networks, see Hugill, 1999; Yang, 2009). Of particular interest to the study of global communications networks is the research on space-biased media, such as writing, newspapers, radio, and television. When the tele-graph severed the connection between communications and transporta-tion, ephemeral information, necessary to control space, began to travel via capital-intensive, durable electrical networks (Peters, 1999, p. 138). The differences between network-based and non-network-based space-biased media, however, are worth exploring because the former are tied to trade routes and, through them, to physical space in unique ways.

Telecommunications networks are embedded in a capitalist world econ-omy and are laid over trade routes, which are central to the organization of space. As cables have been completely replaced several times since the 1860s from submarine telegraph cables to several generations of submarine fiber-optic cables, they have continued to follow the trade routes, whose geographi-cal locations have remained fairly consistent. The map of telecommunications links, in turn, is a representation of what countries and regions matter in the world economy, and they reflect the changing importance of particular long-distance connections. Different nodes of the network may become more valu-able with the transformation of the world economy, as commerce increases in volume between different parts of the world. We are already witnessing a change in the number and thickness of the connections between the United States and the Far East, currently the most dynamic part of the world econ-omy (figure 8.1). Nodes can also gain value because of particular charac-teristics of the technologies that make up the physical infrastructure. The possibility of cables breaking once preoccupied companies and governments

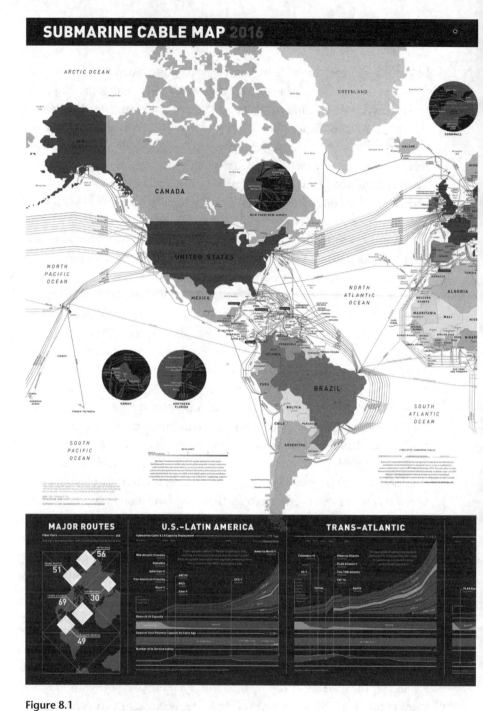

Figure 8.1
Undersea cable links in the 2010s.
Source: https://www.telegeography.com/telecom-resources/map-gallery/submarine
-cable-map-2016/index.html.

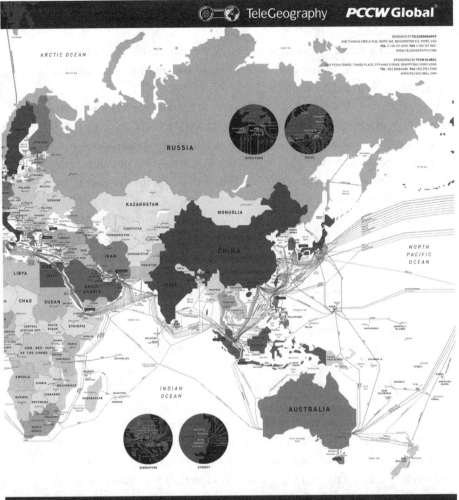

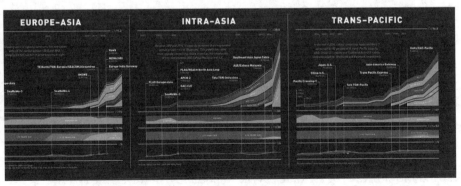

alike, providing islands with an important role. Today, the reduced cost of cooling server farms, crucial to the operation of the internet, increases the importance of Iceland, for example.

Since the early 2010s, U.S. surveillance of the internet has received a great deal of attention, but monitoring the traffic generated in other countries is possible only after the more basic goals of network control have been achieved. Once a state has secured the twin goals of network control, its ability to monitor world communications depends further on (1) the willingness of other states to use its network for their communications and (2) the inability of those states to hide their messages from prying eyes. Free flow is monitored flow. Dependence on others' networks makes states anxious, and national security leaks revealing this dependence simply add insult to injury. Surveillance of global communications networks and the resultant access to confidential information is, therefore, the privilege of an uncontested world leader.

Since global communications networks are weapons of war, geopolitical logics shape both network development and the way traffic is routed. Awareness of U.S. government surveillance of internet platforms has recently prompted countries to scramble for "technological sovereignty," a broader term than the one I use in chapter 3 (Maurer, 2015). Direct communication, free from foreign intermediation, is still the ideal, but how states might secure it depends on the characteristics of the network, which influence the identities of the intermediaries as well as network governance mechanisms. Among the features worth a comparison, the most important seem to be the geopolitical implications of network layers.

In the twentieth century, control over the physical layer was paramount for geopolitical advantage. While radiotelegraphy used the airwaves for connection and the cable network was dependent on relay points, they were separate entities carrying telegraph traffic under the management of different companies. Today, these networks serve as alternative forms of physical infrastructure for the internet, whose common protocols allow traffic to flow seamlessly over them. The varying number of internet layers addressed in the literature fall into one of two main categories, the physical and the "logical," or software, layers. Importantly, however, the logical layer of the internet is far more elaborate than that of earlier networks. It consists of the *application layer*, the home of social networks and search engines, whose millions of offerings obscure the existence of the network's *control software/protocols* to all but specialists (Landau, 2010, pp. 22–23). To what extent, if any, does the United States exercise control over this network? What are the general policy principles and discursive interventions that undergird and justify American power? If control over territory is central to control over the network, where are the choke points of the physical and the logical layers?

In the past, the United States sought control over a global communications network by leveraging its own territory and shaping the identities and actions of intermediaries. The physical network of radio transmitters and receivers was implicitly global from the outset, though radiotelegraphy did not become firmly established as a long-distance alternative to the submarine cable network until the 1910s. As a result, policymakers' attention was fixed on a particular intermediary, early multinational corporations, which pursued their own independent interests and had the ability to control technology, territory, and capital. Since the physical layer still matters, control over the MNCs connecting the country to the outside world would provide the sequel to policymakers' attempts outlined in this book.

Researchers tracing U.S. control over the physical layer must grapple with how the emergence of networks providing program content (broadcasting and cable) influenced the enforcement of foreign ownership provisions either via the court system or the executive branch. Understanding the transformation, if any, in the nature of communications MNCs connecting the world is also in order. In addition, researchers must examine whether the particular characteristics of the internet provide technological sovereignty, narrowly defined as equipment manufacturing, a more important role than in earlier networks. During the early twentieth century, for example, American policymakers would have gladly entrusted British firms with laying cables for the United States, just as long as those cables went only through American territory. By contrast, Huawei, an equipment manufacturer located in China, has faced difficulty in the U.S. market.

Because the internet consists of multiple layers, the number of intermediaries has also increased. Experts have pointed out that the distributed architecture of the internet left states with the option of influencing global internet policy only through a contemporary nonprofit intermediary, the Internet Corporation of Assigned Names and Numbers (ICANN) (Mueller, 2010, p. 80). If so, then the transfer of the Internet Assigned Numbers Authority functions currently under way would signal a larger shift in power.[8] But what exactly is being transferred and what, if anything, is the U.S. holding onto? The software layer of the network requires special attention because it is here that the unique connections between the internet and world power are forged.

Since power passes through choke points, the nature of the network drives what territories need to be controlled on the tactical level. The technology-territory nexus of network control would direct attention to the way centralization and automation create choke points on the software layer. ICANN, for example, is responsible for the management of the domain name system (DNS), which automates the process of matching the numerical IP addresses that computers understand with their plain-language identifiers that internet users understand (DeNardis, 2014, p. 41). The unique control the United States exercises because the A root server is located on American territory is worth special attention. But what is the relationship between control over the various layers of the network, and how does this relationship influence control over the data that flow through the internet? Do the sublayers of the software layer, such as the IP or the transport layer, have different choke points? Could control over the internet be split by the world leader holding onto control over the physical layer while losing control over the software layer?

What's at stake in network control is not primarily citizens' access to websites but instead access to the global network by entire countries. The purpose of denying the ability to communicate on the physical layer is to cut off a country from its allies and sources of supply in wartime. What might be the equivalent of such results on the logical layer of the internet? How do U.S. strengths in network control, if any, match up to the ability of less powerful states to exploit the relative openness of U.S. networked systems and engage in asymmetric warfare in any given instance? Could the internet, long considered to be a symbol of U.S. power, facilitate the decline of the United States? (Goldsmith and Russell, 2018).

Central to some of these questions is whether the centralization and hierarchy present in the world system manifest themselves in the centralization and hierarchy in global networks. Neither the world systems framework nor the network control framework is predictive; there are too many moving parts. Mapping the structure of global communications onto the structure of the world system provides just enough stability to serve as a basis for comparison—a heuristic for thinking about controlling global networks as a tool of geopolitical advancement. Is centralization an unavoidable technological feature of the internet that happens to favor the incumbent? Or does the incumbent actively pursue centralization to maintain its control over the network? In the early twentieth century, as chapter 2 shows, interconnection was an alternative to centralization. What is the relationship between centralization and interconnection today?

From the systemic perspective that informs this study, networks and hierarchies are far from antithetical (cf. Castells, 2013, p. 19). Rather, hierarchy is a key part of network organization because communications networks are the product of a hierarchical world system. The physical infrastructure is situated in the physical world, connecting centers of economic and military power. Network features subject to centralization and hierarchy can also emerge over time as, I suspect, happened with the domain name system. As soon as that happens, states start to compete to exert control over these features. In this framework, then, interconnection would be far from a neutral principle. Incumbents centralize, challengers fragment, but both processes differ based on the network. Many of the questions raised here, however, cannot be answered without unearthing the geopolitical history of the internet.

As for America's geopolitical rivals, the problem is obvious. They cannot rely on an alternative global network; all credible challenges to U.S. power must deal with the internet. But how can rising powers keep the network globally interoperable while prying the fingers of the United States off the tiller? A unified network is not merely an engineering achievement; in the hands of the incumbent, it is a source of leverage. Since sovereign control requires interpretation, these questions must also be investigated from the perspective of policymakers who are straining to figure out today which of the several (likely unsatisfactory) solutions they will accept as "their own" sovereign internet. Steps toward autonomy and expansion are fraught with internal tension: different visions collide about technological and institutional features dimly understood. In the following decades, observers will be treated to the interplay of the changing technological features of a global network and the timeless drive for exercising control over it—yet again.

Notes

Chapter 1

1. This framework describes how researchers have conceptualized these industries. It is not meant to represent the complexity of institutional arrangements in this time period, such as the brief period of public ownership in telephony or the fact that broadcasting did not exist until the 1920s.

2. An expansion of state power is compatible with certain varieties of capitalist state theory, as in historian William Novak's (2010) work.

Chapter 2

Epigraph: International Radio Law, enclosed in Russell Conklin to W. R. Vallance, June 14, 1926, NARA, RG 43, File 574.

1. Promemoria, Imperial German Embassy to the State Department, March 19, 1902, NARA, RG 80, File 12479 (hereafter Promemoria, 1902).

2. *Government control of radio communication: Hearings on H.R. 13159 before the Committee on the Merchant Marine and Fisheries, House of Representatives*, 65th Cong. 195, 211 (1918) (statement of David Sarnoff).

3. F. M. Barber to Chief of Bureau of Equipment, June 1, 1906, NARA, RG 19, File 18301, Box 90.

4. H. Cuthbert Hall to F. M. Barber, May 29, 1906, p. 6, NARA, RG 19, File 18301, Box 89.

5. Post Office to Admiralty, January 17, 1901, BT Archives, PO, File 88/43.

6. Judgment in *The Marconi International Marine Communications Company Limited and Another v. Lloyd's*, May 22, 1906 (hereafter Marconi-Lloyd's court decision, May 1906), BT Archives, PO, File 88/43.

7. Wireless girdle of the globe Marconi's aim, *New York Times*, May 15, 1904, p. 10.

8. Charles Earl, Solicitor, Department of Commerce, Memorandum concerning the International Wireless Telegraph Convention, concluded at Berlin, November 3, 1906, enclosed in Action of War, Navy, and Commerce and Labor Departments on wireless telegraph convention, S. Doc. No. 60-452, at 111 (1908) (hereafter Earl memorandum, 1908).

9. Post Office to Foreign Office, June 11, 1902, TNA: PRO, FO, File 83/1885.

10. Further amendments suggested in draft of Admiralty-Lloyd's agreement, Precis, October 29–December 22, 1902, BT Archives, PO, File 88/43.

11. Evan MacGregor, Admiralty to Lloyd's, June 30, 1902, TNA: PRO, FO, File 83/1885.

12. Postmaster General Lord Stanley to Cabinet, March 4, 1904, TNA: PRO, CAB, File 37/69/39.

13. Admiralty to Treasury, Draft, March 1900, TNA: PRO, ADM, File 116/567.

14. Captain Henry Jackson to First Lord of the Admiralty Lord Selborne, January 10, 1903, TNA: PRO, ADM, File 116/3613.

15. Commander Richardson Clover, Naval Attache, to Bureau of Equipment, October 22, 1901, Confidential, NARA, RG 19, File 18301, Box 15.

16. Marconi-Lloyd's court decision, May 1906.

17. Extract from a letter by John B. Jackson, ambassador to Germany, to the Postmaster General, November 19, 1901, enclosed in Secretary of State John Hay to the Secretary of the Treasury, April 3, 1902, NARA, RG 41, File 30166.

18. Marconi-Lloyd's court decision, May 1906.

19. Memorandum for the Cabinet by Lord Selborne, December 10, 1901, TNA: PRO, CAB, File 37/59/129.

20. Post Office to Foreign Office, June 11, 1902.

21. Selborne to Arthur Balfour, June 21, 1901, Selborne papers, File 157.

22. Memorandum for the Cabinet by Lord Selborne, December 10, 1901, TNA: PRO, CAB, File 37/59/129; Lord Stanley to Cabinet, March 4, 1904.

23. Lord Stanley to Cabinet, March 4, 1904.

24. Chief of Bureau of Equipment to Hall, November 22, 1901, NARA, RG 19, File 18301, Box 16. The exact timing of the non-intercommunication policy and the way it is related to the decision to offer a telegraph service are insufficiently understood and would benefit from research in corporate archives. For current explanations, see Aitken, 1976, pp. 233–236; Douglas, 1989, pp. 69–70; Harlow, 1971, p. 445; Headrick, 1991, p. 119; Pocock, 1988, p. 151.

25. Post Office to Foreign Office, June 11, 1902.

26. Cables (Landing-Rights) Committee, Minutes of Evidence, Testimony of Cuthbert Hall, Marconi Company, February 18, 1903, p. 30, TNA: PRO, FO, File 83/1940 (hereafter Hall testimony, February 18, 1903).

27. Hall to Barber, May 29, 1906, p. 6.

28. International Telecommunication Union, Minutes of the Preliminary Conference at Berlin on Wireless Telegraphy, August 1903, p. 30 (hereafter Minutes of Preliminary Conference, 1903).

29. Concern to establish the Marconi system in the United States, *New York Times*, March 16, 1902, p. 13.

30. Extracts from translation of the Minutes of the Berlin Conference of 1906, transmitted by Mr. Waterbury, p. 20, enclosed in Wireless convention, Report of Ambassador Tower to Secretary Root, November 17, 1906, NARA, RG 80, File 12479 (hereafter *International Wireless Convention extracts*, 1906). These extracts are also available at U.S. Congress, Senate Committee on Foreign Relations, *International Wireless Telegraph. An international wireless telegraph convention with service regulations annexed thereto, a supplementary agreement, and a final protocol and hearings thereon*, 60th Cong., Washington, DC: Government Printing Office, 1908, pp. 149–171.

31. Cables (Landing-Rights) Committee, Minutes of Evidence, Testimony of John Gavey, Engineer-in-Chief of the Post Office, February 11, 1903, TNA: PRO, FO, File 83/1940 (hereafter Gavey testimony, February 11, 1903); Director of Naval Intelligence, General memorandum on wireless telegraphy in the United Kingdom, n.d., 1901, BT Archives, PO, File 30/940.

32. Admiralty to the Marconi Company, March 17, 1902, HIS 131, Marconi collection, Bodleian Library, University of Oxford; Barber to Chief of Bureau of Equipment, June 1, 1906. The British Admiralty received the same information. See Hall to MacGregor, Admiralty, April 19, 1902, HIS 131, Marconi collection, Bodleian Library, University of Oxford.

33. Evan MacGregor, Admiralty, December 12, 1901, TNA: PRO, FO, File 83/1885.

34. Jackson to Selborne, January 10, 1903.

35. Selborne to Austen Chamberlain, Postmaster General, January 11, 1903, TNA: PRO, ADM, File 116/3613.

36. *Pacific Cable: Hearings before the House Committee on Interstate and Foreign Commerce, House of Representatives*, 56th Cong. 24, 35 (1900) (statement of Captain George Owen Squier, Army Signal Corps).

37. By the 1920s, spectrum scarcity, rather than an inadequate amount of traffic to sustain competing stations, would be cited as the reason for the monopolistic tendencies in the radio industry (Prentiss Gilbert, 1921, in Schwoch, 1990, p. 95).

38. Question of international convention and enforced interchange of communication by different systems, n.d., 1904, TNA: PRO, ADM, File 116/3613 (hereafter Question of international convention, 1904).

39. Hall to Babington Smith, July 21, 1905, BT Archives, PO, File 88/43.

40. Wireless Telegraphy, Note on the Berlin Conference Proposal, enclosed in Marconi Company to the Post Office, September 29, 1906, BT Archives, PO, File 88/43, p. 215.

41. Hall to Babington Smith, August 20, 1905, BT Archives, PO, File 88/43.

42. Ibid.

43. Hall statement, *International Wireless Convention extracts*, 1906, p. 27.

44. Ibid.

45. J. Ardron to F. M. Barber, June 29, 1905, NARA, RG 19, File 18301.

46. To experiment against the Marconi system, *New York Times*, March 4, 1902, p. 3; Marconi Company to Foreign Office, July 6, 1904, TNA: PRO, FO, File 83/1982.

47. The total number of transatlantic cables was sixteen. See 57 Cong. Report to Accompany H.R. 5, H.R. Rep. No. 57-568, at 11 (1902).

48. The German-American Cable, *London Times*, September 1, 1900, p. 4; Statement of Edward Sassoon, M.P., in Minutes of evidence taken before the inter-departmental committee on cable communications, p. 6 (London: HMSO, 1902), NARA, RG 38, File 200, Box 355.

49. *Hearing before the Committee on Interstate and Foreign Commerce on the Pacific Cable bills (H.R. 5, H.R. 158, and H.R. 168), House of Representatives*, 57 Cong. 99, 104 (1902) (testimony of R. B. Bradford).

50. Acting Secretary of State Alvey Adee to the Secretary of Treasury, September 12, 1902, enclosed in Secretary of State John Hay to the Secretary of Treasury, May 29, 1903, NARA, RG 41, File 30166.

51. Jackson, Ambassador to Germany, to the Postmaster General, November 19, 1901.

52. F. M. Barber to the Chief of the Bureau of Equipment, December 6, 1901, NARA, RG 19, File 18301.

53. Earl memorandum, 1908, p. 111.

54. Post Office to Foreign Office, June 11, 1902.

55. Ibid.

56. Captain Henry B. Jackson, Assistant D.N.O., The development of practical wireless telegraphy, March 26, 1902, Selborne papers, File 157, Bodleian Library, University of Oxford.

57. Ibid.

58. Admiralty to the Marconi Company, March 17, 1902, HIS 131, Marconi collection, Bodleian Library, University of Oxford.

59. Marconi Company to the Post Office, February 4, 1903, BT Archives, PO, File 88/43.

60. H. Babington Smith, Memorandum of Interview between Representatives of Post Office and Admiralty, January 25, 1904, BT Archives, PO, File 88/43.

61. Agreement between the Admiralty and the Marconi Wireless Telegraph Company, 1903, §3, in Agreements, Etc. relative to wireless telegraphy, London: HMSO, 1912, BT Archives, PO, File 30/1115.

62. Ibid., §7.

63. F. M. Barber to Chief, Bureau of Equipment, July 9, 1906, NARA, RG 19, File 18301.

64. Lamb memorandum, January 29, 1904, BT Archives, PO, File 30/1115.

65. Mackay to Lamb, July 28, 1903, BT Archives, PO, File 30/1298.

66. Ibid.

67. Preliminary Conference at Berlin on Wireless Telegraphy, Memorandum by the British Delegates, August 14, 1903, enclosed in Report on the Proposed International Convention for the regulation of Wireless Telegraphy as affecting the question of Legislation in the United Kingdom, December 8, 1903, BT Archives, PO, File 88/43.

68. Why the Austro-Hungarian monarchy sent two sets of delegates, let alone the position of the country, remains to be explored.

69. Statement of M. Bordelongue, Minutes of Preliminary Conference, 1903, p. 48.

70. Ibid., p. 12.

71. Ibid., pp. 12–13.

72. M. Sydow, Minutes of Preliminary Conference, 1903, p. 7. See also M. Schrader, prioritizing the non-intercommunication policy, at p. 22.

73. Promemoria, 1902, p. 2.

74. M. Sydow, Minutes of Preliminary Conference, 1903, p. 7.

75. Report of the Select Committee to Consider the Report of the Radio-Telegraphic Convention signed in Berlin, 1907, p. 16, Great Britain Parliamentary Papers (hereafter Select Committee Report).

76. F. M. Barber to Chief, Bureau of Equipment, August 14, 1903, NARA, RG 19, File 18301, Box 90.

77. *International Wireless Convention extracts*, 1906, p. 17.

78. J. C. Lamb, Minutes of Preliminary Conference, 1903, p. 15.

79. Solari, Minutes of Preliminary Conference, 1903, p. 11; Del Casale, Minutes of Preliminary Conference, 1903, p. 43.

80. Hall to Babington Smith, August 20, 1905; Marconi Company to Post Office, February 4, 1903, BT Archives, PO, File 88/43.

81. Barber to Chief, Bureau of Equipment, July 9, 1906.

82. Del Casale, Minutes of Preliminary Conference, 1903, pp. 41–43.

83. Hall testimony, February 18, 1903; Hall to Barber, May 29, 1906.

84. Commander Cardarelli, Minutes of Preliminary Conference, 1903, p. 17.

85. German draft proposal enclosed in Minutes of Preliminary Conference, 1903.

86. Solari, Minutes of Preliminary Conference, 1903, p. 11.

87. Radiotelegraphic convention, *London Times*, April 18, 1907, p. 15.

88. Hall testimony, February 18, 1903, p. 30.

89. F. M. Barber, April 30, 1906, NARA, RG 19, File 18301, Box 43; Report of Mr. John I. Waterbury, representing the Department of Commerce and Labor, to Secretary Straus, December 15, 1906, in *International Wireless Convention extracts*, 1906, p. 8 (hereafter Waterbury report, 1906).

90. Post Office to Foreign Office, June 11, 1902.

91. J. C. Lamb, Minutes of Preliminary Conference, 1903, p. 34.

92. James M. Beck, Acting Attorney General, to the Secretary of State, August 18, 1902, enclosed in Acting Secretary Alvey Adee to the Secretary of the Treasury, NARA, RG 41, File 30166; Statement of John I. Waterbury, Minutes of Preliminary Conference, 1903, p. 28.

93. Minutes of Preliminary Conference, 1903, p. 14.

94. Schrader, Minutes of Preliminary Conference, 1903, p. 45.

95. Mackay to Lamb, July 28, 1903, BT Archives, PO, File 30/1298.

96. Minutes of Preliminary Conference, 1903, p. 33.

97. Ibid., p. 16.

98. Minutes of Preliminary Conference, 1903, p. 32.

99. Ibid., 26; Hall to Babington Smith, August 20, 1905.

100. Barber to Chief, Bureau of Equipment, July 9, 1906.

101. Wireless telegraphy troubles the nations, *New York Times*, October 1, 1906, p. 3.

102. Protocole-Final. Conférence Préliminaire concernant la télégraphie sans fil, enclosed in F. M. Barber to Chief, Bureau of Equipment, August 14, 1903, NARA, RG 19, File 18301, Box 90.

103. Lamb memorandum, January 29, 1904.

104. Charles Bright, To the editor of the *Times*, *London Times*, July 29, 1907, p. 10.

105. Imperial German Embassy to the Secretary of State, February 5, 1904, NARA, RG 41, File 30166; F. M. Barber to Chief of the Bureau of Equipment, March 14, 1904, NARA, RG 19, File 18301.

106. Promemoria, 1902.

107. F. M. Barber to Chief of the Bureau of Equipment, March 14, 1904, NARA, RG 19, File 18301.

108. Secretary of Commerce and Labor George Cortelyou to the Secretary of State, February 18, 1904, NARA, RG 41, File 30166.

109. Memorandum relative to the wireless telegraphy plant on the Nantucket Shoal Light-Vessel, enclosed in B. Johnson, Chief Clerk of the Light House Board, to Weaver, May 5, 1904, NARA, RG 40, File 67032.

110. Post Office to Foreign Office, July 25, 1904, TNA: PRO, FO, File 83/1982.

111. Ibid.; Post Office to Foreign Office, July 7, 1906, BT Archive, PO, File 88/43.

112. F. M. Barber to Bureau of Equipment, September 3, 1905, NARA, RG 19, File 18301.

113. Post Office to Foreign Office, July 25, 1904.

114. Hall testimony, February 18, 1903, p. 30; Marconi Company to the Post Office, March 14, 1904, BT Archives, PO, File 88/43.

115. Post Office to Marconi Company, March 31, 1903, BT Archives, PO, File 88/43.

116. Cables (Landing-Rights) Committee, Minutes of Evidence, Testimony of Captain Henry B. Jackson, February 11, 1903, p. 25, TNA: PRO, FO, File 83/1940; Heads of Agreement between the Postmaster General of the one part, and Marconi's Wireless Telegraph Company, Limited, and the Marconi International Marine Communication Company, Limited, of the other part, August 11, 1904, section 7, in Agreements, Etc. relative to wireless telegraphy, London: HMSO, 1912, BT Archive, PO, File 30/1115 (hereafter Heads of Agreement, 1904).

117. Hall testimony, February 18, 1903.

118. Foreign Office to the Marconi Company, July 28, 1904, TNA: PRO, FO, File 83/1982.

119. Babington Smith to Baddeley, July 14, 1904, BT Archives, PO, File 88/43.

120. *International Wireless Telegraph. An international wireless telegraph convention with service regulations annexed thereto, a supplementary agreement, and a final protocol and hearings thereon,* Senate Committee on Foreign Relations, 60th Cong., 1st Sess. (statement of Henry Manney, Bureau of Equipment), Washington, DC: Government Printing Office, 1908 (hereafter Manney testimony, 1908) (hereafter *International Wireless Telegraph Hearings,* 1908).

121. Secretary of Commerce George Cortelyou to the Secretary of State, July 7, 1904, NARA, RG 40, File 67032.

122. Special Notice to Mariners, No. 47a, November 22, 1904, Washington, DC: The Hydrographic Office, NARA, RG 41, File 37554.

123. Chief of Bureau of Equipment to Navy Department, July 11, 1904, 2nd endorsement on a letter from Munroe & Munroe relative to contract with De Forest Wireless Telegraph Company, NARA, RG 19, File 18301, Box 26.

124. *International Wireless Telegraph Hearings,* 1908, p. 211.

125. M. Kraetke, *International Wireless Convention extracts,* 1906, p. 15. For a discussion of other matters, see Douglas, 1989, pp. 137–141.

126. Waterbury report, 1906, p. 8.

127. Manney testimony, 1908, p. 46.

128. Wireless telegraphy conference, *London Times,* November 3, 1906, p. 7.

129. Bethell, *International Wireless Convention extracts,* 1906, p. 13; Hall, *International Wireless Convention extracts,* 1906, p. 28.

130. J. C. Lamb to Lord Stanley, Postmaster General, December 9, 1903, BT Archives, PO, File 30/1298.

131. Marconi Company to the Post Office, February 6, 1904, BT Archives, PO, File 88/43.

132. Memorandum: Notes of discussion at the Admiralty, July 18, 1904, BT Archives, PO, File 88/43.

133. Ibid.

134. Post Office to Admiralty, January 18, 1904, BT Archives, PO, File 88/43.

135. Post Office to Foreign Office, June 11, 1902; Mackay to Lamb, July 28, 1903.

136. Post Office to Foreign Office, August 15, 1904, BT Archives, PO, File 88/43.

137. Heads of Agreement, 1904.

138. Lamb memorandum, January 29, 1904, p. 10.

139. The radio-telegraphic convention, *London Times*, July 22, 1907, p. 11.

140. Sir George Clarke, Wireless Telegraphy, Printed for the Committee of Imperial Defence, September 14, 1906, TNA: PRO, ADM, File 116/3614.

141. Ibid.

142. H. Babington Smith, Memorandum prepared for the Postmaster General, August 16, 1906, BT Archives, PO, File 30/1346.

143. Post Office, Memorandum with reference to the Draft Instructions to the British Delegates to the Berlin Conference on Wireless Telegraphy, August 1906, BT Archives, PO, File 30/1346 (hereafter Memorandum with reference to Draft Instructions, August 1906); Memorandum of interview with Cuthbert Hall, November 1, 1905, BT Archives, PO, File 88/43.

144. Marconi Company to Foreign Office, July 12, 1906, BT Archives, PO, File 88/43; Clarke, Wireless Telegraphy, September 14, 1906.

145. Admiralty Memorandum, August 18, 1906, BT Archives, PO, File 30/1346.

146. Wireless Telegraphy. Note on the Berlin Conference Proposal, enclosed in Marconi Company to the Post Office, September 29, 1906, BT Archives, PO, File 88/43.

147. Fisher to Admiralty, September 10, 1906, TNA: PRO, ADM, File 116/3614.

148. Gavey testimony, February 11, 1903.

149. Lord Stanley to Cabinet, March 4, 1904; Post Office, Draft Memorandum in reply to Sir George Clarke's Memorandum, August 1906, BT Archives, PO, File 30/1346.

150. Clarke, Wireless Telegraphy, September 14, 1906; J. Gavey, Notes on the Admiralty Memorandum dated 18 August 1906, August 31, 1906, TNA: PRO, ADM, File 116/3614 (hereafter Gavey, Notes, 1906).

151. Question of international convention, 1904; Gavey, Notes, 1906.

152. Marconi Company to the Post Office, March 14, 1904.

153. H. Babington Smith, Memorandum, August 16, 1906.

154. Babington Smith to Baddeley, July 14, 1904; Notes of Discussion with Mr. Cuthbert Hall, August 4 and 5, 1904, BT Archives, PO, File 88/43.

155. Memorandum from R. W. Mackay to Postmaster General, August 27, 1906, BT Archives, PO, File 30/1347.

156. Question of international convention, 1904; Gavey, Notes, 1906.

157. Oppose wireless monopoly, *New York Times*, October 10, 1906, p. 1.

158. *International Wireless Convention extracts*, 1906, p. 14.

159. Minutes of Preliminary Conference, 1903, pp. 16, 32; H. Manney to the Bureau of Equipment, November 25, 1906, p. 12, NARA, RG 19, File 18301, Box 60.

160. Post Office to Foreign Office, August 15, 1904; Francis M. Barber to Chief, Bureau of Equipment, May 13, 1906, NARA, RG 19, File 18301, Box 90.

161. Mackay to Lamb, July 28, 1903.

162. Hall statement, *International Wireless Convention extracts*, 1906, p. 27.

163. Barber to Chief of Bureau of Equipment, June 1, 1906.

164. *International Wireless Convention extracts*, 1906, p. 20.

165. H. Manney to the Bureau of Equipment, November 25, 1906, p. 14.

166. Babington-Smith, *International Wireless Convention extracts*, 1906, p. 21.

167. *International Wireless Convention extracts*, 1906, p. 18.

168. Ibid., 22. For a different interpretation of the role of Italy, see Balbi, 2012.

169. Marconi Company to the Post Office, March 14, 1904.

170. Question of international convention, 1904.

171. Gavey, Notes, 1906.

172. Ibid.

173. Babington Smith to Captain Bethell, November 6, 1905, BT Archives, PO, File 88/43; Barber to Bureau of Equipment, June 19, 1905, NARA, RG 19, File 18301.

174. Gavey, Notes, 1906.

175. Ibid.

176. Manney testimony, 1908, p. 49.

177. *International Wireless Telegraph Hearings*, 1908, p. 27.

178. Select Committee Report, p. 23.

179. Telegram from Captain Bethell, October 19, 1906, TNA: PRO, ADM, File 116/3614; H. Babington-Smith, Memorandum, October 22, 1906, TNA: PRO, ADM, File 116/3614.

180. Select Committee Report, p. 6.

181. H. Babington-Smith, Memorandum, August 16, 1906.

182. A. E. Bethell, *International Wireless Convention extracts*, 1906, p. 12.

183. Ibid.

184. Memorandum with reference to Draft Instructions, August 1906.

185. Wireless telegraphy, Memorandum by Lord Stanley, Postmaster General, March 7, 1904, TNA: PRO, ADM, File 116/3613.

186. *International Wireless Telegraph Hearings*, 1908, p. 23.

187. W. M. Cowles, Bureau of Equipment, Memorandum for the Secretary of State, June 17, 1908, NARA, RG 19, File 18301, Box 71.

188. Telegram from Captain Bethell, October 19, 1906, TNA: PRO, ADM, File 116/3614; Lord Tweedmouth to Bethell, October 20, 1906, TNA: PRO, ADM, File 116/3614.

189. British delegates promised to fight "tooth and nail" the provision mandating ships to intercommunicate, but they expressed hope at lunch that the Americans would not take offense. See H. Manney to the Bureau of Equipment, November 25, 1906, pp. 8, 17.

190. Ibid.

191. *International Wireless Convention extracts*, 1906, p. 25.

192. Articles 8 and 9, *International Wireless Telegraph Hearings*, 1908, p. 8.

193. International Radio Law, 1926.

194. Waterbury report, 1906, p. 10.

195. Wireless treaty signed, *New York Times*, November 4, 1906, p. 7.

196. 100 years of ITU radio regulations, 1906–2006, http://www.itu.int/en/history /Pages/100YearsITURadioRegulations.aspx.

197. Radiotelegraphic convention, *London Times*, March 27, 1907, p. 4.

198. By fall 1905, the American DeForest Company had established an English subsidiary, and Reginald Fessenden's National Electric Signaling Company (NESCO) had opened an experimental station in Machrihanish Bay, Scotland. See Barber to Bureau of Equipment, September 3, 1905, NARA, RG 19, File 18301.

199. Waterbury report, 1906, p. 9.

200. H. Cuthbert Hall to Evan MacGregor, Admiralty, April 19, 1902, HIS 131, Marconi collection, Bodleian Library, University of Oxford.

Chapter 3

1. Lieutenant A. M. Beecher, Memorandum for the Chief of Bureau, November 23, 1901, NARA, RG 19, File 18301, Box 16.

2. Royal B. Bradford, Chief of Bureau of Equipment, to the Secretary of the Navy, January 10, 1902, NARA, RG 80, File 12479.

3. Morgan in the wireless, *New-York Daily Tribune*, April 6, 1902, p. 6.

4. A Marconi Wireless Telegraph Company for America, *Electrical World and Engineer, 34*(23), December 2, 1899, 870–871.

5. Statement of Representative Richardson, Alabama, 57th Cong., June 11, 1902, 35 Cong. Rec. 6615 (1902).

6. Morgan in the wireless, *New-York Daily Tribune*, April 6, 1902.

7. Ibid.

8. Marconi Company to the Post Office, March 14, 1904, BT Archives, PO, File 88/43.

9. For a contemporary report on such a requirement, see C. Timberg and E. Nakashima, Agreements with private companies protect U.S. access to cables' data for surveillance, *Washington Post*, July 6, 2013.

10. Bradford to the Secretary of the Navy, December 1, 1899, NARA, RG 19, File 18301, Box 15.

11. Report of Board on transmission of messages, August 29, 1901, NARA, RG 19, File 18301.

12. Chief of Bureau of Equipment, Memorandum for the General Board, April 6, 1904, NARA, RG 19, File 18301.

13. *Hearing before the House Committee on Interstate and Foreign Commerce on the Pacific Cable bills (H.R. 5, H.R. 158, and H.R. 168),* 57 Cong. 99, 107 (1902) (testimony of Admiral R. B. Bradford).

14. Ibid., p. 104. France and Germany were widely discussed as examples in this context. See Report to Accompany H.R. 5, H.R. Rep. No. 57-568, at 9 (1902).

15. Statement of Representative Richardson, Alabama, June 11, 1902.

16. Secretary of the Navy Paul Morton to the Marconi Wireless Telegraph Company of America, January 17, 1905, NARA, RG 41, File 37554.

17. F. M. Barber to Chief of Bureau of Equipment, December 6, 1901, NARA, RG 19, File 18301.

18. E. Rollins Morse to Secretary of the Navy William H. Moody, September 30, 1902, NARA, RG 19, File 18301.

19. Morse to Moody, November 25, 1902, NARA, RG 19, File 18301.

20. Morse to Moody, July 15, 1902, NARA, RG 19, File 18301, Box 16.

21. H.R. Rep. No. 57-568, p. 5 (1902).

22. Ibid., p. 2.

23. Beecher memorandum, November 23, 1901.

24. Unsigned, Wireless Telegraphy for the Navy, 1899, p. 3, NARA, RG 19, File 18301, Box 15.

25. F. M. Barber to Chief of Bureau of Equipment, July 11, 1902, NARA, RG 19, File 18301, Box 85.

26. Bradford, Memorandum for the Secretary of the Navy, October 3, 1902, NARA, RG 19, File 18301, Box 12.

27. The Navy Department to the Marconi Company, January 17, 1905, NARA, RG 19, File 18301, Box 31.

28. The Herald's wireless ship signal service, *New York Times*, May 23, 1901, p. 8.

29. Captain Richardson Clover, U.S. Naval Attache, to the Office of Naval Intelligence, May 29, 1901, NARA, RG 19, File 18301, Box 15.

30. Morton to American Marconi, January 17, 1905.

31. John D. Oppe, Vice President and General Manager, Marconi Wireless Telegraph Company of America, to the Bureau of Equipment, June 21, 1904, enclosed in Wireless telegraphy—Report of the Inter-Departmental Board appointed by the President to consider the entire question of wireless telegraphy in the service of the national government, July 12, 1904, NARA, RG 80, File 12479 (hereafter Report of the Roosevelt Board).

32. U.S. Congress, Senate Committee on Foreign Relations, *International Wireless Telegraph. An international wireless telegraph convention with service regulations annexed thereto, a supplementary agreement, and a final protocol and hearings thereon*, 60th Cong. 43, 48 (1908) (statement of Henry Manney, Chief of the Bureau of Equipment) (hereafter Manney testimony, 1908) (hereafter *International Wireless Telegraph Hearings*, 1908).

33. The Inter-Departmental Board to President Roosevelt, July 29, 1904, p. 5, Hooper papers, LOC.

34. Oppe to Bureau of Equipment, June 21, 1904, in Report of the Roosevelt Board.

35. The Inter-Departmental Board to President Roosevelt, July 29, 1904.

36. Reginald Fessenden to Walker, October 1, 1904, Fessenden papers, State Archives of North Carolina, Box 1140.5.

37. Report of the Roosevelt Board.

38. Chief of Bureau of Equipment to Navy Department, July 11, 1904, 2nd endorsement on a letter from Munroe & Munroe relative to contract with De Forest Wireless Telegraph Company, NARA, RG 19, File 18301, Box 26.

39. Ibid.

40. W. Maxwell Greene, American Consul to Bermuda, to Herbert H. D. Peirce, April 12, 1906, enclosed in Chas. Denby, Chief Clerk, State Department, to the Secretary of the Navy, April 27, 1906, NARA, RG 19, File 18301, Box 43.

41. Annual Report of the Commissioner of Navigation, H.R. Doc. No. 62-143, at 56 (1911).

42. Bureau of Equipment to the Secretary of the Navy, April 10, 1906, NARA, RG 19, File 18301, Box 46.

43. Bradford to Secretary of the Navy, January 10, 1902.

44. Bradford to Secretary of the Navy, February 18, 1902, NARA, RG 19, File 18301, Box 16.

45. Ibid.

46. Bradford, March 10, 1902, 2nd endorsement on March 6, 1902 letter by the Governor of Massachusetts, NARA, RG 19, File 18301, Box 16.

47. W. M. Crane, Commonwealth of Massachusetts, Executive Department, to John D. Long, Secretary of the Navy, March 6, 1902, NARA, RG 19, File 18301, Box 16.

48. Manney testimony, 1908, p. 47.

49. Bradford to Secretary of the Navy, January 10, 1902.

50. Memorandum for the General Board, April 6, 1904.

51. Bradford to Secretary of the Navy, January 10, 1902.

52. G. Converse, Chief of Bureau of Equipment, to the Secretary of the Navy, March 7, 1904, NARA, RG 19, File 18301.

53. Morton to American Marconi, January 17, 1905.

54. *Radio communication: Hearings before the Subcommittee of the Committee on Commerce on S. 3620 and S. 5334*, 62nd Cong. 10, 17 (1912) (statement of Lt. Cmdr David Wooster Todd).

55. Bradford to Secretary of the Navy, January 10, 1902.

56. Secretary of the Navy John D. Long to Senator Eugene Hale, March 14, 1902, NARA, RG 19, File 18301, Box 16.

57. Bradford to Secretary of the Navy, January 10, 1902.

58. Bradford to the Navy Department, April 8, 1902, NARA, RG 19, File 18301, Box 15.

59. *Pacific Cable: Hearings before the House Committee on Interstate and Foreign Commerce*, 56th Cong. 24, 33 (1900) (statement of Captain George Owen Squier); H.R. Rep. No. 57-568, at 1 (1902).

60. James M. Beck, Acting Attorney General, to the Secretary of State, August 18, 1902, enclosed in Acting Secretary Alvey Adee to Secretary of the Treasury, August 22, 1902, NARA, RG 41, File 30166 (hereafter Beck memorandum, 1902).

61. Ibid.

62. Attorney General Joseph McKenna, Foreign cables, 22 Op. Att'y. Gen. 13 (1900) (hereafter McKenna opinion, 1900).

63. *Cable Landing Licenses: Hearings before a subcommittee of the Senate Committee on Commerce on S. 4031*, 66th Cong. 218, 243 (1921) (statement of Fred K. Nielsen, Solicitor for the Department of State).

64. Morton to American Marconi, January 17, 1905; H. Manney, Memorandum for the Secretary of the Navy, May 3, 1904, p. 7, NARA, RG 19, File 18301.

65. Memorandum for the General Board, April 6, 1904.

66. H. Babington Smith, Memorandum prepared for the Postmaster General, August 16, 1906, BT Archives, PO, File 30/1346.

67. Memorandum for the General Board, April 6, 1904.

68. F. M. Barber to the Chief of the Bureau of Equipment, February 28, 1902, NARA, RG 19, File 18301; John B. Jackson, Embassy of the United States, Berlin, to Secretary of State John Hay, enclosed in Hay to the Secretary of Treasury, March 14, 1902, NARA, RG 41, File 30166.

69. Admiral George Dewey, Wireless telegraphy, June 18, 1902, NARA, RG 80, Records of the General Board, File 419. The competition between the General Board and the bureau chiefs is worth more attention in this context. Under Bradford, the Bureau of Equipment jealously eyed the extension of the General Board's authority (Kuehn, 2017, p. 55) and only reluctantly accepted the Board's assessment of the wireless situation.

70. George Dewey, Admiral of the Navy, President, General Board, May 2, 1904, enclosed in Report of the Roosevelt Board, 1904, p. 20.

71. Effect of preponderating control of radio by any one nation, November 22, 1921, p. 6, enclosed in S. W. Bryant, Acting Secretary of the Navy, Memorandum for the Secretary of the General Board, June 1, 1922, NARA, RG 38, File 100.

72. Henry N. Manney. Memorandum for the Secretary of the Navy, Proposed Act to provide for the regulation of wireless telegraphy, October 20, 1904, §11, NARA, RG 41, File 37554 (hereafter Navy draft, October 1904); 47 U.S.C. §§251, 325, 606.

73. Manney to the Secretary of the Navy, January 26, 1905, NARA, RG 40, File 62300.

74. An Act to Provide for the regulation of Wireless Telegraphy, August 15, 1904, BT Archives, PO, File 30/1346.

75. Draft bill for the regulation of wireless telegraphy, n.d., early 1905, NARA, RG 80, File 12479 (hereafter Commerce draft, 1905); James Rudolph Garfield, Uriel Sebree, and Eugene Tyler Chamberlain to the Secretary of Commerce and Labor, January 24, 1905, NARA, RG 40, File 62300.

76. Navy draft, October 1904.

77. Commerce draft, 1905. See also Charles Earl, Solicitor, Department of Commerce, Memorandum concerning the International Wireless Telegraph Convention, concluded at Berlin, November 3, 1906, enclosed in Action of War, Navy, and Commerce and Labor Departments on wireless telegraph convention, S. Doc. No. 60-452 (1908) (hereafter Earl memorandum, 1908).

78. Supervision of wireless, *New York Times*, January 28, 1905, p. 1; Earl memorandum, 1908, p. 17.

79. Bureau of Equipment to Barber, March 8, 1905, NARA, RG 19, File 18301; James Rudolph Garfield, Uriel Sebree, and Eugene Tyler Chamberlain to Secretary of Commerce and Labor, January 24, 1905, NARA, RG 40, File 62300; A. W. Greely, Brigadier General, Chief Signal Officer, to Secretary of War, December 17, 1902, enclosed in Secretary of War to Secretary of Navy, December 29, 1902, NARA, RG 41, File 30166.

80. Secretary of the Navy to the Secretary of State, April 8, 1905, NARA, RG 80, File 12479.

81. Extracts from translation of the Minutes of the Berlin Conference of 1906, transmitted by Mr. Waterbury, p. 10, enclosed in Wireless convention, Report of Ambassador Tower to Secretary Root, November 17, 1906, NARA, RG 80, File 12479.

82. F. M. Barber to Chief, Bureau of Equipment, July 13, 1906, NARA, RG 19, File 18301.

83. Acting Secretary of the Navy to the President, October 27, 1906, NARA, RG 80, File 12479.

84. Barber to Chief, Bureau of Equipment, July 13, 1906.

85. Acting Secretary of the Navy to the President, October 27, 1906, NARA, RG 80, File 12479.

86. Manney testimony, 1908, p. 48.

87. Wm. Cowles, Chief of Bureau of Equipment, to Navy Department, February 27, 1907, NARA, RG 19, File 18301, Box 60.

88. Joint Board to the Secretary of the Navy, March 25, 1905, NARA, RG 80, File 12479.

89. U.S. Congress, Senate Committee on Foreign Relations, *International Wireless Telegraph. An international wireless telegraph convention with service regulations annexed thereto, a supplementary agreement, and a final protocol and hearings thereon*, 60th Cong. 50, 61 (1908) (statement of John Griggs) (hereafter Griggs statement, 1908).

90. S. 5949. A bill to regulate the use of wireless telegraphy, Committee on Naval Affairs, 60th Cong. (1908).

91. F. M. Barber to Bureau of Equipment, September 7, 1905, NARA, RG 19, File 18301.

92. Manney testimony, 1908, p. 43.

93. Earl memorandum, 1908.

94. Griggs statement, 1908, p. 56.

95. Earl memorandum, 1908, pp. 15–16.

96. Ibid., p. 17.

97. Ibid., p. 19.

98. Ibid., p. 16.

99. Griggs statement, 1908, p. 54.

100. Ibid., p. 57.

101. Ibid., p. 51.

102. Ibid., p. 57.

103. Hall to the Under Secretary of State for Foreign Affairs, Commercial Department, Foreign Office, September 30, 1904, p. 3, TNA: PRO, FO, File 83/1982; F. M. Barber to Bureau of Equipment, September 7, 1905, NARA, RG 19, File 18301; Cuthbert Hall, Minutes to 1906 conference, in *International Wireless Telegraph Hearings*, 1908, p. 166.

104. Barber to Bureau of Equipment, September 7, 1905, NARA, RG 19, File 18301.

105. Griggs statement, 1908, p. 57.

106. Express Cases, 117 U.S. 1, 3 (1885).

107. Griggs statement, 1908, p. 59.

108. John D. Oppe, General Manager, Marconi Wireless Telegraph Company of America, to Secretary of the Navy Paul Morton, January 9, 1905, NARA, RG 19, File 18301, Box 31.

109. Griggs statement, 1908, pp. 53–54.

110. Ibid., p. 60.

111. Ibid., p. 55.

112. Morton to American Marconi, January 17, 1905.

113. Earl memorandum, 1908, p. 26.

114. 36 Stat. 545 (1910).

115. Earl memorandum, 1908, p. 13.

116. Ibid.

117. Griggs statement, 1908, p. 58.

118. Ibid., p. 53.

119. John I. Waterbury, Memorandum concerning international wireless telegraphy convention concluded at Berlin, November 3, 1906, January 21, 1908, NARA, RG 40, File 67032 (hereafter Waterbury memorandum, 1908).

120. Earl memorandum, 1908, p. 29.

121. Waterbury memorandum, 1908, pp. 1, 4.

122. Griggs statement, 1908, p. 57.

123. C. C. Wilson, President, United Wireless, to Bureau of Equipment, July 9, 1908, NARA, RG 19, File 18301, Box 71.

124. International Radio Law, 1926, p. 8, enclosed in Russell Conklin to W. R. Vallance, June 14, 1926, NARA, RG 43, File 574.

125. Annual Report of the Commissioner of Navigation, H.R. Doc. No. 62-143, at 53 (1911).

126. Ibid., p. 56.

127. Secretary of the Navy George v. L. Meyer, March 30, 1910, in House of Representatives, Radio Communication, Report to Accompany H.R. 23595, H.R. Rep. No. 61-924, at 4 (1910).

128. *Wireless Telegraphy: Hearings before the House Committee on Interstate and Foreign Commerce.*, 60th Cong. 31, 37 (1909) (statement of Eugene Chamberlain).

129. House Committee on Merchant Marine and Fisheries, Wireless telegraph on certain ocean steamers, Report to accompany S. 7021, H.R. Rep. No. 61-1373, at 3 (1910).

130. Bureau of Equipment to the Navy Department, December 11, 1909, NARA, RG 80, File 12479.

131. Annual Report of the Commissioner of Navigation, Department of Commerce and Labor, H.R. Doc. No. 61-118, at 17 (1909).

132. Bureau of Equipment to Navy Department, December 11, 1909.

133. Annual Report of the Secretary of the Navy, H.R. Doc. No. 62-119, at 264 (1911); Annual Report of the Secretary of the Navy, H.R. Doc. No. 62-932, at 38 (1912).

134. Annual Report of the Secretary of the Navy, H.R. Doc. No. 60-1045, at 283 (1908); Annual Report of the Secretary of the Navy, H.R. Doc. No. 61-1005, at 285 (1910); Annual Report of the Secretary of the Navy, H.R. Doc. No. 62-119, at 263 (1911); Annual Report of the Secretary of the Navy, H.R. Doc. No. 62-932, at 254 (1912).

135. C. C. Wilson, President, United Wireless Telegraph Company, to Hon. Wm. H. Taft, Sec. War, February 13, 1908, p. 3, enclosed in S. Doc. No. 60-452 (1908).

136. Acting Secretary of the Navy to the President, October 27, 1906, NARA, RG 80, File 12479; Bureau of Equipment to the Navy Department, December 11, 1909.

137. *To regulate radio communication: Hearings on S. 7243, Senate Committee on Commerce*, 61st Cong. 23 (1910) (written statement of James H. Hayden, NESCO); *Wireless Telegraphy and Telephony: Hearings on H.R. 19560, House Committee on the Merchant Marine and Fisheries*, 61st Cong. 175 (1910) (statement of Cleland Davis, Bureau of Equipment).

138. *Hearings before a Subcommittee of the Committee on Naval Affairs on H. J. Res. 95, House of Representatives*, 61st Cong. 721, 722 (1910) (statement of Ernest W. Roberts).

139. Waterbury memorandum, 1908.

140. Annual Report of the Commissioner of Navigation, H.R. Doc. No. 62-143, at 54 (1911).

141. *Hearings on H.R. 19560*, House Committee on the Merchant Marine and Fisheries, 61st Cong. 160, 160–163 (1910) (statement of Reginald Fessenden).

142. *Hearings before a Subcommittee of the Committee on Naval Affairs on H. J. Res. 95, House of Representatives*, 61st Cong. 764, 765 (1910) (statement of Eugene Chamberlain); International Radio Law, 1926, p. 9; Hearings on H.R. 19560, House Committee on the Merchant Marine and Fisheries, 61st Cong. 175 (1910).

143. King Alfonso sends wireless to *Times, New York Times*, February 2, 1912, p. 1.

144. James Bryce, British Ambassador to the United States to Secretary of State Philander C. Knox, November 9, 1911, NARA, RG 59, File 574.C1; *International wireless telegraphy: Hearings before the Senate Foreign Relations Committee*, 62nd Cong. 19, 34 (1912) (statement of Rear Admiral John R. Edwards).

145. Wireless delegates plan London work, *New York Times*, May 3, 1912, p. 2.

146. Radio Communication, Report to accompany S. 6412, 62d Cong. S. Rep. No. 62-698, at 5 (1912).

147. The sinking of the *Titanic* did not influence the Radio Act of 1912. The legislative action that did result from the tragedy was a July 1912 amendment to the Wireless Ship Act of 1910 (cf. Douglas, 1989, p. 233; Howeth, 1963); Pub. L. No. 62-238, 37 Stat. 199 (1912).

148. S. 3620, a bill to regulate radio communication (1912); S. 5334, a bill to regulate radio communication (1912); A mischievous bill, *New York Times*, March 31, 1910, p. 10; Radio Communication, Report to accompany S. 6412, 62nd Cong. S. Rep. No. 62-698, at 3 (1912).

149. House Committee on the Merchant Marine and Fisheries, Report to accompany H.R. 15357, 62nd Cong., H.R. Rep. No. 62-582, at 6 (1912). H.R. 15357 was the companion bill to S. 3620 in the House.

150. Eugene Chamberlain, Memorandum for Secretary of Commerce Nagel, May 3, 1912, NARA, RG 40, File 67032.

151. Radio Act of 1912, Pub. L. No. 62-264, 37 Stat. 302 (1912) (hereafter Radio Act of 1912).

152. Ibid.

153. Annual Report of Commissioner of Navigation, H.R. Doc. No. 62-143, at 55 (1911).

154. Radio Act of 1912.

155. H.R. 23595, a bill to regulate radio communication, 61st Cong. (1910); S. 6412, a bill to regulate radio communication, 62nd Cong. (1912).

156. Manney testimony, 1908, pp. 46–47.

157. H.R. Rep. No. 62-582, at 9 (1912).

158. Manney testimony, 1908, p. 49.

159. United States Telephone Co. v. Central Union Telephone Co. et al., 171 F. 130, 144 (1909).

160. Ibid., p. 143.

161. 36 Stat. 545 (1910).

162. Eugene Chamberlain, Memorandum for Secretary Nagel, June 19, 1910, NARA, RG 40, File 67032.

163. An act to require apparatus and operators for radio communion on certain ocean steamers, Pub. L. No. 61-262, 45 Cong. Rec. 629–630 (1910) (hereafter Wireless Ship Act, 1910).

164. H.R. Rep. No. 61-924, at 3 (1910).

165. Wireless Ship Act, 1910, §2.

166. Ibid.

167. To regulate radio communication: Hearings on S. 7243, Senate Committee on Commerce, 61st Cong. 20, 21 (1910) (statement of John Bottomley); H.R. Rep. No. 62-582, at 9 (1912). The provision was then transferred to S. 6412.

168. *Radio communication: Hearings on H.R. 15357, a bill to regulate radio communication before the House Committee on Merchant Marine and Fisheries*, 62nd Cong. 41, 69 (1912) (statement of David W. Todd).

169. *Radio communication: Hearings before the Subcommittee of the Committee on Commerce on S. 3620 and S. 5334*, 62nd Cong. 10, 36 (1912).

170. To regulate wireless, *New York Times*, March 8, 1910, p. 5.

171. Radio Communication, Report to accompany S. 6412, S. Rep. No. 62-698, at 13 (1912).

172. Beecher memorandum, November 23, 1901.

173. S. 6412, §§2 and 3.

174. Radio Act of 1912, §2; Bureau of Steam Engineering to Superintendent of Radio Service, October 13, 1913, 11th endorsement, Secrecy of radio communication, p. 5, NARA, RG 80, Records of the General Board (GB), Subject files, 1900–1947, File 419.

175. Radio Act of 1912, §2.

176. Lamb memorandum, January 29, 1904, BT Archives, PO, File 30/1115.

Chapter 4

Epigraph: General Board to the Secretary of the Navy, June 5, 1915, p. 1, NARA, RG 80, Records of the General Board (GB), File 419 (hereafter NARA, RG 80, GB, File 419).

1. Watch on wireless plant, *New York Times*, August 10, 1912, p. 1.

2. Stanford C. Hooper to Charles J. Badger, Commander-in-Chief, Atlantic Fleet, May 21, 1913, Hooper papers, LOC.

3. Admiral George Dewey, General Board, to the Secretary of the Navy, March 14, 1914, 16th endorsement, Secrecy of radio communication, p. 9, NARA, RG 80, GB, File 419 (hereafter Secrecy).

4. James A. Scrymser, Central and South American Telegraph Company to Benjamin Cable, Acting Secretary of Commerce, October 21, 1912, NARA, RG 59, File 811.74.

5. Attorney General George Wickersham to Department of Commerce and Labor, November 22, 1912, p. 1, enclosed in Acting Secretary of Commerce and Labor to Secretary of State, December 5, 1912, NARA, RG 59, File 811.74.

6. Ibid., p. 2.

7. Wickersham to Department of Commerce and Labor, November 22, 1912, p. 3; Radio communication—Issuance of Licenses, 29 Op. Att'y Gen. 579 (1912).

8. Hoover v. Intercity Radio Co., Inc., 286 F. 1003 (1923).

9. Dewey to the Secretary of the Navy, March 14, 1914, in Secrecy, p. 8.

10. Memorandum to accompany draft of proposed amendment to Radio Act of August 12, 1912, April 24, 1914, p. 1, NARA, RG 38, File 110, Box 3. Policymakers at the Department of Commerce would later view the licensing requirement to erect a station as unconstitutional because it "wipe[d] out all reference to interstate commerce." See V. Ford Greaves to Commissioner of Navigation, Department of Commerce, December 11, 1915, NARA, RG 173, File 70909.

11. Radio Act of 1912, Pub. L. No. 264, 37 Stat. 302 (1912), §18; H.R. 19350, a bill to regulate radio communication, §5, 64th Cong. (1916).

12. W. H. G. Bullard to the Secretary of the Navy, February 6, 1914, 14th endorsement, Secrecy, p. 7.

13. Bureau of Steam Engineering to Superintendent of Radio Service, October 13, 1913, 11th endorsement, Secrecy, p. 5.

14. Chief of Bureau of Steam Engineering to Superintendent of Radio Service, June 2, 1913, in Hooper to Badger, May 21, 1913; *Radio communication: Hearings before the Subcommittee of the Committee on Commerce on S. 3620 and S. 5334*, 62nd Cong. 10, 36 (1912) (statement of Lieut. Cmdr. David W. Todd) (hereafter Todd statement, 62nd Cong. 1912).

15. Bureau of Steam Engineering to Superintendent of Radio Service, October 13, 1913, Secrecy, p. 5.

16. W. H. G. Bullard to the Secretary of the Navy, February 6, 1914, 14th endorsement, Secrecy, p. 9.

17. Admiral Bullard, radio leader, dies, *New York Times*, November 25, 1927, p. 1; Todd statement, 62nd Cong. 10, 87 (1912).

18. Bullard, Memorandum, enclosed in U.S. Naval Radio Service to the Secretary of the Navy, March 28, 1914, pp. 6, 1, Communication by radiotelegraphy, NARA, RG 80, GB, File 419 (hereafter Communication by radiotelegraphy).

19. Wireless delegates plan London work, *New York Times*, May 4, 1912, p. 2.

20. R. P. Schwerin to Robert Lansing, April 9, 1919, p. 1, NARA, RG 59, File 811.74.

21. Navy Department to the Secretary of Commerce, September 2, 1914, p. 2, NARA, RG 38, File 49.

22. Bullard, Memorandum for Secretary, Joint Army and Navy Board, February 9, 1914, p. 3, NARA, RG 38, File 249.

23. F. M. Sammis, Around-the-world-wireless, *Popular Mechanics, 18*(3) (September 1912), 334.

24. John W. Griggs to President Taft, May 3, 1912, enclosed in Edward J. Nally to Secretary of State, December 21, 1915, NARA, RG 59, File 832.74.

25. Wireless around the world in three minutes, *New York Times*, January 24, 1915, p. SM7.

26. Federal's application glossed over the fact that the company's patent rights did not cover either the British Empire or Latin America, so an arrangement with British Marconi would be necessary. See Beach Thompson, Federal Telegraph Company, to the Secretary of the Navy, April 13, 1914, pp. 1–2, NARA, RG 38, File 249; Hobart to Alexanderson, January 30, 1918, Young papers, St. Lawrence University, Box 72.

27. Griggs to Taft, May 3, 1912.

28. Bullard, Memorandum for Secretary, Joint Army and Navy Board, February 9, 1914, p. 2.

29. H. P. Veeder, Federal Telegraph Company, to the Secretary of the Navy, May 7, 1915, p. 3, NARA, RG 38, File 249; Bullard to Chief of Naval Operations, May 17, 1915, p. 1, NARA, RG 38, File 249.

30. Bullard to the General Board, July 3, 1914, 5th endorsement, Communication by radiotelegraphy, p. 2.

31. S. C. Hooper to Commander-in-Chief, Atlantic Fleet, June 12, 1914, 2nd endorsement, Communication by radiotelegraphy, p. 3.

32. *Radio communication: Hearings before the Committee on Merchant Marine and Fisheries on H.R. 19350, a bill to regulate radio communication*, 64th Cong. 13, 49 (1917) (statement of Cmdr. David W. Todd) (hereafter *Radio communication: Hearings on H.R. 19350*, 1917).

33. Unsigned to Duncan U. Fletcher, United States Senate, May 19, 1917, p. 4, NARA, RG 38, File 110, Box 6.

34. Unsigned, Memorandum for the Secretary of the Navy, n.d., NARA, RG 38, File 110, Box 6.

35. Secretary of Navy Josephus Daniels to Secretary of Commerce Redfield, October 15, 1918, p. 3, NARA, RG 38, File 47.

36. Report to accompany H.R. 7716, Amendment of the Radio Act of 1927, S. Rep. No. 72-1004, at 11 (1932).

37. Proposed confidential letter from the Secretary of the Navy to the Secretary of Commerce, June 18, 1915, pp. 1–2, Papers of Assistant Secretary of the Navy, Franklin Delano Roosevelt papers, FDR Library.

38. Dewey to the Secretary of the Navy, March 14, 1914, in Secrecy, p. 9; Admiral Austin M. Knight to the Secretary of the Navy, August 10, 1914, 6th endorsement, Communication by radiotelegraphy, p. 5.

39. General Board to the Secretary of the Navy, June 5, 1915, p. 1, NARA, RG 80, GB, File 419.

40. Navy takes over Sayville radio, New York Times, July 9, 1915, p. 1; Navy Department to the Superintendent of the Radio Service, October 8, 1915, p. 1, NARA, RG 38, File 49.

41. The section did nothing to ensure that the citizen who took out the license was in fact the owner or a manager at the station.

42. Unsigned (likely Daniels), n.d., p. 7, Hooper papers, LOC, Box 1.

43. Ibid.

44. Warning to Japan on Magdalena Bay, New York Times, April 5, 1912, p. 1; Deny German power in wireless plant, New York Times, August 11, 1912, p. 9.

45. Colville Barclay to Secretary of State William Jennings Bryan, August 4, 1914, NARA, RG 173, File 70909.

46. Navy Department to the Secretary of Commerce, September 2, 1914, p. 2.

47. Navy takes over Sayville radio, New York Times, July 9, 1915, p. 1.

48. Wickersham to Department of Commerce and Labor, November 22, 1912, p. 3; Radio communication: Hearings on H.R. 19350, 1917, pp. 36–38.

49. Dewey to the Secretary of the Navy, March 14, 1914, in Secrecy, p. 9.

50. Memorandum to accompany draft of a proposed amendment to Radio Act of August 12, 1912, NARA, RG 38, File 49.

51. Draft bill, July 26, 1915, NARA, RG 38, File 49; Draft bill enclosed in Bullard to Chief of Naval Operations, September 27, 1915, NARA, RG 38, File 49.

52. An act to regulate radio communication (draft bill), December 6, 1915, NARA, RG 173, File 70909. Licensing proposals for radio receivers targeted the amateurs who, the Navy suspected, were "surreptitiously receiving" confidential information and sending it along to the enemy. See Dewey to the Secretary of the Navy, March 14, 1914, in Secrecy, pp. 4–5.

53. Charles Warren, Assistant Attorney General, to Captain William H. G. Bullard, January 5, 1916, p. 2, NARA, RG 38, File 110, Box 4.

54. Daimler Co Ltd v. Continental Tyre and Rubber Co (Great Britain) Ltd [1916] 2 AC 307 (House of Lords).

55. Dartmouth College v. Woodward, 17 U.S. 518 (1819); Salomon v. Salomon & Co. Ltd [1896] UKHL 1, [1897] AC 22. British corporate law experts view the nineteenth-century cases as confirming a principle going back to the seventeenth century rather than developing one (Sealy & Worthington, 2013, p. 52).

56. Continental Tyre and Rubber Co (Great Britain) Ltd v. Daimler Co Ltd [1915] 1 KB 893 (Court of Appeal).

57. Daimler v. Continental Tyre, 1916.

58. Alvey Adee, Second Assistant Secretary to J. Butler-Wright, November 29, 1915, p. 2, NARA, RG 59, File 811.74.

59. An Act to regulate radio communication, nd. (circa spring 1916); An Act to regulate radio communication, August 19, 1916, §5; An Act to regulate radio communication, December 13, 1916, §7.

60. By contrast, countries such as Germany, which experienced emigration, were afraid that their citizens would assimilate in the United States and lose their "Germandom" (Bönker, 2012, p. 31).

61. J. C. Cooper, Government ownership of shore stations, n.d., NARA, RG 38, File 110, Box 6.

62. E. J. Nally to E. W. Rice, President, General Electric Company, June 4, 1915, p. 1, Young papers, St. Lawrence University.

63. Ibid.

64. Honolulu wireless may be seized, *New York Times*, October 17, 1914, p. 4.

65. Wireless around the world in three minutes, *New York Times*, January 24, 1915, SM7.

66. *Radio communication: Hearings on H.R. 19350*, 1917, p. 186 (statement of E. J. Nally, vice president of Marconi Wireless Telegraph Company of America).

67. Naval Communication Service, Office of the Director, Marconi shore radio stations purchased by Navy Department, November 30, 1918, p. 1, NARA, RG 38, File 47; *Government control of radio communication: Hearings on H.R. 13159 before the House Committee on the Merchant Marine and Fisheries*, 65th Cong. 5, 9 (1918) (testimony of Josephus Daniels) (hereafter *Government control of radio communication: Hearings on H.R. 13159*, 1918).

68. Marconi system for Hawaii, *New York Times*, December 3, 1899, p. 16. Naval policymakers quickly realized that it was a mistake to authorize the high-power station and targeted it for takeover. See Memorandum enclosed in U.S. Naval Radio Service to the Secretary of the Navy, March 28, 1914, Communication by radiotelegraphy, p. 5.

69. Marconi wireless soon to span earth, *New York Times*, July 29, 1915, p. 5.

70. H.R. 19350, §§5, 6 (1916).

71. David W. Todd, Memorandum for Chief of Naval Operations, October 5, 1916, p. 1, NARA, RG 38, File 49.

72. David W. Todd, Memoranda, January 15, 1917, p. 5, NARA, RG 38, File 110, Box 3. Based on the stock ownership metric, British Marconi had financial interest in five of the eight high-power stations in the United States. In addition to the four Marconi stations, the station at Tuckerton, New Jersey, was partially owned by the Compagnie Générale de Télégraphie Sans Fil, half of whose stock was owned by British Marconi and the other half by French Marconi and allied interests (Aitken, 1985, p. 391).

73. *Radio communication: Hearings on H.R. 19350*, 1917, p. 362, 370 (statement of David Sarnoff).

74. Ibid.

75. Unsigned, n.d., memorandum prepared for Todd. NARA, RG 38, File 110, Box 6, "Miscellaneous, 1915–1919" folder.

76. Edward J. Nally, The government wireless, January 9, 1917, enclosed in Chief Radio Inspector, Department of Commerce, to Commissioner of Navigation, January 10, 1917, NARA, RG 173, File 70909.

77. D. W. Todd, Memorandum for Chief of Naval Operations, November 6, 1918, p. 3, NARA, RG 80, File 110.

78. Todd, Memorandum for Chief of Naval Operations, October 5, 1916.

79. Ibid.

80. William Redfield to Josephus Daniels, October 19, 1915, p. 1, NARA, RG 173, File 70909.

81. *Radio communication: Hearings on H.R. 19350*, 1917, pp. 13, 21 (Todd statement).

82. H.R. 19350 (1916).

83. *Radio communication: Hearings on H.R. 19350*, 1917, pp. 169, 177 (statement by John W. Griggs).

84. Director of Naval Communications David W. Todd, Memorandum for Chief of Naval Operations, December 13, 1916, NARA, RG 38, File 110.

85. Ibid., p. 2.

86. Chamberlain to Redfield, December 15, 1916, p. 1, NARA, RG 173, File 70909; H.R. 19350 (1916).

87. Todd to Chamberlain, October 28, 1916, p. 1, NARA, RG 173, File 70909.

88. Statement of Edward J. Nally, November 21, 1916, Informal hearing given representatives of commercial and amateur radio interests, by inter-departmental committee on radio legislation, p. 8, NARA, RG 38, File 110, Box 4.

89. H.R. 2573, a bill to further regulate radio communication, 65th Cong. (1917); H.R. 13159, a bill to further regulate radio communication, 65th Cong. (1918), NARA, RG 38, File 47.

90. *Radio communication: Hearings on H.R. 19350*, 1917, p. 13 (Todd statement).

91. J. C. Cooper, Government ownership of shore stations, n.d.

92. The focus of table 4.1 is shore stations, so ship installations are not included, though the Marconi organization played a central role in ship-to-shore traffic.

93. Nally, The government wireless, January 9, 1917.

94. Ibid.

95. Memorandum for Admiral Knapp, February 3, 1919, p. 2, in response to Admiral Harry Shephard Knapp to Captain David W. Todd, February 1, 1919, NARA, RG 38, File 110, Box 6.

96. Daniels to Senator Duncan U. Fletcher, May 19, 1917, p. 5, NARA, RG 38, File 110, Box 6.

97. Secretary of Commerce William G. Redfield to Duncan U. Fletcher, Chairman, Senate Committee on Commerce, January 8, 1917, p. 2, NARA, RG 173, File 70909.

98. Daniels to Fletcher, December 29, 1916, p. 5, enclosed in Press Notice, Office of the Superintendent, U.S. Naval Radio Service, January 2, 1917, NARA, RG 173, File 70909.

99. Admiral Austin M. Knight to the Secretary of the Navy, August 10, 1914, 6th endorsement, Communication by radiotelegraphy, p. 2. See also W. H. G. Bullard, In re proposed new law for regulation of radio communication, Memorandum for heads of all executive departments, March 8, 1916, p. 2, NARA, RG 173, File 70909.

100. S. C. Hooper, Basis of radio organization, U.S.S. America, n.d., enclosed in Rear Admiral Griffin, Bureau of Steam Engineering, Ownership of coastal radio stations by Navy, August 31, 1917, p. 2, NARA, RG 38, File 110, Box 6.

101. *Government control of radio communication: Hearings on H.R. 13159*, 1918, p. 5 (Daniels statement).

102. D. W. Todd, Memorandum, January 15, 1917, p. 7, NARA, RG 38, File 110, Box 6.

103. Secretary of State Robert Lansing to Joshua W. Alexander, February 8, 1917, p. 3, NARA, RG 38, File 110, Box 6.

104. Views of the Navy Department on radio communication, H.R. Doc. No. 66-165, at 4 (1919).

105. Exec. Order No. 2585 (1917); Director of Naval Communications David W. Todd, Statement for the Honorable Josephus Daniels, Secretary of the Navy, before the House Committee on Interstate and Foreign Commerce, July 9, 1918, p. 1, NARA, RG 38, File 32.

106. D. W. Todd, Memorandum on radio legislation, September 12, 1917, p. 4, NARA, RG 38, File 110, Box 6.

107. Chief of Naval Operations Admiral William Benson to Commandants of Naval Districts, Activities of the Naval Communication Service after the War, December 3, 1918, p. 1, NARA, RG 38, File 110, Box 5.

108. Todd, Memorandum for the Secretary of the Navy, September 18, 1918, p. 2, Daniels papers, LOC; Assistant Secretary of the Navy Franklin D. Roosevelt to Secretary of War, Radio legislation, March 29, 1919, p. 4, NARA, RG 38, File 110, Box 6; Howeth, 1963, p. 317.

109. Todd, Memorandum on radio legislation, September 12, 1917, p. 4.

110. Activities of the Naval Communication Service after the War, December 3, 1918, p. 3.

111. Todd, Memorandum for the Secretary of the Navy, September 18, 1918, p. 1.

112. Rear Admiral Robert Griffin, Bureau of Steam Engineering, to the Secretary of the Navy, August 31, 1917, p. 1, NARA, RG 38, File 110.

113. Naval Communication Service, Marconi shore stations purchased by Navy Department, November 30, 1918; Aitken, 1985, p. 287.

114. Secretary of War Newton D. Baker to the Chairman of the Senate Commerce Committee, December 19, 1918, p. 1, NARA, RG 38, File 110, Box 6; Secretary of War Newton D. Baker to the Chairman of the House Committee on Merchant Marine and Fisheries, January 18, 1919, p. 3, NARA, RG 38, File 110, Box 6.

115. Memorandum for Admiral Knapp, February 3, 1919, p. 2.

116. Baker to the Chairman of the House Committee on Merchant Marine and Fisheries, January 18, 1919.

117. Todd, Memorandum for the Secretary of the Navy, September 18, 1918, pp. 1–2; Office of the District Communication Superintendent, Memorandum for Captain

Todd, December 12, 1918, p. 1, NARA, RG 38, File 47. United Fruit was afraid that Central American republics would follow the example of the United States. See Memorandum for Admiral Knapp, February 3, 1919, p. 1.

118. J. W. Elwood, Memorandum on wireless, May 14, 1919, Young papers, St. Lawrence University.

119. Baker to Daniels, May 28, 1919, p. 1, NARA, RG 38, File 110, Box 6. Secretary Daniels's final attempt at government ownership, later that summer, received no support (Winkler, 2008, p. 254). See also Burwell S. Cutler, Chief, Bureau of Foreign and Domestic Commerce, to William C. Redfield, Secretary of Commerce, June 26, 1919, NARA, RG 40, File 75334.

120. Cutler to Redfield, Secretary of Commerce, June 26, 1919.

121. An Act Relating to the landing and operation of submarine cables in the United States, Pub. L. No. 67-8 (1921), 47 U.S.C. §§34–39.

122. Naval Communication Service, Marconi shore stations purchased by Navy Department, November 30, 1918; *Government control of radio communication: Hearings on H.R. 13159*, 1918, pp. 5, 9 (Daniels statement).

Chapter 5

1. D. W. Todd, Memorandum on radio legislation, September 12, 1917, NARA, RG 38, File 110, Box 6.

2. W. Henry Robertson, Consul General, Argentina, September 27, 1915, NARA, RG 38, File 49; American Consul General to Secretary of State, August 26, 1913, NARA, RG 59, File 832.74.

3. Albert Davis to Owen D. Young, August 8, 1919, p. 3, Young papers, St. Lawrence University, File 11-14, Box 72.

4. John W. Griggs to President Taft, May 3, 1912, enclosed in Edward J. Nally to Secretary of State, December 21, 1915, NARA, RG 59, File 832.74.

5. S. C. Hooper, Memorandum relative to attached letter, November 13, 1913, Hooper papers, LOC.

6. Josephus Daniels to the Secretary of State, August 27, 1913, NARA, RG 59, File 819.74.

7. Division of Latin American Affairs to Weitzel, December 9, 1911, NARA, RG 59, File 819.74.

8. Griggs to President Taft, May 3, 1912.

9. Ibid.

10. H. Breckinridge, Acting Secretary of War, to Secretary of State, August 26, 1913, NARA, RG 59, File 819.74.

11. W. J. Price to George Washington Goethals, September 15, 1914, NARA, RG 185, File 43-D-8.

12. Ibid.; Notes on Navy Department redraft (1931), in Charles Francis Adams to Henry L. Stimson, March 27, 1931, NARA, RG 80, File 310109.

13. Admiral William S. Benson, Memorandum for the Secretary of the Navy, March 12, 1918, p. 3, NARA, RG 38, File 49.

14. Daniels to the State Department, January 11, 1916, p. 2, NARA, RG 38, File 240.

15. Benson, Memorandum for the Secretary of the Navy, March 12, 1918.

16. Bullard to Benson, November 3, 1915, p. 1, NARA, RG 38, Division of Naval Communications, Confidential Correspondence, 1917–1926, Box 17.

17. Ibid.

18. General Board to the Secretary of the Navy, November 17, 1915, p. 2, 2nd endorsement re: proposed radio station at San Juan Bautista, Mexico, NARA, RG 80, GB, File 419.

19. Ibid.

20. Chauncey Eldridge to the State Department, November 3, 1915, p. 1, NARA, RG 38, File 240.

21. J. Butler Wright, Memorandum, In re wireless telegraph in Central and South America, September 21, 1915, p. 1, NARA, RG 59, File 832.74.

22. Edwin H. Morgan to the State Department, August 24, 1915, NARA, RG 59, File 832.74.

23. Edward J. Nally to Secretary of State Robert Lansing, September 16, 1915, NARA, RG 59, File 832.74.

24. Robert Lansing to Marconi Wireless Telegraph Company of America, October 9, 1915, p. 1, NARA, RG 59, File 832.74.

25. Bullard to Chief of Naval Operations, Letter prepared for the Secretary's signature, November 18, 1915, p. 2, NARA, RG 38, File 240.

26. Alvey Adee, Second Assistant Secretary to J. Butler-Wright, November 29, 1915, p. 1, NARA, RG 59, File 811.74.

27. Lansing to American Marconi, October 9, 1915, p.1.

28. Nally to Lansing, December 21, 1915, p. 2.

29. Nally to Lansing, November 4, 1915, p. 2, NARA, RG 59, File 832.74; Nally to Lansing, December 21, 1915.

30. J. Butler Wright, Memorandum re Marconi Wireless Telegraph Company, October 26, 1915, p. 1, NARA, RG 59, File 832.74; Nally to Lansing, November 4, 1915, p. 2, NARA, RG 59, File 832.74.

31. Nally to Lansing, December 21, 1915, p. 1.

32. Bullard to Chief of Naval Operations, November 18, 1915, p. 1.

33. Josephus Daniels to the Secretary of State, December 6, 1915, NARA, RG 80, File 12479.

34. Bullard to Chief of Naval Operations, November 18, 1915, p. 1.

35. Nally to Lansing, December 21, 1915, p. 1.

36. Assistant Secretary Franklin D. Roosevelt to State Department, January 14, 1916, p. 2, NARA, RG 59, File 832.74.

37. J. Butler-Wright, Memorandum, November 24, 1915, p. 1, NARA, RG 59, File 832.74.

38. J. Butler Wright, Memorandum re Marconi Wireless Telegraph Company, October 26, 1915, p. 1.

39. Nally to Lansing, December 21, 1915, pp. 2–3.

40. Ibid., pp. 3–4.

41. Ibid.

42. Ibid.

43. Bullard to Chief of Naval Operations, November 18, 1915, p. 1 (see also in Winkler, 2008, p. 95, as a memorandum by Secretary Daniels).

44. Alvey Adee, Second Assistant Secretary to J. Butler-Wright, November 29, 1915, p. 2, NARA, RG 59, File 811.74.

45. J. Butler Wright, Memorandum re Marconi Wireless Telegraph Company, October 26, 1915, p. 1; J. Butler Wright, Memorandum re Wireless in Brazil, December 2, 1915, pp. 1–2, NARA, RG 59, File 832.74.

46. Secretary of the Treasury William Gibbs McAdoo to the Secretary of the Navy, November 18, 1915, NARA, RG 38, File 49.

47. Lieutenant Guy Whitlock to Director of Naval Intelligence, January 11, 1915, p. 1, enclosed in Director of Naval Intelligence to Superintendent of Naval Radio Service, January 16, 1915, NARA, RG 38, File 49.

48. Circular dated March 11, 1916, prepared by the Navy Department and presented by the State Department to the representatives of the Latin American Republics at an informal conference in January 1916, NARA, RG 59, File 810.74, p. 2 (hereafter Circular, March 11, 1916). See also *Foreign Relations of the United States*, Vol. 1, 1916, p. 1.

49. Bullard to the Secretary of the Treasury, December 3, 1915, pp. 1–2, NARA, RG 38, File 49.

50. Bullard, Radio organization for the Western Hemisphere, Letter prepared for the Secretary's signature, January 24, 1916, p. 4, in Bullard to Daniels, January 26, 1916, NARA, RG 38, File 240.

51. Circular, March 11, 1916, p. 7.

52. Ibid.

53. Ibid., p. 8.

54. Office of the Solicitor to Boaz Long, August 9, 1915, p. 2, NARA, RG 59, File 810.74.

55. Circular, March 11, 1916, p. 1.

56. Ibid., pp. 2–3.

57. Ibid., pp. 3, 7.

58. Ibid., p. 4.

59. Rear Admiral S. Valdes, Memorandum relative to radio-telegraphic service on the American continent, September 13, 1916, in Secretary of the State to the Secretary of the Navy, January 31, 1917, NARA, RG 38, Division of Naval Communications, Confidential Correspondence, 1917–1926, Box 17.

60. Edwin Morgan, Ambassador to Brazil, to the State Department, December 8, 1915, p. 3, in State Department to the Navy Department, January 5, 1915, NARA, RG 38, File 240.

61. Jordan Stabler, Division of Latin American Affairs, Memorandum, December 29, 1916, NARA, RG 59, File 835.74/8. Just how the emerging geopolitical significance of the spectrum fit with concerns about control over stations is yet to be analyzed.

62. S. C. Hooper to Lieutenant P. H. Bastedo, Commander, U.S. naval forces operating in European waters, November 3, 1917, Hooper papers, LOC.

63. Secretary of the Navy Josephus Daniels to the Secretary of State, April 12, 1917, NARA, RG 80, File 12479. The State Department had already investigated the German ties of Federal's previous chairman. See Jordan Stabler, Division of Latin American Affairs, December 29, 1916.

64. Department of State, Office of the Solicitor, Memorandum, n.d., RG 59, File 811.74; Sidney Steadman to the Secretary of State, October 28, 1917, p. 1, NARA, RG 59, File 811.74.

65. Secretary of State Robert Lansing to the Pan American Wireless Telegraph and Telephone Company, November 2, 1917, NARA, RG 59, File 811.74.

66. Pan American Wireless Telegraph and Telephone Company, Amended certificate of incorporation, October 31, 1917, pp. 4–5, NARA, RG 59, File 811.74; Bureau of Steam Engineering to the Secretary of the Navy, February 9, 1918, NARA, RG 19, File 917, p. 1; Benson, Memorandum for the Secretary of the Navy, March 12, 1918.

67. David W. Todd, Memorandum for the Secretary of the Navy, January 2, 1918, p. 2, NARA, RG 38, Division of Naval Communications, Confidential Correspondence, 1917–1926, Box 17.

68. Charles Warren to Bullard, June 8, 1916, p. 2, NARA, RG 38, File 110.

69. Solicitor to Navy Department, March 11, 1918, pp. 2–3, NARA, RG 38, File 110.

70. Ibid.

71. Ibid.

72. Memorandum for the Secretary of the Navy, unsigned, n.d., p. 3, NARA, RG 38, Division of Naval Communications, Confidential Correspondence, 1917–1926.

73. Nally to the Secretary of the Navy, March 4, 1918, p. 1, NARA, RG 38, Division of Naval Communications, Confidential correspondence, 1917–1926, Box 17.

74. S. C. Hooper, Basis of radio organization, U.S.S. America, n.d., enclosed in Rear Admiral Griffin, Bureau of Steam Engineering, Ownership of coastal radio stations by Navy, August 31, 1917, p. 2, NARA, RG 38, File 110, Box 6 (hereafter Hooper, Basis of radio organization, 1917).

75. Ibid., p. 2; Hooper's record of service, August 10, 1921, p. 2, enclosed in Young to Hooper, August 11, 1921, Young papers, St. Lawrence University, Box 147. At the time, Hooper did not publicly take credit for his plan, but he would seek recognition for it from various sources during the rest of his career. See Affidavit of Stanford C. Hooper before the War Claims Arbiter, December 18, 1930, p. 8, Hooper papers, LOC.

76. Hooper, Basis of radio organization, 1917, p. 1.

77. Boaz Long to the Secretary of State, April 28, 1917, NARA, RG 80, File 12479; Daniels to the Secretary of State, April 20, 1917, NARA, RG 80, File 12479.

78. I. M. Thames, Memorandum for Chief of Naval Operations, March 2, 1918, NARA, RG 38, File 49.

79. George Sweet, Memorandum for the Bureau of Steam Engineering, April 4, 1919, NARA, RG 19, File 917.

80. Hooper, Basis of radio organization, 1917, p. 3.

81. The Radio Corporation of America, History of the Radio Corporation and its relation to the art of radio communication and to the requirements of public communication, April 25, 1921, p. 5, Wallace White papers, LOC.

82. Hooper, Memorandum for Commander Parsons, March 2, 1920, Hooper papers, LOC.

83. Benson to Daniels, May 5, 1919, p. 3, Daniels papers, LOC, Reel 42.

84. Walter S. Rogers to the Secretary of the Navy, n.d., 1919, p. 3, Daniels papers, LOC, Reel 42.

85. Ibid., p. 7.

Chapter 6

1. Unsigned, A bill to further regulate radio communication. Comments in support of H.R. 13159 introduced on November 21, 1918, n.d., p. 5, NARA, RG 38, File 47.

2. Walter S. Rogers, Outlines of a communications program, September 11, 1918, p. 5, NARA, RG 38, File 110, Box 6.

3. Ibid., p. 2.

4. John Cutter, Acting Chief of Service to Secretary of Commerce, January 31, 1919, NARA, RG 40, File 78332.

5. Secretary of State to Chargé d'Affaires, Great Britain, November 5, 1920, in *Foreign Relations of the United States*, Vol. 1 (Washington, DC: US Government Printing Office, 1920), pp. 137–138; Walter S. Rogers to Josephus Daniels, n.d., 1919, pp. 5–6, Daniels papers, LOC, Reel 42.

6. The citations from Baker, 1960, pp. 427–442, refer to a reprint of Walter S. Rogers, Memorandum on wire and radio communications, February 12, 1919.

7. Rogers, Outlines of a communications program, September 11, 1918, pp. 5–6.

8. Ibid., p. 3.

9. Ibid., p. 6.

10. Ernest E. Power, General report on the international cable situation, January 15, 1919, Davis papers, LOC, Box 30.

11. Rogers, Outlines of a communications program, September 11, 1918, p. 5.

12. Charles Neave to J. W. Elwood, November 19, 1920, p. 2, Young papers, St. Lawrence University, Box 124.

13. Sub-Committee of Imperial Communications Committee, Committee of Imperial Defence, Report on proposed international conference at Washington, June 30, 1920, p. 12, Secret, I.C.C. No. 288, TNA PRO, CAB, File 35/14 (hereafter C.I.D. report, 1920).

14. Lansing to Pichon, June 4, 1919, in *Foreign Relations of the United States*, Vol. 1, 1920, p. 107.

15. Secretary of State Bainbridge Colby to All American Diplomatic Representatives, March 30, 1920, in *Foreign Relations of the United States*, Vol. 1, 1920, p. 116.

16. C.I.D. report, 1920, p. 8.

17. Ibid., p. 9.

18. Secretary of Commerce Joshua Alexander to the Secretary of State, July 13, 1920, p. 2, NARA, RG 40, File 67032; S. W. Stratton, Bureau of Standards, to Secretary of Commerce, November 30, 1922, p. 1, NARA, RG 40, File 67032.

19. Press release of the Department of State, December 14, 1920, *Foreign Relations of the United States*, Vol. 1, 1920, pp. 147–148.

20. RCA to Rogers, November 19, 1920, p. 5, Young papers, St. Lawrence University, Box 124; RCA to Rogers, November 10, 1920, p. 5, Young papers, St. Lawrence University, Box 124.

21. Rogers to RCA, November 13, 1920, p. 4, Young papers, St. Lawrence University, Box 124.

22. Rogers to Josephus Daniels, n.d., 1919, p. 6; John Jacob Rogers, Cables, wireless and American trade, *New York Times*, November 23, 1919, p. X8.

23. Rogers to RCA, November 13, 1920, p. 3, Young papers, St. Lawrence University, Box 124.

24. Young to Rogers, November 17, 1920, p. 1, Young papers, St. Lawrence University, Box 124.

25. Ibid., pp. 1–2.

26. Radio Corporation of America, History of Radio Corporation and its relation to the art of radio communication and to the requirements of public communication, April 25, 1921, p. 23, Wallace White papers, LOC (hereafter History of RCA, 1921).

27. Young to Rogers, November 17, 1920, p. 1.

28. Milton S. Davis to Stanford C. Hooper, July 24, 1928, Hooper papers, LOC.

29. Appendix to accompany the third endorsement, enclosed in General Board to the Secretary of the Navy, June 19, 1923, NARA, RG 80, GB, File 419.

30. Secretary of the Navy Edwin Denby to Senator Root, December 19, 1921, Hooper papers, LOC.

31. Effect of preponderating control of radio by any one nation, November 22, 1921, p. 7, enclosed in S. W. Bryant, Acting Secretary of the Navy, Memorandum for the Secretary of the General Board, June 1, 1922, NARA, RG 38, File 100. Later in the decade, Hooper looked back to 1920–1921 as the time when British dominance was broken. See S. C. Hooper, Memorandum to Director of Naval Communications, September 29, 1927, p. 1, Hooper papers, LOC.

32. Ibid.; S. C. Hooper, Memorandum of conference with Senator Root, December 21, 1921, p. 1, Hooper papers, LOC.

33. Power, General report, January 15, 1919.

34. Rogers to Daniels, n.d., 1919, p. 5.

35. Power, General report, January 15, 1919.

36. American Commission to Negotiate Peace, Secretary's notes of a conversation held in M. Pichon's room at the Quai d'Orsay, Paris, on Thursday May 1, 1919, at 4 p.m., p. 3, Davis papers, LOC.

37. Hooper to J. G. Harbord, President of RCA, April 23, 1929, p. 2, Hooper papers, LOC.

38. Young to Denby, December 22, 1921, Hooper papers, LOC.

39. Ibid., p. 2.

40. Radio Act of 1927, Pub. L. No. 639, 44 Stat. 1163 (1927).

41. E. T. Chamberlain, Department of Commerce to Rogers, October 12, 1920, p. 1, NARA, RG 40, File 67032.

42. Unsigned, Amalgamation of International Conventions, n.d., p. 3, NARA, RG 38, Miscellaneous folder.

43. Unsigned to Charles Neave, November 24, 1920, p. 2, Young papers, St. Lawrence University, Box 124.

44. History of RCA, 1921, p. 18; Unsigned, Memorandum Re: Universal Electrical Communications Convention and Regulations, March 24, 1921, p. 1, Young papers, St. Lawrence University, Box 124.

45. Charles Neave to H. B. Thayer, April 5, 1921, p. 2, Young papers, St. Lawrence University, Box 124.

46. History of RCA, 1921, p. 20.

47. Ibid., p. 24.

48. Memorandum of Radio Corporation of America with reference to the proposed Universal Electrical Communications Union, p. 16, enclosed in J. W. Elwood to Frank B. Kellogg, May 25, 1921, Kellogg papers, Minnesota Historical Society, Microfilm Roll 8 (hereafter RCA memorandum, May 25, 1921).

49. Unsigned to Secretary of Commerce, Communications conference, October 21, 1922, p. 2, NARA, RG 40, File 67032.

50. RCA memorandum, May 25, 1921, p. 13.

51. Unsigned, Memorandum Re: Universal Electrical Communications Convention and Regulations, March 24, 1921, pp. 2, 4, Young papers, St. Lawrence University, Box 124.

52. RCA memorandum, May 25, 1921, p. 5.

53. Ibid.

54. J. W. Elwood, Memorandum on wireless, May 14, 1919, p. 4, Young papers, St. Lawrence University.

55. J. W. Elwood, Memorandum, June 2, 1919, p. 4, Young papers, St. Lawrence University.

56. Elwood, Memorandum on wireless, May 14, 1919, p. 4.

57. Captain Milton S. Davis, Pacific Communication Officer, to S. C. Hooper, May 5, 1929, Hooper papers, LOC.

58. S. C. Hooper, Memorandum relative to attached letter, November 13, 1931, p. 1, Hooper papers, LOC.

59. Albert Davis to Young, August 22, 1919, Young papers, St. Lawrence University, Box 71.

60. Hobart to Alexanderson, January 30, 1918; Edwards to Young, June 7, 1918, Young papers, St. Lawrence University, Box 72.

61. Young to Glaser, August 22, 1919, Young papers, St. Lawrence University, Box 72; Davis to Young, August 6, 1919, p. 1, Young papers, St. Lawrence University.

62. Davis to Young, August 6, 1919, p. 2, Young papers, St. Lawrence University.

63. Young to Glaser, August 22, 1919, p. 1, Young papers, St. Lawrence University, Box 72; Advantages of proposed agreement with General Electric Co., September 18, 1919, p. 2, Young papers, St. Lawrence University, Box 73.

64. Advantages of proposed agreement with General Electric Co., September 18, 1919, Young papers, St. Lawrence University, Box 73.

65. J. G. Harbord, RCA, to F. Perry, Lazard Brothers, October 6, 1927, p. 1, Young papers, St. Lawrence University.

66. Davis to Young, August 22, 1919.

67. Hooper to Young, December 20, 1919, Hooper papers, LOC.

68. Hooper to Young, October 3, 1922, Hooper papers, LOC.

69. *Cable-landing licenses: Hearings before a subcommittee of the Committee on Interstate Commerce, United States Senate*, 66th Cong. 337, 337–338 (1921) (statement by W. A. Winterbottom, Traffic Manager, RCA).

70. Draft of Principal Agreement, November 1919, p. 14, Young papers, St. Lawrence University.

71. Godfrey Isaacs to Young, July 12, 1921, pp. 4–5, Young papers, St. Lawrence University.

72. AEFG traffic agreement, October 14, 1921, in Report of the Federal Trade Commission on the Radio Industry, 67th Cong., 4th Sess. (Washington, DC: Government Printing Office, 1924), p. 313 (hereafter AEFG traffic agreement, 1921), in *The making of modern law* (Farmington Hills, MI: Gale Cengage Learning, 2018).

73. Ibid., p. 317.

74. Ibid., p. 313.

75. Ibid., p. 314.

76. Ibid.

77. Ibid.

78. Ibid., p. 316.

79. Hooper to Young, September 20, 1921, Young papers, St. Lawrence University.

80. Ibid.

81. Hooper to Young, August 1, 1921, p. 2, Hooper papers, LOC.

82. Young to Sheffield, December 7, 1921, p. 7; Young to Hooper, October 9, 1922, Hooper papers, LOC.

83. Young to Bullard, December 12, 1921, p. 2, Young papers, St. Lawrence University.

84. AEFG traffic agreement, 1921, p. 318.

85. Theodore Roosevelt, Jr., Acting Secretary of the Navy, to the Secretary of State, December 19, 1923, Hooper papers, LOC.

86. Hooper to Young, n.d., 1921, Hooper papers, LOC.

87. Ibid.

88. Hooper, n.d., 1929, p. 5, Hooper papers, LOC.

89. Hooper, Memorandum of conference with Senator Root, December 21, 1921.

90. World's greatest wireless, *New York Times*, November 6, 1921, p. 1.

91. Unsigned, Attention of Mr. Woolsey, January 12, 1922, p. 2, Young papers, St. Lawrence University, Disarmament Conference files.

92. Young to Bullard, December 12, 1921, p. 3, Young papers, St. Lawrence University.

93. Young to James R. Sheffield, December 7, 1921, p. 7, Young papers, St. Lawrence University, Disarmament Conference files.

94. Advantages of proposed agreement with General Electric Co., September 18, 1919, p. 3, Young papers, St. Lawrence University, Box 73; Young to J. R. Geary, General Electric, Japan, October 7, 1920, p. 1, Young papers, St. Lawrence University.

95. Albert G. Davis to Owen D. Young, August 18, 1919, Young papers, St. Lawrence University, Box 71.

96. Davis to Edward J. Nally, October 13, 1919, pp. 1–2, Young papers, St. Lawrence University.

97. R. P. Schwerin to Robert Lansing, April 9, 1919, p. 3, NARA, RG 59, File 811.74.

98. Charles Crane, Minister in China, to the Chinese Premier, January 21, 1921, reprinted in "The Federal Telegraph Company's contract with the Chinese government: Correspondence and documents" (Washington, DC: Department of State, Division of Publications, 1925), p. 9 (hereafter Federal Telegraph contract correspondence, 1925).

99. H. C. Hopson to John W. Elwood, December 29, 1921, p. 1, Young papers, St. Lawrence University.

100. T. W. Lamont, J.P. Morgan and Co., to Under Secretary of State, March 11, 1921, reprinted in Federal Telegraph contract correspondence, 1925, p. 28.

101. Young to Denby, December 12, 1921, Young papers, St. Lawrence University, Disarmament Conference files.

102. Hooper, Memorandum regarding Owen D. Young, November 17, 1921, p. 1, Hooper papers, LOC.

103. Hooper, Memorandum of conference with Senator Root, December 21, 1921, p. 5.

104. Ibid.

105. Ibid.

106. Denby to Young, December 16, 1921, Hooper papers, LOC.

107. Young to Denby, December 22, 1921, Young papers, St. Lawrence University.

108. Young to Secretary of State Charles Evans Hughes, January 9, 1922, Young papers, St. Lawrence University.

109. Ibid.

110. Unsigned to James R. Sheffield, January 9, 1922, p. 2, Young papers, St. Lawrence University, Disarmament Conference files.

111. Mackay and I. T. & T. close wire merger, *New York Times*, March 21, 1928, p. 35.

112. *Commission on Communications: Hearings before the Committee on Interstate Commerce, United States Senate, on S. 6*, 71st Cong. 305, 326 (1929) (statement of Captain S. C. Hooper, May 22, 1929) (hereafter Hooper testimony, 1929).

113. Denies radio deal for Western Union, *New York Times*, March 10, 1929, sec. II, p. 44.

114. Radio—I. T. & T. step termed an "accord," *New York Times*, March 30, 1929, p. 12.

115. Secretary of Commerce Daniel C. Roper to the President, A study of communications by an interdepartmental committee, January 23, 1934, p. 4, President's Official File, FDR Library, File 859a.

116. Radio subsidiary sold for $100,000,000, *New York Times*, March 29, 1929, p. 1.

117. Hooper testimony, 1929, p. 323.

118. S. C. Hooper, Memorandum for Judge Sykes, March 21, 1928, p. 1, Hooper papers, LOC.

119. S. C. Hooper to William E. Beakes, Manager, Tropical Radio Telegraph Company, January 30, 1929, p. 1, Hooper papers, LOC; Milton S. Davis to Hooper, May 5, 1929, Hooper papers, LOC.

120. S. C. Hooper, Some principles involved in legislating for rapid communications, p. 4, enclosed in Hooper to William E. Beakes, Manager, Tropical Radio Telegraph Company, January 30, 1929, Hooper papers, LOC.

121. George S. Gibbs, Chief Signal Officer, U.S. Army, to S. C. Hooper, June 22, 1928, Hooper papers, LOC.

122. Milton S. Davis, Review of international communications with special reference to the Pacific Situation, *U.S. Naval Institute Proceedings, 55*, no. 12 (1929), p. 1040, Hooper papers, LOC.

123. S. C. Hooper, Some principles involved in legislating for rapid communications, Revision, April 4, 1929, p. 4, Hooper papers, LOC.

124. Hooper to Admiral S. S. Robison, September 28, 1927, Hooper papers, LOC.

125. Radio subsidiary sold for $100,000,000, *New York Times*, March 29, 1929, p. 1.

126. Hooper to F. B. Jewett, Vice President of American Telephone and Telegraph, March 20, 1930, Hooper papers, LOC.

127. Hooper testimony, 1929, pp. 322, 325.

128. Hooper, Some principles involved in legislating for rapid communications, Revision, April 4, 1929, p. 3.

129. Hooper, Some principles involved in legislating for rapid communications, January 30, 1929, p. 1.

130. Ibid., p. 2.

131. Ibid.

132. Ibid.

133. Ibid.

134. Ibid.; Hooper, Memorandum relative to attached letter, November 13, 1931.

135. Hooper to J. G. Harbord, President of RCA, April 23, 1929, p. 2, Hooper papers, LOC.

136. David Sarnoff, Vice President of RCA, to Hooper, January 31, 1929, Hooper papers, LOC.

137. Harbord to Hooper, April 17, 1929, p. 3, Hooper papers, LOC.

138. Ibid., p. 3.

139. Hooper, Some principles involved in legislating for rapid communications, Revision, April 4, 1929, p. 3.

140. S. C. Hooper to Lieutenant Commander A. N. Offley, Assistant Pacific Communication Officer, March 17, 1930, p. 1, Hooper papers, LOC.

Chapter 7

1. Admiral William S. Benson to Secretary of the Navy Josephus Daniels, May 5, 1919, p. 4, Daniels papers, LOC, Reel 42.

2. Ibid.

3. Albert G. Davis to Young, enclosed in Glaser to Young, n.d., August 1919, Young papers, St. Lawrence University, Box 72.

4. Owen D. Young to Glaser, August 22, 1919, Young papers, St. Lawrence University, Box 72.

5. Radio Corporation of America, History of Radio Corporation and its relation to the art of radio communication and to the requirements of public communication, April 25, 1921, Wallace White papers, LOC.

6. At issue was the 1920 patent cross-licensing agreement that Federal Telegraph now sought to join. See William G. H. Bullard to E. W. Rice, April 6, 1921, Young papers, St. Lawrence University, Box 147.

7. Guy E. Tripp, Chairman of Westinghouse, to Young, March 9, 1922, Young papers, St. Lawrence University, File 11-14-65, Box 147.

8. Norway wireless to Massachusetts, *New York Times*, October 1, 1913, p. 6.

9. Memorandum on communications. Communication policy, April 1921, enclosed in S. W. Bryant, Acting Secretary of the Navy, Memorandum for the Secretary of the General Board, June 1, 1922, p. 1, NARA, RG 38, File 100.

10. Effect of preponderating control of radio by any one nation, November 22, 1921, p. 6, enclosed in S. W. Bryant, Acting Secretary of the Navy, Memorandum for the Secretary of the General Board, June 1, 1922, NARA, RG 38, File 100.

11. S. 4038, a bill to regulate the operation of and to foster the development of radiocommunication in the United States, 1920, Kellogg papers, Minnesota Historical Society.

12. Young to Secretary of the Navy Edwin Denby, December 22, 1921, Hooper papers, LOC; Davis to William Brown, May 13, 1921, Young papers, St. Lawrence University, Box 122.

13. Minutes of open meetings of Department of Commerce on Radio Telephony, February 27 and 28, 1922, p. 2, Kellogg papers, Minnesota Historical Society, Roll 9; House Committee on Merchant Marine and Fisheries, Report to accompany H.R. 13773, H.R. Rep. No. 67-1416, at 2 (1923).

14. Radio Act of 1927, Pub. L. No. 639, 44 Stat. 1163 (1927).

15. Ibid.

16. S. C. Hooper, Memorandum to Director of Naval Communications, September 29, 1927, p. 1, Hooper papers, LOC.

17. Radio Act of 1927.

18. S. C. Hooper, Lecture delivered at the Naval War College, April 26, 1934, p. 21, Hooper papers, LOC.

19. Davis, M. to S. C. Hooper, March 7, 1929. Hooper papers, LOC.

20. Ibid.

21. Mackay now enters the wireless field, *New York Times*, August 25, 1927, p. 1.

22. Hooper memorandum, September 29, 1927, p. 1.

23. Ibid., p. 3.

24. Ibid., p. 4.

25. Bethuel M. Webster, Jr., Special Assistant to the Attorney General, to Eugene O. Sykes, Acting Chairman, Federal Radio Commission, April 23, 1928, p. 1, Hooper papers, LOC.

26. Hooper to Milton Davis, August 2, 1928, Hooper papers, LOC; Minutes, Federal Radio Commission, May 24, 1928, Hooper papers, LOC.

27. *Commission on Communications: Hearings before the Committee on Interstate Commerce, United States Senate, on. S.6*, 71st Cong. 305, 322 (1929) (statement of Captain S. C. Hooper, May 22, 1929) (hereafter Hooper testimony, May 22, 1929).

28. Hooper to Davis, August 2, 1928.

29. Milton S. Davis, Memorandum, November 14, 1928, Hooper papers, LOC.

30. Hooper to Davis, August 2, 1928; S. C. Hooper, Some principles involved in legislating for rapid communications, January 30, 1929, p. 4, Hooper papers, LOC; Hooper testimony, May 22, 1929, p. 328.

31. Secretary of Commerce Daniel C. Roper to the President, A study of communications by an interdepartmental committee, January 23, 1934, p. 4, President's Official File, FDR Library, File 859a (hereafter Roper Committee report, 1934).

32. Radio subsidiary sold for $100,000,000, *New York Times*, March 29, 1929, p. 1.

33. S. C. Hooper, Memorandum, November 27, 1931, Hooper papers, LOC.

34. S. C. Hooper, Memorandum relative to attached letter, November 13, 1931, Hooper papers, LOC.

35. Ibid.

36. S. C. Hooper to Captain D. W. Todd, June 25, 1928, Hooper papers, LOC; Todd to Hooper, July 6, 1928, Hooper papers, LOC.

37. J. L. Merrill, President of All America Cables Inc., to Todd, August 28, 1928, Hooper papers, LOC; Todd to Hooper, February 6, 1929, Hooper papers, LOC.

38. J. R. Barnes, Solicitor, State Department, to Allan Dawson, August 10, 1931, NARA, RG 59, File 819.74/All America.

39. Benedict Crowell, Acting Secretary of War, to Senator Carroll S. Page, April 22, 1920, NARA, RG 185, File 43-D-8.

40. Radio Act of 1927.

41. Joint Board memorandum to the Secretary of War, April 5, 1924, NARA, RG 185, File 43-D-8; Lester H. Woolsey, Attorney for Tropical Radio Telegraph Company, to the Secretary of the Navy, July 20, 1933, NARA, RG 80, File 310109.

42. V. M. Cutter, President, Tropical Radio Telegraph Company, to Secretary of War Dwight F. Davis, June 16, 1928, p. 1, NARA, RG 185, File 43-D-50. In this case, United Fruit proposed to transfer a permission that a subsidiary received from Panama to another subsidiary. See Lester H. Woolsey, Attorney for Tropical Radio Telegraph Company, to the Secretary of the Navy, July 20, 1933, p. 4, NARA, RG 80, File 310109.

43. Cutter to Davis, June 16, 1928, pp. 1–2.

44. S. C. Hooper, Director of Naval Communications, to Admiral William C. Cole, October 24, 1928, Hooper papers, LOC.

45. N. E. Irwin, Commandant, 15th Naval District, to Chief of Naval Operations, January 31, 1924, p. 2, NARA, RG 185, File 43-D-50.

46. Admiral H. H. Christy, Commandant of the 15th Naval District, Memorandum for Governor, Panama Canal, February 3, 1928, p. 2, NARA, RG 185, File 43-D-50.

47. Hooper to Cole, October 24, 1928.

48. For the company's assurances of its loyalty, see Cutter to Davis, June 16, 1928, p. 3. For the Navy's recognition of the company's loyalty, see W. R. Sexton, Acting Chief of Naval Operations, to the Secretary of Navy, September 28, 1928, NARA, RG 59, File 819.74; Christy memorandum, February 3, 1928, p. 2.

49. Major General B. H. Wells, Acting Chief of Staff, Memorandum for the Secretary of War, May 31, 1929, NARA, RG 185, File 43-D-8; Sexton to the Secretary of Navy, September 28, 1928, pp. 1–2.

50. Local Joint Board to the Governor of the Panama Canal, July 8, 1929, NARA, RG 185, File 43-D-50.

51. Lester H. Woolsey, Attorney for Tropical Radio Telegraph Company, to the Secretary of the Navy, July 20, 1933, p. 6, NARA, RG 80, File 310109.

52. Memorandum for Commandant covering conference held in the Governor's office at 10:30 this morning in connection with the reported concession of certain radio privileges to the Panama Corporation by the Government of Panama, enclosed in N. E. Irwin, Commandant of 15th Naval District, to Chief of Naval Operations, May 1, 1931, NARA, RG 80, File 310109.

53. Secretary of State Henry L. Stimson to Secretary of the Navy Charles Francis Adams, January 9, 1931, NARA, RG 80, File 310109.

54. Secretary of State Charles Evans Hughes to the Secretary of War, May 20, 1924, cited in Francis White, Memorandum, July 21, 1925, p. 5, Francis White papers, HHPL.

55. Allan Dawson to Francis White, Memorandum, April 1, 1931, p. 8, NARA, RG 59, File 819.74.

56. Douglas MacArthur, Chief of Staff, Memorandum for the Assistant Chief of Staff, War Plans Division, November 25, 1931, NARA, RG 165, File 1652.

57. Allan Dawson to Walter C. Thurston, February 14, 1931, p. 2, NARA, RG 59, File 819.74.

58. DGM, Conversation with Mr. Elihu Root, representing All America Cables Inc., August 26, 1929, NARA, RG 59, File 819.74/All America.

59. This, of course, is to overstate matters. Though Panama had abrogated the 1914 decree, the U.S. Navy still acted as the chief arbiter of license applications. See American Minister to Panama to the Secretary of State, March 30, 1932, NARA, RG 59, File 819.74.

60. Report of conference held in the Office of the Assistant Secretary of State, March 11, 1932, to discuss the application of All-America Cables, I. N. C. for permit to establish a radiotelephone station in the Republic of Panama, March 11, 1932, NARA, RG 165, File WPD 1652 (hereafter Report of conference, March 1932); Hooper, Memorandum relative to attached letter, November 13, 1931, p. 2.

61. Hooper, Memorandum relative to attached letter, November 13, 1931, p. 2.

62. Telephone conversation between Frank Page, International Telephone and Telegraph Corporation, and Irwin Stewart, Treaty Division, September 3, 1931, NARA, RG 59, File 819.74.

63. Ibid.; Francis White (for the Secretary of State) to Secretary of the Navy Charles F. Adams, September 23, 1931, NARA, RG 80, File 310109.

64. Admiral William V. Pratt, Acting Secretary of the Navy, to Secretary of State Henry L. Stimson, August 8, 1932, p. 2, NARA, RG 165, File 2372-8; American owned communication company with international links, Prepared for Captain Hooper, December 20, 1932, p. 2, Hooper papers, LOC.

65. Pratt to Stimson, August 8, 1932, p. 2.

66. Ibid.; American owned communication company with international links, December 20, 1932, p. 2; S. C. Hooper, Untitled draft, December 22, 1932, Hooper papers, LOC.

67. Acting Secretary of the Navy William V. Pratt to Secretary of State Henry L. Stimson, August 8, 1932, NARA, RG 80, File 310109 (hereafter Pratt to Stimson, August 8, 1932 II).

68. Local Joint Board to the Governor of the Panama Canal, July 8, 1929, NARA, RG 185, File 43-D-50.

69. Pratt to Stimson, August 8, 1932; Edwin C. Wilson, Division of Latin American Affairs, to Francis White, November 11, 1931, NARA, RG 59, File 819.74.

70. Irwin Stewart, Radiotelephony in Panama, November 14, 1931, NARA, RG 59, File 819.74/All America.

71. Undersecretary of State William Castle, Memorandum of conversation with the Secretary of the Navy, December 21, 1932, p. 3, NARA, RG 59, File 819.74/All America.

72. W. McClure, Treaty Division, "Control by the United States of radio in Panama," Policy memo 503, February 6, 1931, NARA, RG 59, File 819.74/190.

73. Ibid.

74. Lester H. Woolsey, Memorandum for Mr. White, January 26, 1932, NARA, RG 59, File 819.74; Irwin Stewart to Merrill, February 3, 1932, NARA, RG 59, File 819.74.

75. Castle memorandum, December 21, 1932.

76. Edwin C. Wilson to Francis White, December 7, 1931, NARA, RG 59, File 819.74.

77. Stimson to Adams, March 26, 1932, NARA, RG 80, File 310109.

78. Stimson to Adams, November 23, 1932, NARA, RG 80, File 310109.

79. Commander C. C. Gill, Office of Naval Intelligence, Memorandum, June 15, 1931, NARA, RG 80, File 310109.

80. H. Burgess, Governor of the Panama Canal, to Paul West, Manager of the United Fruit Company, July 10, 1931, NARA, RG 185, File 43-D-8.

81. Rear Admiral N. E. Irwin, Commandant of the 15th Naval District, to the Governor of the Panama Canal, July 8, 1931, NARA, RG 185, File 43-D-50.

82. Memorandum of conference in the office of the Secretary of State, February 3, 1933, p. 3, NARA, RG 165, File 2372-8.

83. Admiral Crosley, Commandant, 15th Naval District, to Chief of Naval Operations, February 3, 1934, NARA, RG 185, File 43-D-8; Crosley to U.S. Minister Gonzalez, May 11, 1934, NARA, RG 185, File 43-D-8.

84. Hooper, Memorandum, November 27, 1931.

85. Pratt to Stimson, August 8, 1932, p. 4.

86. Sexton to the Secretary of Navy, September 28, 1928, p. 2.

87. Ibid.

88. Admiral N. E. Irwin, Commandant of the 15th Naval District, October 6, 1932, NARA, RG 185, File 43-D-8.

89. Hooper to J. G. Harbord, President of RCA, April 23, 1929, p. 2, Hooper papers, LOC.

90. S. C. Hooper, National ownership of American radio companies, January 10, 1933, p. 1, NARA, RG 80, File 310109; Hooper, Untitled draft, December 22, 1932; Pratt to Stimson, August 8, 1932, p. 4. Secretary Adams explained the same thing to the State Department. See Castle memorandum, December 21, 1932, p. 2.

91. *Hearings before the Senate Committee on Interstate Commerce on S. 2910, a bill to provide for the regulation of interstate and foreign communication by wire and radio and for other purposes*, 73rd Cong. 160, 172 (1934) (statement of S. C. Hooper, Director of Naval Communications) (hereafter Hooper statement, March 15, 1934) (hereafter *Hearings on S. 2910*, 1934).

92. American owned communication company with international links, December 20, 1932, p. 3.

93. Pratt to Stimson, August 8, 1932, p. 4.

94. Pratt to Stimson, August 8, 1932 II, p. 4; Hooper to Commander B. V. McCandlish, April 7, 1932, Hooper papers, LOC.

95. Hooper, Memorandum relative to attached letter, November 13, 1931, p. 3.

96. American owned communication company with international links, December 20, 1932, pp. 1–2.

97. Pratt to Stimson, August 8, 1932, p. 3.

98. Ibid., p. 2.

99. General Douglas MacArthur, Chief of Staff to Secretary of State Henry L. Stimson, December 23, 1931, NARA, RG 165, File 2372-8.

100. Commander H. M. Lammers to Assistant Secretary of State Francis White, August 15, 1932, p. 1, NARA, RG 80, File 320815.

101. Ibid.

102. Pratt to Stimson, August 8, 1932 II, pp. 4–5.

103. Ibid., p. 3.

104. Secretary of the Navy Charles Francis Adams to Senator Clarence C. Dill, Chairman of the Interstate Commerce Committee, March 22, 1932, enclosed in *Hearings before the Senate Committee on Interstate Commerce on H.R. 7716 to amend the Radio Act of 1927*, 72nd Cong. 19, 23 (1932) (statement of Secretary of the Navy Charles Francis Adams) (hereafter Adams statement, 1932).

105. Pratt to Stimson, August 8, 1932, p. 3.

106. Hooper, National ownership, January 10, 1933, p. 3.

107. Adams to Dill, March 22, 1932, enclosed in Adams statement, 1932, p. 24.

108. American owned communication company with international links, December 20, 1932, pp. 1, 3.

109. Conversation between Francis White and Hernand Behn, Recognition of new Spanish regime, April 21, 1931, Francis White papers, HHPL, Box 1.

110. American owned communication company with international links, December 20, 1932, p. 3.

111. Adams statement, 1932, p. 23.

112. Hooper to Brown, Undated, handwritten draft, in December 1934 folder, Hooper papers, LOC; Hooper, Memorandum, September 11, 1934, p. 4, enclosed in Secretary of the Navy Claude A. Swanson to Secretary of State Cordell Hull, September 15, 1934, NARA, RG 59, File 811.70.

113. Davis to Hooper, March 7, 1929.

114. Hooper, Memorandum relative to attached letter, November 13, 1931.

115. S. C. Hooper, Lecture delivered at the Naval War College, April 26, 1934, pp. 53–54, Hooper papers, LOC.

116. Ibid., p. 64.

117. Admiral William V. Pratt, A plan for the equalization and limitation of armaments amongst the seven great military nations, May 19, 1933, p. 25, President's Secretary's Files, FDR Library, Box 7.

118. Hooper, Untitled draft, December 22, 1932.

119. Spain denies plea of phone company, *New York Times*, November 26, 1932, p. 23.

120. American owned communication company with international links, December 20, 1932, p. 3.

121. Spain in note to US mild on phone deal, *New York Times*, December 4, 1932, p. 27.

122. Castle memorandum, December 21, 1932, p. 1.

123. Ibid., p. 2.

124. Report of conference, March 1932.

125. G. R. Merrell, Division of Latin American Affairs, to Assistant Secretary of State Francis White, October 1, 1931, p. 2, NARA, RG 59, File 819.74.

126. Henry Fletcher, Handwritten note, enclosed in G. R. Merrell, Division of Latin American Affairs to Assistant Secretary of State Francis White, October 1, 1931, NARA, RG 59, File 819.74.

127. William R. Castle, Under Secretary of State, Handwritten note, October 1, 1931, NARA, RG 59, File 819.74/All America.

128. Charles E. Hughes to Charles McKinley Saltzman, Undated, 1931, enclosed in Charles McKinley Saltzman to the Secretary of State, November 4, 1931, NARA, RG 59, File 819.74/All America.

129. Ibid.

130. Irwin Stewart, Treaty Division, Handwritten note, November 7, 1931, NARA, RG 59, File 819.74/All America.

131. Assistant Secretary of State Francis White to Secretary of State Henry L. Stimson, March 24, 1932, Francis White papers, HHPL, Box 18.

132. Report of conference, March 1932.

133. Stimson to Adams, November 23, 1932, p. 2.

134. Pratt to Stimson, August 8, 1932, p. 4.

135. Stimson to Adams, November 23, 1932, pp. 2–3.

136. Castle memorandum, December 21, 1932. How the personal relationships between Sosthenes Behn and officials in various government departments had evolved, facilitating either trust or the opposite, is for future researchers to discover. Such research in combination with studies about the relationship between the U.S. government and other U.S.-headquartered MNCs would highlight the extent to which the Navy's concerns about ITT were unique to this firm in the early 1930s.

137. Ibid.

138. Ibid.

139. Secretary of State Henry L. Stimson, Handwritten note, enclosed in Castle memorandum, December 21, 1932.

140. Irwin Stewart, Radiotelephony in Panama, November 14, 1931, NARA, RG 59, File 819.74/All America.

141. Hooper statement, March 15, 1934, pp. 165–166.

142. Hooper, Memorandum relative to attached letter, November 13, 1931, p. 2.

143. Memorandum re Paragraph 310(a), Section 5, enclosed in Secretary of State Cordell Hull, Memorandum of conversation with Frank Page, Vice President of ITT, April 5, 1934, NARA, RG 59, File 811.70.

144. Roper Committee report, 1934, p. 10; Clarence C. Dill, Comment on report of committee on communications, enclosed in Dill to Roper, January 9, 1934, President's Official File, FDR Library, File 859a.

145. *Hearings on Commission on Communications*, 1929; H.R. 11635, 71 Cong. Rec. 8050 (1930).

146. Senate Committee on Interstate Commerce, Report to accompany H.R. 11635 to amend the Radio Act of 1927, S. Rep. No. 71-1578 (1931); H.R. 11635, 71st Cong., 74 Cong. Rec. 5204 (1931).

147. *Hearings on H.R. 7716*, March 1932, 72nd Cong. 27, 32 (statement of S. C. Hooper); Adams statement, 1932, 19, 20.

148. Conversation between Assistant Secretary of State Francis White, Colonel Sosthenes Behn, President of ITT, and Frank Page, Vice President of ITT, January 8, 1932, Francis White papers, HHPL, Box 18; Telephone conversation between White and Hooper, July 5, 1932, Francis White papers, HHPL, Box 18.

149. Hooper to McCandlish, April 7, 1932.

150. S. C. Hooper, Policies of the Army and Navy relative to U.S. commercial communication systems, July 31, 1934, p. 2, NARA, RG 59, File 819.74/All America; Hooper statement, March 15, 1934, p. 172.

151. Roper Committee report, 1934, p. 10.

152. Hooper to McCandlish, April 7, 1932.

153. *Hearings on H.R. 7716*, Hooper statement, March 1932, 72nd Cong. 27, 35. See also Policies of the Army and Navy relative to U.S. commercial communication systems, July 31, 1934, p. 3.

154. Policies of the Army and Navy relative to U.S. commercial communication systems, July 31, 1934, p. 3.

155. Hooper lecture at the Naval War College, April 26, 1934, p. 57.

156. *Hearings on H.R. 7716*, March 1932, 72nd Cong. 39, 52 (statement of Frank C. Page, ITT).

157. Ibid.

158. Sosthenes Behn, President of ITT, to Representative Sam Rayburn, May 15, 1934, enclosed in *Hearings before the House Committee on Interstate and Foreign Commerce on H.R. 8301, a bill to provide for the regulation of interstate and foreign communication by wire or radio, and for other purposes*, 73rd Cong. 206, 222 (1934) (hereafter *Hearings on H.R. 8301*, 1934).

159. Behn to Secretary of State Cordell Hull, May 26, 1934, NARA, RG 59, File 811.70.

160. Hull memorandum of conversation with Page, April 5, 1934.

161. Behn to FDR, June 4, 1934, p. 4, President's Official File, FDR Library, File 859a.

162. Behn statement, May 15, 1934, in *Hearings on H.R. 8301*, 1934, p. 218.

163. Memorandum filed by Sosthenes Behn with the Interstate Commerce Committee of the United States Senate, March 22, 1934, enclosed in John K. Roosevelt, Vice President of All America Cables, to FDR, March 26, 1934, NARA, RG 59, File 811.70.

164. Statement of Sosthenes Behn, March 9–15, 1934, in *Hearings on S. 2910*, 1934, pp. 123–124, 218.

165. Behn to Rayburn, May 15, 1934.

166. Behn statement, May 15, 1934, p. 218. In Hooper's eyes, of course, the State Department's interest in national security also left a lot to be desired. That the diplomats pursued their own approach in Panama led him to conclude that the State Department didn't "care a rap about our own defense." See S. C. Hooper, Memorandum for Chief of Naval Operations, October 12, 1933, NARA, RG 80, File 310109.

167. Page statement, in *Hearings on H.R. 7716*, March 1932, p. 40. Behn statement, March 9–15, 1934, pp. 122, 131.

168. Memorandum re Paragraph 310(a), Section 5, enclosed in Hull memorandum of conversation with Page, April 5, 1934.

169. I. T. T. elects directors, *New York Times*, May 12, 1932, p. 29.

170. Behn statement, May 15, 1934, in *Hearings on H.R. 8301*, p. 214.

171. Report to accompany H.R. 7716 to amend the Radio Act of 1927, H.R. Rep. No. 72-221 (1932).

172. John K. Roosevelt, Vice President of All America Cables, to FDR, February 2, 1934, enclosed in M. H. McIntyre to Rayburn, February 20, 1934, President's Official File, FDR Library, File 859a.

173. S. C. Hooper to Chairman, President's communications committee, December 7, 1933, p. 3, President's Official File, FDR Library, File 859a.

174. John K. Roosevelt to FDR, March 26, 1934, p. 2, NARA, RG 59, File 811.70.

175. Roosevelt to FDR, February 2, 1934.

176. Ibid.

177. Ibid.

178. *Hearings on S. 2910*, 1934, p. 17.

179. Joint Board to Secretary of the Navy Claude A. Swanson, American communications systems in their relation to national defense, January 19, 1934, enclosed

in H. L. Roosevelt, Acting Secretary of the Navy, to Secretary of State Cordell Hull, March 16, 1934, NARA, RG 59, File 811.70.

180. Hull memorandum of conversation with Page, April 5, 1934, p. 3.

181. Ibid.

182. Irwin Stewart to Dunn, April 19, 1934, p. 6, NARA, RG 59, File 811.70.

183. Ibid., p. 3.

184. Ibid., p. 4.

185. Senator Clarence C. Dill to FDR, February 15, 1934, enclosed in FDR to Dill, February 17, 1934, President's Official File, FDR Library, File 859a. See also Stewart to Dunn, April 19, 1934, p. 4.

186. Albert Stephen, Clerk of the Senate Committee on Interstate Commerce, Memorandum for Senator Dill, February 15, 1934, p. 3, enclosed in FDR to Dill, February 17, 1934.

187. Irwin Stewart, Treaty Division, to Dunn, April 19, 1934, p. 6, NARA, RG 59, File 811.70.

188. Adams statement, 1932, p. 20.

189. Statement of Senator Wallace H. White, in *Hearings on H.R. 7716*, March 1932, p. 15. See also *Hearings on S. 2910*, 1934, p. 125.

190. Adams statement, 1932, p. 24.

191. Page statement, in *Hearings on H.R. 7716*, March 1932, p. 42; White statement, in *Hearings on H.R. 7716*, March 1932, p. 17.

192. White statement, in *Hearings on H.R. 7716*, March 1932, p. 16.

193. Handwritten comments on S. Rep. No. 221 (1932), Wallace White papers, LOC.

194. Behn statement, March 9–15, 1934, p. 123.

195. Ibid., pp. 126–127.

196. Comments by Senator Dill during the debate on S. 3285, 73rd Cong., 78 Cong. Rec. 8825 (1934); Hull memorandum of conversation with Page, April 5, 1934.

197. Draft letter from Secretary of the Navy Claude A. Swanson to Secretary of State Cordell Hull, July 12, 1934, p. 2, NARA, RG 80, File 310109.

198. *Hearings before the House Committee on Interstate and Foreign Commerce on H.R. 8301, a bill to provide for the regulation of interstate and foreign communication by wire or radio, and for other purposes, April, 1934*, 73rd Cong. 25 (1934) (statement of S. C. Hooper).

199. Memorandum re Paragraph 310(a), Section 5, enclosed in Hull memorandum of conversation with Page, April 5, 1934.

200. Behn to Hull, May 26, 1934.

201. Hooper testimony, May 22, 1929.

202. Hooper to Chairman, December 7, 1933, p. 3.

203. Ibid.

204. Ibid.

205. Behn to FDR, June 4, 1934, p. 4, President's Official File, FDR Library, File 859a; Acting Secretary of State William Phillips to Senator Clarence C. Dill, June 4, 1934, NARA, RG 59, File 811.70.

206. Conference report on Communications Act of 1934, H.R. Rep. No. 1918, presented to the House of Representatives, 73rd Cong., 1934; 78 Cong. Rec. 10969 (1934); Communications Act of 1934, 47 U.S.C. §§310 (b)(3), 310 (b) (4).

207. Draft letter from Swanson to Hull, July 12, 1934, pp. 2–3, NARA, RG 80, File 310109.

208. Ibid. The letter was not sent, but the matter was taken up in person by Admiral Standley and Secretary Hull.

209. Draft letter from Swanson to Hull, July 12, 1934, pp. 1–2.

210. Assistant Secretary of State Francis White to Secretary of State Henry L. Stimson, March 24, 1932, p. 2, Francis White papers, HHPL, Box 18.

211. White to Stewart, June 30, 1933, p. 2, Francis White papers, HHPL, Box 18.

212. Policies of the Army and Navy relative to U.S. commercial communication systems, July 31, 1934, p. 7.

213. Hooper to Paul Shoup, President, Southern Pacific Railway Co., July 19, 1934, Hooper papers, LOC.

214. Hooper to Brown, Undated, handwritten draft, in December 1934 folder, Hooper papers, LOC.

215. Policies of the Army and Navy relative to U.S. commercial communication systems, July 31, 1934, p. 2.

216. Josephus Daniels, Ambassador to Mexico, to Hooper, December 4, 1933, Hooper papers, LOC.

217. Unsigned, undated, 1929 folder, Hooper papers, LOC.

Chapter 8

1. S. C. Hooper to Major Louis B. Bender, War Department, October 7, 1931, Hooper papers, LOC.

2. Whether thinking about the airwaves as a resource was preferable to thinking about them as a form of commodity or, in fact, facilitated commodification is subject to debate (Benkler, 1997; Streeter, 1996).

3. The first step toward answering this question would require working through the differences between the literature on perception and misperception in international relations and constructivist scholarship.

4. General Post Office, Memorandum on points raised in Mr. Cuthbert Hall's letter of 20 August, October 2, 1905, BT Archives, PO, File 30/1299.

5. Sir George Clarke, Wireless Telegraphy, Printed for the Committee of Imperial Defence, September 14, 1906, TNA: PRO, ADM, File 116/3614.

6. S. C. Hooper, National ownership of American radio companies, January 10, 1933, p. 1, NARA, RG 80, File 310109.

7. Unsigned, undated, 1929. Submarine cables of the world, Hooper papers, LOC.

8. Maria Farrell, Quietly, symbolically, U.S. control over the Internet was just ended, *The Guardian*, March 14, 2016.

References

Primary Sources

Archive and Manuscript Collections, United States
Private papers
    Library of Congress, Washington, DC (LOC)
        Papers of Josephus Daniels
        Papers of Norman Davis
        Papers of Rear Admiral Stanford C. Hooper
        Papers of Wallace White
    Papers of Reginald Fessenden, State Archives of North Carolina, Raleigh, NC
    Papers of Frank B. Kellogg, Minnesota Historical Society, St. Paul
    Papers of Franklin Delano Roosevelt, FDR Library, Hyde Park, NY
        Papers of Assistant Secretary of the Navy
        President's Official File, File 859a
        President's Secretary's Files
    Papers of Owen D. Young, St. Lawrence University, Canton, NY
        Communications, Disarmament Conference, File 11-14-49

Government Documents
National Archives and Record Administration, College Park, MD, and Washington,
        DC (NARA)
    Record Group (RG) 19, Records of the Bureau of Ships, Files 917, 918, 18301
    RG 38, Records of the Office of the Chief of Naval Operations, Files 32, 47, 49,
        240, 249
        Records of the Director of Naval Communications
            Office Files of Captain David W. Todd, 1916–1919, File 110
            Office Files of Rear Admiral W. H. G. Bullard, 1919–1921
        Division of Naval Communications, Confidential Correspondence, 1917–1926
    RG 40, Records of the Department of Commerce, Files 62300, 67032, 75334, 78332
    RG 41, Records of the Bureau of Marine Inspection and Navigation, Files 30166,
        37554

RG 43, Records of International Conferences, Commissions, and Expositions, File 574

RG 59, Records of the Department of State

Central Decimal Files, 1910–1949, Files 810.74, 811.70, 811.74, 819.74/All America, 835.74

Country-specific records for Brazil and Panama, Files 819.74, 832.74

RG 80, Records of the Office of the Secretary of the Navy

Office Files of the Secretary of the Navy

General Correspondence, 1896–1915, 1916–1926, 1926–1936, Files 12479, 310109, 320815

Records of the General Board (GB), Subject Files, 1900–1947, File 419

RG 165, Records of the War Department, File 2372-8, WPD 1652

RG 173, Records of the Federal Communications Commission, File 70909

RG 185, Records of the Panama Canal, 1914–1951, Files 43-D-8, 43-D-50

Papers of Francis White, Herbert Hoover Presidential Library, West Liberty, IA (HHPL)

Archive and Manuscript Collections, United Kingdom

Archives of British Telecommunications, London (BT Archives)

Records of the British Post Office (PO), Files 30/940, 30/1115, 30/1298, 88/43

HIS 131, Marconi collection, Bodleian Library, University of Oxford

The National Archives of the United Kingdom, Public Record Office, Kew, London (TNA: PRO)

Records of the British Admiralty (ADM), Files 116/567, 116/3613, 116/3614

Records of the Cabinet (CAB), Files 35/14, 37/59/129, 37/69/39

Records of the Foreign Office (FO), Files 83/1885, 83/1940, 83/1982

Papers of William Waldegrave Palmer, second Earl of Selborne, File 157, Bodleian Library, Oxford

Secondary Sources

Aitken, H. G. J. (1976). *Syntony and spark: The origins of radio.* New York: Wiley.

Aitken, H. G. J. (1985). *The continuous wave: Technology and American radio, 1900–1932.* Princeton, NJ: Princeton University Press.

Aitken, H. G. J. (1994). Allocating the spectrum: The origins of radio regulation. *Technology and Culture, 35*(4), 686–716.

Altman, R. (2004). *Silent film sound.* New York: Columbia University Press.

Alvarez, J. E. (2009). Contemporary foreign investment law: An "empire of law" or "a law of empire"? *Alabama Law Review, 60*(4), 943–975.

Amoore, L., Dodgson, R., Germain, R. D., Gills, B. K., Langley, P., & Watson, I. (2000). Paths to a historicized international political economy. *Review of International Political Economy, 7*(1), 53–71.

Andelman, D. A. (2007). *A shattered peace: Versailles 1919 and the price we pay today.* Hoboken, NJ: Wiley.

Archer, G. (1938). *History of radio to 1926.* New York: American Historical Society.

Arrighi, G. (1998). Globalization and the rise of East Asia. *International Sociology, 13*(1), 59–77.

Arrighi, G. (2010). *The long twentieth century: Money, power, and the origins of our times* (2nd ed.). New York: Verso.

Baer, G. W. (1994). *One hundred years of sea power: The U.S. Navy, 1890–1990.* Stanford, CA: Stanford University Press.

Bailey, T. A. (1933). The Lodge corollary to the Monroe Doctrine. *Political Science Quarterly, 48*(2), 220–239.

Bairoch, P. (1996). Globalization myths and realities. In R. Boyer & D. Drache (Eds.), *States against markets: The limits of globalization* (pp. 173–192). London, England: Routledge.

Baker, R. S. (1960). *Woodrow Wilson and world settlement.* Gloucester, MA: Peter Smith.

Balbi, G. (2012). *Marconi's diktats: How Italian international wireless policy was shaped by a private company, 1903–1911.* Paper presented at the History of Electrotechnology Conference, Pavia, Italy.

Bar, F., & Sandvig, C. (2008). U.S. communication policy after convergence. *Media, Culture and Society, 30*(4), 531–550.

Barber, B. R. (1995). *Jihad vs. McWorld.* New York: Times Books.

Beale, H. K. (1956). *Theodore Roosevelt and the rise of America to world power.* New York: Collier Books.

Beloff, M. (1970). *Imperial sunset: Britain's liberal empire, 1897–1921* (Vol. 1). New York: Knopf.

Benjamin, L. M. (2001). *Freedom of the air and the public interest: First Amendment rights in broadcasting to 1935.* Carbondale: Southern Illinois University Press.

Benkler, Y. (1998). Overcoming agoraphobia: Building the commons of the digitally networked environment. *Harvard Journal of Law and Technology, 11*(2), 290–400.

Black, M. (1979). More about metaphor. In A. Ortony (Ed.), *Metaphor and thought* (pp. 19–43). New York: Cambridge University Press.

Bönker, D. (2012). *Militarism in a global age: Naval ambitions in the United States and Germany before World War I.* Ithaca, NY: Cornell University Press.

Bowman, S. R. (1996). *The modern corporation and American political thought.* University Park: Pennsylvania State University Press.

Boyd-Barrett, O. (1977). Media imperialism: Towards an international framework for an analysis of media systems. In J. Curran, M. Gurevitch & J. Woollacott (Eds.), *Mass communication and society* (pp. 116–135). London, England: Edward Arnold.

Brewer, S. A. (2009). *Why America fights*. New York: Oxford University Press.

Castells, M. (1997). *The power of identity*. Malden, MA: Blackwell.

Castells, M. (2013). *Communication power*. New York: Oxford University Press.

Challener, R. (1973). *Admirals, generals and American foreign policy, 1898–1914*. Princeton, NJ: Princeton University Press.

Cherry, B. A. (2008). Back to the future: How transportation deregulatory policies foreshadow evolution of communications policies. *Information Society, 24*(5), 273–291.

Clarke, R., & Knake, R. K. (2010). *Cyber war*. New York: Ecco.

Codding (1995). The International Telecommunications Union: 130 years of telecommunications regulation. *Denver Journal of International Law and Policy, 23*(3), 501–511.

Cowhey, P. F. (1990). The international telecommunications regime: The political roots of regimes for high technology. *International Organization, 44*(2), 169–199.

Cox, K. A., & Byrnes, W. J. (1989). The common carrier provisions—a product of evolutionary development. In M. D. Paglin (Ed.), *A legislative history of the Communications Act of 1934* (pp. 25–60). New York: Oxford University Press.

Cox, M. (2004). Empire, imperialism and the Bush doctrine. *Review of International Studies, 30*(4), 585–608.

Cronon, D. E. (Ed.). (1963). *The cabinet diaries of Josephus Daniels*. Lincoln: University of Nebraska Press.

Davis, M. S. (1929). Review of international communications with special reference to the Pacific Situation. *U.S. Naval Institute Proceedings, 55*(12), 1039–1044.

De Grazia, V. (2005). *Irresistible empire: America's advance through 20th-century Europe*. Cambridge, MA: Belknap Press of Harvard University Press.

DeNardis, L. (2014). *The global war for internet governance*. New Haven, CT: Yale University Press.

Der Derian, J. (2009). *Virtuous war: Mapping the military-industrial-media-entertainment network* (2nd ed.). New York: Routledge.

Dorsey, K. (1995). Scientists, citizens and statesmen: U.S.-Canadian wildlife protection treaties in the Progressive Era. *Diplomatic History, 19*(3), 407–429.

Douglas, S. J. (1989). *Inventing American broadcasting, 1899–1922.* Baltimore, MD: Johns Hopkins University Press.

Doyle, M. W. (1997). *Ways of war and peace.* New York: W. W. Norton.

Edwards, P. N. (2003). Infrastructure and modernity: Force, time, and social organization in the history of sociotechnical systems. In T. J. Misa, P. Brey, & A. Feenberg (Eds.), *Modernity and technology* (pp. 185–225). Cambridge, MA: MIT Press.

Edwards, P. N. (2010). *A vast machine: Computer models, climate data, and the politics of global warming.* Cambridge, MA: MIT Press.

Elton, G. R. (1967). *The practice of history.* New York: Thomas Y. Crowell.

Evans, P. B. (1981). Recent research on multinational corporations. *Annual Review of Sociology, 7,* 199–233.

Evenett, S. J., Levenstein, M. C., & Suslow, V. Y. (2001). International cartel enforcement: Lessons from the 1990s. *World Economy, 24*(9), 1221–1245.

Faltesek, D. (2018). *Selling social media: The political economy of social networking.* New York: Bloomsbury Academic.

Feldman, M. L. B. (1975). *The role of the United States in the International Telecommunication Union and pre-ITU conferences.* [s.l.]: Author.

Fieldhouse, D. K. (1986). The multinational: A critique of a concept. In A. Teichova, M. Lévy-Leboyer, & H. Nussbaum (Eds.), *Multinational enterprise in historical perspective* (pp. 9–29). Cambridge, England: Cambridge University Press.

Fouraker, L. E., & Stopford, J. M. (1968). Organizational structure and the multinational strategy. *Administrative Science Quarterly, 13*(1), 47–64.

French, P. A. (1979). The corporation as a moral person. *American Philosophical Quarterly, 16*(3), 207–215.

Friedberg, A. (1988). *The weary titan: Britain and the experience of relative decline, 1895–1905.* Princeton, NJ: Princeton University Press.

Gaines, B. J., & Cho, W. K. T. (2004). On California's 1920 Alien Land Law: The psychology and economics of racial discrimination. *State Politics and Policy Quarterly, 4*(3), 271–293.

Garraty, A. J., & Carnes, M. C. (1999). James Harbord. *American national biography* (Vol. 10). New York: Oxford University Press.

Gilderhus, M. T. (1986). *Pan American visions: Woodrow Wilson and the Western Hemisphere, 1913–1921.* Tucson: University of Arizona Press.

Gilpin, R. (1975). *U.S. power and the multinational corporation: The political economy of foreign direct investment.* New York: Basic Books.

Gilpin, R. (1977). Economic interdependence and national security in perspective. In K. Knorr & F. N. Tager (Eds.), *Economic issues and national security* (pp. 19–66). [Lawrence]: The Regents Press of Kansas.

Gilpin, R., & Gilpin, J. M. (2001). *Global political economy: Understanding the international economic order*. Princeton, NJ: Princeton University Press.

Gioia, D., Schultz, M., & Corley, K. G. (2000). Organizational identity, image, and adaptive instability. *Academy of Management Review, 25*(1), 63–81.

Goldsmith, J. L., & Russell, S. (2018). *Strengths become vulnerabilities*. Aegis Series Paper No. 1806. Palo Alto, CA: Hoover Institution at Stanford University.

Goldsmith, J. L., & Wu, T. (2008). *Who controls the internet? Illusions of a borderless world*. New York: Oxford University Press.

Gooch, J. (1994). The weary titan: strategy and policy in Great Britain, 1890–1918. In W. Murray, M. Knox, & A. Bernstein (Eds.), *The making of strategy: Rulers, states and war* (pp. 278–306). Cambridge, England: Cambridge University Press.

Gorman, D. (2010). Freedom of the ether or the electromagnetic commons? Globality, the public interest, and multilateral radio negotiations in the 1920s. In S. M. Streeter, J. C. Weaver, & W. D. Coleman (Eds.), *Empires and autonomy: Moments in the history of globalization* (pp. 138–156). Vancouver, Canada: UBC Press.

Government regulation of wireless telegraphy. (1908). *Electrical World, 51* (March 21), 589.

Gunder Frank, A. (1996). *Re-Orient: Global economy in the Asian age*. Berkeley: University of California Press.

Hall, P., & Preston, P. (1988). *The carrier wave: New information technology and the geography of innovation, 1846–2003*. London, England: Unwin Hyman.

Hallberg, B. A. (2010). *Networking: A beginner's guide*. New York: McGraw-Hill.

Hampf, M. M., & Müller-Pohl, S. (2013). Global communication electric: Business, news and politics in the world of telegraphy. In M. M. Hampf & S. Müller-Pohl (Eds.), *Global communication electric: Business, news and politics in the world of telegraphy* (pp. 7–27). New York: Campus Verlag.

Hancock, H. E. (1974). *Wireless at sea*. New York: Arno Press.

Hannigan, R. E. (2002). *The new world power: American foreign policy, 1898–1917*. Philadelphia: University of Pennsylvania Press.

Hansmann, H., & Kraakman, R. (2000). *The end of history for corporate law*. Harvard Law School John M. Olin Center for Law, Economics and Business Discussion Paper Series, Paper 280.

Harlow, A. F. (1971). *Old wires, new waves: The history of the telegraph*. New York: Arno Press.

Harvey, D. (2003). *The new imperialism*. Oxford, England: Oxford University Press.

Headrick, D. R. (1991). *The invisible weapon: Telecommunications and international politics, 1851–1945*. New York: Oxford University Press.

Headrick, D. R. (1994). Shortwave radio and its impact on international telecommunications between the wars. *History and Technology, 11*(1), 21–32.

Headrick, D. R., & Griset, P. (2001). Submarine telegraph cables: Business and politics, 1838–1939. *Business History Review, 75*(3), 543–578.

Herring, G. C. (2008). *From colony to superpower: US foreign relations since 1776*. New York: Oxford University Press.

Heydarian, R. J. (2018). This is how a superpower commits suicide. *New Perspectives Quarterly, 35*(1), 11–14.

Higham, J. (1955). *Strangers in the land: Patterns of American nativism, 1860–1925*. New Brunswick, NJ: Rutgers University Press.

Hills, J. (2002). *The struggle for control of global communication*. Urbana: University of Illinois Press.

Hills, J. (2007). *Telecommunications and empire*. Urbana: University of Illinois Press.

Hodgson, G. (1984). *Lloyd's of London*. New York: Viking Press.

Hogan, M. J. (1991). *Informal entente: The private structure of cooperation in Anglo-American economic relations, 1918–1928*. Chicago: Imprint Publications.

Hollis, M., & Smith, S. (1990). *Explaining and understanding international relations*. Oxford, England: Clarendon Press.

Honig, B. (2001). *Democracy and the foreigner*. Princeton, NJ: Princeton University Press.

Hood, J. (1900). The Pacific submarine cable. *United States Naval Institute Proceedings, 26*(3), 477–488.

Horwitz, R. B. (1989). *The irony of regulatory reform: The deregulation of American telecommunications*. New York: Oxford University Press.

Hovenkamp, H. (1991). *Enterprise and American law, 1836–1937*. Cambridge, MA: Harvard University Press.

Howeth, L. S. (1963). *History of communications electronics in the United States Navy*. Washington, DC: U.S. Government Printing Office.

Hughes, B. A. (1969). *Owen D. Young and American foreign policy, 1919–1929* (PhD dissertation, University of Wisconsin).

Hugill, P. J. (1999). *Global communications since 1844: Geopolitics and technology.* Baltimore, MD: Johns Hopkins University Press.

Hugill, P. J. (2009). The geopolitical implications of communication under the seas. In B. Finn and D. Yang (Ed.), *Communications under the seas: The evolving cable network and its implications* (pp. 257–277). Cambridge, MA: MIT Press.

Hugill, P. J. (2014). Petroleum supply, marine transportation technology, and the emerging international order of the post World War One period. In M. Mayer, M. Carpes, & R. Knoblich (Eds.), *The global politics of science and technology* (Vol. 1, pp. 141–159). Berlin: Springer-Verlag.

Hunter, D. (2003). Cyberspace as place. *California Law Review, 91*(2), 439–519.

Iriye, A. (1965). *After imperialism: The search for a new order in the Far East, 1921–1931.* Cambridge: MA: Harvard University Press.

Jacobsen, K. (2010). Wasted opportunities? The Great Northern Telegraph Company and the wireless challenge. *Business History, 52*(2), 231–250.

Janson, M. A., & Yoo, C. S. (2013). The wires go to war: The U.S. experiment with government ownership of the telephone system during World War I. *Texas Law Review, 91*(5), 983–1050.

John, R. R. (2008). Telecommunications. *Enterprise and Society, 9*(3), 507–520.

John, R. R. (2010). *Network nation.* Cambridge, MA: The Belknap Press of Harvard University Press.

Katz, M. L., & Shapiro, C. (1994). Systems competition and network effects. *Journal of Economic Perspectives, 8*(2), 93–115.

Kennedy, P. (1971). Imperial cable communications and strategy. *English Historical Review, 86*(341), 728–752.

Kennedy, P. (1987). *The rise and fall of the great powers.* New York: Random House.

Kostova, T., & Zaheer, S. (1999). Organizational legitimacy under conditions of complexity: The case of the multinational enterprise. *Academy of Management Review, 24*(1), 1–15.

Kramer, P. A. (2006). *The blood of government: Race, empire, the United States and the Philippines.* Chapel Hill: University of North Carolina Press.

Krasner, S. D. (1978). *Defending the national interest: Raw materials investments and US foreign policy.* Princeton, NJ: Princeton University Press.

Krasner, S. D. (1995). State power and the structure of international trade. In J. A. Frieden & D. A. Lake (Eds.), *International political economy: Perspectives on global power and wealth* (pp. 19–36). New York: St. Martin's Press.

Krasner, S. D. (1999). *Sovereignty: Organized hypocrisy.* Princeton, NJ: Princeton University Press.

Krysko, M. A. (2011). *American radio in China: International encounters with technology and communications, 1919–41.* New York: Palgrave Macmillan.

Kuehn, J. T. (2017). *America's first general staff: A short history of the rise and fall of the General Board of the US Navy, 1900–1950.* Annapolis, MD: Naval Institute Press.

Kurylo, F., & Susskind, C. (1981). *Ferdinand Braun, a life of the Nobel-prize winner and inventor of the cathode-ray oscilloscope.* Cambridge, MA: MIT Press.

Lake, D. (1988). *Power, protection and free trade: International sources of U.S. commercial strategy, 1887–1939.* Ithaca, NY: Cornell University Press.

Landau, S. (2010). *Surveillance or security? The risks posed by new wiretapping technologies.* Cambridge, MA: MIT Press.

Lee, C.-C. (1979). *Media imperialism reconsidered: The homogenizing of television culture.* Beverly Hills, CA: Sage Publications.

Levenstein, M. C., & Suslow, V. Y. (2006). What determines cartel success? *Journal of Economic Literature, 44*(1), 43–95.

Lipsky, A. B., & Sidak, J. G. (1999). Essential facilities. *Stanford Law Review, 51*(5), 1187–1248.

Lipson, C. (1985). *Standing guard: Protecting foreign capital in the nineteenth and twentieth centuries.* Berkeley: University of California Press.

Little, D. J. (1979). Twenty years of turmoil: I.T.T., the State Department and Spain, 1924–1944. *Business History Review, 53*(4), 449–472.

Maclaurin, W. R. (1949). *Invention and innovation in the radio industry.* New York: Macmillan.

Major, J. (2003). *Prize possession: The United States and the Panama Canal, 1903–1979.* New York: Cambridge University Press.

Masini, G. (1995). *Marconi.* New York: Marsilio.

Maurer, T. E. A. (2015). *Technological sovereignty: Missing the point?* Paper presented at the 2015 7th International Conference on Cyber Conflict: Architectures in Cyberspace, Tallinn, Estonia.

McChesney, R. W. (1993). *Telecommunications, mass media and democracy.* New York: Oxford University Press.

McMurria, J. (2007). A taste of class: Pay-TV and the commodification of television in postwar America. In S. Benet-Weiser, C. Chris, & A. Freitas (Eds.), *Cable visions* (pp. 44–65). New York: New York University Press.

Modelski, G., & Thompson, W. R. (1996). *Leading sectors and world powers: The coevolution of global politics and world economics*. Columbia: University of South Carolina Press.

Moran, T. H. (1990). The globalization of America's defense industries. *International Security, 15*(1), 57–99.

Morgon, W. (2011). *Pacific Gibraltar: U.S.-Japanese rivalry over the annexation of Hawaii, 1885–1898*. Annapolis, MD: Naval Institute Press.

Morley, D. (2010). Communications and transport: The mobility of information, people and commodities. *Media, Culture and Society, 33*(5), 743–759.

Morrow, R. W. (2011). Nationalizing American radio: Anti-monopoly, nationalism, and the first Alexander bill, 1915–1917. *Journal of Radio and Audio Media, 18*(1), 17–32.

Mueller, M. (1997). *Universal service: Competition, interconnection and monopoly in the making of the American telephone system*. Cambridge, MA: MIT Press.

Mueller, M. (2010). *Networks and states: The global politics of internet governance*. Cambridge, MA: MIT Press.

Neuman, W. R., McKnight, L., & Solomon, R. J. (1997). *The Gordian knot: Political gridlock on the information highway*. Cambridge, MA: MIT Press.

Ngai, M. M. (2004). *Impossible subjects: Illegal aliens and the making of modern America*. Princeton, NJ: Princeton University Press.

Novak, W. J. (2010). Law and the social control of American capitalism. *Emory Law Journal, 60*(2), 377–405.

Nye, J. S. (2011). Nuclear lessons for cyber security? *Strategic Studies Quarterly, 5*(4), 18–38.

O'Brien, P. P. (1998). *British and American naval power: Politics and policy, 1900–1936*. Westport, CT: Praeger.

O'Hara, G. (2010). New histories of British imperial communication and the "networked world" of the 19th and early 20th centuries. *History Compass, 8*(7), 609–625.

Ohmae, K. (2000). *The invisible continent: Four strategic imperatives of the new economy*. New York: HarperBusiness.

Ouellette, L. (2002). *Viewers like you? How public TV failed the people*. New York: Columbia University Press.

Perlmutter, H. J. (1969). The tortuous evolution of the multinational corporation. *Columbia Journal of World Business, 4*(1), 9–18.

Peters, J. D. (1999). *Speaking into the air: A history of the idea of communication.* Chicago: University of Chicago Press.

Peters, J. D. (2013). Calendar, clock, tower. In J. Stolow (Ed.), *Deus in machina: Religion, technology and the things in between.* (pp. 25–42). New York: Fordham University Press.

Pocock, R. F. (1988). *The early British radio industry.* Manchester, England: Manchester University Press.

Pool, I. D. S. (1983). *Technologies of freedom.* Cambridge, MA: The Belknap Press of Harvard University Press.

Posen, B. R. (2003). Command of the commons: The military foundation of U.S. hegemony. *International Security, 28*(1), 5–46.

Price, M. E. (1994). The market for loyalties and a global communications commission. *Intermedia, 22*(5), 15–21.

Raboy, M. (2016). *Marconi: The man who networked the world.* New York: Oxford University Press.

Raymond, L. (2003). *Private rights in public resources: Equity and property allocation in market-based environmental policy.* Washington, DC: Resources for the Future.

Rein, M., & Schön, D. (1993). Reframing policy discourse. In F. Fischer & J. Forester (Eds.), *The argumentative turn in policy analysis and planning* (pp. 145–166). Durham, NC: Duke University Press.

Robinson, W. I. (2005). Gramsci and globalisation: From nation-state to transnational hegemony. *Critical Review of International Social and Political Philosophy, 8*(4), 1–16.

Rogers, W. S. (1922a). *Electrical communications with special reference to China and the North Pacific: Papers related to Pacific and Far Eastern affairs prepared for the use of the American delegation to the Conference on the Limitation of Armament, Washington, 1921–1922.* Washington, DC: Government Printing Office.

Rogers, W. S. (1922b). International electrical communications. *Foreign Affairs, 1*(2), 144–157.

Rosenberg, E. (1982). *Spreading the American dream: American economic and cultural expansion, 1890–1945.* New York: Hill and Wang.

Roskill, S. (1968). *Naval policy between the wars: The period of Anglo-American antagonism, 1919–1929* (Vol. 1). London, England: Collins.

Ross, R. S. (2009). China's naval nationalism. *International Security, 34*(2), 46–81.

Rossi, J. P. (1985). A "silent partnership"? The U.S. government, RCA and radio communications with East Asia, 1919–1928. *Radical History Review, 33,* 32–52.

Sawhney, H. (1996). Information superhighway: Metaphors as midwives. *Media, Culture and Society, 18*(2), 291–314.

Sawhney, H. (2012). Beyond the path of least resistance: The system quest. *Info, 14*(1), 20–35.

Schake, K. (2017). *Safe passage: The transition from British to American hegemony.* Cambridge, MA: Harvard University Press.

Schiller, H. (1992). *Mass communications and American empire* (2nd ed.). Boulder, CO: Westview Press.

Schoultz, L. (1998). *Beneath the United States: History of U.S. policy toward Latin America.* Cambridge, MA: Harvard University Press.

Schwoch, J. (1990). *The American radio industry and its Latin American activities, 1900–1939.* Urbana: University of Illinois Press.

Sealy, L., & Worthington, S. (2013). *Sealy & Worthington's cases and materials in company law* (10th ed.). Oxford, England: Oxford University Press.

Sidak, J. G. (1997). *Foreign investment in American telecommunications.* Chicago: University of Chicago Press.

Sinclair, J. (2007). Cultural globalization and American empire. In J. Wasko & G. Murdock (Eds.), *Media in the age of marketization* (pp. 131–150). New York: Hampton Press.

Skocpol, T. (1985). Bringing the state back in: Strategies of analysis in current research. In P. B. Evans, D. Rueschemeyer, & T. Skocpol (Eds.), *Bringing the state back in* (pp. 3–29). Cambridge, MA: Harvard University Press.

Smith, H. L. (1942). *Airways: The history of commercial aviation in the United States.* New York: Knopf.

Smith, T. (1981). *The pattern of imperialism: The United States, Great Britain, and the late-industrializing world since 1815.* New York: Cambridge University Press.

Sobel, R. (1982). *ITT: The management of opportunity.* New York: Truman Talley Books.

Speta, J. B. (2001). A regulatory approach to internet interconnection. *Federal Communications Law Journal, 54*(2), 225–280.

Starr, P. (2004). *The creation of the media: Political origins of modern communications.* New York: Basic Books.

Stewart, I. (1929). Recent radio legislation. *American Political Science Review, 33*(2), 421–426.

Stone, A. (1991). *Public service liberalism: Telecommunications and transitions in public policy*. Princeton, NJ: Princeton University Press.

Strange, S. (1996). *The retreat of the state: The diffusion of power in the world economy*. Cambridge, England: Cambridge University Press.

Strange, S. (1997). An international political economy perspective. In. J. H. Dunning (Ed.), *Governments, globalization and international business* (pp. 132–145) New York: Oxford University Press.

Streeter, T. (1987). The cable fable revisited: Discourse, policy and the making of cable television. *Critical Studies in Mass Communication, 4*(2), 174–200.

Streeter, T. (1996). *Selling the air: The critique of the policy of commercial broadcasting in the United States*. Chicago: University of Chicago Press.

Taylor, P. J. (1993). *Political geography: World-economy, nation-state and locality* (3rd ed.). New York: Longman.

Taylor, P. J. (1996). *The way the modern world works: World economy to world impasse*. New York: Wiley.

Teichova, A. (1986). Multinationals in perspective. In A. Teichova, M. Lévy-Leboyer, & H. Nussbaum (Eds.), *Multinational enterprise in historical perspective* (pp. 362–371). Cambridge, England: Cambridge University Press.

Thompson, W. (2000). *The emergence of the global political economy*. New York: Routledge.

Thomson Gale (2018). *The making of modern law*. Farmington Hills, MI: Gale Cengage Learning.

Till, G. (2013). *Seapower: A guide for the twenty-first century* (3rd ed.). London, England: Routledge.

Todd, D. W. (1911). The Navy's Coast Signal Service. *Journal of the American Society of Naval Engineers, 23*(4), 1092–1116.

Tomlinson, J. D. (1948). *International control of radiocommunications*. Geneva, Switzerland: Université de Genève.

Trumpbour, J. (2002). *Selling Hollywood to the world: U.S. and European struggles for mastery of the global film industry, 1920–1950*. New York: Cambridge University Press.

Turner, S. (1974). Missions of the U.S. Navy. *Naval War College Review, 27*(2) (March–April), 2–17.

Tworek, H. J. S. (2019). *News from Germany: The project to control world communications, 1900–1945*. Cambridge, MA: Harvard University Press.

Tyson, L. D. A. (1991). They are not US. *American Prospect, 2*(4), 37–49.

Vagts, D. F. (1961). The corporate alien: Definitional questions in federal restraints on foreign enterprise. *Harvard Law Review, 74*(8), 1489–1551.

Vagts, D. F. (1970). The multinational enterprise: A new challenge for transnational law. *Harvard Law Review, 83*(4), 739–792.

Vernon, R. (1971). *Sovereignty at bay: The multinational spread of US enterprises.* New York: Basic Books.

Vernon, R. (1974). *Multinational enterprise and national security.* London, England: Institute for Strategic Studies.

Wallerstein, I. (2004). *World-systems analysis: An introduction.* Durham, NC: Duke University Press.

Waterbury, J. I. (1903). The International Preliminary Conference to Formulate Regulations Governing Wireless Telegraphy. *North American Review, 177*(564), 655–666.

Wetter, J. G. (1962). Diplomatic assistance to private investment: A study of the theory and practice of the United States during the twentieth century. *University of Chicago Law Review, 29*(2), 275–326.

White, L. J. (2001). Propertyzing the radio spectrum: Why it is important and how to begin. In J. A. Eisenach & R. May (Eds.), *Communications deregulation and FCC reform: Finishing the job* (pp. 111–143). New York: Springer.

Wilkins, M. (1974). *The maturing of the multinational enterprise: American business abroad from 1914 to 1970.* Cambridge, MA: Harvard University Press.

Wilkins, M. (1989). *The history of foreign investment in the United States to 1914.* Cambridge, MA: Harvard University Press.

Williams, W. A. (1972). *The tragedy of American diplomacy* (2nd ed.). New York: Dell.

Winder, G. M. (2006). Webs of enterprise 1850–1914: Applying a broad definition of FDI. *Annals of the Association of American Geographers, 96*(4), 788–806.

Winkler, J. R. (2008). *Nexus: Strategic communications and American security in World War I.* Cambridge, MA: Harvard University Press.

Winkler, J. R. (2009). Information warfare in World War I. *Journal of Military History, 73*(3), 845–867.

Winseck, D. (2008). Information operations "blowback." *International Communication Gazette, 70*(6), 419–441.

Winseck, D. (2013). Globalizing telecommunications and media history: Beyond methodological nationalism and the struggle for control model of communication history. In M. M. Hampf & S. Müller-Pohl (Eds.), *Global communication electric* (pp. 35–62). New York: Campus Verlag.

Winseck, D., & Pike, R. M. (2007). *Communication and empire: Media, markets and globalization, 1860–1930*. Durham, NC: Duke University Press.

Winseck, D., & Pike, R. M. (2009). The global media and the empire of liberal internationalism, circa 1910–30. *Media History, 15*(1), 31–54.

Wu, T. (2010). *Master switch: The rise and fall of information empires*. New York: Knopf.

Yang, D. (2009). Submarine cables and the two Japanese empires. In B. Finn & D. Yang (Eds.), *Communications under the seas* (pp. 227–249). Cambridge, MA: MIT Press.

Yang, D. (2010). *Technology and empire: Telecommunications and Japanese expansion in Asia, 1883–1945*. Cambridge, MA: Harvard University Press.

Zajácz, R. (2004). Foreign ownership regulations from the Radio Act of 1912 to the Radio Act of 1927. *Journal of Broadcasting and Electronic Media, 48*(2), 157–178.

Zajácz, R. (2012). Fragmented imperialism: U.S. control over radio in Panama, 1914–1936. *International Communication Gazette, 7*(1), 78–94.

Zajácz, R. (2013). WikiLeaks and the problem of anonymity: A network control perspective. *Media, Culture and Society, 35*(4), 487–503.

Zajácz, R. (2015). *The development of spheres of interest in global communications, 1919–1921*. Paper presented at the International Communication Association, San Juan, Puerto Rico.

Zakaria, F. (2008). The future of American power. *Foreign Affairs, 87*(3).

Index